Golden®

SOCIAL SCIENCE

Study Material

Based on New NCERT Textbook

EXPLORING SOCIETY: INDIA AND BEYOND

Golden®

SOCIAL SCIENCE

Study Material

EXPLORING SOCIETY: INDIA AND BEYOND

Based on New NCERT Textbook

CLASS VI

Multi Colour EDITION

- **Interesting Mind Map**
- **Facts to Remember/Summary**
- **Textbook Keywords/Glossary/Date Line**
- **The Big Questions (*Solved*)**
- **NCERT Intext/Textbook Exercises (*Solved*)**
- **NCERT Questions, Activities and Projects (*Solved*)**
- **Exam Oriented Questions (*with Answers*)**
- **Objective Type Questions (*with Answers*)**
- **Map Work for Practice**
- **Test Your Knowledge Exercises for Self Evaluation**
- **Three Golden Sample Papers (*for Practice*)**

By

Mr. Prem Kant Mishra
MA (*History-Gold Medalist, Political Science, Economics-Distance*)
BEd (CIE-Delhi University)
Former, Faculty-GD Goenka, VIS, New Delhi

Ms. Manju Arora
MA (*Economics*)
Former, Head of Economics
HT learning Centres *and*
Former, Economics, PGT-DPS, RK Puram, New Delhi

S Gupta
&
Editorial Team

Committed to Educate the Nation

NEW AGE

Publishing Globally

IN INDIA

NEW AGE INTERNATIONAL (P) LIMITED, PUBLISHERS
LONDON • NEW DELHI
Bengaluru • Chennai • Cochin • Guwahati
Hyderabad • Kolkata • Mumbai
Visit us at www.newagegolden.com

Published by New Age International (P) Ltd., Publishers
New Edition

GLOBAL OFFICES

- **New Delhi** — **NEW AGE INTERNATIONAL (P) LIMITED, PUBLISHERS**
  7/30 A, Daryaganj, New Delhi-110002, (INDIA), **Tel.:** (011) 23253472, 23253771, **Mob.:** 9315905300
  E-mail: contactus@newagepublishers.com • Visit us at www.newagepublishers.com
- **London** — **NEW AGE INTERNATIONAL (UK) LTD.**
  27 Old Gloucester Street, London, WC1N 3AX, UK
  E-mail: info@newacademicscience.co.uk • Visit us at www.newacademicscience.co.uk

BRANCHES

- **Bengaluru** — 167, 1st Floor, 11th Cross, Mulkatamma Temple Road,Near Rajiv Gandhi Sports Complex, Vittal Nagar Bengaluru – 560026, **Tel.:** (080) 26756823, **Mob.:** 9315905288, **E-mail: bangalore@newagepublishers.com**
- **Chennai** — 26, Damodaran Street, T. Nagar, Chennai-600 017, **Tel.:** (044) 24353401, **Mob.:** 9315905309 **E-mail: chennai@newagepublishers.com**
- **Cochin** — CC-39/1016, Carrier Station Road, Ernakulam South, Cochin-682 016 **Tel.:** (0484) 4051304, **Mob.:** 9315905289, **E-mail: cochin@newagepublishers.com**
- **Guwahati** — Hemsen Complex, Mohd. Shah Road, Paltan Bazar, Near Starline Hotel Guwahati-781 008, **Tel.:** (0361) 2513881, **Mob.:** 9315905296 **E-mail: guwahati@newagepublishers.com**
- **Hyderabad** — 105, 1st Floor, Madhiray Kaveri Tower, 3-2-19, Azam Jahi Road, Near Kumar Theater Nimboliadda Kachiguda, Hyderabad-500 027, **Tel.:** (040) 24652456, **Mob.:** 9315905326 **E-mail: hyderabad@newagepublishers.com**
- **Kolkata** — RDB Chambers (Formerly Lotus Cinema) 106A, 1st Floor, S N Banerjee Road Kolkata-700 014, **Tel.:** (033) 22273773, **Mob.:** 9315905319, **E-mail: kolkata@newagepublishers.com**
- **Mumbai** — 142C, Victor House, Ground Floor, N.M. Joshi Marg, Lower Parel, Mumbai-400 013 **Tel.:** (022) 24927869, 24915415, **Mob.:** 9315905282, **E-mail: mumbai@newagepublishers.com**
- **New Delhi** — 22, Golden House, Daryaganj, New Delhi-110 002, **Tel.:** (011) 23262368, 23262370 **Mob.:** 9315905300, **E-mail: sales@newagepublishers.com**

C-26-02-15384

Printed in India at Goyal Offset Work (P) Ltd., Sonipat, Haryana.
Typeset at In-house, Delhi.

NEW AGE INTERNATIONAL (P) LIMITED, PUBLISHERS
7/30 A, Daryaganj, New Delhi-110002
Visit us at **www.newagegolden.com**
(CIN: U74899DL1966PTC004618)

PREFACE

We are pleased to introduce the revised and updated edition of Golden **Social Science** for Class VI, aligned with the latest new NCERT textbook **EXPLORING SOCIETY: INDIA AND BEYOND** this edition follows the **National Education Policy (NEP) 2020** and **National Curriculum Framework for School Education (NCF-SE) 2023**. It has been meticulously crafted to ensure seamless alignment with the current academic requirements.

Special Features of the Book are:

- Interesting Mind Map
- Facts to Remember/Summary
- Textbook Keywords/Glossary
- The Big Questions? (*Solved*)
- NCERT Intext/Textbook Exercises (*Solved*)
- NCERT Questions, Activities and Projects (*Solved*)
- Exam Oriented Questions (*with Answers*)
- Map Skills (*Solved*)
- Objective Type Questions (*with Answers*)
    - Multiple Choice Questions
    - Fill in the Blanks
    - True or False
    - Match the Columns
    - Assertion and Reasoning Questions
- Test Your Knowledge Questions (*for Self Evaluation*)
- Three Golden Sample Papers (*for Practice*)

To help students better understand the chapters, **Video animations** of the book's content are available. A **QR Code** has been provided at the back cover of the book, allowing students to access these animated explanations easily.

We highly value the feedback and suggestions from educators and students, which have played a crucial role in refining and updating this edition. Their insights will continue to guide us in future updates.

We are confident that this book will serve as an indispensable resource in your academic journey, helping you achieve excellence in Social Science. Our goal is to provide a comprehensive learning experience and support your academic success.

AUTHORS

CONTENTS

Theme B — Tapestry of the Past

Theme C — Our Cultural Heritage and Knowledge Traditions

Theme D — Governance and Democracy

Theme E — Economic Life Around Us

THEME A

INDIA AND THE WORLD: LAND AND THE PEOPLE

Locating Places on the Earth

1 Introduction

- Maps help us find places in a new city
- A map shows important places like the station, bank, school, and market
- Maps help us choose the right route between places
- Direction arrows make maps easy to understand

2 A Map and Its Components

- Maps show areas from a top view, small or large
- An atlas is a collection of maps
- Types of maps include:
  - Physical maps: show natural features like mountains, rivers, oceans
  - Political maps: show boundaries, cities, states, countries
  - Thematic maps: show specific information, like population or resources
- Key map components are:
  - Distance: Scale shows how real distances are reduced on the map
  - Directions:
    - Cardinal directions also called cardinal points: North, East, South, West
    - Intermediate directions: North-East, South-East, South-West, North-West
  - Symbols: represent features to save space
    - Standard symbols make maps easy to read

3 Mapping the Earth

- Earth is nearly spherical
- Flat maps cannot show it accurately
- A globe is a spherical model showing Earth more accurately than flat maps

3(a) Understanding Coordinates

- Coordinates: A system using two values to show exact locations
- For example: In a market, row and shop number help find a shop; on a chessboard, letters and numbers mark each square
- On a map: The system of coordinates is used to find the exact location of any place

3(b) Latitudes

- Latitude is the distance from the Equator; shown by east-west lines called parallel of latitude
- The measurement of latitude is given in degrees
- Equator is 0°, poles are 90°North and 90°South
- Climate: Hot near the Equator, moderate in middle latitudes, cold near the poles

3(c) Longitudes

- Meridians of Longitude: Lines that run from the North Pole to the South Pole as half-circles
- Prime Meridian: The imaginary line at 0° longitude used as the starting point to measure longitudes
- Longitude: The distance of a place east or west from the Prime Meridian, up to 180° east (E) or west (W)
- Coordinates: Latitude and longitude together help identify the exact position of any place
- Grid: Latitude and longitude lines that form a network to find places

4 Understanding Time Zones

- Earth rotates 360° in 24 hours
- Local time: The actual time at a place based on its position on the Earth
- Standard time: The official time that a whole country follows, based on a chosen meridian
- Greenwich Mean Time (GMT): The time at the Prime Meridian, used as a reference worldwide
- The world is divided into zones; moving east adds hours, moving west subtracts hours from GMT
- International Date Line: Line at about 180° longitude; crossing it forward or backward changes the calendar day

CHAPTER 1

THEME A
India and the World: Land and the People

LOCATING PLACES ON THE EARTH

I. FACTS TO REMEMBER/SUMMARY

A MAP AND ITS COMPONENTS

- A map is a representation or a drawing of the Earth's surface on a flat sheet of paper, drawn to scale. For example; village, district, city, state, country or world.
- An atlas is a collection of maps.
- There are many kinds of maps:
  - physical maps: they show natural features *e.g.* mountains, oceans etc.
  - political maps: they show details of countries or boundaries.
  - thematic maps: they depict specific information, for example showing coal mines on a map.
- The three components of maps are:
  - distance ❖ direction ❖ symbols.
- Maps reduce the entire world or part of it, to fit on a sheet of paper. A map scale represented in the bottom left corner by a ruler is important for people to understand actual distance based on a small map.
- A map scale is the ratio between two points in the printed map and the actual distance on the ground.
- Directions on a map are indicated by an arrow marked with the letter 'N' on the upper right side, called 'north line'.
- Four cardinal directions are marked clockwise:
  ❖ N–North ❖ E–East ❖ S–South ❖ W–West
- Intermediate directions are marked clockwise:
  - NE North East – SE South East
  - SW South West – NW North West
- Since it is not possible to draw actual shape and size of features, symbols and colours are used to represent features like roads, rivers, bridges, hospitals, post offices etc.

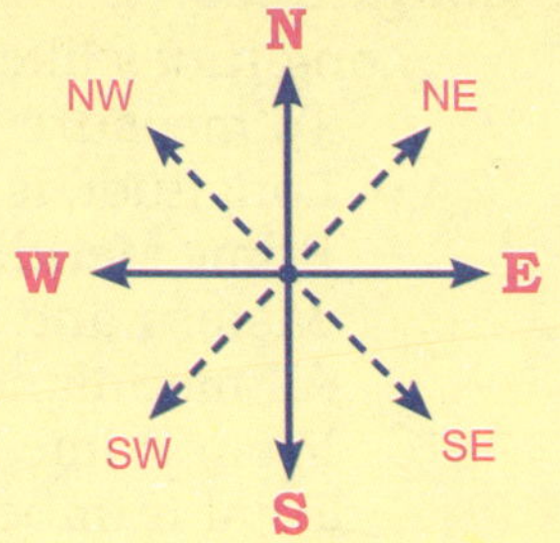

MAPPING THE EARTH

- Mapping the Earth is difficult because it is not a flat surface and has an almost spherical shape.
- A Globe is a three-dimensional model of the Earth.
- The fixed points on the globe at the top and bottom are the two poles – the North Pole and the South Pole.
- Axis of the Earth joins the North Pole with the South Pole. It is inclined toward the east by 23½°.
- The Earth spins on its axis. The Earth completes one rotation in 24 hours. The Sun illuminates the Earth.
  - Due to the spherical shape of the Earth only half of it gets sunlight at a time and the other half remains in darkness causing day and night.

Understanding Coordinates

- Coordinates are used in the world of maps to determine the location of any place on a map.
- Latitudes and longitudes are imaginary lines that are used in world maps as coordinates to provide systematic network of lines to determine location of any place or surface feature of the Earth.

Latitudes

- The Equator is the largest circle that runs halfway between the poles — East to West. It divides the Earth into 2 hemispheres: North Hemisphere and South Hemisphere.
  - By convention equator is 0° parallel of latitude.
  - Latitudes are parallel and the size of the parallels decrease as we move Northward or Southward.
  - Latitudes are expressed in degrees.
  - 90° N latitude marks the North Pole and 90° S latitude marks the South Pole.
- Important parallels of latitude are:
  - Equator (0°)
  - Tropic of Cancer (23½° N)
  - Tropic of Capricorn (23½° S)
  - Arctic Circle (66½° N)
  - Antarctic Circle (66½° S)
  - North Pole (90° N)
  - South Pole (90° S)

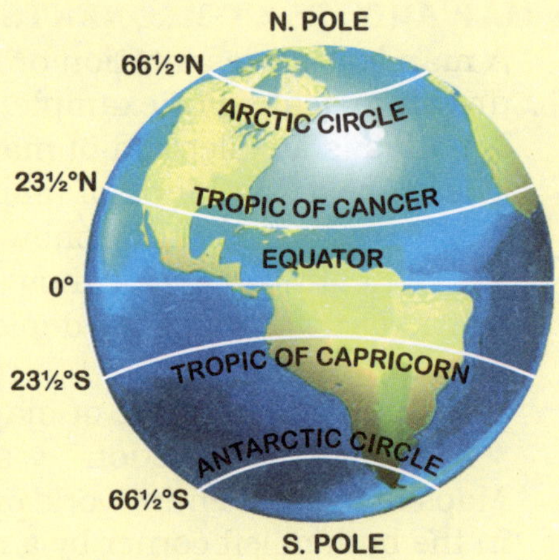

Fig. Major parallels of latitudes

- Latitudes and climate are intimately linked.
- On the globe, lines that are half circles running from one pole to the other are called Meridians of Longitude. Longitudes mark the time and define the time zones.

Longitudes

- Longitudes like latitudes are measured in degrees.
  - To measure longitude, Prime Meridian 0° is point of reference.
  - Longitude is measure of distance from the Prime Meridian.
  - Prime Meridian (0°) or Greenwich Meridian divides the Earth into 2 hemispheres—eastern and western.
  - All meridians are of equal length.
  - From Prime Meridian (0°) we count 180° eastwards and westwards.
  - Total number of longitudes are 360°.
  - 180° E and 180° W are on the same line.

UNDERSTANDING TIME ZONES

- The Earth rotates from West to East on its axis
  - It completes one rotation of 360° in 24 hours *i.e.* 15° per hour or say 1° per 4 minutes.
  - To calculate time the Earth has been divided into 24 time zones 15° apart.
  - From Prime Meridian 0° local time is ahead in the east by an hour every 15°E from Greenwich. Likewise westward local time is behind by an hour every 15° W.
  - It is not convenient for a country to use many local times.
- Countries use Standard Time based on a meridian.
  - Indian standard time (IST) is based on 82½°E meridian.
  - Standard time are organised in time zones at 15° or 7.5°.
  - The line opposite to the Prime Meridian located at approximately 180° longitude, is known as the International Date Line (IDL).
  - Crossing the IDL changes the date by one day.

II. TEXTBOOK KEYWORDS/GLOSSARY

1. **Sphere:** It is a three-dimensional, round geometrical shape.
2. **Map:** It is a representation of the earth's surface or its part on a flat surface according to a scale.
3. **Globe:** Three-dimensional model of the earth is called globe. It is a sphere on which a map is drawn.
4. **Atlas:** Atlas is a book or collection of maps.
5. **Physical Maps:** Maps depicting physical/natural features such as mountains, rivers, plateaus, oceans and plains.
6. **Political Maps:** Maps showing details of countries— boundaries, states, union territories and their capitals etc.
7. **Thematic Maps:** Maps representing a particular theme or topic – rainfall, forests, distribution of minerals etc.
8. **Cartography:** Science of map-making.
9. **Scale:** Ratio between the distance of two points on a map and the actual distance of these points on the ground.
10. **Compass:** An instrument which indicates the directions.
11. **Cardinal Points or Directions:** The four major directions such as North, South, East and West are termed cardinal points.
12. **Intermediate Directions:** The directions lying exactly between – N-E, E-S, S-W and W-N *i.e.* NE, SE, SW and NW.
13. **Symbols:** Is a mark or sign that is understood as representing an object, or an idea.
14. **Coordinates:** On a map they are points of intersection in a grid system expressed as combination of latitude and longitude.
15. **Conventional Symbols:** Symbols used in various maps all over the world.
16. **Axis:** The imaginary line joining the North Pole and the South Pole.
17. **Poles:** The two ends of the axis.
18. **North Pole:** The northern-most end of the axis.
19. **South Pole:** The southern-most end of the axis.
20. **Parallels of Latitudes:** The imaginary lines drawn parallel to the equator in both the hemispheres (N and S) upto the poles (They run east to west).
21. **Equator:** 0° parallel of latitude. This is an imaginary line passing through centre of the earth and perpendicular to the axis.
22. **Tropic of Cancer:** Parallel of latitude of 23½° N of the equator.
23. **Tropic of Capricorn:** Parallel of latitude of 23½° S of the equator.
24. **Arctic Circle:** Parallel of latitude of 66½° N.
25. **Antarctic Circle:** Parallel of latitude of 66½° S.
26. **Torrid Zone:** Zone with high temperatures throughout the year and lying between the Tropic of Cancer and the Tropic of Capricorn.
27. **Temperate Zone:** Zones with moderate temperatures lying between Tropic of Cancer and Arctic circle in the Northern hemisphere and between the Tropic of Capricorn and the Antarctic Circle in the Southern hemisphere.
28. **Frigid Zone:** Zones with extreme cold climate and lying between the Arctic circle and the North Pole in the Northern hemisphere and between the Antarctic Circle and the South Pole in the Southern hemisphere.
29. **Meridians of Longitude:** Imaginary lines, all half-circles, joining the North and South Poles with reference to Prime Meridian.
30. **Prime Meridian:** 0° longitude passing through Greenwich (London). It is also called Greenwich Mean Time (GMT).

31. **Grid Lines:** A network of horizontal and vertical lines or latitudes and longitudes drawn on a map or globe. It helps in locating places on the map or the globe.

32. **Rotation:** Movement of a heavenly body on its axis.

33. **Local Time:** Time of a meridian.

34. **Standard Time:** The local time of a meridian of longitude which is considered valid for the whole country, is called Standard Time of that country. This meridian is called Standard Meridian of that country. (*e.g.* 82½° E is Standard Meridian of India/Bharat).

35. **Greenwich Mean Time (GMT):** The time of the Greenwich meridian.

36. **Indian Standard Time (IST):** The time of 82½° E Longitude is taken as the standard time for the whole country (India/Bharat).

37. **International Date Line (IDL):** The 180° Longitude is called the International Date Line. It functions as a line of demarcation, separating each calendar day from the next.

38. **Estuary:** Where the river meets the sea.

III. DATE LINE

1884: Some nations decided that the meridian passing through Greenwich, in London would be the international standard for the Prime Meridian marked as 0° Longitude.

IV. THE BIG QUESTIONS *(Page 7)*

Q. 1. ***What is a map and how do we use it? What are its main components?***

Ans. Map is a representation or drawing of an area of the Earth on a flat surface whether small or large – say of a district or a village or a very large area like India or even the world at a specific scale.

– One map contains many facts.

– Collection of maps is called an Atlas.

• Maps can be used to represent details of areas and features of the Earth.

Types of Maps:

(*i*) **Physical Maps:** Physical features of the Earth such as mountains, oceans, rivers, plains and plateaus.

(*ii*) **Political Maps:** Political division of the Earth – countries, states, boundaries, capitals, cities, villages etc.

(*iii*) **Thematic Maps:** Specific information like rainfall, forests, minerals, roads, industries, population density etc.

• The main components of maps are: (*i*) distance (*ii*) direction and (*iii*) symbols.

Q. 2. ***What are coordinates? How can latitude and longitude be used to mark any location on the Earth?***

Ans.

• Coordinates are two numbers or sometimes a letter and a number (Example: Chess board) that locate a specific point on a grid.

• On a map latitudes and longitudes are referred to as two coordinates of a place. They provide systematic network of lines (grid lines) upon which the position of various surface features of the Earth can be represented, located and identified.

• Latitudes are horizontal lines that measure distances North and South of the Equator. Longitudes are vertical lines that measure East or West of the Prime Meridian. But there exists only one point where they intersect. By combining these two coordinates and identifying the point of intersection of latitudes and longitudes one can mark and locate any location on the earth.

Q. 3. *How are local time and standard time related to longitude?*

Ans.

- Longitudes are related to local time and standard time as they help us to calculate time.
  - Time is measured by the movement of the earth.
  - The earth spins on its axis West to East making a full turn of 360° in 24 hours (rotation).
  - This means 15° per hour (15° × 24 = 360°) or say 4 minutes for one degree of longitude.
  - Accordingly the earth has been divided into 24 time zones of one hour each.
  - Moving eastwards from the Prime Meridian we get 12 time zones, 15° apart example: 0°, 15°E, 30°E etc. and likewise westwards (example 0°, 15°W, 30°W).
  - Each place has different time of sunrise and sunset.
  - Places east of Prime Meridian/ Greenwich Meridian experience sunrise (day) earlier than places lying west of the Meridian.
- Local time of a place is based on the longitude of that place *i.e.* local time varies when places are situated on different meridians.
  - To solve confusion in a country every country fixes its central meridian, passing through it as the standard meridian. The standard times are organised in time zones of 15° or 7.5°.
  - The local time of the meridian is considered standard for the whole country. It is called standard time.

    Example: In India the longitude of 82½° E is treated as the standard meridian. The local time of the Meridian is known as Indian Standard Time (IST).
  - Through an international agreement, the local time of all places is linked to the Greenwich Mean Time. The IST is 5 hours 30 minutes ahead of GMT.

    Both local and standard time are related to longitude.
  - Local time refers to the time of a place as defined by the apparent motion of the Sun. Standard time is agreed time of places along the same meridian established by law in the same country.
  - While local time changes continuously as longitude changes, the standard time stays the same for a specific nation.

V. NCERT INTEXT/TEXTBOOK EXERCISES

Let's Explore

(Page 9)

Q. 1. *On the map in Fig. 1.1 given on (Page 08 of NCERT textbook)*

- ***Mark the hospital.***
- ***What is the meaning of the blue-coloured areas?***

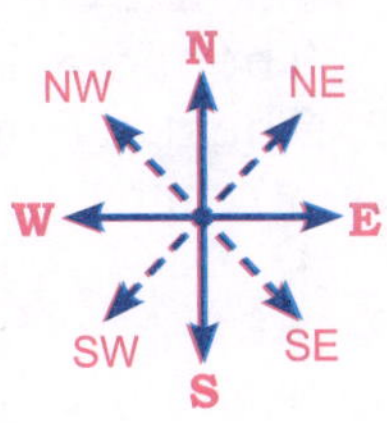

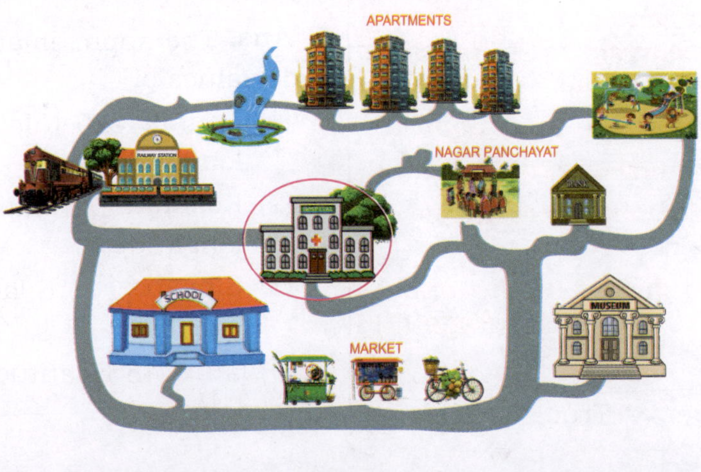

Ans.

- The hospital is marked by a circle above.
- Blue coloured areas represent water bodies, lake/pond and stream.
- ***Which is farther away from the railway station—the school, the Nagar Panchayat or the public garden?*** *(Page 9)*

Ans. Public garden.

Q. 2. ***Draw a simple map of a school's playground. Let us assume it is a rectangle, 40 m in length and 30m in width. Draw it precisely with your ruler on a scale of 1 cm = 10 m.*** *(Page 10)*

Ans. As 1 cm = 10 m

Hence,

length should be: 40 m = 4 cm on the map

width should be: 30 m = 3 cm on the map

Q. 3. ***Now measure the diagonal of the rectangle. How many centimetres do you get? Using the scale, calculate the real length of the playground's diagonal, in metres.*** *(Page 10)*

Ans. The diagonal of the rectangle is 5 cms.

So, if 1 cm as per scale equals 10 metres

Then, 5 × 10 metres = 50 metres

The real length of the playground's diagonal is 50 metres.

Q. 4. ***Consider the map of the small city again. Identify the correct and incorrect statements in the list below:***

- ***The market is north of the hospital.***
- ***The museum is southeast of the bank.***
- ***The railway station is northwest of the hospital.***
- ***The lake is northwest of the apartment blocks.*** *(Page 11)*

Ans.

1. False **2.** True **3.** True **4.** False

Q. 5. ***Draw a rough map of your locality or your village, including your home, school and a few other important landmarks. Show the cardinal directions and use a few of the symbols shown in Fig. 1.2 on page 12 to mark some important features.*** *(Page 11)*

What do the following symbolise on a map? *(Page 12)*

Ans.

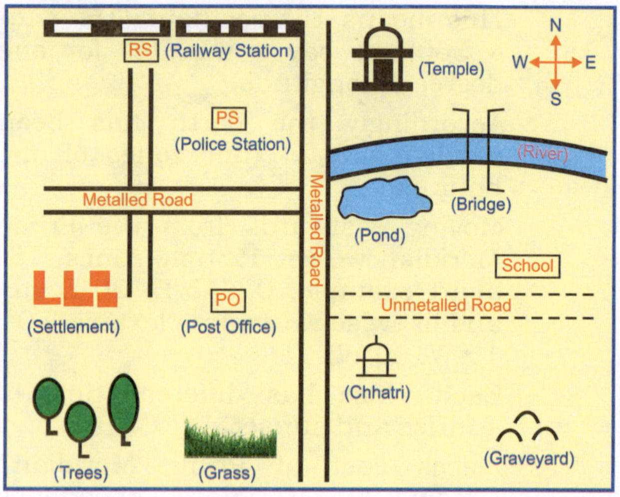

Q. 6. ***Using the same terms, write down your move if you play black and respond with the same move.*** *(Page 13)*

Ans. The black side has just opened the game by moving the queen's pawn two squares forward. The pawn has moved from d7 to d5.

Q. 7. ***If the globe or atlas in your class has well-marked latitudes and longitudes, try to note down approximate values for the latitude and longitude of (1) Mumbai, (2) Kolkata, (3) Singapore, (4) Paris.*** *(Page 17)*

Ans. The approximate latitude and longitude values of

(1) Mumbai: 19°N latitude and 72°E longitude

(2) Kolkata: 22°N latitude and 8°E longitude

(3) Singapore: 1°N latitude and 103°E longitude

(4) Paris: 48°N latitude and 2°E longitude

Q.8. ***Two friends, one sitting in Porbandar (Gujarat) and the other in Tinsukia (Assam), are speaking on the phone late afternoon. The latter remarks that the sun has set in Assam and it's now dark. The former is surprised and says, "But it's still full daylight here!" Explain why. And, as a class activity, calculate the difference in local time between those two cities. (Hint: for now, consider the difference in longitude between Porbandar and Tinsukia to be 30°; later, you can find out the precise value.)*** (Page 21)

Ans. Explanation: There is a difference of 30° between Porbandar (Gujarat) and Tinsukia (Assam). That is the local time difference is 4 min × 30 = 120 minutes or 2 hours. Also the sunrises in Assam (Tinsukia) before it rises in Gujarat (Porbandar) as Assam is in North East of India and Gujarat in West of India.

The time both cities follow is the IST set at 82½° E. So while the standard time is the same the sun rise and sun set follows local time.

Calculation: Tinsukia is 30° East of Porbandar

Since 1° = 4 minutes

30° = 4 minutes × 30 = 120 min.

= 120 minutes ÷ 60 = 2 hours.

The time difference in local time is 2 hours.

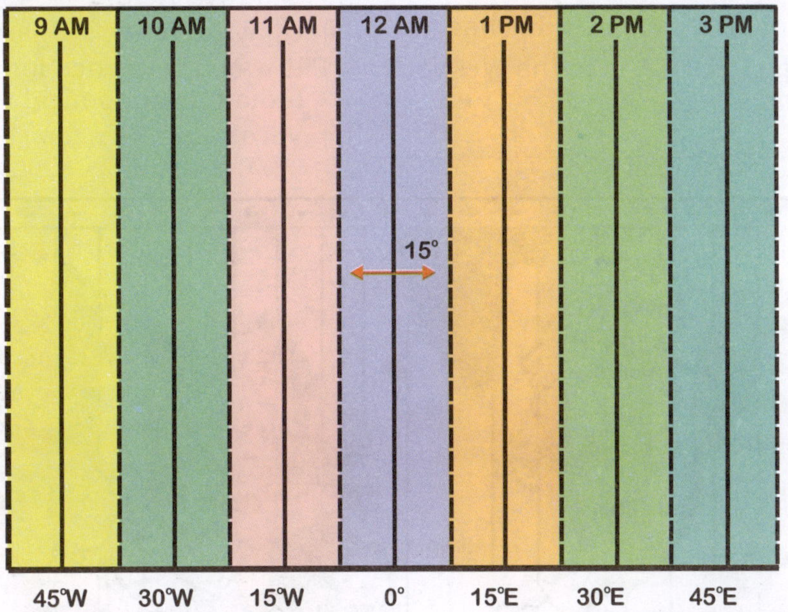

Q. 9. ***Return to the two friends sitting in Gujarat and Assam. Use this example to explain the difference between local time and standard time.*** (Page 21)

Ans. While local time varies with longitude, standard time always stays the same in the whole country at a particular moment, no matter where you are (as it is fixed as per the standard meridian).

Don't Miss Out

Q. 1. ***As you can see on the globe of meridians of longitudes, 180°W and 180°E are the same longitude; so this longitude is noted 180°, omitting the letter W or E.*** (Page 16)

Ans.

- Yes the 180° longitude is not marked 180° E or 180°W as other meridians East or West of the Prime Median (0°).
- The 180° longitude is called the International Date Line opposite the Prime Meridian.
- Crossing the IDL changes the date by one day.
- If you cross to its East you add a day.
- If you cross to its West you subtract a day.
- You would have heard people say they reached the US from India on the same day because for the US we have to cross the imaginary IDL. While India has to the East of the IDL USA is to the West of the IDL 0°.

Read the passage under Don't Miss Out on page 17 and answer the following questions:

(*Source Based Questions*)

Q.2 (*i*) ***Is Greenwich the 1st prime meridian?***

(*ii*) ***What was India's prime meridian centuries ago?***

(*iii*) ***The ancient India's own prime meridian passed through which old city?***

(*iv*) ***Why was this meridian famous?***

(*v*) ***Give the name of the famous Indian astronomer who lived 1500 years ago in the city.***

Ans.

(*i*) No

(*ii*) 'Madhya Rekha' (or middle line).

(*iii*) Ujjayini (today's Ujjain).

(*iv*) It was a reference for calculations in all Indian astronomical texts.

(*v*) Varahamihira.

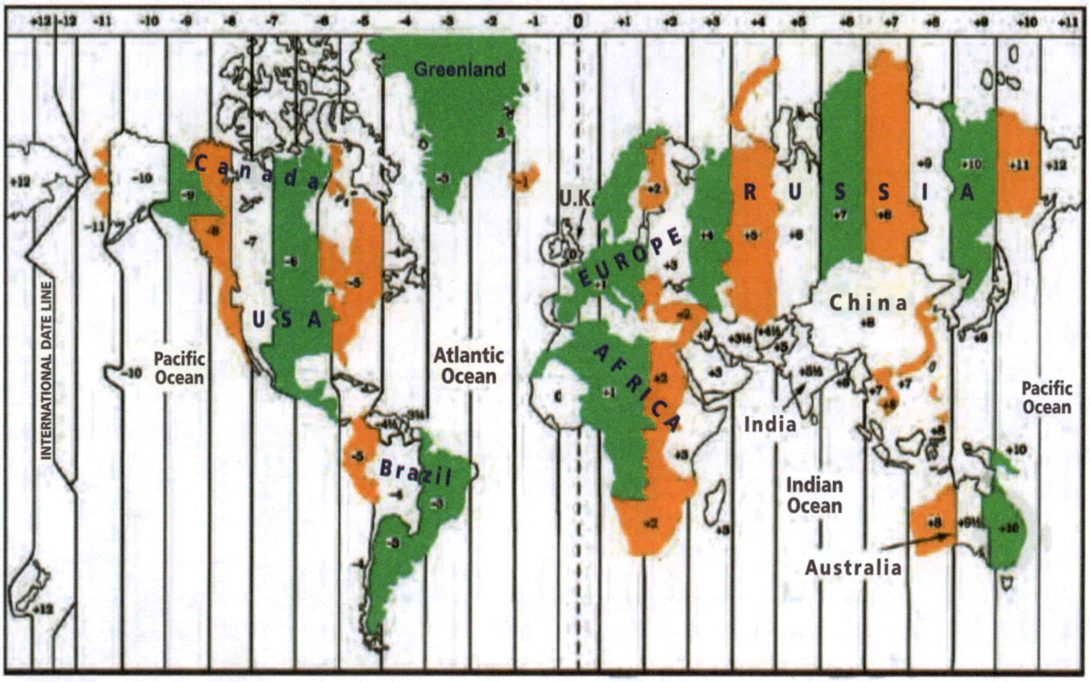

Q. 3. ***Do all countries have one standard time?***

(*a*) ***Give examples of any 2 countries which have more than one time zone.***

(*b*) ***Why do these countries have more time zones.*** (*Page 22*)

Ans. Not all but most countries have one time zone.

(*a*) Russia has 11 time zones and USA has 6 time zones.

(*b*) These countries have more time zones because of the longitudinal extent.

NCERT Questions, Activities and Projects
(*Pages 24-25*)

Q. 1. ***Returning to page 10 and to Fig. 5.2 in Chapter 5 of this textbook, taking the scale to be 2.5 cm = 500 km, calculate the real distance from the estuary of the Narmada River to the estuary of the Ganga river. (Hint: round off your measurement on the map to an easy number.)***

Ans. Distance between estuary of the Narmada river and of the Ganga river is 10 cms. So, if 2.5 cms is equal to 500 kms on ground, then 10 cms will be 500 km × 4 = 2,000 kms.

Q. 2. ***Why is it 5:30 pm in India when it is 12 pm (noon) in London?***

Ans. It is 5.30 pm in India when it is 12 pm (noon) in London because:

- London is located at 0° longitude, (the Prime Meridian).
- In India, the 82½°E longitude is considered standard meridian and time based on this meridian is the Indian Standard Time (IST).
- India is ahead of London in time. The time difference is calculated as 4 minutes for every 1° of longitude towards the east.
- Therefore, for India's longitude the time difference is: – 82½°×4 minutes = 330 minutes *i.e.* 330 ÷ 60 = 5 hours 30 minutes.

  "This explains why when it is 12:00 PM in London, it is 5:30 PM in India."

Q. 3. ***Why do we need symbols and colours in the map?***

Ans. Symbols and colours are important components of maps and are needed in maps because:

- It is not possible to draw actual shapes and sizes of different features like buildings, roads, temples, rivers, mountains etc. due to lack of space, so we use various symbols and colours to show these features.
- In this way numerous details and more information can be shown in limited space.
- Symbols and colours enable easy understanding of maps by a variety of users.
- They help tide over language barriers as maps have a universal language. These are called conventional symbols.
- The Survey of India, a government body, has fixed a set of symbols and colours for maps of India.

Q. 4. ***Find out what you have in the eight directions from your home or school.***

Ans. *Do it yourself.*

Example: South Extension II in New Delhi.

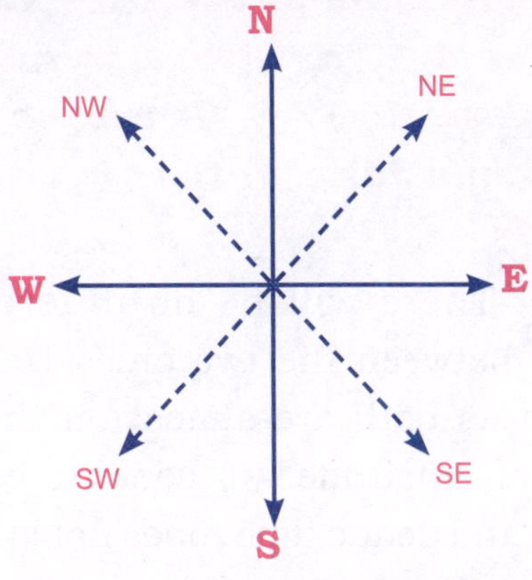

North : INA Market
North East : Defence Colony
East : Nature Basket
South East : Gautam Nagar
South : Asiad Village
South West : Ansal Plaza
West : Yusuf Sarai

Q. 5. ***What is the difference between local time and standard time? Discuss it in groups, with each group writing an answer in 100 to 150 words. Compare the answers.***

Ans.

- Both local time and standard time are based on meridians.
- Local time is based on the local meridian passing through that place. The places lying North and South on the same meridian will have the same local time. On the other hand the places lying East or West of that meridian will have different local times. It varies by 4 minutes for every 1° of Prime meridian East or West. While in the East it is plus 4 minutes going West from Prime Meridian it is 4° behind. (If it is 12 noon at Greenwich it would be 12:04 pm in the 1° East and 11:56 a.m. in the 1° west).

- Standard time is local time of a meridian of longitude which is considered valid for the whole country. This meridian is called Standard Meridian of the country. Example in Indian Standard Meridian is 82½° E and time on it is Indian Standard Time (IST). **[For more details, students can lookup The Big Question 3.]**

Q. 6. ***Delhi's and Bengaluru's latitudes are 29°N and 13°N; their longitudes are almost the same, 77°E. How much will be the difference in local time between the two cities?***

Ans. (*i*) There will be no difference in local time between the two cities Delhi and Bengaluru as both are almost on the same meridian of longitude. (*ii*) Longitudes alone mark time and define time zones not latitudes.

Q. 7. ***Mark the following statements as true or false; explain your answers with a sentence or two.***

(*a*) All parallels of latitude have the same length.
(*b*) The length of a meridian of longitude is half of that of the Equator.
(*c*) The South Pole has a latitude of 90°S.
(*d*) In Assam, the local time and the IST are identical.
(*e*) Lines separating the time zones are identical with meridians of longitude.
(*f*) The Equator is also a parallel of latitude.
(*g*) Solve the crossword below.

Ans. (*a*) False.

Explanation: The earth is almost like a sphere and latitudes are imaginary horizontal lines — complete circles that remain equidistant from each other. The Earth bulges at the equator and flattens at the poles. They vary in size from the longest at the equator (great circle) to the smallest, and are just points at the North and South pole.

Ans. (*b*) True.

Explanation: All meridians are of equal length, and approximately half the length of the equator. All meridians converge at the poles and are true North-South lines.

Ans. (*c*) True.

Explanation: Imaginary lines of latitude are labelled 90°N and 90°S of the equator (0°). The South pole is the southern most point on Earth. It is the precise point of the southern intersection of Earth's axis and Earth's surface.

Ans. (*d*) False.

Explanation: It is false because IST is calculated on the Standard Meridian of 82½°E, while Assam is further east of the 82½°E meridian. Since local time changes every 1° by 4 minutes, the local time of Assam and IST cannot be the same.

However, Assam uses IST as standard time because all states and UT in India follows IST to maintain consistency.

Ans. (*e*) True.

Explanation: Time zones are spaces of 15° of longitude that change by one hour with regard to the local time. As the circle has 360°, there are 24 time zones pertaining to 24 hours that are in a day. Thus time zones are identical with meridian of longitude – 0°, 15°, 30°, 45°, 60°, 75°, till 180° Eastwards and Westwards.

Ans. (*f*) True.

Explanation: The equator is the most well known parallel of latitude. At 0° latitude running east to west it equally divides the Earth into the Northern and Southern hemispheres. The equator is also known as the great circle. From the equator size of parallels of latitudes decreases both Northwards and Southwards.

Across		Down	
1.	Let's you squeeze a huge area into your map	2.	A measure of the distance from the Prime Meridian
4.	A convenient sphere	3.	These two together allow us to locate a place
5.	The longest parallel of latitude	6	What latitudes and longitudes together create
6.	The place the Prime Meridian is attached to	7	The time we all follow in India
8.	So convenient to find your way	9	These two are poles apart
10.	A measure of the distance from the Equator	11	An abbreviation for a line across which the day and date change.

Locating places on Earth

Ans. (*g*)

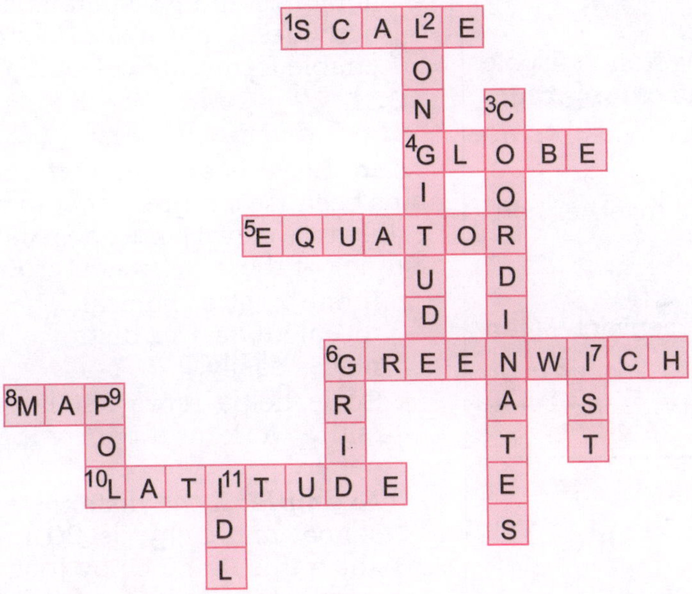

VI. EXAM ORIENTED QUESTIONS

A. Very Short Answer Type Questions

Q. 1. ***What is an atlas?***

Ans. An atlas is a book or collection of maps.

Q. 2. ***What is a north line?***

Ans. It is simply an arrow marked with the letter 'N' at the upper right hand corner of the map which points towards the north direction.

Q. 3. ***Why do maps use specific symbols?***

Ans. Maps use specific symbols to represent different features and information clearly and concisely. By using symbols maps provide an effective and efficient way to navigate and understand geographical information.

Q. 4. ***Which authority in India fixes a set of symbols for maps of India?***

Ans. The Survey of India, a government body, has the authority to fix a set of symbols for maps of India.

Q. 5. ***Why do we use the term 'nearly' the shape of a 'sphere' to describe the shape of the Earth?***

Ans. We use the term 'nearly' because the Earth, our planet is not a perfect sphere, but is slightly flattened at the poles.

Q. 6. ***What term best describes the four main directions—North, South, East and West on a map?***

Ans. The term **Cardinal** directions is used to describe the four main directions—North, South, East and West on a map.

Q. 7. ***What are the imaginary lines on the globe that measure the distance North and South of the Equator called?***

Ans. The imaginary lines on the globe that measure the distance North and South of the Equator are called **parallels of latitude**.

Q. 8. ***What are the half circles running from one pole to another called?***

Ans. The half circles running from one pole to another are called **meridians of longitude**.

Q. 9. ***What constitute the two coordinates of a place?***

Ans. Latitude and longitude together constitute two coordinates of a place.

Q. 10. ***What does GMT mean?***

Ans. GMT is short form of Greenwich Mean Time.

B. Short Answer Type Questions

Q. 1. ***How do symbols help in reading maps?***

Ans.

- Symbols help in making maps more informative. They enable representation of numerous details in limited space — rivers, buildings, railway line, etc.
- Symbols help overcome barriers of language, communication etc.
- They make maps easier to understand by wide range of users. For example, less educated.
- Maps have a universal language. The Survey of India has fixed a set of symbols for maps of India.
- There is an international agreement on the use of these symbols. They are called 'Conventional symbols'.

Q. 2. ***Describe the various types of Maps and their uses.***

Ans. There are several kinds of maps—

- **Physical maps:** They mainly show natural features such as mountains, oceans, rivers and forests. They help us to understand landscape and environment of a region.
- **Political maps:** They show details of countries or states, boundaries, cities etc. ***Example:*** A map of India shows the states and union territories and their capitals. They help us to understand geopolitical divisions, administrative areas and location of settlements.
- **Thematic maps:** They show a specific kind of information. *Example:* Road maps, rainfall maps, forest distribution maps, industries map etc. They help us to understand patterns, economic activities and give details about human activities, natural phenomena and enable formulate co-relations.

Q. 3. ***Why is scale for distance an important component of maps? Give example.***

Ans. Scale is an important component of maps because it represents the ratio between the distance of two points on a map and actual distance of these points on ground.

- If one knows the scale then one is able to calculate the distance between two places easily.
- Scale helps represent large areas, the entire world or a part of it on a sheet of paper.
  Example: If the distance between your school and home is 20 kms. You can show this distance by just 4 cms using the scale — 1 cm = 5 kms. Therefore, 4 cms × 5 kms = 20 kms.
- Scale helps in precise measurement and plays a crucial role in our planning. ***Example:*** for a playground, shopping complex etc.

Q. 4. ***How are directions known?***

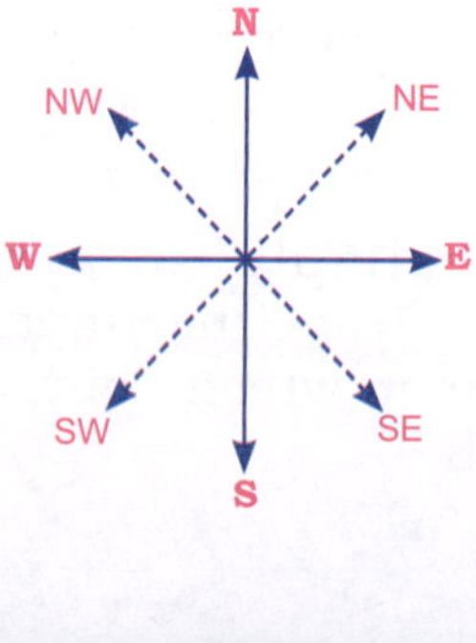

Ans.

- Maps contain an arrow marked with the letter 'N' on the upper right side.
- This arrow shows the North direction. It is called the north line.
- With this moving clockwise we find other directions East, South and West-called cardinal points.
- The directions between the cardinal directions are called intermediate directions. They are: North-East (NE) South-East (SE), South-West (SW) and North-West (NW). With the help of these directions we can locate any place of accurately.
- One can also find directions with the help of an instrument called compass.

Q. 5. ***What are parallels of latitudes and meridians of longitude?***

Ans.

- All imaginary lines that run east to west parallel to the equator (0°) to the poles are called parallels of latitudes.
- All imaginary half circles (semi circles) which run from north pole to the south pole are termed as meridians of longitude.

Q. 6. ***Give three differences between parallels of latitude and meridians of longitude.***

Ans. Both latitudes and longitudes are imaginary lines expressed in degrees but they are different.

- Equator at 0° is the longest latitude. Other latitudes are of shorter length as they progress towards the poles. While all longitudes including Prime Meridian (0°) are of equal length.
- Distance between the latitudes is equal except at the poles where it is slightly less. Distance between the longitudes varies as they converge at the poles and extends at the Equator 0°.
- Each latitude is a circle. While each longitude is a semicircle. There are 180 latitudes in total while there are 360 longitudes.

Q. 7. ***Briefly discuss the significance of the International Date Line (IDL).***

Ans.

- The International Date Line (IDL) is located exactly opposite the Prime Meridian at 180° longitude in Greenwich.
- The earth rotates from west to east, 360° in 24 hours i.e. 15° in 1 hour. The regions East of Greenwich are ahead of those West of Greenwich in time. There are 24 time zones— + (plus) 12 time zone and – (minus) 12 time zone touch each other on the IDL.
- If you cross the IDL by ship or plane you need to change the date. If you travel from West on Sunday it would be Monday in the East i.e., you subtract a day. While if you travel from East on a Sunday, it would still be Sunday in the west i.e., you add a day. Crossing the IDL changes the date by one day.

[***Example:*** Travelling from USA to India and from India to the USA.]

C. Long Answer Type Questions

Q. 1. ***Why is globe considered the perfect representation of the Earth? Give reasons.***

Ans.

- A globe represents the three-dimensional view of the Earth. Earth is spherical in shape and can accurately depict its geography including the shapes of oceans, and continents.
- It also shows their correct relationship to one another as they are on earth.
- The distances based on scale and the directions of places are fairly accurate on the globe.
- A globe provides a better understanding of parallels of latitudes and meridians of longitude.
- It helps us understand how day and night occur and how seasons are caused.

Q. 2. ***What is standard time?***

Ans. Standard Time:

- Local time of a place is based on its longitude. It means that places situated on different meridians will have different local times.

- This variation creates confusion and makes it difficult for people to function efficiently within a country.
- There is a time difference of 1 hour and 45 minutes between Dwarka (Gujarat) and Dibrugarh (in Assam).
- To address this issue, every country designates a central meridian, which is considered the standard meridian of that country.
- The local time of this meridian is taken as the standard time for the entire country. This is known as standard time.
- In India, the longitude of 82½° E (82° 30° E) is treated as the standard meridian.
- The local time of this meridian is followed all over the country.
- This is known as Indian Standard Time (IST).
- Through an international agreement, the local time of all places is linked to the Greenwich Mean Time (GMT). Different places have different times.

D. Assertion & Reasoning Questions

There are two statements marked as Assertion (A) and Reason (R). Mark your answer as per the codes provided below:

Q. 1. Assertion (A): A globe is the most accurate way of representing the Earth and its geography.

Reason (R): A map is a representation of the Earth but a flat map cannot show the curved surface of the Earth.

Codes:

(*a*) Both (A) and (R) are true but (R) is not the correct explanation of (A).

(*b*) Both (A) and (R) are true and (R) is the correct explanation of (A).

(*c*) (A) is true but (R) is false.

(*d*) (A) is false but (R) is true.

Q. 2. Assertion (A): Ships and aircrafts wherever possible follow the Great Circle routes in order to save time and fuel.

Reason (R): The shortest distance between two points on spherical Earth is the route following the arc of the Great Circle passing through them.

Codes:

(*a*) Both (A) and (R) are true but (R) is not the correct explanation of (A).

(*b*) Both (A) and (R) are true and (R) is the correct explanation of (A).

(*c*) (A) is true but (R) is false.

(*d*) (A) is false but (R) is true.

[**Attention:** The Equator and all pairs of meridians divide the Earth into two equal halves and therefore called Great Circles.]

Q. 3. Assertion (A): There is a connection between latitude and climate.

Reason (R): As we travel away from the Equator Eastward or Westward the climate becomes more moderate and colder.

Codes:

(*a*) Both (A) and (R) are true but (R) is not the correct explanation of (A).

(*b*) Both (A) and (R) are true and (R) is the correct explanation of (A).

(*c*) (A) is true but (R) is false.

(*d*) (A) is false but (R) is true.

Q. 4. Assertion (A): By measuring longitude of a place we will also be measuring the time at that place.

Reason (R): Longitude is a measure of distance from the Prime Meridian (0°) Eastward or Westward.

Codes:

(*a*) Both (A) and (R) are true but (R) is not the correct explanation of (A).

(*b*) Both (A) and (R) are true and (R) is the correct explanation of (A).

(*c*) (A) is true but (R) is false.

(*d*) (A) is false but (R) is true.

Q. 5. Assertion (A): The earth completes one full rotation on its axis every 24 hours.

Reason (R): The Earth rotates 15° an hour or 1° in four minutes.

Codes:

(*a*) Both (A) and (R) are true but (R) is not the correct explanation of (A).

(*b*) Both (A) and (R) are true and (R) is the correct explanation of (A).

(*c*) (A) is true but (R) is false.

(*d*) (A) is false but (R) is true.

Ans. **1.** (*a*) **2.** (*a*) **3.** (*c*) **4.** (*b*) **5.** (*a*)

E. Case/Source Based Questions

Read the passages given below and answer the questions that follow:

I. Every map has certain components which help us to read it easily and properly. One such component are symbols. Symbols for different kinds of buildings—railway station, a school, a post office, for roads, and colours for natural elements such as a river, a pond or a forest. In that way, numerous details can be shown in the limited space available on a map. The common standard symbols that are Internationally accepted and used in maps are called conventional symbols. These help us to easily draw maps, show details, also read, interpret and surmount barrier of language and culture world over.

(*i*) Why are symbols used on maps?

(*ii*) What are the benefits of using symbols on maps?

(*iii*) What colours are used to represent major physical features on physical maps— mountains, plateaus, rivers, and plains?

(*iv*) What are the common symbols called?

(*v*) Give two main components of a map.

(*vi*) Which government body in India is responsible to fix symbols for map of India?

Ans.

(*i*) Symbols are used on maps to represent numerous details—like roads, buildings, bridges, trees etc. in limited space.

(*ii*) Benefits of using symbols on maps are:

(*a*) Simplify information: Represent complex features in a simple way.

(*b*) Save space: Allow more details to be shown without overcrowding.

(*c*) Easy to understand: Provide a universal way to interpret maps.

(*d*) Show important features: Indicate roads, rivers, landmarks etc.

(*e*) Enhance clarity: Improve readability and quick reference.

(*iii*) Colours are used to represent physical features:

Mountains—Brown

Plateaus—Yellow

Rivers—Blue

Plains—Green

(*iv*) Common symbols are called conventional symbols.

(*v*) Two main components of maps are—(*a*) Distance and (*b*) Direction

(*vi*) Survey of India.

II. The Earth rotates from west to east. This is obvious from the fact that sun rises in the east and sets in the west.

When sun rises at a particular place any place to its east has already seen sunrise and it is morning there. However, at places to its west, it is still dark. It takes the earth 24 hours to complete one rotation of 360°. Geographers have divided the entire globe into 24 time zones, each with its own time. The difference between each time zone is 15° or one hour. The middle longitude of each time zone is taken as the standard meridian and the local time on that meridian is generally followed all over the time zone as the standard time. This creates uniformity and avoids confusion.

(*i*) The Earth is divided into how many time zones?

(*ii*) What is the difference in degrees and minutes between one time zone and the next?

(*iii*) State the relationship between standard meridian and standard time.

(*iv*) What is the standard meridian of India?

(*v*) What is the time followed by India called?

(*vi*) By how many hours IST is ahead of Greenwich Mean Time. Why so? Explain briefly.

Ans.

(*i*) The Earth is divided into 24 time zones.

(*ii*) Difference in degree: 15°,
Difference in minutes: 60 minutes (4 min × 15 = 60 min)

(*iii*) Every country has few meridians passing through it—(for example India has 30 meridians passing through it. So if each meridian were to follow its own local time, there would be a lot of confusion within the country. Local time of some central meridian of a country is taken as the time for the whole country. This meridian is called standard meridian and its local time is called the standard time of that country.

(*iv*) Standard meridian of India—82½° E.

(*v*) Time followed by India is called Indian Standard Time (IST).

(*vi*) IST is ahead of Greenwich Mean Time by 5 hours 30 minutes because the Standard Meridian of India is 82½°E i.e.

4 minutes for every 1°
= 82½° × 4 minutes = 330 minutes
= 330 minutes ÷ 60 = 5 hours 30 minutes ahead of GMT.

III. While Prime Meridian was fixed at Greenwich, the opposite line at approximately 180° is called the International Date Line (IDL). If we cross it by ship or plane you need to change the date in your watch. If you say cross the line travelling from west to east. We adjust our watches by adding a day, while we subtract a day when we cross the date line east to west. It passes through many Islands in the Pacific Ocean, it is a zig zag line and deviates in places to avoid dividing some countries into two different days.

(*i*) The Prime Meridian fixed at Greenwich, London is fixed at.

(*a*) 0° Latitude
(*b*) 0° Longitude
(*c*) 180° Latitude
(*d*) 180° E longitude

(*ii*) The International Date Line that approximately is opposite to the Prime Meridian is

(*a*) 180° E (*b*) 180° W
(*c*) 0° (*d*) 180°

(*iii*) Unlike the Prime Meridian, the International Date Line (IDL).

(*a*) is a straight imaginary meridian of longitude
(*b*) deviates in certain places.
(*c*) passes through the Atlantic Ocean
(*d*) requires to change the time on your watch when crossing it.

(*iv*) The opposite line at approximately 180° is called the IDL because

(*a*) If we cross this meridian of longitude we have to subtract a day.
(*b*) This meridian of longitude determines standard time.
(*c*) If we cross this meridian we need to change the date on our watch.
(*d*) If we cross the meridian, we have to add a day.

Ans. (*i*) (*b*) (*ii*) (*d*) (*iii*) (*b*) (*iv*) (*c*)

F. Competency Based Questions

Q. 1. ***How do cardinal points and intermediate directions in maps help reach destination?***

Ans. Everything is understood in relation to the other. So is the case with direction—to ones left or right. But this is possible if one is aware of the area and surroundings. Take an example of two friends who are standing at different points with their back facing each other. If they are asked to go left — each would go in different directions but if they are told to go towards the north or say south they will go in one direction. Thus, cardinal points and intermediate directions are important to help guide us reach our destinations.

Q. 2. ***How do grid lines formed by the two coordinates—latitudes and longitudes, help locate places on map or globe? Support your answer with an example.***

Ans. Maps and globes have a network of horizontal and vertical lines called parallels of latitude and meridians of longitude.

(i) Latitudes are imaginary lines expressed in degrees that measure distance North or South of the Equator (0°). Longitudes are also expressed in degrees and measure the distance East or West of the Prime Meridian (0°).

(ii) The values of latitudes range from 90° North of the Equator (0°) to 90° South of the Equator. Similarly, longitudes range from 180° E to 180° W of the Prime Meridian (0°). 180° E and 180° W Meridians lie on the same line. Latitudes are represented by the letters 'N' or 'S' and longitudes by the letters 'E' or 'W'.

(iii) These imaginary lines intersect to form a grid pattern creating squares of latitude and longitude. This grid helps in locating any place on a map or globe. ***Example:*** Dhubri in Assam, is situated 26° N latitude and 90° E longitude. The point where these two lines intersect represents the exact location of Dhubri.

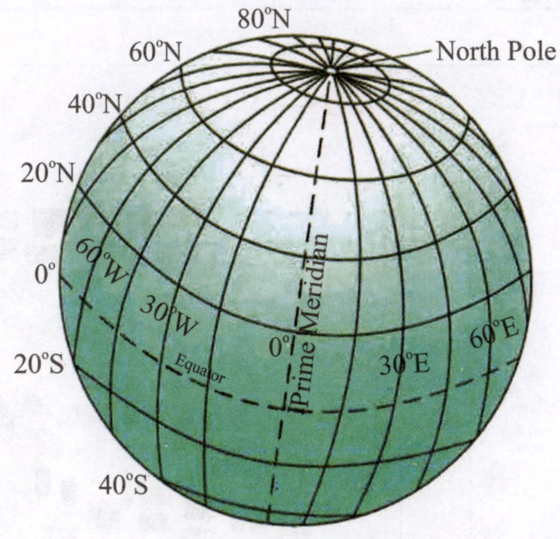

(Fig. 1.3)

Q. 3. ***Explain why the standard meridian of any country is usually a multiple of 15° or 7.5° as per international agreement.***

Ans. As per international agreement the standard meridian of any country is usually a multiple of 15° or 7.5°. So that the difference between its standard time and Greenwich Mean Time (GMT) can easily be expressed as multiple of one hour (15°) or half and hour (7.5°).

G. Skill Based Questions

Q. 1. ***What would be the local time at a place situated 60° W and 90° E of London if it is 10 am at London.***

Ans. Time at London: 10 am.

Local time 60° W of London :

60 × 4 mins = 240 minutes

240 minutes ÷ 60 = 4 hours.

10 am – 4 hours = 6 am.

Time at London : 10 am.

Local time at 90° E of London : 90 × 4 mins = 360 minutes.

= 360 minutes ÷ 60 = 6 hours.

= 10 am + 6 hours = 4 pm.

H. Picture Based Questions

Q. 1. ***Look at the map of the Sunderpur Village and its surroundings and answer the questions that follow.***

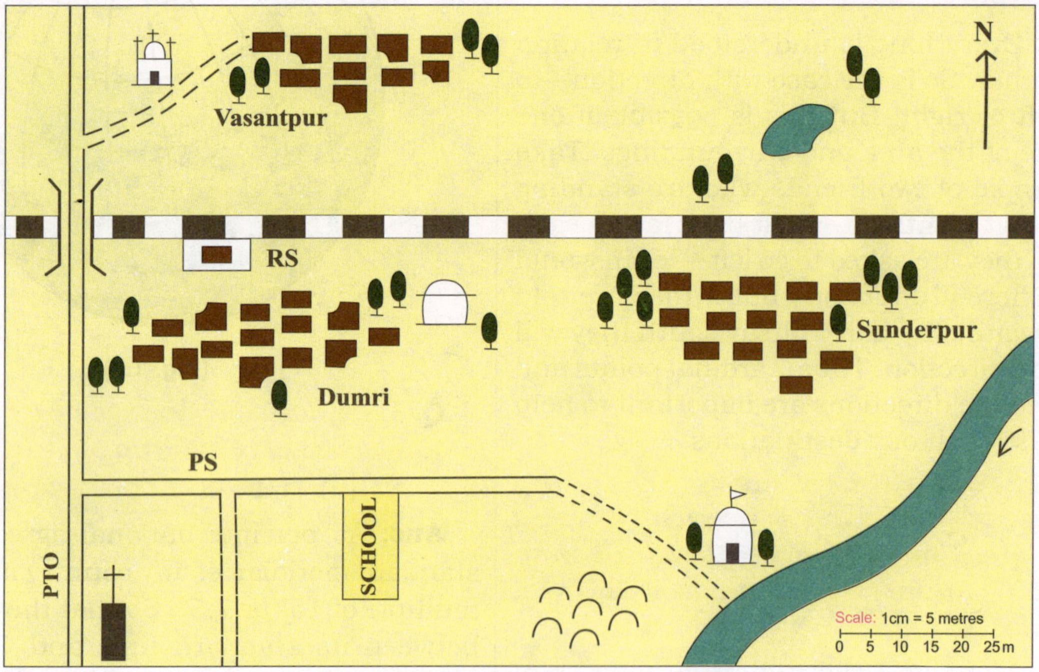

(Fig. 4.4)

(*i*) In which direction is the river flowing?

(*ii*) What kind of road passes by the side of village Dumri?

(*iii*) On what type of railway line is Sunderpur situated?

(*iv*) On which side of the railway bridge is the Police Station situated?

(*v*) On which side of the railway line do the following lie?

(*a*) River

(*b*) Post and Telegraph Office

(*c*) School

(*vi*) Measure with scale and answer how far is the school from the river?

Ans.

(*i*) South

(*ii*) Metalled

(*iii*) Broad gauge railway line

(*iv*) South

(*v*) (*a*) South East

(*b*) South West

(*c*) South

(*vi*) The school is 25 metres away from the river i.e. 5 cm if we draw and measure diagonally 5 × 5 metres = 25 metres.

Q.2. *Look at the picture below and answer the questions that follow:*

(*i*) *The direction of the Community Centre.*

(*ii*) *The direction of the playground from Vikas's house.*

(*iii*) *The direction of the school from shops.*

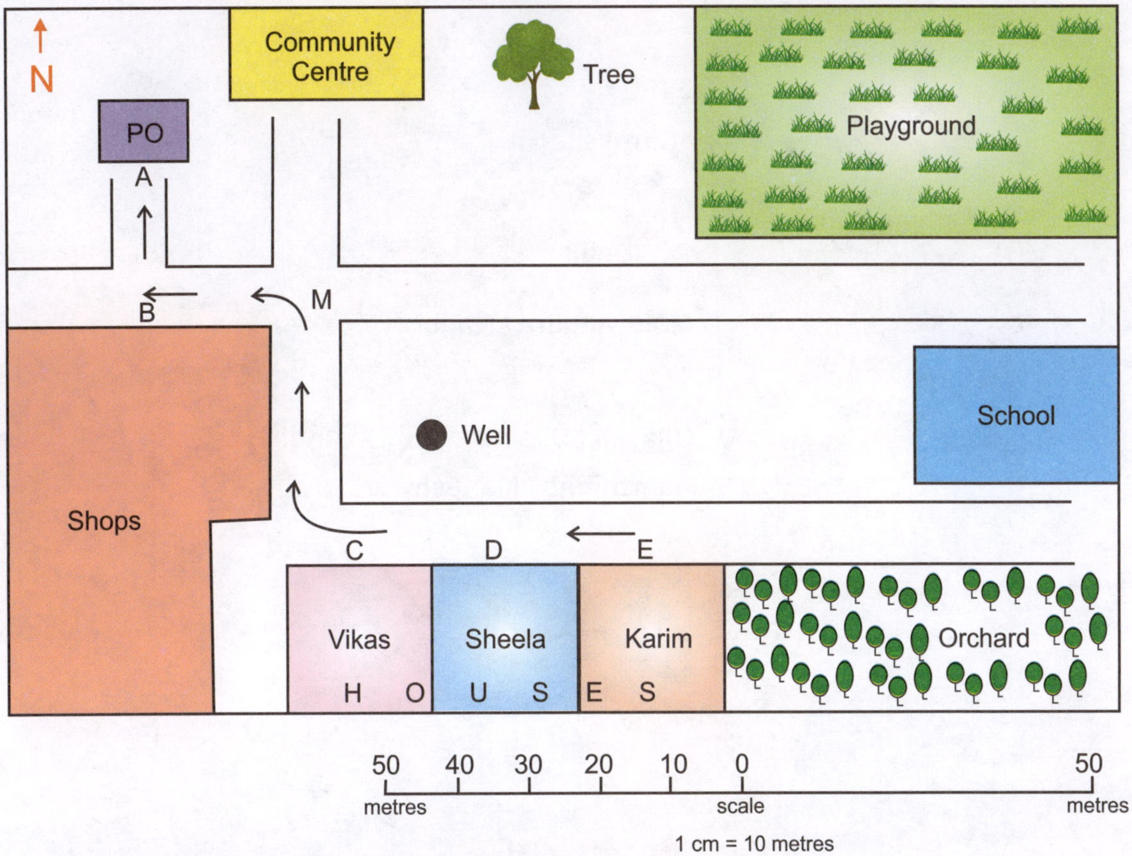

Ans. (*i*) **Community Centre**—North direction

(*ii*) **Playground**—North East direction

(*iii*) **School**—East

VII. MAP SKILLS

Q.1. *Look at the map (See NCERT Page 18)*

(*i*) *What is the value of (degree) of 'Madhya rekha'?*

(*ii*) *Give names of any 5 cities which according to ancient texts were on the madhya rekha.*

(*iii*) *Why are some cities marked away from the 'Madhya rekha'?*

(*iv*) *Look at the atlas and write down the approximate latitude and longitude of Delhi, Mumbai, Kolkata, Bengaluru, Chennai and Kanyakumari.*

(*v*) *Identify which of the following places would be having the some local time. Give reason.*

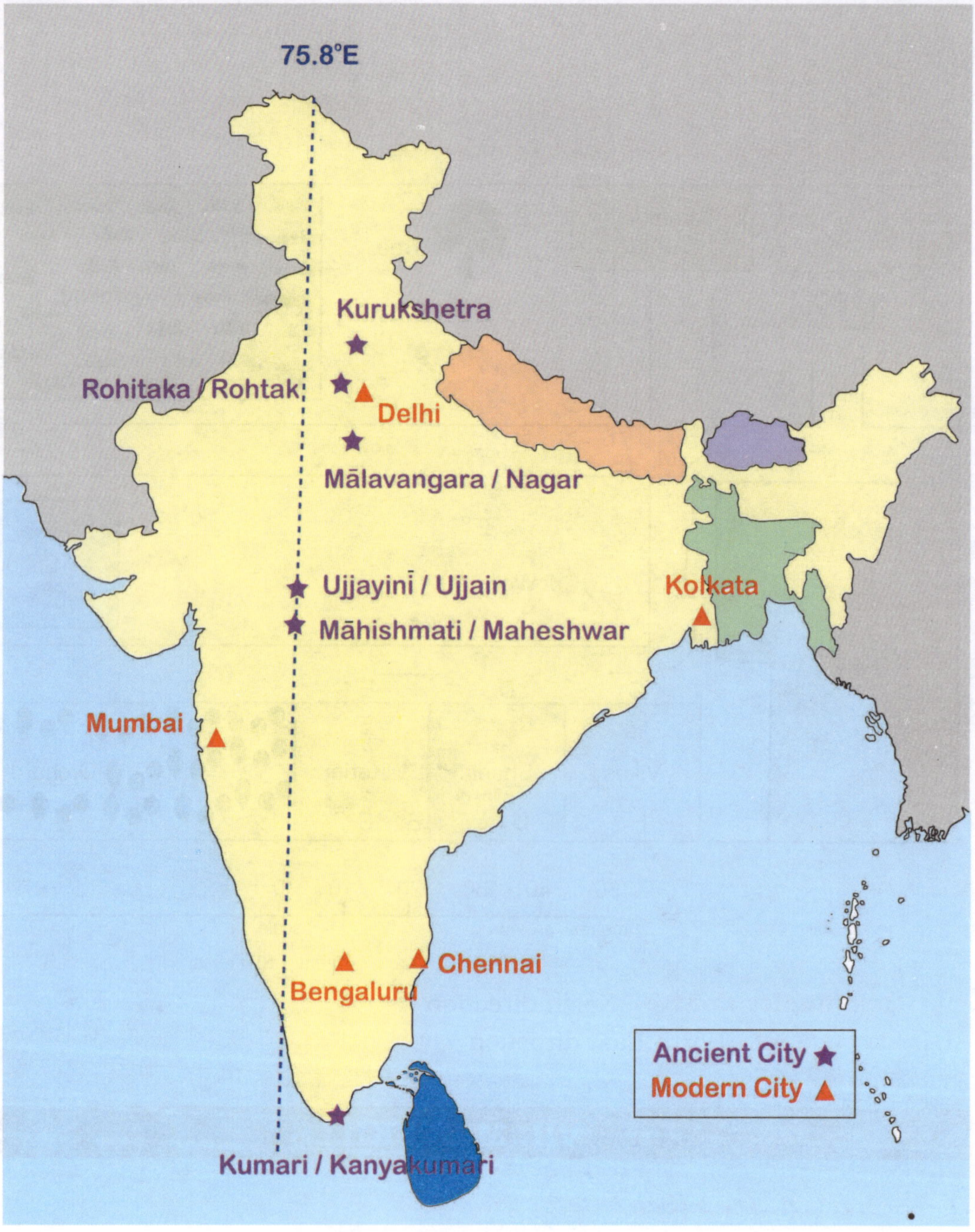

Ans.

(*i*) 75.8°E.

(*ii*) Kurukshetra, Rohitaka [Rohtak], Malāvangara [Nagar], Ujjayini [Ujjain] and Māhishmati [Maheshwar].

(*iii*) That is because measuring longitude required accurate time keeping which was not as precise then as it is today.

(*iv*) Delhi – 28°N 77° E
Mumbai – 19°N 72° E
Kolkata – 22°N 88° E
Bengaluru – 12°N 77° E
Chennai – 13°N 80° E
Kanyakumari – 8°N 77° E

(*v*) Delhi, Bengaluru and Kanyakumari have same local time as they are approximately on the same longitude 77° E.

Q.2. ***Look at the globe and answer the following questions:***

(*i*) *What is the value of the Prime Meridian?*

(*ii*) *Which important latitude passes nearly midway through India?*

(*iii*) *What is an equator?*

(*iv*) *What is the latitudinal value of the Tropic of Cancer?*

(*v*) *What is the name given to the top half of the globe?*

Ans. (*i*) 0° Longitude

(*ii*) Tropic of Cancer.

(*iii*) An equator is an imaginary line running horizontally on the globe dividing it into two equal halves.

(*iv*) The Tropic of Cancer lies 23½°N of the equator.

(*v*) Northern Hemisphere.

The Earth

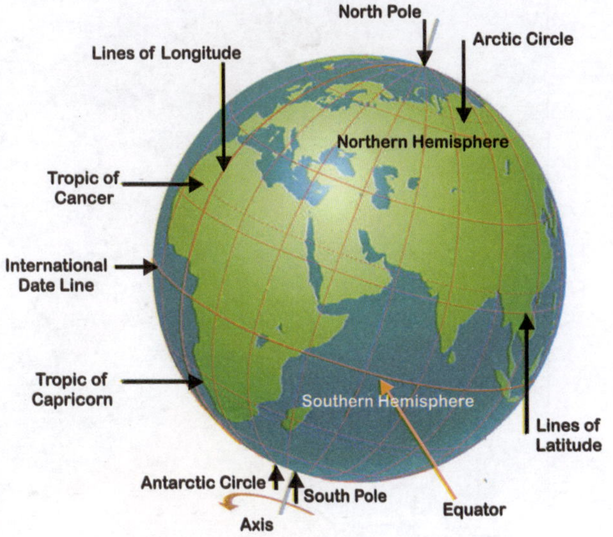

Q.3. (*i*) ***What is the degree of Prime Meridian?***

(*ii*) ***What is the degree of International Date Line?***

(*iii*) ***India lies in which hemisphere?***

(*iv*) ***What is time at zero time known as?***

Ans. (*i*) Prime Meridian— 0°.

(*ii*) International Date Line— 180°.

(*iii*) Northern Hemisphere.

(*iv*) Greenwich Mean Time (GMT).

Q.4. (*i*) ***What is represented in the map given below?***

(*ii*) ***How would you classify this map?***

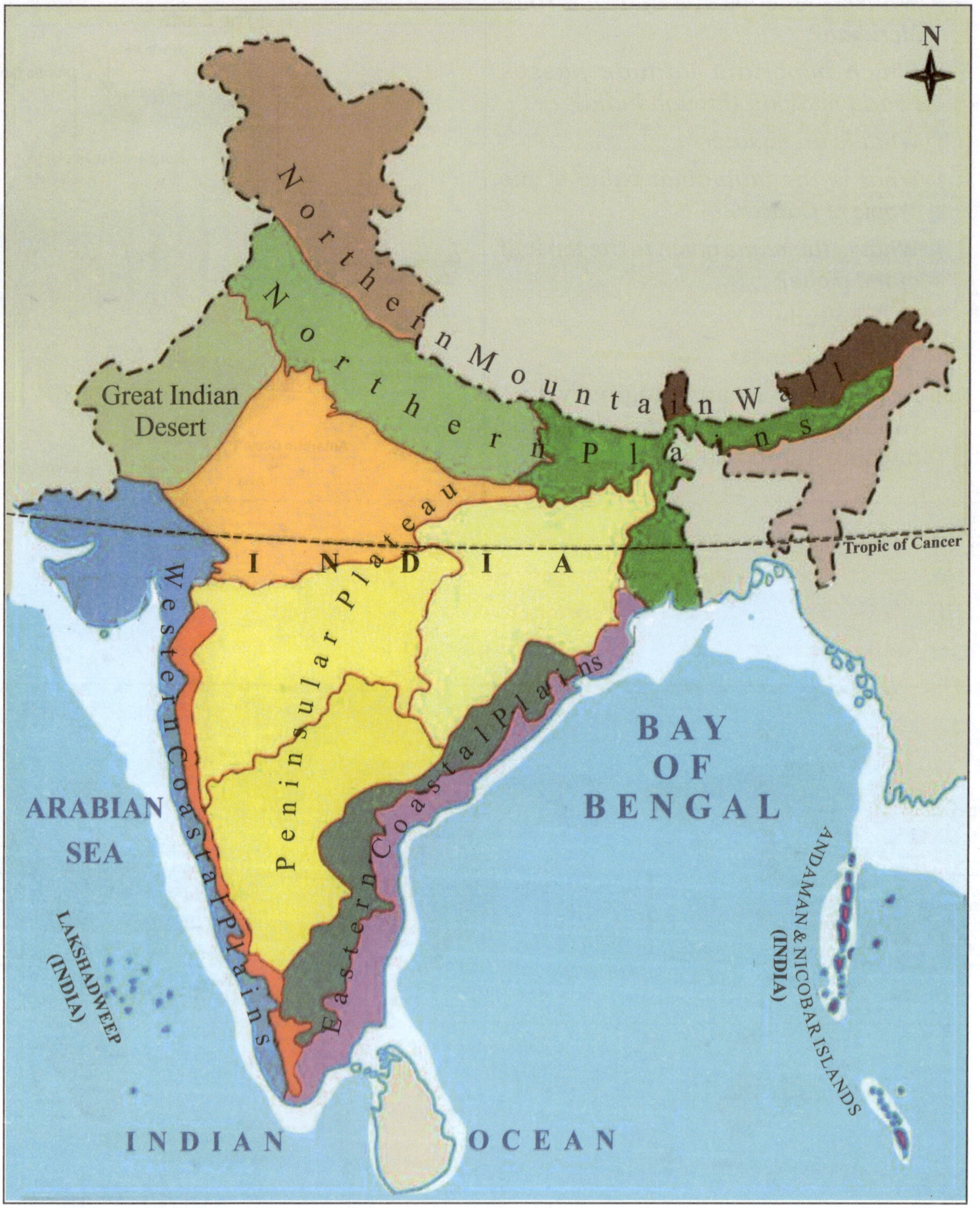

Ans. (*i*) Physical features of India

(*a*) Northern Mountains (*b*) Northern Plains (*c*) Great Indian Desert (Thar) (*d*) Peninsula Plateau (*e*) Western and Eastern Coastal Plains (*f*) Islands—Lakshadweep and Andaman & Nicobar Islands (*g*) The Indian Ocean and Seas — Arabian Sea and Bay of Bengal

(*ii*) Physical Map.

VIII. MULTIPLE CHOICE QUESTIONS

1. *Which of the following tool would you use to understand the layout of your city?*

(*a*) a globe (*b*) a sketch
(*c*) a map (*d*) an atlas

2. *Which of the following statements are **true:***

(*i*) Map is a drawing or representation of some area—small or big.
(*ii*) Maps give a top view of the surface represented.
(*iii*) Maps are a projection on a sheet of paper.
(*iv*) Maps give a rough idea of a globe on a sheet of paper.

(*a*) (i) & (ii) (*b*) (i), (iii) & (iv)
(*c*) (ii) & (iii) (*d*) (iii) & (iv)

3. *Map showing distribution of forests are called _______.*

(*a*) Political map (*b*) Physical map
(*c*) Thematic map (*d*) Colourful map

4. *A scale is necessary for*

(*a*) a plan (*b*) symbols
(*c*) accuracy (*d*) a map.

5. *Which of the following is **not** an important component of a map?*

(*a*) Symbols (*b*) Direction
(*c*) Theme (*d*) Distance

6. *Which of the following are cardinal directions?*

(*a*) East and South
(*b*) South east and West
(*c*) North and North east
(*d*) West and South west

7. *An arrow marked with a letter 'N' on a map signifies.*

(*a*) North west (*b*) North east
(*c*) North (*d*) Top corner

8. *Grid is a network of:*

(*a*) lines of latitude
(*b*) lines converging at the poles
(*c*) total number of longitudes
(*d*) parallels of latitudes and meridians of longitudes.

9. *The longest circle drawn midway between the two poles is*

(*a*) The Prime Meridian
(*b*) The Equator
(*c*) The Tropic of Cancer
(*d*) The Tropic of Capricorn.

10. *The Equator does not pass through which of the following continents?*

(*a*) Europe (*b*) Africa
(*c*) Asia (*d*) South America.

11. *Which two imaginary lines help in locating a place on the globe?*

(*a*) Equator and Prime Meridian
(*b*) Equator and International Date Line
(*c*) Prime Meridian and Tropic of Cancer
(*d*) Latitudes and Longitudes.

12. *What is the longitude for IST?*

(*a*) 82½° W (*b*) 82½° E
(*c*) 80½° W (*d*) 80½° E

13. *Opposite imaginary line to Prime Meridian is called.*

(*a*) IDL (*b*) Equator
(*c*) South Pole (*d*) North Pole

14. *Which of the following statements are **correct** regarding the rotation of the Earth?*

(*i*) The Earth rotates on its axis and takes full circle in 24 hours
(*ii*) Earth rotates West to East
(*iii*) Earth covers 15° in one hour
(*iv*) Earth rotates East to West.

(*a*) (i), (ii) & (iii)
(*b*) (i), (ii) & (iv)
(*c*) (i), (iii) & (iv)
(*d*) (ii), (iii) & (iv)

15. *Which of the following statements are* ***correct*** *regarding the time in India and Greenwich?*

(*i*) If it is 4 pm in India it is 10:30 am at Greenwich.

(*ii*) The time in India is ahead of Greenwich because India is to the East of Greenwich.

(*iii*) Since IST is calculated as per 82½° E longitude of Greenwich for every 1° there is a difference of 4 minutes i.e., 1 hour for 15°.

(*iv*) The time in India is behind that of Greenwich.

(*a*) (i), (ii) & (iv)

(*b*) (i), (ii) & (iii)

(*c*) (ii), (iii) & (iv)

(*d*) (i), (iii) & (iv)

Ans.

1. (*c*) **2.** (*a*) **3.** (*c*) **4.** (*d*) **5.** (*c*)
6. (*a*) **7.** (*c*) **8.** (*d*) **9.** (*b*) **10.** (*a*)
11. (*d*) **12.** (*b*) **13.** (*a*) **14.** (*a*) **15.** (*b*)

IX. OBJECTIVE TYPE QUESTIONS

A. True or False

1. Distance between two points represented on maps depend on symbols and colours that a map is using.

2. Both latitudes and longitudes are expressed in degrees.

3. It takes the Earth 365 days to complete one spin on its axis called rotation.

4. India's (Bharat's) Prime Meridian many centuries ago was called 'madhya rekha' and passed through the city of Ujjayini.

5. India's latitudes extend approximately from 8°N to 37°N and longitudes from 68°E to 97°E.

Ans.

1. False **2.** True
3. False **4.** True
5. True

B. Fill in the Blanks

1. The Earth rotates from _____ to _____.

2. Each degree of longitude corresponds to a time difference of _____ minutes.

3. International Date Line passes through the _____ Ocean.

4. Prime Meridian passes through Greenwich near _____.

5. Standard Meridian of India is _____.

Ans.

1. West/East

2. 4 minutes

3. Pacific

4. London

5. 82½° E longitude

C. Match Column A with Column B

	Column A		Column B
1.	Coordinates	*a.*	Scale
2.	Distance	*b.*	North
3.	Cardinal directions	*c.*	Latitudes and Longitudes
4.	Axis	*d.*	Model of Earth
5.	Globe	*e.*	23½°

Ans.

1. → (*c*) **2.** → (*a*)
3. → (*b*) **4.** → (*e*)
5. → (*d*)

X. TEST YOUR KNOWLEDGE

A. Multiple Choice Questions

1. *Maps representing, rivers, plains, plateaus mountains and oceans are called:*

   (*a*) Political maps (*b*) Feature maps

   (*c*) Physical maps (*d*) Thematic maps

2. *Which of the following statements relate to scale, integral to the important component distance in maps?*

   (*i*) scale is very important in maps to represent distance

   (*ii*) scale is the ratio between actual distance on ground and distance shown on the map

   (*iii*) Maps are drawn to a large scale.

   (*iv*) Maps are drawn to a reduced scale.

   (*a*) (i), (ii) & (iii)

   (*b*) (ii), (iii) & (iv)

   (*c*) (i), (ii) & (iv)

   (*d*) (i), (iii) & (iv)

3. *The pointer or arrow on maps points towards:*

   (*a*) the North

   (*b*) the South

   (*c*) the direction

   (*d*) the North and South

4. *Which of the following statements relate to meridian of longitude?*

   (*i*) The local time of a place is calculated with the help of its longitude.

   (*ii*) Longitudes are expressed in degrees.

   (*iii*) Difference of 7.5° between longitudes amounts to one hour difference.

   (*iv*) All longitudes are not of equal length and form great circles.

   (*a*) (i), (ii) & (iii)

   (*b*) (i), (ii) & (iv)

   (*c*) (i), (iii) & (iv)

   (*d*) (i) & (ii)

5. *Find the **odd** one out.*

   (*a*) The area between Tropic of Cancer and Tropic of Capricorn is the Torrid Zone.

   (*b*) The Equator divides the Earth into Northern and Southern Hemispheres.

   (*c*) All parallels of latitude are equal and expressed in degrees.

   (*d*) The Tropic of Cancer nearly runs to the middle of the subcontinent of India.

Ans.

1. (*c*) **2.** (*c*) **3.** (*a*) **4.** (*d*) **5.** (*c*)

B. Very Short Answer Type Questions

Q. 1. *How many types of maps are there?*

Q. 2. *What do you mean by the term 'the scale of a map'?*

Q. 3. *What are the three heat zones of the Earth?*

Q. 4. *How is the globe more advantageous than a map?*

Q. 5. *How much time does the Earth take to complete one spin on its axis?*

C. Short Answer Type Questions

Q. 1. *How is distance measured?*

Q. 2. *Distinguish between Equator and Prime Meridian.*

Q. 3. *Define the term 'Grid lines'.*

Q. 4. *Give reason:*

(*i*) *Why the lines dividing the time zones are not fully straight?*

(*ii*) *Why meridians selected for standard are divisible by 7.5°?*

Q. 5. *Briefly discuss with examples some of the colour schemes used in physical maps.*

D. Long Answer Type Questions

Q. 1. *There is a connection between latitude and climate. Discuss.*

Q. 2. *Compare and contrast parallels of latitude and meridians of longitude.*

INTERESTING MIND MAP

Oceans and Continents

1 Introduction

- Earth looks blue as three-fourths is water
- Large water bodies are **oceans** and land is one-fourth
- **Landmass** is a large land area; a **continent** is a bigger landmass
- Oceans and continents affect climate, life, and culture

2 The Distribution of Water and Land on the Earth

- Oceans and land are unevenly spread in two hemispheres, the Northern and Southern Hemispheres
- **Seas**, **bays**, **gulfs** are smaller parts of oceans
- Most of the ocean water is salty and undrinkable
- Freshwater is limited and found in rivers, lakes, glaciers, air, and underground

3 Oceans

- **Five oceans:** Pacific, Atlantic, Indian, Arctic, and Southern
- Ocean boundaries on maps are conventional, not natural
- Seawater flows freely, connecting all oceans
- **Marine flora and fauna:** Include algae, seaweeds, colourful fish, dolphins, whales, and deep-sea creatures
- Pacific is largest, followed by the Atlantic, Indian, Southern, and Arctic

3(a) Oceans and disasters

- **Oceans** bring rain that supports life and agriculture
- Storms, cyclones, and tsunamis cause damage
- **Tsunami:** A huge sea wave caused by an underwater earthquake or volcanic eruption, leading to great damage in coastal areas
- 2004 tsunami affected Andaman & Nicobar Islands, Tamil Nadu, and Kerala
- Warning systems and disaster management help save lives

4 Continents

- **Seven Continents:** Africa, Antarctica, Asia, Australia, Europe, North America, & South America
- North & South America can sometimes be counted as one continent
- Europe & Asia can be counted together as one continent called Eurasia

4(a) Islands

- Land surrounded by water on all sides
- Continents are not islands because they are very large
- Lakhs of islands exist in different sizes worldwide

5 Oceans and Life

- Oceans provide rainfall and support the water cycle
- Produce over half of Earth's oxygen; called planet's lungs
- Regulate climate and sustain life
- Used for trade, fishing, travel and shape coastal cultures and stories

CHAPTER

2

THEME A
India and the World:
Land and the People

OCEANS AND CONTINENTS

I. FACTS TO REMEMBER/SUMMARY

PRELUDE

- The most widespread colour in the picture of the Earth seen from the Moon is '*Blue*'.
- Almost 3/4th of Earth's surface is actually covered with water.
- Land covers a little over 1/4th of the globe.
- A large body of land is called a '*Landmass*'.
- Early astronauts lovingly called the Earth the '*blue planet*'.
- The largest water bodies seen on the globe are called '*Oceans*', that are represented by blue colour.

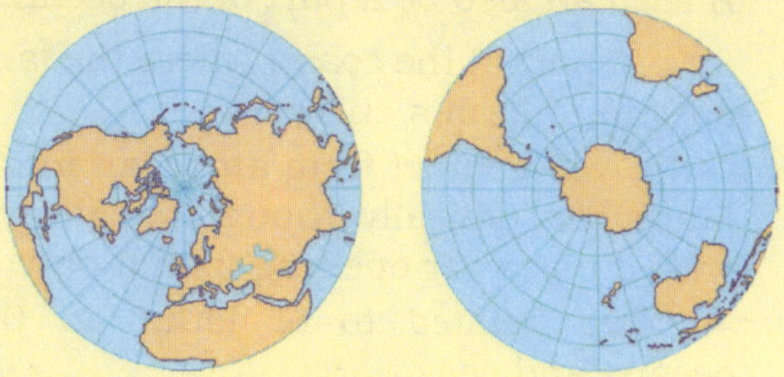

Fig.: Earth as seen from above – the North Pole (Left) and the South Pole (Right)

- The other colour shown is brown. This colour is that of the land.
- Large continuous expanse of land is called a '*continent*'.
- Oceans and continents play a vital role in shaping the climate and all aspects of life.

THE DISTRIBUTION OF WATER AND LAND ON THE EARTH

- Oceans and continents are not distributed equally between the Northern and the Southern Hemisphere.
- While oceans hold most of the water, this water is salty and unfit for consumption.
- Freshwater makes up for small proportion of planet's water.

OCEANS

- There are five oceans in the world **(the Pacific Ocean, the Atlantic Ocean, the Indian Ocean, the Arctic Ocean and the Southern** (or Antarctic) **Ocean).**
- On a map oceans are shown separately but actually they are interconnected.
- Many plants (*flora*) and animals species (*fauna*) can be found across multiple oceans.
- The Pacific ocean is the largest and the Arctic ocean is the smallest ocean.

Oceans and Disasters

- While oceans are a boon they are also home to natural disasters. Example Tsunamis, Cyclones.

CONTINENTS

- There are seven continents in the world **(Africa, Antarctica, Asia, Australia, Europe, North America, South America)**. However, geologists consider North America and South America as one continent. Similarly, although Europe and Asia are considered separate continents, some regard them as a single continent called Eurasia.
- Among the continents Asia is the largest and Australia is the smallest.

Islands

- Smaller pieces of land surrounded by water from all sides are called islands.
- Greenland is the largest island in the world.

OCEANS AND LIFE

- Oceans and continents are vital parts of the environment and affect most aspects of our life.

II. TEXTBOOK KEYWORDS/GLOSSARY

1. **Oceans:** Largest water bodies.
2. **Landmass:** A large body of land.
3. **Continent:** A large continuous expanse of land.
4. **Earth:** Blue planet.
5. **Varuna:** A Vedic deity
6. **Sea:** A particular large area of salt water. A sea can also be a part of the ocean.
7. **Bay:** A part of the coast, where the land goes in to form a curve.
8. **Gulf:** A large inlet from an ocean into a landmass, typically (though not always) with a narrower opening than a bay.
9. **Marine:** Related to or found in the oceans and seas.
10. **Flora:** The plant life of a particular region or period of time.
11. **Fauna:** The animal life of a particular region or period of time.
12. **Tsunami:** A natural disaster that originates in the ocean. It is a huge powerful wave caused due to strong earthquake or a volcanic eruption at the bottom of the ocean.
13. **Geologists:** A scientist who studies the structure composition and history of the Earth.
14. **Islands:** Smaller pieces of land surrounded by water from all sides.

III. DATE LINE

- **26 December 2004:** India and 13 other countries around the Indian Ocean were struck by a powerful Tsunami.
- **1981:** Indian Antarctica Programme.
- **1983:** India established its first scientific base station in Antarctica.
- **8 June:** World Oceans Day.

IV. THE BIG QUESTIONS *(Page 27)*

Q. 1. *What are oceans and continents? What are their names and their distribution?*

Ans.

- The Earth's surface is divided into oceans and continents of which almost three-fourths is covered with water and 1/4th with land. 97% of this water is in Oceans. That is why, Earth is called the 'Blue planet'.
- The largest water bodies, we see on the globe are called 'Oceans'. They are all interconnected and level of water remains same everywhere (MSL i.e. Mean Sea Level).
- A large continuous expanse of land is called a continent.
- There are **five** major Oceans of the world from the largest to the smallest they are:

  (*a*) The Pacific Ocean.

  (*b*) The Atlantic Ocean.

  (*c*) The Indian Ocean.

  (*d*) The Southern Ocean.

  (*e*) The Arctic Ocean.
- The Pacific Ocean is the largest and spreads on about 30% area of the earth.
- It is circular in shape. The world's deepest part of the earth — Mariana Trench lies under the Pacific Ocean.
- It is bounded by Asia and Australia on one side and North the South America on the other.
- The Atlantic Ocean is the second largest and is 'S' shaped.
  - It is flanked by the North and South Americas on the western side and Europe and Africa on the eastern side.
  - It has a highly irregular indented coastline, helpful in development of natural harbours.
  - It is the busiest ocean from the point of commerce.

- The Indian Ocean is the third largest and the only Ocean named after a country (India/Bharat). It is shaped almost like a triangular and some say it is 'M' in shape.
  - Its boundaries are: North-Asia, West-Africa, East-Australia and South-Southern Ocean.
  - The Arabian Sea lies to the west, while the Bay of Bengal is to the east.
- The Southern Ocean surrounds the continent of Antarctica.
  - It includes the waters from the Atlantic, Pacific and Indian Oceans around Antarctica.
  - 60°S latitude is often considered its boundary.
  - Some people refer to it as the Antarctic Ocean.
- The Arctic Ocean is smallest of all the Oceans and is located within the Arctic Circle surrounding the North Pole.
  - It is actually a northward extension of the Atlantic Ocean.
  - A narrow water body, Bering Strait connects it to the Pacific Ocean.
  - It is bordered by the northern coasts of North America and Eurasia.

There are seven continents. In order of size they are: Asia, Africa, North America, South America, Antarctica, Europe, and Australia.

Asia: It occupies about 1/3 rd of the Earth land area. It is separated from Europe by the Ural Mountains. Asia and Europe together are known as Eurasia. Asia is surrounded by three oceans- Arctic (N) Pacific (E) & Indian (S).

Africa: Three important latitudes pass through it - Tropic of Cancer, the Equator and Tropic of Capricorn. The Prime Meridian too passes through this landmass. Like Asia it is bound on three sides by water bodies. The Suez Canal separates Asia and Africa.

North America: North America is bound by three oceans -the Arctic Ocean (N), the Atlantic Ocean (E) and the Pacific Ocean. While earlier the Panama Isthmus joined North and South Americas today separates them.

South America: It is too surrounded by oceans on almost all sides— *e.g.* Pacific Ocean on the west side and Atlantic Ocean on the east, the Southern Ocean in the south.

Antarctica: This continent lies to the extreme end of the Southern Hemisphere. The South Pole is almost at the centre. Its other names are frozen continent or the white continent as it is permanently covered with ice. Out of all the continents here people do not live on a permanent basis.

Europe: It is joined to the continent of Asia. In the north it is bound by the Arctic Ocean, in the west by the Atlantic Ocean and in the south by the Mediterranean Sea.

Australia: It is the smallest of the seven continents. It is bound on all sides by seas and oceans and thus also known as an island continent.

Q. 2. ***In what ways do oceans and continents impact life on Earth, including human life?***

Ans. Oceans and continents impact life on Earth including human life in a number of ways.

- They play a vital role in shaping the climate of the Earth. Oceans through currents transport heat from the equator to the poles regulating our climate.
- 98% of the heat from Sun's rays are absorbed by the Oceans.
- They help deliver rain to the continents. They are a part of the water cycle which sustains agriculture, life on earth and replenishes the useable fresh water resources.
- Our Oceans produce over half the world's oxygen we breathe and captures an estimate of 40% of the CO_2 produced which is why they are called 'planet's lungs'.
- The Oceans feed us, example- fishes. Its biodiversity provide our global community with animal protein. In many developed countries seafood is the primary source of protein.

- Oceans provide jobs and livelihoods. From early times people have used oceans and seas to migrate to other regions, to trade in all kinds of goods and to conduct military campaign; and exchange ideas.
- Oceans have impacted history and culture, example seafarers, discovery of sea routes to various continents led to colonisation and imperialisation—even to enslavement.
- However, Oceans are not all a story of gains. Oceans give rise to violent events with extreme rainfall, or strong winds such as cyclones which cause widespread damage to men and material.
- Tsunami, a natural disaster originates in the ocean. The sea waves travel thousands of km, submerge coastal areas and cause loss to life and property.

Like Oceans continents too impact life on Earth. Continents (7) are home to various landforms— mountains, plains, plateaus and deserts. They support variety of plant and animal life giving rise to many interesting eco systems in nature.

The soil cover provides us various forms of vegetation like, forests and grasslands for grazing, agriculture and human settlements.

Continents along with oceans are a rich source of minerals essential for economic development.

The landmass supports all structures like buildings, roads, rails, that are essential for living and transport. Continents are home to vast variety of fauna. The animals range from tigers to lizards to moles, bacteria and organisms that live underground and overground.

The vast and ever growing human population with its wasteful, modern life style and green house gases to contribute to climate change. This inturn impacts life in oceans and on continents. What is needed is a sustainable way of life.

V. NCERT INTEXT/TEXTBOOK EXERCISES

Let's Explore

Q. 1. ***What are the circular lines in each map called? And do you know what the lines radiating out of the two poles are called? (Hint: you studied them in the previous chapter, but here they are presented differently.)*** *(Page 29)*

Ans. The circular lines in each map are called – parallels of latitudes. Lines radiating from the two poles are called – meridians of longitudes.

Q. 2. ***Which hemisphere holds more water?*** *(Page 29)*

Ans. The Southern Hemisphere holds more water than the Northern Hemisphere.

Q. 3. ***What do you think could be the approximate proportion of water to land in the Northern Hemisphere? And in the Southern Hemisphere? Discuss in groups.*** *(Page 29)*

Ans.

- **Northern Hemisphere:** The proportion of water to land 40% land, 60% water.
- **Southern Hemisphere:** The proportion of water to land 20% land, 80% water.

Q. 4. ***Are all the oceans connected with one another, or are there separations between them?*** *(Page 29)*

Ans. Yes, all the five oceans are interconnected.

- Some are connected via the Arctic Ocean.

  Example: The narrow water body named Bering Strait connects the Pacific and the Arctic Ocean.
- Still others are connected by the narrow gap between the land masses of South America and the Antarctica.

Q. 5. *Locate the five oceans and, in the table below, mark the hemisphere or hemispheres they belong to (See fig. 2.3 on NCERT book page 32).*

Ans.

	Northern Hemisphere	Southern Hemisphere
Pacific Ocean	Northern Hemisphere	Southern Hemisphere
Atlantic Ocean	Northern Hemisphere	Southern Hemisphere
Indian Ocean	Northern Hemisphere	Southern Hemisphere
Southern Ocean	–	Southern Hemisphere
Arctic Ocean	Northern Hemisphere	–

For questions 6 to 9

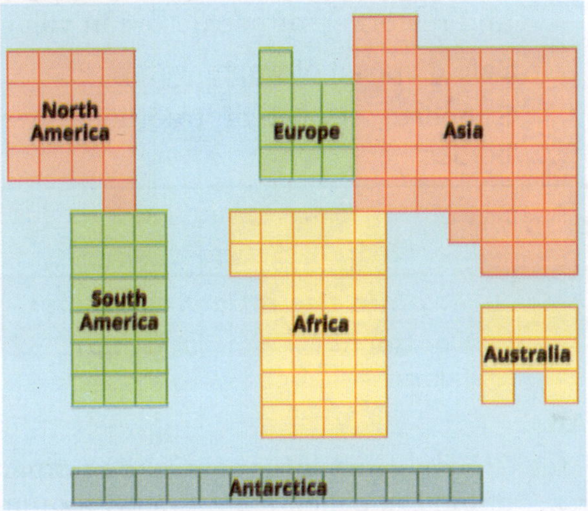

Q. 6. *Counting the numbers of squares, name the largest continent and the smallest.* *(Page 36)*

Ans. The largest continent is Asia and the smallest continent is Australia.

Q. 7. *Which one is larger — North America or South America? Africa or North America? Antarctica or Australia?* *(Page 36)*

Ans. South America is larger than North America.

Africa is larger than North America.

Antarctica is larger than Australia.

Q. 8. *Re-colour the diagram by having a single colour for Europe and Asia and rename the result as 'Eurasia'. Compare its size with South America's.* *(Page 36)*

Ans. 'Eurasia' (54 squares) is three times the size of South America (18 squares).

Q. 9. *Write down the list of continents from the smallest to the largest.* *(Page 36)*

Ans. List of smallest to the largest continents.

1. Australia
2. Europe
3. Antarctica
4. South America
5. North America
6. Africa
7. Asia.

Think About it

Q. 1. *If there is such abundance of water on the planet, why is there so much talk of 'water scarcity' or a 'water crisis'?* *(Page 31)*

Ans.

- The oceans together hold 3/4th of the water available on our planet.
- But the seawater is salty and unfit for consumption by most animals and humans.
- Fresh water (3%) that is fit for consumption constitutes only 1.2% and is available only in rivers and lakes. The rest is locked up in glaciers, ice caps and buried deep under the ground (ground water).
- As there is limited availability of fresh water, we need to use it judiciously *i.e.* with care.
- Other contributing factors which are adding to the scarcity are –
  - Climate change and natural calamities like droughts and floods.
  - Increased human consumption.
  - Pollution of available resources, overuse and wastage.
  - Increased global demand due to population increase and resource intensive economic development.

Q. 2. *What ways of saving water are you aware of? Which ones have you seen practised at home, at your school, and in your village, town or city?* (*Page 31*)

Ans. Water being a precious gift of nature, and an essential and scarce resource needs to be used judiciously.

(*i*) Home:

- Take shorter showers and mostly with bucket and mug.
- Fix leaks.
- Turn off tap and also not put the tap full on.
- Turn off water i.e. not let taps run while brushing teeth or while shaving.
- Do rain water harvesting in which rain water from terrace, veranda goes in underground pit through a separate pipe.
- Mopping the floor instead of washing.
- Reusing water used for washing vegetables by watering plants.
- Ensuring the water tank does not overflow when it is being filled.
- Running washing machine only with full load.
- Wiping the cars with wet mop instead of using hose for cleaning them.
- Low flow flush toilets.

(*ii*) School:

- Turn off water tap after use.
- Report tap or pipes that are leaking.
- Form a water action plan team.
- Encourage students to use refill water bottles and educate them to pour their leftover, water in pots or the play field.
- Raise awareness among students about importance of water by preparing colourful posters on water use and water saving.
- Avoid flushing the toilets unnecessarily.
- Dispose waste like tissues in dustbins rather than in the toilet.
- Designate a water saving week in school calendar to spread awareness and save water.

(*iii*) Village/Town/City:

- Harvest and reuse water
- Educate and engage community to harvest and store water.
- Check for openings or leaks in water distribution pipes.
- Better irrigation practices like drip irrigation.
- Invest in water harvesting by digging ponds, canals or installing water collecting ducts.
- Replenish ground water by building and restoring infrastructure in villages.
- Safe disposal of waste water.
- Support revival of traditional water bodies.

NCERT Questions, Activities and Projects
(*Pages 39-40*)

Q. 1. *Explain the following terms:*

(*a*) Continent (*b*) Ocean
(*c*) Island

Ans.

(*a*) **Continent:** A large continuous expanse of land is called a continent. Example: Asia, North America.

(*b*) **Oceans:** Vast water bodies on the surface of the earth are called oceans. Example: Pacific Ocean, Indian Ocean.

(*c*) **Island:** Some smaller places of land surrounded by water from all sides are called Islands. Example: Lakshadweep Islands, Andaman and Nicobar Islands.

Q. 2. *Let us draw – Without looking at the maps in this chapter, draw the continents free hand on a sheet of paper and colour them. Then compare your drawing with the map of oceans and continents in the chapter.*

Ans. Do it yourself.

Q. 3. ***Let us do – On the outline map of the world given below, label all the continents and oceans.***

Ans.

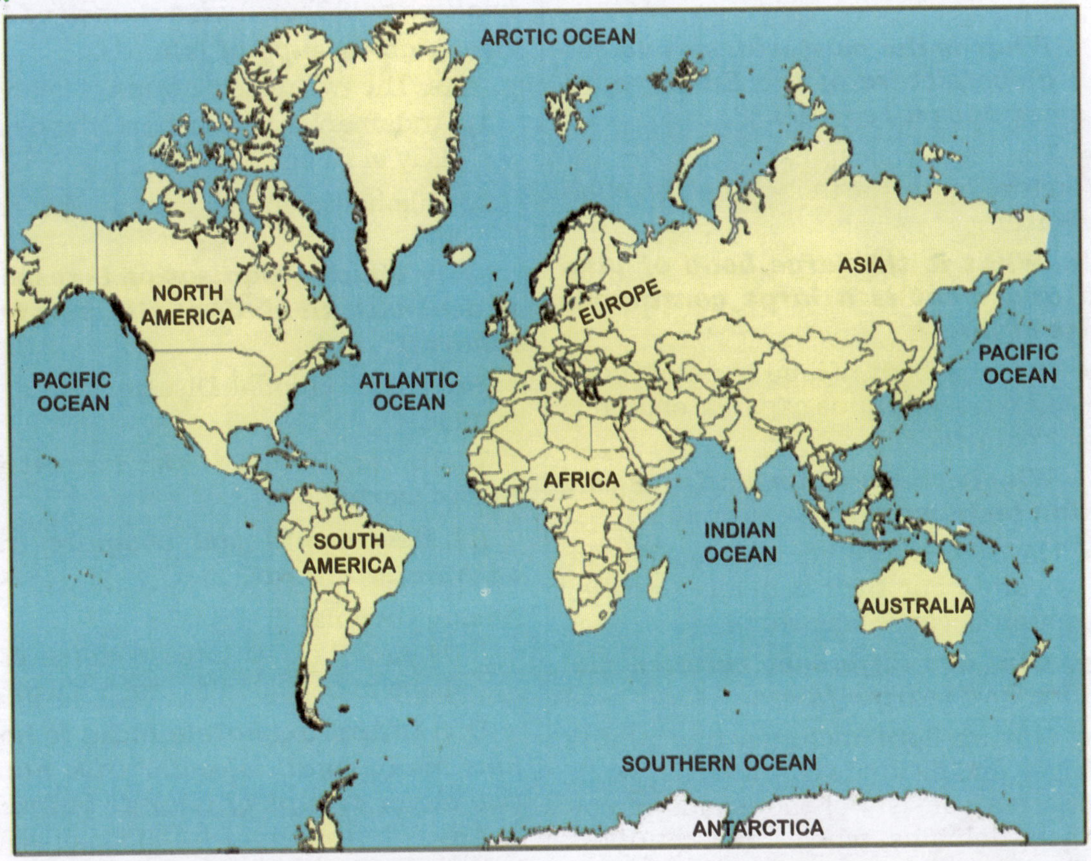

Q. 4. ***Solve this crossword.***

ACROSS		DOWN	
1.	Abundantly produced by the oceans	2.	The largest island on Earth
3.	A large expanse of landmass	4.	A huge destructive wave from the ocean
6.	A large continent of which India is a part	5.	The smallest continent
8.	A major source of pollution of the oceans	7.	The largest body of water on the Earth
10	The coldest continent	9.	A landmass (but not a continent) surrounded by the sea or ocean

Ans.

VI. EXAM ORIENTED QUESTIONS

A. Very Short Answer Type Questions

Q. 1. ***What is the most widespread colour on globe/picture of the Earth represent, what does it represent?***

Ans. The most widespread colour on the globe/picture of the Earth is **'Blue'**. It represents **'Water'**.

Q. 2. ***What is the large body of land called and what is a large continuous expanse of land?***

Ans. The large body of land is called *'landmass'*. A large continuous expanse of land is called a *'continent'*.

Q. 3. ***Why is ocean water unfit for consumption by humans?***

Ans. The oceans together hold most of the water available but their water is unfit for consumption because it is *salty*.

Q. 4. ***Give one difference between marine flora and marine fauna.***

Ans. Marine flora includes tiny plants called algae and all kinds of seaweeds. While marine fauna consists of thousands of colourful fish, dolphins, whales and countless mysterious deep-sea creatures.

Q. 5. ***Enumerate limits of the Indian Ocean.***

Ans. The main limits of the Indian Ocean are : Asia to the north, Africa to the west, Australia to the east and the Southern Ocean in the south.

Q. 6. ***What are the main limits of the Indian Ocean?***

Ans. The main limits of the Indian Ocean are:

Asia to the north, Africa to the west, Australia to the east Southern Ocean in the south.

Q. 7. ***Give names of two parts of the Indian Ocean which are on either side of India?***

Ans. The two parts of the Indian Ocean to the east and west of the Indian sub-continent are:

- the Bay of Bengal to the east
- the Arabian sea to the west.

Q. 8. ***Look at the map given on (NCERT book page 33) and give names of India's two major groups of Islands.***

Ans. The two major groups of islands are:

1. Andaman and Nicobar Islands in the Bay of Bengal.
2. Lakshadweep Islands in the Arabian Sea.

Q. 9. ***Which organisation is responsible to deal with all kinds of disasters in India (Bharat).***

Ans. The National Disaster Management Authority.

Q. 10. ***(a) Which is the largest island in the world?***

(b) How would you compare its size with India/Bharat?

Ans. (*a*) Greenland.

(*b*) Areas of 10 largest states of India have to be added to reach its size.

Q. 11. ***Approximately India is home to how many small islands? Give names of two major groups of islands in India.***

Ans. – More than 1,300 small islands.

– Andaman and Nicobar Islands in the Bay of Bengal and Lakshadweep Islands in the Arabian Sea.

Q. 12. ***Mention the World Oceans Day, designated by the United Nations (UN).***

Ans. June 8th.

B. Short Answer Type Questions

Q. 1. ***Explain what brown colour represents in the Earth's picture?***

Ans.

(*a*) Brown is the colour of land.

(*b*) It covers 1/4th of the globe.

(*c*) A large body of land is called a landmass.

(*d*) A large continuous expanse of land is called a continent. There are seven continents in the world. Of them the largest is Asia and smallest is Australia.

(*e*) The second largest is Africa followed by North America and South America.

(*f*) Fifth is Antarctica followed by Europe.

Q. 2. *Briefly list out some of India's engagement with the continent of Antarctica.*

Ans.

(*a*) Since 1981, the Antarctica programme has been exploring Antarctica, a continent with a very cold climate and harsh environment.

(*b*) In 1983, India established its first scientific base station there called 'Dakshin Gangotri'. Since then two other stations 'Maitri' and 'Bharat' have been set up.

(*c*) About 40 teams of Indian scientists have conducted research especially on evolution of climate and environment.

Q. 3. *How do Oceans impact climate?*

Ans.

(*a*) The oceans affect climate by absorbing solar radiation. About 98% of the heat from the sun's rays are absorbed by the oceans.

(*b*) They redistribute the heat across the globe, example—through ocean currents.

(*c*) Oceans are estimated to capture about 40% of CO_2 from the atmosphere.

(*d*) They help increase atmospheric humidity and send rain to the continents. Example: In India, the monsoons originate from the Oceans.

Q. 4. *'All Oceans are interconnected'. Explain.*

Ans. Although we list five oceans, the lines that divide them on the map are mere conventions.

(*a*) The natural world does not follow such boundaries—sea water constantly flow across different oceans. Many plants and animal species can be found across multiple oceans.

(*b*) Marine fauna consists of thousands of colourful fish, dolphins, whales, mysterious sea creatures. Each part of ocean has its own diverse life forms from sun-lit surface to the dark depths but through pattern of migration many can be found across oceans.

(*c*) Moreover if we look at the map carefully, some are connected via the Arctic Ocean and some via the relatively narrow gap between South America and the Antarctica. Earlier it was known as Isthmus of Panama, today it is called the 'Panama Canal'.

Q. 5. (*i*) *What is the motto of the emblem of the Indian Navy?*

(*ii*) *Give the meaning.*

(*iii*) *Which Vedic deity does it invoke?*

Ans. (*i*) The motto of the emblem of the Indian Navy is '*Sam noh Varunah*'.

(*ii*) It means 'Be auspicious to us, O Varuna'.

(*iii*) It invokes the Vedic deity Lord, Varuna, who is associated with the oceans, the sky and water.

Q. 6. *Give reasons why 26 December 2004, is related with natural disaster.*

Ans.
- On 26 December 2004, India and 13 countries around the Indian Ocean were struck by a powerful Tsunami. Tsunamis are rare but very destructive.
- By the Tsunami, caused by an earthquake in Indonesia, more than 2 lakh people lost their lives.
- In India, the islands of Andaman and Nicobar and coasts of Tamil Nadu and Kerala were severely affected, suffered much damage and loss of life.

Q. 7. *Are Tsunamis common? How can we protect lives and property?*

Ans. Tsunamis are not very common, but they do occur few times in few years around the world. However destructive tsunamis that cause significant damage and loss are rare. Tsunami of the magnitude of 26th December 2004 that occurred in the Indian Ocean is one of the rarest.

Tsunamis can often be detected before they hit a coast.

Many countries have come together in 'early warning system'.

There is an Indian Ocean Tsunami Warning System to which India contributes with other countries. This enables and helps take measures to protect lives and property.

Q.8. ***Enumerate some measures that help protect lives and property in the event of warning of approaching Tsunami.***

Ans.
- Stay away from the beach.
- Plan evacuation routes from your home, school, work place, or any other place you could be where Tsunami present a risk.
- If you are near a coast or experience shaking from an earthquake – Drop, cover and hold on to protect yourself.
- If possible pick areas above sea level or go as far as 3 kms inland, away from the coast line.
- If you cannot get this far or high go as far as you can.
- Listen to emergency information and alerts (through scene or notification by voice or texts).

Q.9. ***Mention continents names.***

Ans.

Count of continents (in alphabetical order)	
Four continents	Africa-Eurasia, America, Antarctica, Australia
Five continents	Africa, America, Antarctica, Australia, Eurasia
Six continents	Africa, Antarctica, Australia, Eurasia, North America, South America (this is reflected in Fig. 2.3 on page 32 of the textbook)
Seven continents	Africa, Antarctica, Asia, Australia, Europe, North America, South America

Q. 10. ***Look at the table above and answer, in practice which of the above count is the most widely adopted and used.***

Ans. The count of seven continents – Africa, Antarctica, Asia, Australia, Europe, North America, South America.

Q. 11. ***(a) Give name of the continent with a very cold climate and harsh environment.***

(b) When did India start its Antarctica programme and establish its first scientific base station? What is it called?

(c) Have any new bases been established since then? If so, how many? Give their names.

(d) How many teams of Indian scientists have conducted research in Antarctica? Mention the main area of their interest.

Ans.

(a) Antarctica

(b) India started the Indian Antarctica programme in 1981 and established its first scientific research base station in 1983 called 'Dakshin Gangotri'.

(c) Since 'Dakshin Gangotri', 2 more bases have been established, called 'Maitri' and 'Bharati'.

(d) About 40 teams of Indian scientists have conducted research in this faraway region. Their main area of interest is evolution of climate and environment. The settlement where the scientists live has a library and even a post office.

Q. 12. ***Why did UN designate a day as World Ocean Day?***

Ans. The UN has designated June 8th as World Oceans Day to remind us all of

(i) the major role the Oceans play in everyday life.

(ii) how oceans serve as 'lungs' of our planet Earth, and

(iii) that they are a major source of food and medicinal resources and a critical part of the biosphere.

C. Long Answer Type Questions

Q. 1. ***Oceans are integral to sustenance of life on Earth. Discuss.***

Ans. For sustenance of any life on Earth the three essentials are: Air, Water and Food for all of which the Oceans play a vital role.

(*a*) More than half of the world's oxygen is produced by the oceans' flora which is why they are called the 'planet's lungs'. They capture an estimated 40% of the CO_2 produced.

(*b*) They help deliver rain to the continents. They are a part of the water cycle. Rains sustain agriculture (food) on earth and replenish fresh water resources. Example: The monsoon in India originates in the ocean.

(*c*) The Oceans sustain life on earth, for example marine animals. Its biodiversity provides our global community with animal protein. In many developed countries seafood is their staple food and primary source of protein.

(*d*) Apart from these essentials, oceans regulate climate, provide jobs and livelihoods and have nourished cultures around the world. They provide adventure and are store house of minerals—*e.g.* petroleum for developing and sustaining economic development of mankind and nations.

Q. 2. *Oceans sustain life but are not without perils for mankind? Discuss by giving examples.*

Ans. Yes, oceans are a boon, but, not without perils.

(*a*) Oceans often give rise to storms—violent events with extreme rainfall and very strong winds such as cyclones which cause widespread damage to coastal regions of the world.

(*b*) A tsunami is another natural disaster that originates in the ocean. It is a huge and powerful wave generally caused by a strong earthquake or a volcanic eruption at the bottom of the ocean.

(*c*) Tsunamis travel thousands of kilometres, submerge coastal areas, causing widespread damage to life and property.

Example: On 26th December 2004, India and 13 other countries around the Indian Ocean were struck by a powerful Tsunami caused by an earthquake in Indonesia. More than 2 lakh people lost their lives. In India, the Andaman and Nicobar Islands and the coasts of Tamil Nadu and Kerala were severely affected and suffered much danger and loss of life.

Q. 3. *(a) Draw and colour the symbol of the Olympic Games.*

(b) How many rings are there?

(c) What does the symbol symbolise?

(d) The widely adopted practice lists seven continents. Why are there only 5 rings?

(e) In which city/country were Olympics held in the year 2024.

Ans.

(*a*) 

(*b*) There are five interlocked rings.

(*c*) The symbol symbolises the gathering of sports people from all over the world.

(*d*) The rings are only 5, because they were chosen to represent five inhabited continents – Africa, America, Asia, Australia and Europe.

(*e*) Paris (France)

Q. 4. *Discuss briefly how the oceans are polluted by human activities.*

Ans. Human activities have led to the pollution of oceans.

(*i*) Dumping of several million tonnes of plastic wastes every year in sea and oceans has led to choking of marine life. Fish, seabirds, sea turtles, marine mammals not only get entangled in plastic, but plastic debris causes suffocation and starvation of marine life.

(*ii*) Excessive fishing *i.e.* overfishing has led to decline in marine life.

(*iii*) Chemicals, fertilisers etc. used in industries and agriculture plus trash are washed, thrown or intentionally dumped into oceans.

(*iv*) **Warning:** Greenhouse gases in the atmosphere trap energy from the sun. The oceans absorb much of this energy, causing ocean waters to warm— whereby there is less available dissolved oxygen for native sea life which negatively impacts the biological process.

Q. 5. *When and why, was the Indian Ocean Tsunami Warning System established? Briefly discuss its role and significance.*

Ans. The Indian Ocean Tsunami Warning System is a collaborative effort of many countries including India. It was inaugurated on 15th October, 2007. It was established in response to the devastating tsunami of 26th December, 2004 which caused a massive loss of life and property in India and another 13 countries around the Indian Ocean. More than two lakh people lost their lives.

Role and Significance: The system is designed to provide early warning of potential tsunamis, to enable nations to undertake timely evacuations and other safety measures for their coastal communities at risk.

(*i*) This allows people to evacuate to safer areas and take necessary precautions, reducing the loss of life and property.

(*ii*) Plays, a, critical role is safeguarding coastal communities.

(*iii*) Serves to help prevent a natural hazard from becoming a disaster.

(*iv*) Lesson in collaborative efforts.

D. Assertion & Reasoning Questions

There are two statements marked as Assertion (A) and Reason (R). Mark your answer as per the codes provided below:

Q. 1. Assertion (A): Oceans are not really separate the lines that divide them are no more than conventions.

Reason (R): Many plant and animal species can be found across multiple oceans.

Codes:

(*a*) Both (A) and (R) are true but (R) is not the correct explanation of (A).

(*b*) Both (A) and (R) are true and (R) is the correct explanation of (A).

(*c*) (A) is true but (R) is false.

(*d*) (A) is false but (R) is true.

Q. 2. Assertion (A): Oceans play a crucial role in sustaining life on Earth.

Reason (R): Coastal people all over the world have tales and legends about the oceans dangers and also their blessings.

Codes:

(*a*) Both (A) and (R) are true but (R) is not the correct explanation of (A).

(*b*) Both (A) and (R) are true and (R) is the correct explanation of (A).

(*c*) (A) is true but (R) is false.

(*d*) (A) is false but (R) is true.

Q. 3. Assertion (A): Continents can be counted in several ways; the list of 7 continents is most widely adopted.

Reason (R): Depending on our choice, we may list continents between four and seven.

Codes:

(*a*) Both (A) and (R) are true but (R) is not the correct explanation of (A).

(*b*) Both (A) and (R) are true and (R) is the correct explanation of (A).

(*c*) (A) is true but (R) is false.

(*d*) (A) is false but (R) is true.

Q. 4. Assertion (A): Fresh water makes up for a very small proportion of the planets water resources.

Reason (R): Most of the fresh water is found in glaciers, rivers, lakes in the atmosphere and overground.

Codes:

(*a*) Both (A) and (R) are true but (R) is not the correct explanation of (A).

(*b*) Both (A) and (R) are true and (R) is the correct explanation of (A).

(*c*) (A) is true but (R) is false.

(*d*) (A) is false but (R) is true.

Q. 5. Assertion (A): Indian Ocean is the only ocean named after a country. India is surrounded on three sides by the waters of Ocean.

Reason (R): The Arabian Sea to the west and the Bay of Bengal to the east are parts of the Indian Ocean.

Codes:

(*a*) Both (A) and (R) are true but (R) is not the correct explanation of (A).

(*b*) Both (A) and (R) are true and (R) is the correct explanation of (A).

(*c*) (A) is true but (R) is false.

(*d*) (A) is false but (R) is true.

Ans.

1. (*a*) **2.** (*b*) **3.** (*a*) **4.** (*c*) **5.** (*a*)

E. Case/Source Based Questions

Read the passages given below and answer the questions that follow:

I. Seawater, for example, constantly flows across different oceans, sustaining a rich diversity of marine life. Many plant and animal species can be found across multiple oceans.

The marine flora includes tiny plants called algae and all kinds of seaweeds; the marine fauna consists of thousands of species of colourful fish, dolphins, whales, and countless mysterious deep-sea creatures. Each part of the ocean, from the sun-lit surface to the dark depths, has its own diverse life forms.

(Page 31)

(*i*) Oceans sustain diverse life forms. Give 2 points in support.

(*ii*) Give names of oceans in descending order.

(*iii*) You have listed more than one ocean, **but the natural world does not follow such boundaries.** Give reason in support of the statement.

(*iv*) Which ocean is almost circular in shape and which is truly a circle?

Ans.

(*i*) Oceans sustain diverse life forms as a rich diversity of marine life can be found across oceans.

(*a*) Marine **flora** includes tiny plants called algae and all kinds of seaweeds.

(*b*) Marine **fauna** consists of thousands of species of colourful fish, dolphins, whales and other deep-sea mysterious creatures. The sunlit to dark depths has its own diverse life forms.

(*ii*) The five major oceans in descending order are:

- Pacific • Atlantic • Indian
- Arctic, and • Southern

(*iii*) Though we list five major oceans the natural world does not follow such boundaries as all oceans are not really separate but connected as sea water constantly flows across different oceans and plant and animal species can be found across multiple oceans.

(*iv*) (*a*) The Pacific Ocean—almost circular

(*b*) The Antarctic Ocean — truly a circle.

II. Continents do not include all landmass. Some smaller pieces of land are left out; surrounded by water on all sides, they are called islands. (Continents are also surrounded by water, but because they are so large, they are not considered islands.)

There are lakhs of islands on the planet, of very different sizes. *(Page 37)*

(*i*) What are smaller pieces left out land called? Why?

(*ii*) Name, the largest island of the world.

(*iii*) Give names of two major group of islands of India.

(*iv*) India has more than ________.

(*a*) 1300 small islands

(*b*) 1100 small islands

(*c*) 1200 small islands

(*d*) 1320 small islands

Ans.

(*i*) Smaller pieces of left out lands are called islands.

Why: They are called islands because they are surrounded by water on all sides.

(*ii*) Greenland is the largest island in the world.

(*iii*) (*a*) Andaman and Nicobar Islands.

(*b*) Lakshadweep Island

(*iv*) (*a*) 1300 small islands

III. From early times, people have used oceans and seas to migrate to other regions, to trade in all kinds of goods, to conduct military campaigns, and as a source of food through fishing. Oceans have also nourished the cultures of coastal people all over the world. Almost all of them have tales and legends about the sea, sea gods and goddesses, sea monsters and treasures from the sea — the oceans' dangers but also their blessings.

(Page 38)

(i) How are oceans a blessing for people?

(ii) How have oceans impacted humanity negatively?

(iii) Almost all cultures world over have tales and legends of ocean dangers. Give any 2 dangers that oceans are home too.

Ans.

(i) (a) Oceans are a blessing for people as they are a source of protein rich food through fishing.

(b) They have nourished cultures of coastal people all over the world and enabled exchange of ideas, goods and people.

(ii) Oceans have impacted humanity in both positive and negative ways. They enable trade and movement of goods, ideas and people but at the same time they act negatively. Movement of people, goods and ideas have also slavery, indentured labourers, conquests, subjugation of weaker people and countries, enforcement of ideas, rules and laws of the superior powers—eg. colonialism and imperialism.

(iii) Oceans while a blessing are also a home to dangers. They give rise to storms, tsunamis and other violent events like extreme rainfall and strong winds such as cyclones.

F. Competency Based Questions

Q. 1. *'Continents can be counted in several ways'. Explain why and how?*

Ans. The most widely adopted and used way lists seven continents. Depending on our choice we may list continents between four and seven. These variations rely on historical, cultural or geographical considerations.

(i) North and South Americas are generally considered to be two continents but they can be seen as single landmass as they are connected by a narrow strip of land.

(ii) Similarly Europe and Asia are considered as two continents, while they form a single landmass. Geologist regard them as a single continent called Eurasia.

(iii) Yet another point of difference in count is Africa and Eurasia. Africa which today is separated by the Suez Canal was connected to the Asian continent by the Suez Isthmus.

(iv) The table below lists the variations in counting the continents.

Number	Names of Continents
4 Continents:	Africa–Eurasia, America, Antarctica, Australia
5 Continents:	Africa, America, Antarctica, Australia, Eurasia
6 Continents:	Africa, Antarctica, Australia, Eurasia, North America, South America
7 Continents	Africa, Antarctica, Asia, Australia, Europe, North America, South America

Q. 2. *The oceans together hold 97% of the water on planet Earth which is salty and unfit for consumption by land animals and humans, but it is crucial to sustain life. Give three points in support of the above statement.*

Ans. Ocean water though salty and unfit for consumption is crucial to sustain life —

(*i*) Oceans support a rich diversity for marine life—flora and fauna. Each part of the ocean from sun-lit to dark depths has its own life forms—algae, colourful fish, whales etc.

(*ii*) Ocean waters provide food through fishing. For many people, especially those in coastal areas, fish is a basic food item and a source of protein.

(*iii*) These ocean waters, are a part of the water cycle and send rain to continents eg. monsoon rains in India which sustain our agriculture.

(*iv*) Ocean waters sustain livelihoods, transport, commerce and economic growth.

(*v*) Oceans absorb CO_2 from the atmosphere and regulate climate.

Q. 3. *Briefly discuss the role of oceans in regulating climate?*

Ans. Ocean waters fluidity render it a significant player in regulating our climate.

(*i*) Ocean's ability to absorb, store and transport heat by the sun (solar heat) help in regulating temperatures and influencing weather pattern around the world. Coastal areas world over have a moderate climate. For example: through ocean currents, oceans distribute heat from warm tropical areas near the equator to colder areas near the poles.

(*ii*) Oceans are an integral part of the water cycle—evaporation, condensation and precipitation. If there is no rainfall the earth would be a desert. The monsoon rain in India originates from the ocean. Without such rains our agriculture and all life will suffer.

(*iii*) The oceans generate 50% of the oxygen we need, absorb large amount of all carbon dioxide emissions and capture 90% of excess heat generated by these emissions. They are not just lungs of the planet but they are the largest 'carbon sink'— a vital player in regulating climate and buffer against climate change.

Q. 4. *Why is ground water significant. This resource is fast depleting or getting contaminated. Suggest any three ways to regenerate this resource?*

Ans. Fresh water makes up a very small proportion of planets water resources and ground water to one such source along with waters in glaciers, rivers, lakes and the atmosphere.

(*i*) Groundwater is vital source of water on Earth providing to more than 50% of the global populations drinking water supply and 40% to irrigate crops.

(*ii*) In many parts of the world say dry and remote areas it is the only source of fresh water for all human needs.

(*iii*) Ground water provides a buffer to climate variability and acts as storage during droughts. Rainwater is the main source to replenish our water sources. Some other ways in which we can replenish our water sources are:

(*a*) Reforestation.

(*b*) Wetland restoration.

(*c*) Injecting water directly into the aquifers by deep dug wells.

(*d*) Guide run off water inside the ground by manual activities to recharge aquifers.

Q. 5. *Why do geologist regard Europe and Asia as one continent Eurasia. On what ground are they widely accepted as two continents—Europe and Asia?*

Ans.

(*i*) A large continuous expanse of land is defined a 'continent'. Looking at this definition. Europe and Asia are one single landmass and are on the same tectonic plate—geologists, consider it as one continent Eurasia.

(*ii*) The widely accepted view of two separate continents—Europe and Asia gained ground because while other continents are separated by clear physical boundaries Europe and Asia are separated due to historical and cultural reasons as Europe evolution has been very different from Asia.

(*iii*) The Ural Mountains that run in north-south direction and Caucasus Mountains in the south along with the Caspian and Black Seas mark the geographical boundaries of the two continents is North America and South America.

G. Skill Based Questions

Q. 1. *Conservation of water is the urgent need of the hour. Suggest ways in which you as a citizen of the country and the world can help in water conservation.*

Ans.

(*i*) To conserve water the essential steps are forward consciousness, minimal waste or judicious use, optimal use and reuse.

(*ii*) First and foremost I would begin by conservation from my home—install water efficient attachments, consciously try not to waste water and undertake measures which will help me to reuse waste water.

Ways to conserve water are:

(*a*) Install low flow efficient shower heads, taps and flush toilets.

(*b*) Stop all overflows, turn off taps when not in use, and fix leakages immediately.

(*c*) Mop floors, wipe cars instead of washing.

(*d*) Reuse waste water for gardening—use sprinklers for watering plants, grass, trees etc.

(*e*) To conserve run off water from terraces, balconies and verandas', rain water harvesting should be undertaken.

(*f*) Be mindful that tanks do not overflow, or taps do not run while brushing, shaving, bathing, washing clothes, cooking etc. Ensure washing machines are worked on full load.

Q. 2. *Oceans have played a significant role human lives—exchange of goods, peoples and ideas. But today health of ocean and ocean systems are in danger from humans. Give any three threats to ocean health. and suggest three measures to reduce/ ease these threats/dangers.*

Ans. Among the threats/dangers to ocean health and ocean systems, the three major ones are:

(*i*) Pollution and plastic debris.

(*ii*) Chemical run offs fishing and overfishing. These harm marine life and disrupts ocean eco-systems. Studies show that more than 80% of marine pollution originates on land and caused by direct human impact. Majority of the plastic debris is caused by unmindful littering—food wrappers, plastic bags, razors, bottles are not disposed of properly which end in water ways and eventually oceans. Plastic pollution has a devastating impact on eco-system—cause marine life to suffocate, cause entanglements, infections and internal injuries. Chemical runoffs, comes both from urban and agricultural areas. Still other sources of pollutants are waste from industrial plants which is often toxic, oil spills, disposal of waste from ships and sewage plants. Fishing gear made of plastic leaves a great amount of debris which destroys habitats and threatens marine eco-systems. Fishing nets left or lost in the ocean water threatens wildlife as they get trapped or are dragged for miles. Due to commercial whaling many species are on the brink of extinction. Overfishing is destructive for the ocean and is threatening food security of millions of people. Bluefin tuna which were once extremely common are becoming endangered species. Subsidies by government unregulated illegal fishing is not only costing, huge amounts of loss governments negatively impacting ocean eco-system.

Measures:

(*i*) Controlling the production of coastal pollutants.

(*ii*) Involving local communities for better monitoring of all processes.

(*iii*) Implementing a ban on single use plastic items like straws, plastic bags to reduce plastic in our environment.

(*iv*) Strict regulations for treatment of industrial and sewage waste before disposed.

Q. 3. *India is home to two major group of islands. Discuss with specific reference to these islands groups how natural phenomena and human activities have adversely impacted them.*

Ans. The two major group of islands are Andaman and Nicobar Islands in the Bay of Bengal and the Lakshadweep Islands in the Arabian Sea. While Andaman Islands are volcanic, Lakshadweep Islands are coral. Both are home to rich flora and fauna and adversely impacted by human activities. Human activities also play a role in acceleration of disasters caused by natural phenomena like extreme rainfall, strong winds such as cyclones which cause widespread damage to coastal regions.

Human activities have led to climate change, for example: excess emission of CO_2 due to use of fossil fuels, industrial activities, increased mining etc.

Andaman and Nicobar Islands are grappling with man made problem of deforestation and marine pollution. Also there is habitat loss, and problem of invasive species. These have adversely impacted the biodiversity and the unique flora and fauna of these islands. In 2004 because of tsunami these islands suffered significant loss of life and property. These islands are home to some of the oldest indigenous tribes who have preserved their traditional way of life.

The Lakshadweep Islands are facing threat from rising sea waters due to warming of seas which inturn are due to global warming, human activities contributing to climate change. These islands are witnessing coral bleachings. The decline of corals is a major concern as corals form the bedrock of marine life. There is constant threat of biodiversity, loss and extreme weather events.

Q. 4. *The Northern Hemisphere lies above the Equator while the Southern-Hemisphere lies below the Equator. Give any five difference in the Hemisphere in relation to oceans and continents.*

Ans. The planet Earth is divided into two hemisphere North and South by the imaginary line of latitude — the Equator at 0°. Differences:

(*i*) Both hemispheres are of the same size but most of the continents are in the Northern hemisphere. Much of Southern hemisphere is made up of seas and oceans (81%).

(*ii*) Some continents have parts in both the hemispheres. Europe and North America lie completely in the Northern hemisphere Australia and Antarctica lie completely in the Southern hemisphere.

(*iii*) The world's smallest, shallowest, coldest ocean, the Arctic Ocean is located entirely in the Northern hemisphere and the Southern Ocean totally lies in the Southern hemisphere. The other three oceans i.e., Atlantic, Pacific and Indian Oceans span both the hemispheres.

(*iv*) The Earth rotates on its axis west to east, this impacts the ocean currents. In the Northern hemisphere the ocean currents move clockwise, while in the Southern hemisphere they move counter clockwise.

(v) The Northern hemisphere, especially the North Atlantic Ocean usually has higher salinity compared to Southern hemisphere due to higher evaporation, fewer large fresh water inputs, and the enclosed nature of seas such as the Mediterranean sea.

(vi) The Northern and Southern hemi-spheres experience different weather conditions during different times of the year— when one experiences cold, the other experiences warmer conditions. The seasons in the Southern hemi-sphere are less extreme than Northern hemisphere because Southern hemisphere has more seas, while Northern has more landmass and landmass returns heat.

(vii) The Southern hemisphere is less populated and polluted than the Northern hemisphere. About 90% of the population lives in the Northern hemisphere.

(viii) The Arid regions warm more than other areas, land areas warm more than ocean surface and the Northern hemisphere warms more than the Southern hemisphere.

VII. MAP WORK

Q.1. ***On the given outline map of India mark the following:***

1. Indian Ocean
2. Major group of islands to east side.
3. Major group of islands to west side.

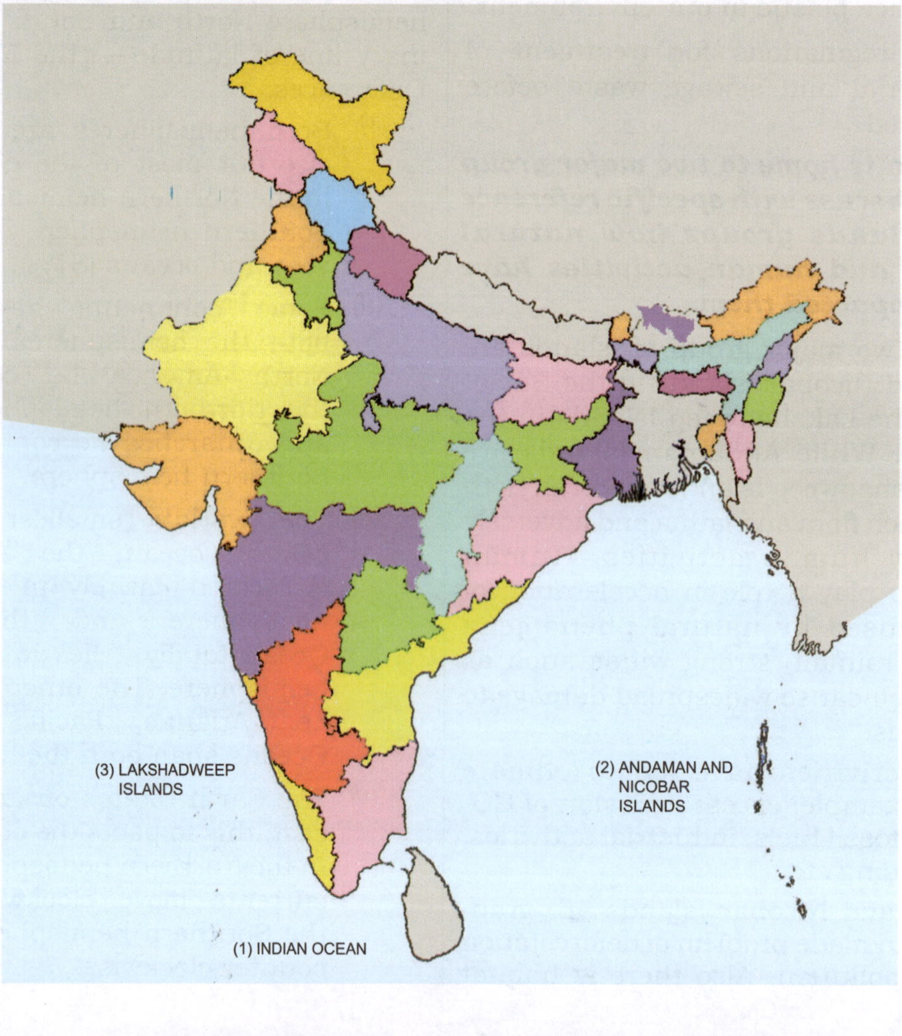

Q.2. *On the given outline map of the world mark the following:*

1. World's largest ocean
2. World's smallest ocean
3. World's largest island
4. Smallest continent
5. Eurasia
6. Frozen continent

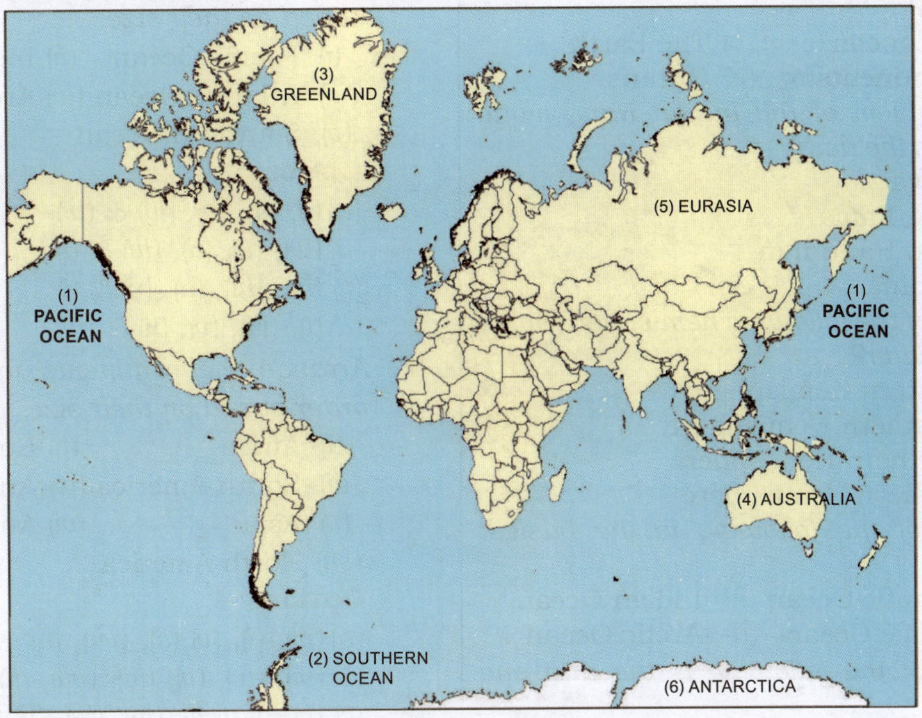

Q.3. *On the given outline map of the world mark and label the largest water bodies to which the Earth owes the nickname—Blue Planet.*

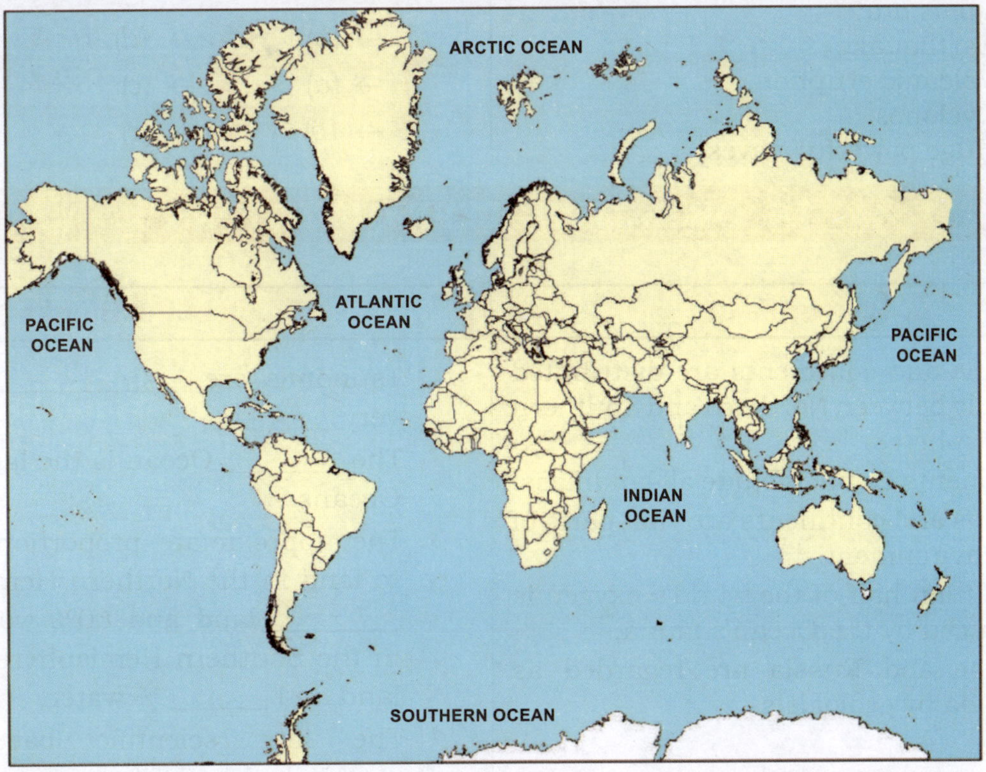

VIII. MULTIPLE CHOICE QUESTIONS

1. *Which of the following is called the 'blue planet'?*
   (*a*) The moon (*b*) The Earth
   (*c*) Continents (*d*) Oceans
2. *The emblem of the Indian Navy motto invokes the deity.*
   (*a*) Shiva
   (*b*) Lord Rama
   (*c*) Lord Hanuman
   (*d*) Varuna
3. *Which of the following hemisphere holds more water?*
   (*a*) Eastern Hemisphere
   (*b*) Southern Hemisphere
   (*c*) Northern Hemisphere
   (*d*) Western Hemisphere
4. *Which of the following is the busiest ocean?*
   (*a*) Atlantic Ocean (*b*) Indian Ocean
   (*c*) Pacific Ocean (*d*) Arctic Ocean
5. *Which of the following is the* ***odd*** *one out?*
   (*a*) Rivers (*b*) Lakes
   (*c*) Sea (*d*) Ground water
6. *Tsunamis are:*
   (*a*) Earthquake
   (*b*) Volcanic eruption
   (*c*) Cyclones
   (*d*) Huge powerful waves
7. *Arrange the oceans in ascending order based on their size.*
   (*i*) Pacific Ocean (*ii*) Indian Ocean
   (*iii*) Atlantic Ocean (*iv*) Arctic Ocean
   (*v*) Southern Ocean

   Options:
   (*a*) (*i*), (*ii*), (*v*), (*iii*) & (*iv*)
   (*b*) (*iv*), (*v*), (*ii*), (*iii*) & (*i*)
   (*c*) (*iv*), (*iii*), (*ii*), (*v*) & (*i*)
   (*d*) (*i*), (*iii*), (*v*), (*ii*) & (*iv*)
8. *Arrange the continents in descending order based on their size.*
   (*i*) Africa (*ii*) Europe
   (*iii*) South America (*iv*) Antarctica
   (*v*) Asia (*vi*) Australia
   (*vii*) North America

   Options:
   (*a*) (*vi*), (*i*), (*v*),(*ii*), (*vii*), (*iii*) & (*iv*)
   (*b*) (*vi*), (*iv*), (*v*), (*iii*), (*vii*), (*ii*) & (*i*)
   (*c*) (*v*), (*i*), (*vii*), (*iii*), (*iv*), (*ii*) & (*vi*)
   (*d*) (*iv*), (*vi*), (*i*), (*vii*), (*v*), (*ii*) & (*iii*)

Ans.

1. → (*b*) 2. → (*d*) 3. → (*b*)
4. → (*a*) 5. → (*c*) 6. → (*d*)
7. → (*b*) 8. → (*c*)

IX. OBJECTIVE TYPE QUESTIONS

A. True or False

1. Oceans and continents are distributed equally between Northern and Southern Hemisphere.
2. Continents do not include all landmass.
3. Oceans and continents are vital parts of the environment.
4. More than half of the world's oxygen is produced by the Ocean's fauna.
5. Europe and Russia are regarded as Eurasia by geologists.

Ans.

1. → False 2. → True 3. → True
4. → False 5. → False

B. Fill in the Blanks

1. Tsunamis are____________ but very________.
2. The________ Ocean is the largest of all Oceans.
3. The approximate proportion of water to land in the Northern Hemisphere is ________ land and 60% water. While in the Southern Hemisphere it is 20% land and _______ % water.
4. The first scientific base station established by India at Antarctica was called _______.

5. Oceans also send rain and are an integral part of the Earth's __________.

Ans.

1. rare/destructive
2. Pacific
3. 40%, 80%
4. Dakshin Gangotri
5. Water cycle

C. Match Column A with Column B

1.

Column A	Column B
1. Maitri	(*a*) Surrounded by water on all sides
2. Australia	(*b*) Caused by earthquake or volcanic eruption at the bottom of the ocean
3. Islands	(*c*) Scientific base station
4. Algae	(*d*) Smallest continent
5. Tsunami	(*e*) Flora

Ans.

1. → (*c*) **2.** → (*d*) **3.** → (*a*)
4. → (*e*) **5.** → (*b*)

2.

	Column A		Column B
1.	Frozen continent	(*a*)	Dolphins
2.	Largest island	(*b*)	Antarctica
3.	Water cycle	(*c*)	Arabian Sea
4.	Lakshadweep islands	(*d*)	Oceans
5.	Fauna	(*e*)	Greenland

(*a*) 1 – A, 2 – B, 3 – C, 4 – D, 5 – E
(*b*) 1 – B, 2 – E, 3 – A, 4 – C, 5 – D
(*c*) 1 – B, 2 – E, 3 – D, 4 – C, 5 – A
(*d*) 1 – A, 2 – B, 3 – E, 4 – D, 5 – C

Ans. (*c*) 1 – B, 2 – E, 3 – D, 4 – C, 5 – A

X. TEST YOUR KNOWLEDGE

A. Multiple Choice Question

1. *A continent that lies on both sides of the equator.*

(*a*) Antarctica (*b*) Africa
(*c*) North America (*d*) Europe

B. Fill in the Blanks

1. __________ Ocean has indented coastlines which provide excellent location for ports.

2. ________, __________ is the process by which water circulates between the Earth oceans, atmosphere and land.

3. __________ are large continuous expanse of land.

C. True or False

1. Climate change and global warming are not factors in rise in water level of ocean.

2. Europe is a continent surrounded by water on all three sides.

3. For generations there is adequate water on Earth to sustain all life.

D. Very Short Answer Type Questions

Q.1. *What are the sources of fresh water?*

Q.2. *Give names of oceans in a descending order.*

Q.3. *Give name of the organisation responsible for natural disaster in India. Support with example.*

Q.4. *Europe and Asia form a single land-mass yet they are widely seen as two continents. Give reasons.*

Q.5. *The Olympic games symbol has five rings. Which is the continent that is missing?*

Q.6. *Enumerate some of the disasters linked to oceans?*

Q.7. *Under Indian Antarctica Programme India has established scientific base stations. Give names of two stations.*

E. Short Answer Type Questions

Q.1. *What are Islands? Why every land-mass surrounded by water is not called an Island?*

Q.2. *Why is marine environment under threat?*

Q.3. *Give three ways by which we can collectively protect oceans for the future of our planet.*

Q.4. *Without oceans the Earth would be a desert? Give three ways in which oceans regulate climate.*

Q.5. *Oceans are 'planet's lungs' 'carbon sink'. Give reasons in support of the statement.*

Q.6. *How do 'early warning system' safeguard natural disasters from becoming a human disaster.*

F. Long Answer Type Questions

Q.1. *How have oceans imported cultures of coastal people all over the world?*

Q.2. *'The Northern hemisphere has more land than Southern hemisphere.' Discuss.*

Q.3. *Briefly discuss the Andaman and Nicobar Islands with emphasis on location, biodiversity, tsunami of 2004 and uniqueness.*

Q.4. *Discuss the significance of Earth's waterbodies. (Hint: fresh water and salty water).*

G. Assertion & Reasoning Questions

There are two statements marked as Assertion (A) and Reason (R). Mark your answer as per the codes provided below:

Q. 1. Assertion (A): Early astronauts lovingly called the Earth 'the blue planet'.

Reason (R): It covers seven-tenth of the terrestrial globe.

Codes:

(*a*) Both (A) and (R) are true but (R) is not the correct explanation of (A).
(*b*) Both (A) and (R) are true and (R) is the correct explanation of (A).
(*c*) (A) is true but (R) is false.
(*d*) (A) is false but (R) is true.

Q. 2. Assertion (A): Oceans play a crucial role in regulating climate.

Reason (R): Half of the world's oxygen is produced by the ocean's flora.

Codes:

(*a*) Both (A) and (R) are true but (R) is not the correct explanation of (A).
(*b*) Both (A) and (R) are true and (R) is the correct explanation of (A).
(*c*) (A) is true but (R) is false.
(*d*) (A) is false but (R) is true.

Q. 3. Assertion (A): Tsunami is a huge powerful wave that can travel thousands of kilometres and cause widespread damage.

Reason (R): Tsunamis are caused by a strong earthquake or volcanic eruptions at the bottom of the ocean.

Codes:

(*a*) Both (A) and (R) are true but (R) is not the correct explanation of (A).
(*b*) Both (A) and (R) are true and (R) is the correct explanation of (A).
(*c*) (A) is true but (R) is false.
(*d*) (A) is false but (R) is true.

H. Match Column A with Column B

	Column A		Column B
1.	Largest	(*a*)	Australia
2.	Smallest	(*b*)	Oxygen
3.	Indented	(*c*)	Asia
4.	Bering Strait	(*d*)	Atlantic Ocean
5.	Flora	(*e*)	Arctic Ocean

(*a*) 1 – C 2 – E 3 – D 4 – A 5 – B
(*b*) 1 – C 2 – A 3 – D 4 – E 5 – B
(*c*) 1 – C 2 – E 3 – A 4 – B 5 – D
(*d*) 1 – C 2 – D 3 – E 4 – B 5 – A

NOTES

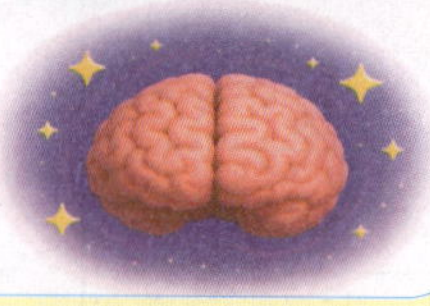

INTERESTING MIND MAP

Landforms and Life

1 Introduction

- Humans live on land that varies by region
- Landforms are Earth's physical features formed over millions of years
- Three main types: mountains, plains, plateaus
- Each has different climate, plants, animals, and population

2 Mountains

- Mountains are tall landforms with steep slopes and narrow tops
- Snow melts at lower altitudes or stays permanent at higher peaks, feeding rivers
- Hills are smaller, rounded highlands
- Mountains are grouped ranges like Himalayas, Alps, Andes
- Young mountains are sharp, old ones are rounded by erosion

2(a) Mountain Environment

- Slopes often have montane forests with conifer trees like pines, firs, spruce, deodar
- Higher areas have grasses, mosses, lichens
- Forests, rivers, lakes, grasslands, caves support many animals
- Animals include snow leopard, ibex, yak, golden eagle

2(b) Life in the Mountains

- Mountain land is rough and has steep slopes
- Farming uses terraces, herding is common
- Tourism brings income but can damage the environment

3 Plateaus

- Plateaus are raised land with flat tops and steep sides
- Rich in minerals, mining is common
- Soil is often rocky, farming is limited (except lava plateaus with fertile soil)
- Many plateaus have waterfalls like Victoria Falls, Jog Falls, Hundru Falls, and Nohkalikai Falls

4 Plains

- Plains are flat or gently wavy land, usually up to 300 metres above sea level
- Rivers bring fertile soil to the plains
- Plains are good for farming and home to many plants and animals

4(a) Life in the plains

- Fertile plains supported early civilisations and have high population
- Main occupation is farming and fishing
- Irrigation boosts farming but lowers groundwater levels
- Rivers are considered sacred and used for festivals, ceremonies, rituals, and navigation
- Landforms like deserts are dry, with unique life and human adaptations

CHAPTER 3

LANDFORMS AND LIFE

I. FACTS TO REMEMBER/SUMMARY

INTRODUCTION

- A landform is a physical feature on earth's surface that is a part of the terrain. Landforms take shape over millions of years and have a significant connection with environment and life.
- These landforms are divided into three categories — **mountains**, **plateaus** and **plains**. They have different climates and are home to a variety of **flora** and **fauna**.
- Humans have adapted to all landforms but the number of people living on different kinds of landforms varies throughout the world.

MOUNTAINS

- Mountains are the landforms that are much higher than the surrounding landscape. They can be recognised by a broad base, steep slopes and a narrow summit.
  — Mountains are grouped in mountain ranges. eg., The Himalayas in Asia, The Alps in Europe.
  — Mountains can be old or young.
  — Young mountains have tall sharp peaks/summit. e.g., The Himalayas.
- Other highlands with lower height, less steep slopes and rounded tops are called **hills**.

MOUNTAIN ENVIRONMENT

- Mountain forests are called 'montane forests'.
  — conifer forests have trees such as pine, spruce, deodar.
  — at higher altitudes trees give way to grasses.
  — mountains are home to diverse fauna.

LIFE IN THE MOUNTAINS

- Mountain terrain is rugged with steep slopes.
  — farming practised here is called 'terrace farming'.
  — herding is a preferred occupation.
  — tourism is an important source of income.
- Mountains are susceptible to natural disasters.
- Excessive flow of visitors has put the fragile mountain environment under pressure.

PLATEAUS

- A plateau is a landform that rises up from the surrounding land and has a more or less flat surface, some of its sides have often steep slopes.
  - Tibetan plateau is the highest and largest plateau of the world.
  - Deccan plateau is one of the oldest plateaus of the world.
  - Plateaus are called 'store houses of minerals'.
  - Environment is very diverse across the world.
  - They are home to spectacular waterfalls.

PLAINS

- Plains are landforms that have an extensive flat or gently undulating surface. They do not have any large hills or deep valleys.
  - Flood plains are a type of plain formed by deposition of sediments carried by rivers originating in mountain ranges. These sediments make the soil very fertile. *For example*, the Gangetic plains.

LIFE IN THE PLAINS

- Plains have been home to some of the earliest civilisations, such as the Indus Valley Civilisation and the Mesopotamian Civilisation.
- A large population of the world resides within the plain areas.
- One-fourth of the India's population lives on the Gangetic plains.
  - Major occupation here includes river fishing and agriculture.
  - Traditionally agriculture is mostly rain-fed but in recent decades irrigation facilities have led to increased production and have contributed to depletion of ground water resources.
  - Other problems are high population and pollution.

- Rivers and plains have great cultural value and support a lot of economic activities.
- Deserts are large and dry expanses with little precipitation and unique flora and fauna.
  - They can be hot like Sahara Desert in Africa and cold like Gobi Desert in Asia. Some experts consider the Antarctica continent as a cold desert.
  - Deserts have rich cultural traditions related to folk songs, festivals and legends. *For example*, Thar Desert.
- Despite unique challenges and opportunities of each landform, human beings' adaptation and spirit of resilience has enabled mankind to make all landforms their home.

II. TEXTBOOK KEYWORDS/GLOSSARY

1. **Landform:** A landform is any natural feature of the earth's surface such as a hill, lake, beach, etc.
2. **Mountain Range:** A mountain range or hill range is a series of mountains or hills arranged in a line and connected by high ground.
3. **Altitude:** Height of a landform above the sea level.
4. **Precipitation:** Water from the atmosphere reaching the ground in any form—rain, snow and hail are most common forms of precipitation.
5. **Montane forests:** A type of forest that grows in mountainous regions— pines, spruce and other varieties of trees are found here.
6. **Lichen:** A plant like organism that generally clings to rocks, walls or trees.
7. **Moss:** A small green plant without roots or flowers often spreading in a cushion-like cover on higher altitudes.
8. **Internal forces:** The forces that act suddenly from within the Earth towards the surface such as volcano and earthquake.
9. **External forces:** The forces that act slowly on the surface of the Earth like wind, running water, moving ice.
10. **Erosion:** To gradually erode the surface of something through action of wind or rain etc.
11. **Undulating:** A smooth curving shape with gentle rises and pills.
12. **Flash flood:** A sudden local flood often caused by a cloud burst.
13. **Landslide:** A sudden collapse of a mass of earth or rock from a mountain side.
14. **Avalanche:** A very large amount of snow that slides quickly down the side of a mountain.
15. **Confluence:** The meeting point of two or more rivers.
16. **Sea level:** The average level of the surface of the oceans. It is also called mean sea level.
17. **Resilience:** The capacity to meet challenges and difficulties, adapt them to overcome them.
18. **Alluvial deposits:** Very fine soils brought by rivers and deposited on the river basins.
19. **Tributary:** A river or stream which contributes its water to a main river.
20. **Glaciers:** Moving rivers of ice or masses of ice.
21. **Mouth:** The place where river enters a lake, a larger river or an ocean is called its mouth.
22. **Terrain:** The lay of the land or a stretch of land especially with regard to its physical features example elevation, roughness etc.
23. **Sediments:** They are small particles of rock, soil etc. carried by wind, water or ice.
24. **Cloud burst:** A sudden violent rainstorm.
25. **Adaptation:** Change or evolution in an animal or plant that helps it to survive in its environment.

III. PHYSICAL MAP OF INDIA

Major Cities are Based on the Fertile Plain of Main Rivers

PHYSICAL FEATURES OF INDIA

Mountain Ranges, Mountain Peaks, Plateau, Coastal Plains, Desert

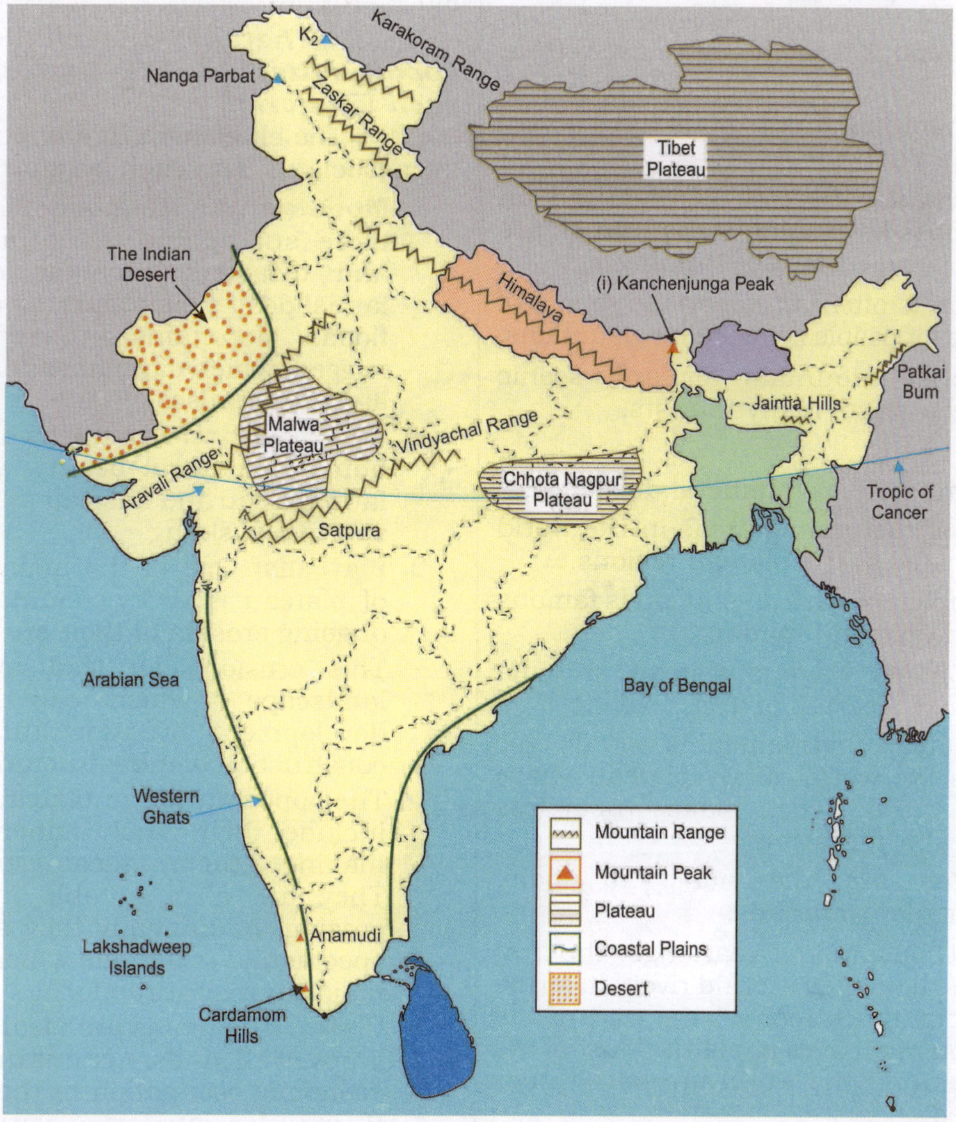

IV. THE BIG QUESTIONS *(Page 41)*

Q. 1. *What are the major types of landforms and their significance to life and culture?*

Ans. The major types of landforms are the mountains, the plateaus and the plains.

Mountains: Mountains are the landforms that are much higher than the surrounding landscape. Depending on their height, some mountains are covered with snow. At lower altitudes, the snow melts every summer and turns into water that feeds rivers. At high altitudes, the snow may never melt, leaving the mountain permanently snow-capped.

Plateaus: A plateau is a land form that rises up from the surrounding land and has a more or less flat surface; some of its sides are often steep slopes. Tibetan Plateau is the largest and highest plateau in the world. Plateaus are the 'store house of minerals'. Mining is the major activity on plateaus where many of the world's largest mines are found.

Plains: Plains are the landforms that have an extensive flat or gently undulating surface. They do not have any large hills. They are generally not more than 300 metres above the sea level.

Significance of mountains, plateaus and plains in human life and culture.

Mountains:

- Mountainous regions have rich **flora** and **fauna**.
- Most mountainous regions have a very low population.
- Here regular farming is practised on the slopes by cutting steps into slopes which is called terrace farming.
- Tourism is often an important source of income for people living in the mountains.
- The crisp mountain air and scenic beauty attracts many tourists.

Plateaus:

- Plateaus have rich mineral deposits.
- Many of the mining areas in the world are located in the plateau regions.

For example, the African plateau is famous for gold and diamond mining.

- The Chhota Nagpur plateau in India has huge reserves of iron, coal etc.
- The plateau environment is very diverse across the world. Many plateaus have a rocky soil, which makes them less favourable for farming.
- Plateaus are the home to many spectacular waterfalls.

Plains: Thousands of years ago, the first civilisations developed around rivers in fertile plains. In our times too, a large part of the world's population lives in plains. Most of the big cities around the world are based near the river bed.

- Plains in many areas are important for doing agriculture work on a large scale.
- Plains have a gentle slope, river navigation is easy and supports a lot of economic activities.

Even today there are stretches along the Ganga where people prefer to use boats to move around.

Q. 2. ***What are the challenges and opportunities of life associated with each landform?***

Ans. The challenges and opportunities of life associated with each landform are:

1. **Mountains:** Mountain areas are more susceptible to natural hazards and disasters such as avalanches, landslides, cloudburst and flash floods. Mountains are very steep and rugged, which can impact daily life and agriculture also.

   Opportunities: Mountains are the store house of natural beauty with diverse fauna, clean and crisp air and mountain sports like skiing.
2. **Plateaus:** One of the main challenges of plateau is rocky mountain and the ongoing erosion of their surface.

   This erosion can lead to a patchy landscape which can hinder the development of agriculture and the construction of infrastructure like roads.

   The opportunities in plateau landforms include their rich mineral deposits making them ideal for mining. They are also suitable for livestock grazing. Additionally they are home to spectacular waterfalls which serve as a major tourist attractions.
3. **Plains:** The plains are ideal for growing crops of all kinds. Agriculture is a major economic occupation in the landforms. Plains also support a variety of flora and fauna.

   Among the challenges faced by plains are overpopulation, pollution, and the depletion of natural resources like groundwater.

V. NCERT INTEXT/TEXTBOOK EXERCISES

Let's Explore

Q. 1. ***As a class activity, form groups of four or five students and observe the school's surroundings. What kind of landscape do you see? will the landscape change a few kilometres away? Or within some 50 kilometres? Compare with other groups.*** *(Page 42)*

Ans. The landscape we see in our surroundings varies—(*a*) plains (*b*) undulating surface (*c*) rocky land similar to landform of plateau or (*d*) hills— mountains eroded with time.

The landscape can or may not change within 50 kms.

Q. 2. *In the same groups, discuss a journey that any of you has made through a region of India. List the different landscapes seen on the way. Compare with other groups.* *(Page 42)*

Ans. When we make a journey through a region in India, landscapes we can observe through the journey are:

(*a*) Mountains

(*b*) Plains

(*c*) Plateaus

(*d*) Deserts

(*e*) Coastal region

Q. 3. *These images (Fig. 3.6, Page 50) depict a few challenges that people living in the mountains may face. Discuss them in groups in the class and write one paragraph on each. Also discuss, why, despite many such challenges, people still choose to live in the mountains.* *(Page 49)*

(A) Flash flood

(B) Avalanche

(C) Cloudburst

(D) Landslide

(E) Uncontrolled tourism

(F) Heavy snowfall

(G) Cold weather

Ans. The above pictures show the problems faced by people living in mountains, which make their lives challenging. Even though they live under these harsh conditions, they continue to adapt and survive.

(*a*) **Flash Floods:** A sudden flood, caused by heavy rainfall in a short period of time generally less than 6 hours is known as flash flood. Flash floods are often caused by cloudburst resulting in heavy rainfall or dam break. They are very fatal, cause mass destruction as these are almost sudden and people do not get time to take caution. *Example:* Mumbai flood of 2005, Uttarakhand (2013).

(*b*) **Avalanche:** A large amount of snow that slides down a slope is an avalanche. It starts when the snow breaks loose from the ground and quickly collects more snow as it moves down. Avalanches often happen when the snow begins to melt. *Example:* Uttarakhand April 2021 and in February 2025. These avalanches occurred after a glacier broke near the Indo-China border.

(*c*) **Cloudburst:** Short bursts of heavy rainfall leading to floods, erosion and blockages.

(*d*) **Landslide:** A landslide is a mass of rock, debris or earth moving from a mountain slope. Landslides can destroy homes and block roads. *Example:* Wayanad landslide in 2024.

(*e*) **Uncontrolled tourism:** Excessive footfall of visitors puts pressure on limited local resources, disturbs mountain eco-system causing harm to both environment and local communities.

(*f*) **Heavy snowfall:** It refers to excessive snowfall. This impacts life by causing road blocks, limiting access and movement and damage to houses.

(*g*) **Cold weather:** Extremely cold weather, that hinders daily life, movement and accessibility.

Q. 4. ***Use the colour code in Fig. 3.8 to add a landform to each name. For instance, 'Tibetan plateau', 'Rocky range', 'Nile plain'. (You do not have to remember the names in this map.)*** (*Page 53*)

Ans.

1. For Tibetan Plateau, we will use dark brown colour.
2. For the Rocky range, we will use light brown colour.
3. For the Nile, Amazon, Mississipi and Ganges Plains, we will use light green colour.

Q. 5. ***The picture in Fig. 3.9 has been taken from a satellite. It captures a portion of north India from a high altitude. Observe and discuss the image as a class activity.***

→ ***Which colour is the Ganga plain?*** (*Page 52*)

Ans. Ganga plain is green in colour.

→ ***What does the white expanse represent?***

Ans. The white expanse represent the snow or ice sleets on the mountains (*Himalayan range*).

→ ***What does the brown expanse at the bottom left of the image represent?***

Ans. Deccan Plateau.

Q. 6. ***Can you give examples of river sources or confluences from your region that are regarded sacred by any community?*** (*Page 55*)

Ans. The Ganges river is one of the most sacred rivers for Hindus. Its source, Gangotri glacier in the Himalayas, is considered highly sacred. Hindus believe the river as a goddess and million of pilgrims visit the Ganges to bathe in its water to purify themselves of sins. The confluence of the Ganges and the Yamuna rivers at Prayagraj, known as the Triveni Sangam, is another highly revered site for Hindus, especially, during the Kumbh Mela festival.

Q. 7. *Visit a nearby river and observe all activities there, whether economic or cultural. Note them down and discuss with your classmates.* *(Page 55)*

Ans. Do it yourself.

Q. 8. *Name some popular tourist destinations in India and identify the category of landform they are associated with.* *(Page 56)*

Ans. India has diverse tourist destinations linked to various landforms. Few are as follows:

(*i*) **Himalayas (Mountains):** Shimla, Manali, Leh.

(*ii*) **Thar Desert (Desert):** Jaisalmer, Bikaner.

(*iii*) **Western Ghats (Plateaus):** Matheran, Lonavala.

(*iv*) **Gangetic Plains (Plains):** Varanasi, Rishikesh and Haridwar.

(*v*) **Andaman and Nicobar (Islands):** Havelock, Neil Island.

Think About It

Read the paragraph under section Think About It on Page 43 and answer the following questions.

Q. 1. *What is snow?*

Ans. Snow is the precipitation of water in a solid state. It is soft, and looks just like a beautiful white blanket.

Q. 2. *In India most precipitation is in what form?*

Ans. Most precipitation in India is in the form of rain and hail.

Q. 3. *Where in India you may see snow? Support by giving examples.*

Ans. In India, snow can be seen in high-altitude regions like Ladakh, Kashmir, Himachal Pradesh, Uttarakhand, Sikkim, and Arunachal Pradesh.

Intext Questions

Q. 1. (*a*) *What are the 'western to eastern oceans'? Can you locate them as well as the "Lord of mountains' on Fig. 5.2?* *(Page 46)*

Ans. The phrase "western to the eastern oceans", here refers that India is flanked by the Arabian Sea to the west and the Bay of Bengal to the east.

Yes, "Lord of Mountains" i.e, the Himalayas can easily be located in Fig. 5.2, running across northern India, Nepal, Bhutan and Tibet (China).

(*b*) *Why is Ganga mentioned?* *(Page 46)*

Ans. In Kumarsambhava, the Ganga is mentioned for multiple reasons. She symbolises purity and divinity, serves as a celestial river descending to Earth, and plays a role in the birth of Kartikeya. Her sacred waters also signify life, fertility and spiritual cleansing.

NCERT Questions, Activities and Projects
(Page 58)

Q. 1. *In what type of landform is your town/village/city located? Which features mentioned in this chapter do you see around you?*

Ans. I am living in a town where the landform is quite plain. We can do agriculture work on this land as the soil is quite fertile. Black soil is found in very large scale. So, we can do cultivation of cotton on a very large scale. Farmers grow crops on large scale as they have their own lands near the river.

Q. 2. *Let us go back to our initial trip from Chhota Nagpur to Prayagraj and Almora. Describe the three landforms you came across on the way.*

Ans. As we move from Chhota Nagpur to Prayagraj and Almora, we come across three major landforms:

(*a*) Chhota Nagpur is a plateau. It is rugged, yet rich in minerals, with dissected hills and river valleys. It lies in the eastern part of India and covers Jharkhand as well as parts of Chhattisgarh, Odisha, West Bengal and Bihar.

(*b*) Prayagraj is located in the Gangetic plains in the state of Uttar Pradesh which have fertile alluvial soil making them ideal for agriculture. Prayagraj is one of the most ancient and sacred cities of India, renowned for the confluence of three rivers.

(*c*) Almora lies in the beautiful Kumaon mountain range in the state of Uttarakhand. It is famous for its scenic beauty and pleasant weather.

Q. 3. *List a few famous pilgrimage spots in India along with the landforms in which they are found.*

Ans. Some of the pilgrimage sites as per their landforms are:

Mountains

(i) Amarnath Cave
(ii) Vaishno Devi
(iii) Badrinath
(iv) Mount Abu
(v) Shirdi

Plains

(i) Prayagraj (Allahabad)
(ii) Haridwar
(iii) Rishikesh
(iv) Mathura
(v) Amritsar
(vi) Varanasi

Plateau

(i) Deogarh
(ii) Ujjain

Coastal region

(i) Rameswaram

Q. 4. *State whether True or false—*

1. The Himalayas are young mountains with rounded tops.
2. Plateaus usually rise sharply at least on one side.
3. Mountains and hills belong to the same type of landform.
4. Mountains, plateaus and rivers in India have the same types of flora and fauna.
5. Ganga is a tributary to the Yamuna.
6. Deserts have unique flora and fauna.
7. Melting snow feeds rivers.
8. Sediments from rivers deposited in the plains makes the land fertile.
9. All deserts are hot.

Ans.

1. → False 2. → True 3. → True
4. → False 5. → False 6. → True
7. → True 8. → True 9. → False

Q. 5. *Match words in pairs:*

Ans:

(a) Mount Everest	**climbing**
(b) rafting	**river**
(c) camels	**desert**
(d) plateau	**roof of the world**
(e) Gangetic plains	**rice fields**
(f) waterway	**Ganga**
(g) Mount Kilimanjaro	**Africa**
(h) Yamuna	**Tributary**

VI. EXAM ORIENTED QUESTIONS

A. Very Short Answer Type Questions

Q. 1. *Into how many categories are landforms classified?*

Ans. The landforms are classified into three categories.

(i) Mountains (ii) Plateaus
(iii) Plains

Q. 2. *Name the mountain that is not the part of any range.*

Ans. Mount Kilimanjaro in eastern Africa is an isolated mountain that is not a part of any range.

Q. 3. *What are hills? Support with example.*

Ans. Hills are highlands i.e., naturally raised area of land. Compared to mountains they are lower in height, have less steep slopes and have rounded tops. *Examples* (a) Cardamom Hills (b) Annamalai Hills.

Q. 4. *Plateaus differ from plains in their surface features? Give reason.*

Ans. While both are flat and in horizontal position, plateaus differ from plains in their surface features. Plateaus have at least one side with a steep slope, while plains are vast undulating land.

Q. 5. *What is precipitation and its forms?*

Ans. Water from the atmosphere reaching the ground is defined as precipitation. The most common forms of precipitation are rain, snow and hail.

Q. 6. *Flood plains are ideal for agriculture. Give reason.*

Ans. Flood plains are ideal for agriculture because they are fertile due to the nutrient rich sediment (sand, silt and other soil forming material) deposited by rivers especially during floods.

Q. 7. *Irrigation has increased agricultural production in the Gangetic plains but it presents a challenge for the future. What is the challenge?*

Ans. The challenge posed by increased irrigation in Gangetic plains is that it has contributed to depletion of ground water which threatens the future of agriculture in the region.

Q. 8. *Give any two ways in which human activities are a factor in landslides.*

Ans. Human activities that are contributing to the disaster of landslides in mountainous regions are:

(*a*) deforestation.

(*b*) uncontrolled construction activities on hill slopes. For example, roads and railways.

(*c*) poorly planned drainage system.

Q. 9. *Give names of hottest desert in Africa and a cold desert in India.*

Ans. Hottest desert in Africa — The Sahara.

Cold desert in India — Ladakh.

B. Short Answer Type Questions

Q. 1. *State the differences between 'young' and 'old' mountains. Support with examples.*

Ans. Mountains can be categorised as 'young' and 'old' mountains.

(*a*) Young mountains

(*i*) Young mountains are those that were formed in Earth's recent history—but that too is still millions of years ago.

(*ii*) They have tall steep peaks.

(*iii*) Upliftment and erosion continue to this day. *Example*: the Himalayas, the Alps, the Andes.

(*b*) Old mountains

(*i*) They are low in height, have gentle slopes and rounded peaks.

(*ii*) Forces of erosion have acted on them for millions of years and worn them out. *Example:* the Aravallis, and the Urals.

Q. 2. *What type of farming is practised in mountainous regions. Why? Explain with an example.*

Ans. Terrace farming is the form of agriculture practised in mountainous regions. Steps or terraces are built into mountain slopes. Terrace farming is practised to maximise arable land area in diverse landscape and to reduce soil erosion. Water runoff or loss is a major concern in these regions. Terrace *i.e.*, steps help hold water, slow down the speed of flow of rain water, thereby preventing damage to crops. *Example*: In India it is practised in Himachal Pradesh, Uttarakhand and North Eastern States.

Q. 3. *Plateaus are a major landform however many plateaus are less favourable to farming? Give reasons.*

Ans. A plateau is a landform that rises up from the surrounding land and has more or less flat surface. One or more of its sides are often steep. They are storehouses of minerals.

However, the plateaus environment is very diverse across the world.

Many plateaus are made up of rocky infertile soil. *For example*: Chhota Nagpur plateau in India, Patagonia in South America (Argentina). This makes them less fertile than plains and therefore are less favourable to farming.

Exceptions are Lava plateaus like Deccan plateau rich in black soil which consists of minerals and nutrients fit for cultivation. *For example*: Cotton.

Q. 4. *How are flood plains formed? How are they useful? Support your answer with an example.*

Ans.

1. Flood plains are formed by rivers originating in mountain ranges.
2. These rivers collect particles of rock, sand and silt called sediments or alluvium.
3. These sediments are carried all the way, to the plains (extensive flat, gently undulating surface) and deposited on their banks making the soil fertile.
4. The fertile soil of plains is ideal for growing all kinds of crops, and agriculture is a major economic occupation here.
5. Plains are home to a large part of world population as this landform is well suited to settlement. In India the Ganga plains supports one-fourth of the country's population. Plains also support a variety of flora and fauna. *For Example*: Gangetic plains in India, the Amazon plains in South America, Nile plains in Egypt, the Mississippi Basin in North America.
6. The rivers are suitable for navigation.

Q. 5. *Discuss some of the significant features of a desert. Give examples in support.*

Ans. (*i*) Deserts are large dry expanses with very little precipitation. Deserts can be divided into two groups— hot or cold desert.

Example: the Sahara desert in Africa and the Thar desert to the north west of Aravalli hills in India are examples of hot deserts.

The Gobi desert in Asia, Ladakh in India, and some experts say that even the Antarctica continent are examples of cold deserts.

(*ii*) The flora and fauna of deserts is unique.

(*iii*) These deserts have harsh living conditions, but humans due to their adaptability and resilience have adapted to life in most deserts. Communities living or migrating through them have rich cultural traditions. *For example*: In India communities living in the Thar Desert have rich cultural traditions—they have their own folk songs, dances, music, art, craft, culinary skills etc. that are related to desert life.

C. Long Answer Type Questions

Q. 1. *Give some features of Himalayas?*

Ans. 1. Himalayas are a crescent shaped mountain range with tall sharp peaks, spanning five countries—India, Pakistan, Nepal, China and Bhutan, the word Himalaya means 'abode of snow'.

2. They are 'young' mountains, formed recently in Earth's history. 'Young' but still millions of years old. Upliftment and erosion continues to this day.

3. Mount Everest and Kanchenjunga are the two highest peaks of the Himalayan range. Mount Everest is also the highest mountain peak in the world.

4. Its slopes are covered with montane forest where conifer trees such as pines, firs, spruce and deodar grow. These Conifer trees grow tall and are cone shaped, with thin pointed leaves. It is home to thousands of species of flowering plants, many endemic plants and fauna.

Q. 2. *Excessive inflow of visitors put the fragile mountain environment under pressure. Suggest ways to maintain the right balance.*

Ans. Ways to maintain right balance between mountain environment and excessive inflow of tourists are:

1. Educate and ensure visitors stay on trails and footpath.
   - that they do not litter
   - do not pluck plants or feed animals or disturb their habitat by playing loud music, use of mobiles etc.
2. Increase public appreciation of environment.
3. Speed awareness of environmental problems when people come into close contact with nature.

4. Proper planning and management of tourism facilities to enhance the safeguarding of natural surroundings.
5. Use of energy efficient and non-polluting construction materials, minimisation technique and proper waste management.

D. Assertion & Reasoning Questions

There are two statements marked as Assertion (A) and Reason (R). Mark your answer as per the codes provided below:

Q. 1. Assertion (A): Altitude of mountains determine whether mountains are permanently snow-capped.

Reason (R): At lower altitudes, snow melts every summer and turns into water that feeds rivers.

Codes:

(*a*) Both (A) and (R) are true but (R) is not the correct explanation of (A).
(*b*) Both (A) and (R) are true and (R) is the correct explanation of (A).
(*c*) (A) is true but (R) is false.
(*d*) (A) is false but (R) is true.

Q. 2. Assertion (A): All world's mountains are grouped in mountain ranges.

Reason (R): Mount Kilimanjaro in eastern Africa is an isolated mountain that is not a part of any range.

Codes:

(*a*) Both (A) and (R) are true but (R) is not the correct explanation of (A).
(*b*) Both (A) and (R) are true and (R) is the correct explanation of (A).
(*c*) (A) is true but (R) is false.
(*d*) (A) is false but (R) is true.

Q. 3. Assertion (A): The Aravalli range are much older than the Himalayas.

Reason (R): Himalayas are tall with sharp peaks and are still growing/uplifting.

Codes:

(*a*) Both (A) and (R) are true but (R) is not the correct explanation of (A).
(*b*) Both (A) and (R) are true and (R) is the correct explanation of (A).
(*c*) (A) is true but (R) is false.
(*d*) (A) is false but (R) is true.

Q. 4. Assertion (A): Ganga is the largest river originating in the Himalayas.

Reason (R): Some of its numerous tributaries also originate in the Himalayas.

Codes:

(*a*) Both (A) and (R) are true but (R) is not the correct explanation of (A).
(*b*) Both (A) and (R) are true and (R) is the correct explanation of (A).
(*c*) (A) is true but (R) is false.
(*d*) (A) is false but (R) is true.

Ans.

1. (*b*) 2. (*d*) 3. (*a*) 4. (*b*)

E. Case/Source Based Questions

Read the passage given below and answer the questions that follow:

I. Thousands of years ago, the first civilisations developed around rivers in fertile plains. In our times too, a large part of the world's population lives in plains. About 40 crore people, more than one-fourth of the total Indian population, live in India's Ganga plain (often called the 'Gangetic plain'). As with many other plains of the world, the major occupations of people in this region include river fishing and agriculture.

Whether in mountain ranges or plains, rivers around the world have carried immense cultural value. In particular, many communities have considered a river's source and its confluence with one or two other rivers to be sacred. In India, numerous festivals, ceremonies and rituals are conducted at such locations.

(*i*) Why first civilisations developed around river plains?
(*ii*) Give two major occupations of people in this region.
(*iii*) Name some fibre crops grown in India's Gangetic plains.
(*iv*) What are the two problems affecting Gangetic plains?
(*v*) Why do rivers around the world carry immense cultural value?

Ans.

(*i*) First civilisations (Indus Valley, Mesopotamian civilisations) developed around river plains because of fertility of the soil that was ideal for agriculture and availability of water.

(*ii*) River fishing and agriculture.

(*iii*) Jute, cotton and hemp.

(*iv*) High population and pollution.

(*v*) (*a*) Rivers around the world carry immense cultural value because many communities consider a river's source and its confluence with other rivers to be sacred.

(*b*) Numerous festivals, ceremonies and rituals are conducted at these locations.

F. Competency Based Questions

Q. 1. *Mountains and plateaus are two major type of landforms. Identify and briefly discuss any three similarities between there landforms.*

Ans. Despite being two different types of major landforms mountains and plateaus share some similarities.

(*i*) Like mountains, plateaus can be young or old in terms of the Earth's history.

(*ii*) Like mountains, plateaus are rich in mineral deposits. They are called 'storehouses of minerals'?

(*iii*) Mountains are very important for tourism—the snow-capped peaks, wooded slopes, swift rivers, fresh cool air are great attractions. Similarly, plateaus too are great tourist attraction with their spectacular waterfalls e.g. Nohkalikai Falls of Cherrapunji Plateau.

(*iv*) Many rivers of these landforms are sources of hydroelectric power.

Q. 2. *'Reverence of mountain summits is found in communities around the world'. Give examples in support of the statement.*

Or

Mountains hold spiritual significance in many cultures. Discuss with example.

Ans.

(*i*) Kālidāsa's poem *Kumārasambhava* begins with the invocation to the Himalayas—Lord of the Mountains, like a living god.

(*ii*) Mount Everest (8849 m) the highest mountain in the world is regarded as sacred by both the Tibetans and Nepalis Tibetans name it 'Chomolungma' meaning Mother Goddess of the world.

Nepalis in reverence call it 'Sagarmatha' meaning 'Goddess of the Sky'.

(*iii*) Yet another mountain Mount Kailash held sacred by followers of Hinduism, Buddhism, Jainism and Bon.

(*iv*) Mount Sinai or Mount Moses located in the Peninsula of Egypt.

G. Skill Based Questions

Q. 1. *Why is the Tibetan Plateau nicknamed as the 'Roof of the World'?*

Ans. The Tibetan Plateau is nicknamed the 'roof of the world' due to its enormous height.

(*i*) It is the largest, highest flat land in the world with an average altitude of 4500 metres above sea level.

(*ii*) Its east to west length is nearly 2,500 kms.

(*iii*) It is angled like a house roof.

Q. 2. (a) 'Mountains contribute to river formation.' Elaborate. Support with the help of an example.

(b) How do rivers originating in mountains enable formation of flood plains?

Ans. (a) Mountains contribute to river formation as:

(i) Mountains are at higher elevation—they receive more precipitation in the form of rain or snow. This abundant source helps in formation of rivers.

(ii) Many mountain ranges have glaciers and snow fields, melting of snow and they provide a continuous source of water that flows down the slopes forming streams and rivers.

Example: The Ganges and its biggest tributary the Yamuna river originate from the Himalayan ranges—the Gangotri glacier and Yamunotri glacier respectively. These rivers are snow fed—they receive water from the melting ice of the glaciers as well as the rains.

(b) Rivers originating in mountain ranges collect nutrient rich sediments which they deposit on way to plains making the soil fertile. This fertile soil is ideal for agriculture and supporting diverse ecosystems.

H. Picture Based Questions

Q. 1. Study the illustration and answer the questions that follow:

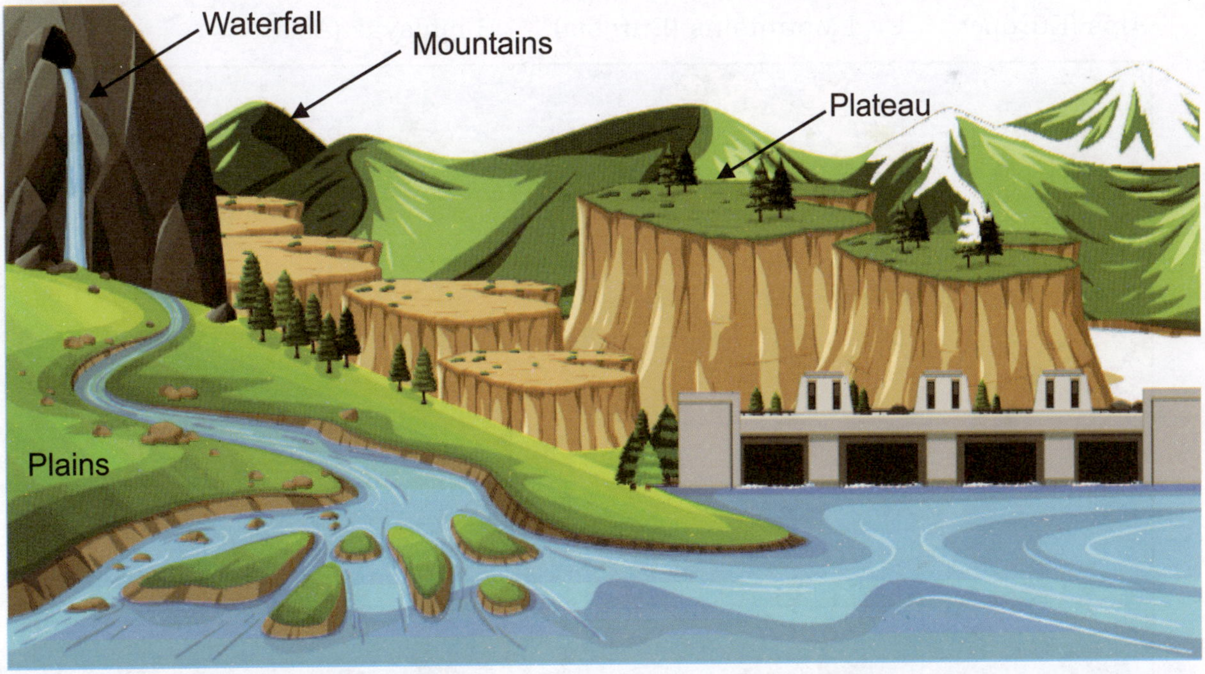

Fig. This drawing illustrates three landforms — mountains in the background (two of them snow-capped), a plateau on the left and a plain in the foreground, with a river emerging from the mountains and a waterfall.

(*i*) Which of the following landform is **not** represented.

(*a*) Mountains (*b*) Plain

(*c*) Plateau (*d*) Desert

(*ii*) Find the **odd** one out.

(*a*) Mountains have broad base, steep slopes, and narrow summit.

(*b*) Plateaus have somewhat a flat surface and are always a result of volcanic activity.

(*c*) Plains have extensive flat, low lying, gently undulating surface.

(*d*) Two mountains which are at higher altitude are snow-capped.

(*iii*) Choose the correct one

(*a*) The blue curves represent a river.

(*b*) The rivers source is the mountains.

(*c*) It is a snow fed river.

(*d*) All of the above.

(*iv*) Which of the statements are **True** about sparsely populated landforms.

(*a*) rugged terrain.

(*b*) extreme climate and lack of agricultural land.

(*c*) lack of transport facilities.

(*d*) All of the above.

Ans. (*i*) (*d*), (*ii*) (*b*), (*iii*) (*d*), (*iv*) (*d*)

VII. MAP SKILLS

Q. 1. ***On the given outline map of the world locate and label the world's famous mountain ranges.***

1. Rocky Mountains (North America), **2.** Andes (South America) **3.** Atlas Mountains (Africa) **4.** Alps (Europe), **5.** Ural Mountains (Eurasia), **6.** Himalayas (Asia)

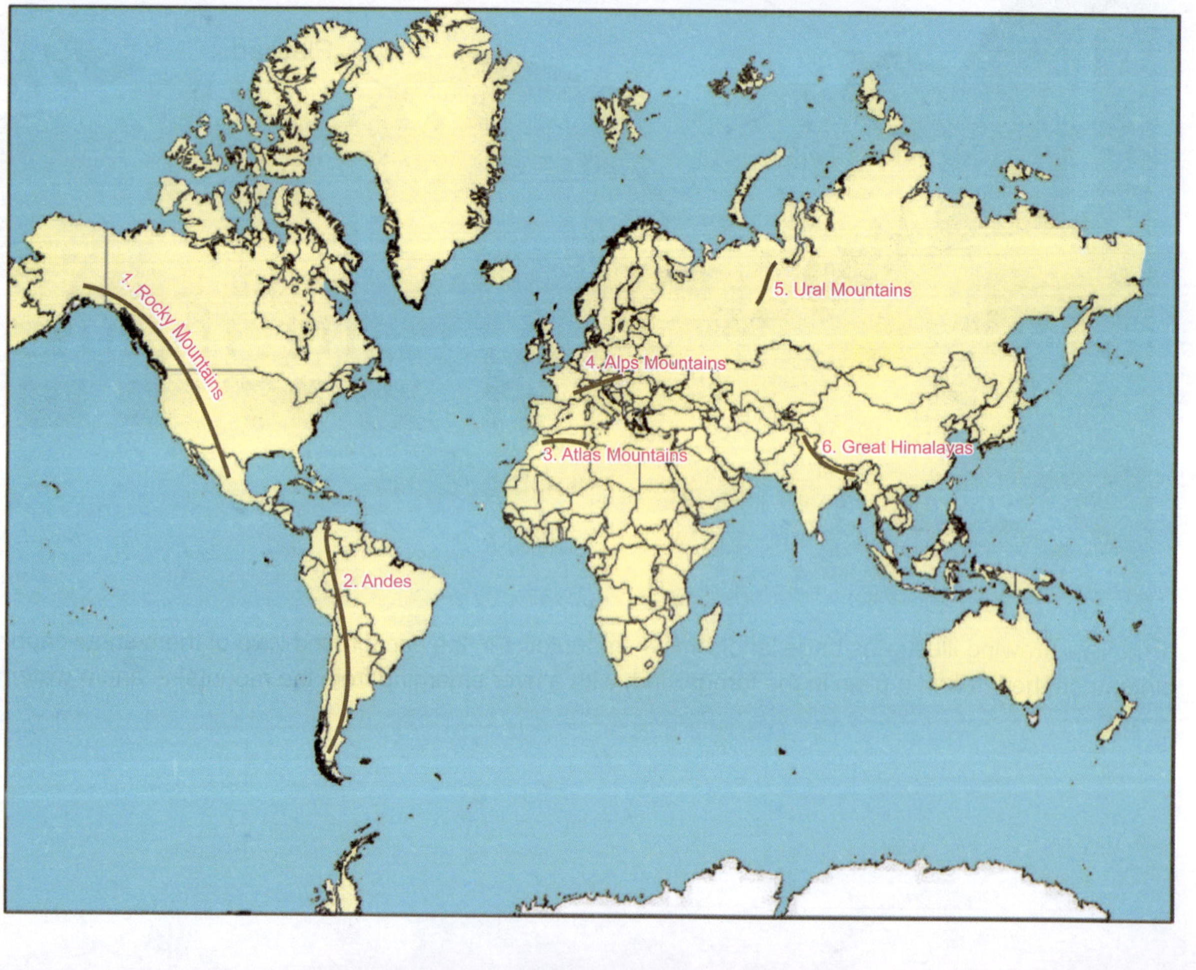

Q. 2. *On the given map of India locate and label the following:*

1. Vindhya Range
2. Satpura Range
3. Aravalli Range
4. Himalayan Range in India
5. Deccan Plateau
6. Ganges Plains
7. Thar Desert
8. Chhota Nagpur Plateau

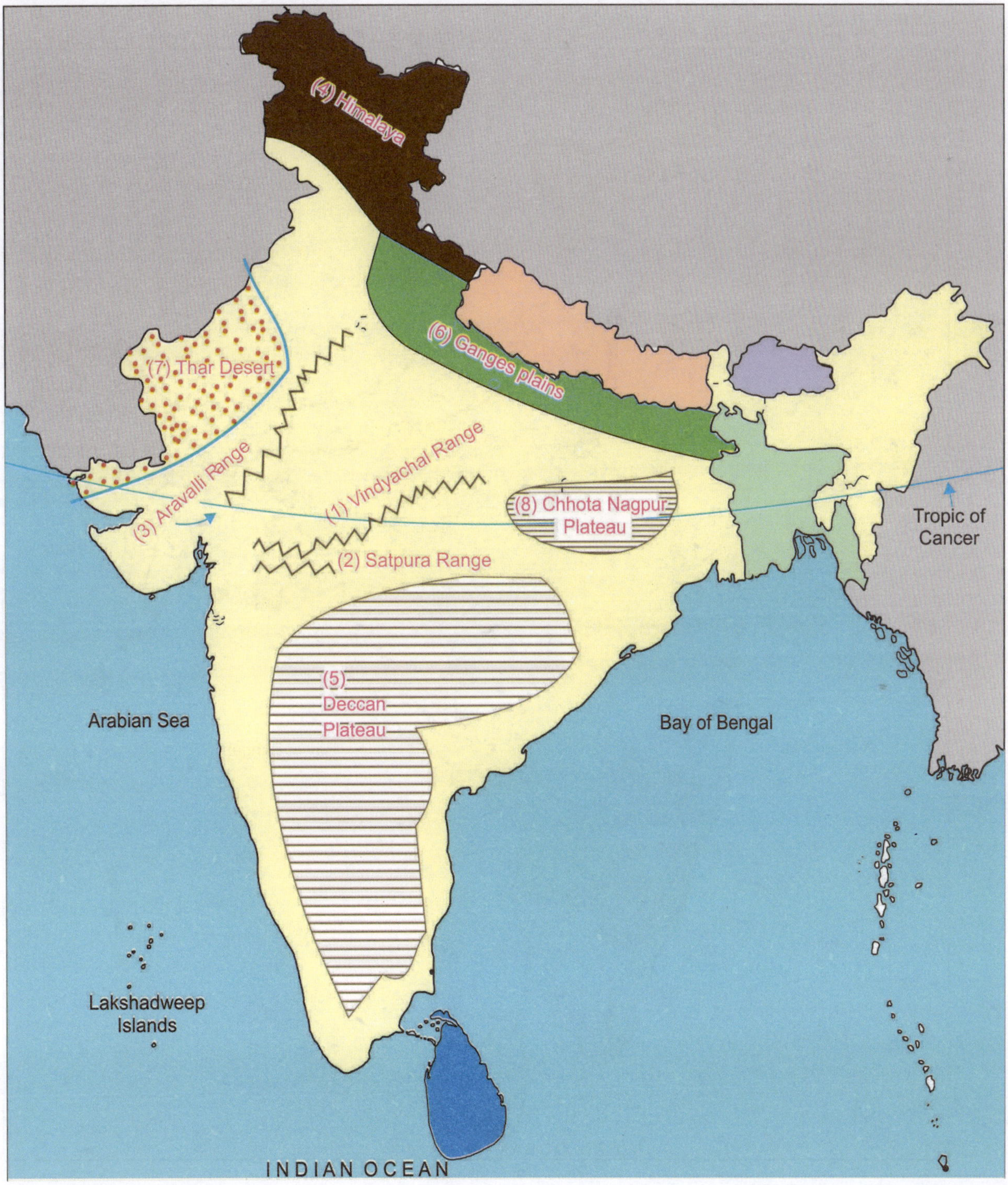

Q. 3. On the given map of India locate and mark states of

1. Uttarakhand	2. Uttar Pradesh	3. Jharkhand
4. Kashmir	5. Ladakh	6. Himachal Pradesh
7. Sikkim	8. Arunachal Pradesh	9. Karnataka
10. Tamil Nadu	11. Kerala	12. Odisha

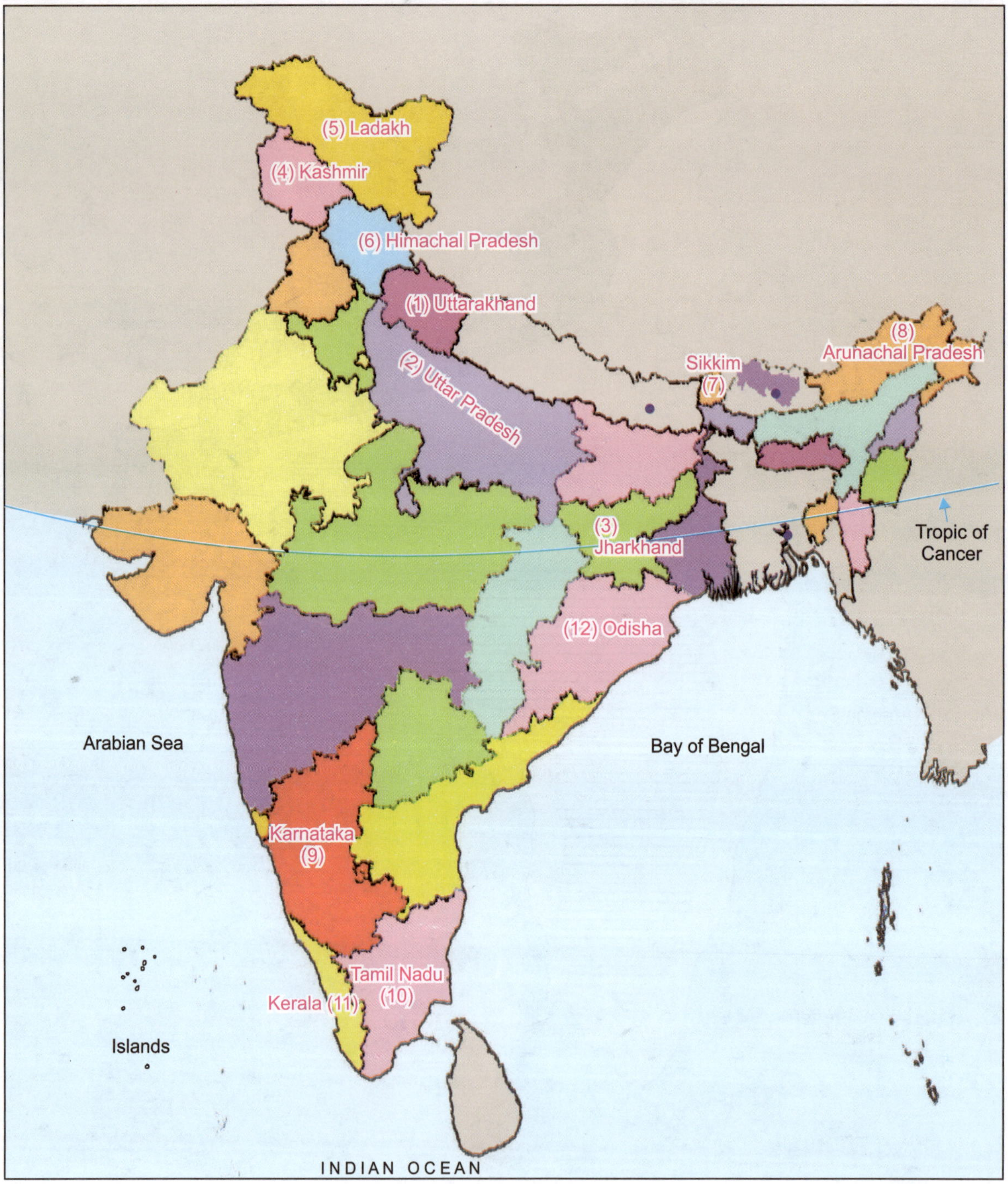

VIII. MULTIPLE CHOICE QUESTIONS

1. *Mountains can be recognised by*
   (*a*) steep slopes (*b*) gentle slopes
   (*c*) narrow slopes (*d*) broad slopes
2. *Highlands with a lower height, less steep slopes and rounded tops are called*
   (*a*) Mountain (*b*) Valleys
   (*c*) Hills (*d*) Range
3. *Mount Aconcagua is the highest peak of*
   (*a*) Mont Blanc (*b*) The Aravallis
   (*c*) The Andes (*d*) The Alps
4. *At higher altitudes the trees give way to*
   (*a*) grasses
   (*b*) grasses, mosses and lichens
   (*c*) pines
   (*d*) rains
5. *________ is the Indian name of the largest river originating from Himalayas.*
   (*a*) The Son (*b*) The Ganga
   (*c*) The Narmada (*d*) The Yamuna
6. *African Plateau is famous for*
   (*a*) gold, silver
   (*b*) gold, diamond
   (*c*) silver and brass
   (*d*) copper
7. *Floodplains are one type of plains formed by________*
   (*a*) sea (*b*) rivers
   (*c*) lake (*d*) all of these
8. *Plains also support a variety of________ .*
   (*a*) animals (*b*) flora and fauna
   (*c*) plants (*d*) all of these
9. *The Himalayas are young mountains with ________ peaks.*
   (*a*) sharp (*b*) elliptical
   (*c*) spherical (*d*) round

Ans.

1. → (*a*) 2. → (*c*) 3. → (*c*)
4. → (*b*) 5. → (*b*) 6. → (*b*)
7. → (*b*) 8. → (*b*) 9. → (*a*)

IX. OBJECTIVE TYPE QUESTIONS

A. True or False

1. The Bhumi Sukta is 'Hymn to the Earth'.
2. In the Himalayan region most precipitation as in the rest of India is in the form of monsoons.
3. Permanently frozen rivers of ice in mountains are called glaciers.
4. Lava plateaus have fertile soil rich in minerals.
5. Rivers originating in mountain ranges carry rich sediments made up of rocks silt and clay.
6. The five tinais of ancient Tamil Sangam poetry reflect a deep connection between humanity and the natural environment.

Ans.

1. → True 2. → False
3. → True 4. → False
5. → True 6. → True

B. Fill in the Blanks

1. With the Himalayan ranges ________ and ______ continue to this day.
2. The highest plateau in the world is the __________ plateau.
3. Alluvial plains are made up of _______, __________ and _________.
4. Earthquakes and volcanoes are a result of _________ processes.
5. _________ and _________ are two highest peaks of the Himalayan range.
6. Life in mountains involves potential challenges both _______ and ________ made.

Ans.

1. upliftment; erosion 2. Tibetan
3. rocks; silt; sand 4. internal
5. Mount Everest; Kanchenjunga
6. natural; human

C. Match Column A with Column B

1.

Column A		Column B	
1.	Mountain which is not a range	(*a*)	Anamudi
2.	Confluence of rivers	(*b*)	Ganga plains
3.	Highest mountain in South India	(*c*)	Cherrapunji Plateau
4.	High population	(*d*)	Kilimanjaro
5.	Nohkalikai Falls	(*e*)	Sacred

(*a*) 1 – (*e*) 2 – (*a*) 3 – (*b*) 4 – (*c*) 5 – (*d*)
(*b*) 1 – (*d*) 2 – (*e*) 3 – (*a*) 4 – (*b*) 5 – (*c*)
(*c*) 1 – (*b*) 2 – (*c*) 3 – (*d*) 4 – (*e*) 5 – (*a*)
(*d*) 1 – (*c*) 2 – (*d*) 3 – (*e*) 4 – (*a*) 5 – (*b*)

Ans. (*b*) 1 – (*d*) 2 – (*e*) 3 – (*a*) 4 – (*b*) 5 – (*c*)

X. TEST YOUR KNOWLEDGE

A. Multiple Choice Questions

1. *Which of the following is not a part of landform?*
(*a*) Glacier (*b*) Hill
(*c*) Mountain (*d*) Plateau

2. *A plateau is an elevated flat land. It is a flat topped ________ land.*
(*a*) irregular (*b*) regular
(*c*) rectangular (*d*) conical

3. *Find the* ***odd*** *one out*
(*a*) Flash flood
(*b*) Avalanche
(*c*) Uncontrolled tourism
(*d*) Cloud burst

4. *Which of the following is not a mountain animal?*
(*a*) Lion (*b*) Yak
(*c*) Leopard (*d*) Ibex

5. *Which of the following world's religion does not regard Mount Kailash as sacred?*
(*a*) Hindus (*b*) Islam
(*c*) Buddhism (*d*) Bon

6. *In ancient Tamil Sangam poetry which landforms are associated with farming and cattle rearing respectively?*
(*a*) Palai and Kurinji
(*b*) Marudam and Mullai
(*c*) Neydal and Mullai
(*d*) Palai and Marudam

7. *Which of the following are* ***cold*** *deserts?*
(*i*) Gobi (*ii*) Leh
(*iii*) Thar (*iv*) Arabian
(*a*) (*i*) and (*ii*)
(*b*) (*ii*) and (*iii*)
(*c*) (*iii*) and (*iv*)
(*d*) (*iv*) and (*i*)

8. *Given below are names of some mountains, arrange them in descending order.*
(*i*) Mt Aconcagua
(*ii*) Mt Kanchenjunga
(*iii*) Mont Blanc
(*iv*) Mt Everest
(*a*) (*iv*), (*i*), (*iii*) and (*ii*)
(*b*) (*iv*), (*iii*), (*ii*) and (*i*)
(*c*) (*iv*), (*ii*), (*iii*) and (*i*)
(*d*) (*iv*), (*ii*), (*i*) and (*iii*)

9. *Given below are names of famous waterfalls. Which of the following are correctly matched?*
(*i*) Hundru Falls — Subarnarekha river
(*ii*) Victoria Falls — Zambezi river
(*iii*) Jog Falls — Periyar river
(*iv*) Nohkalikai Falls—Brahmaputra river
(*a*) (*i*), (*iii*), and (*iv*)
(*b*) (*i*), and (*ii*)
(*c*) (*ii*), (*iii*), and (*iv*)
(*d*) (*i*), (*ii*), and (*iii*)

B. True or False

1. Indian culture celebrates different landforms in common ways.
2. Mount Everest is the highest mountain in the world located between Tibet (China) and Nepal.

C. Fill in the Blanks

1. Plains have a _______ slope.
2. Each landform offers different challenges as well as an _________.
3. Mountains and hills belong to the same type of _______
4. Major landforms are _______, _______, and _______.
5. A plateau is a landform that rises up from the surrounding _______ and has a more or _______ flat surface.

D. Very Short Answer Type Questions

Q. 1. *Why cultivation is not possible in the mountainous areas on very large scale?*

Q. 2. *Define Precipitation.*

Q. 3. *Why plains are densely populated?*

Q. 4. *What is the difference between mountains and plateaus?*

Q. 5. *Give any two ways in which we can safeguard mountains from disaster.*

E. Short Answer Type Questions

Q. 1. *Write a short note on terraced farming.*

Q. 2. *Explain the classification of landforms.*

Q. 3. *Differentiate between Plateaus and Plains.*

Q. 4. *How flood plains are formed?*

Q. 5. *Give few examples of river sources from your region that are regarded sacred by your community.*

F. Long Answer Type Questions

Q. 1. *Define plains. How the plains are formed? Explain the importance of plains.*

Q. 2. *Differentiate between mountains and hills.*

Q. 3. *Explain the significance of mountains.*

Q. 4. *Explain the challenges and opportunities of life linked or associated with each landforms.*

Q. 5. *Do you think agriculture work is possible on the plateaus? Give reason for your answer.*

XI. PICTURE STUDY

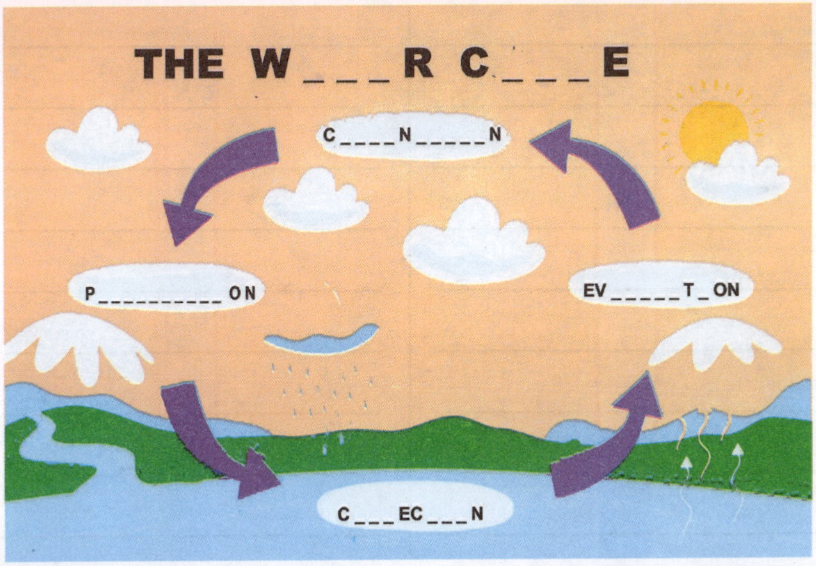

(*i*) Identify the given picture.

(*ii*) Name the four processes involved in the hydrological cycle which is the life line of the landforms?

NOTES

THEME B
TAPESTRY OF THE PAST

INTERESTING MIND MAP

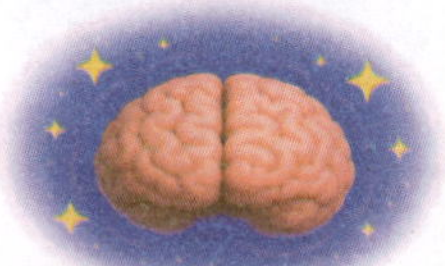

Timeline and Sources of History

1 How Do We Learn About the Past?

- **History:** The study of past events (especially about humans).
- **History Experts**

  Geologists: Study earth's physical features (rocks, soil, rivers, seas, mountains).

  Palaeontologists: Study fossils (remains) of plants, animals, humans from a million years ago.

  Anthropologists: Study societies & cultures (ancient & present).

  Archaeologists: Study past life via excavations (tools, pottery, beads, toys, figurines, bones, houses, grains).

2 How Is Time Measured in History?

- Societies measured time with new eras (king's reign, leader's birth).
- **New era:** A special & separate period of time.
- **Gregorian Calendar:** Widely used across the world.
- Hindu, Muslim, Jewish & Chinese (festivals & auspicious events).
- In the West, birth year of Jesus Christ = New Era called AD (Anno Domini), now replaced by CE (Common Era).
- Ex. 1914: Beginning of World War I.
- Years before Jesus' birth = BC (Before Christ); Now known as BCE (Before Common Era).
- Ex. 322 BCE: The Rise of Maratha Empire.
- **Timeline:** Tool to show order of events (earlier/later).
- **Century:** Period of 100 years.
- **Millennium:** Period of 1000 years.

3 What Are the Sources of History?

- **Sources:**

  Inscriptions: Manuscripts, copper plates, coins.

  Archaeological Sources: monuments, mounds.

  Excavation: Fossils (human, plant, animals), tools & weapons, statues & ornaments, pottery & toys, burials.

  Artistic Sources: Paintings, sculptures, panels.

  Foreign Accounts: Historical chronicles & travelogues.

  Indian Literature: The Vedas, historical texts, poems, plays & stories.

  Oral Sources: Genealogical & folklore (local stories).
- Historians compare + cross-check information from different sources (sometimes match, sometimes contradict) and recreate history.
- **Experts contribute to sources:** Archaeologists, Epigraphists, Anthropologists, Linguists, Literary Scholars.
- **Epigraphists:** Study ancient inscriptions.
- **Linguists:** Expert in different languages.
- **Scientific studies:** ancient climate studies, chemical tests, DNA/genetic research of excavated resources.
- Recent history (last 200–300 yrs): Newspapers, TV, Internet, digital media.

4 The Beginnings of Human History

- **Modern humans (Homo sapiens):** appeared ~300,000 years ago.
- **Early humans:** hunters & gatherers, lived in caves/rock shelters, temporary camps
- **Early beliefs:** respect for nature, **afterlife** ideas (life begins after death).
- Early humans communicated in **lost languages**.
- They used fire to create stone tools (axes, blades, arrowheads).
- Rock paintings (shows aspects of life): animals, humans, symbols.
- **Ornaments:** stone/shell beads, teeth pendants, exchanged between groups.

5 The First Crops

- **Ice Age:** When the climate warmed, glaciers melted, rivers swelled, and drained into oceans.
- The **Ice Age** lasted from over 100,000 years ago to 12,000 years ago.
- Humans settled near rivers, started farming (cereals, grains) & animal domestication (cattle, goats).
- Large communities settled near rivers due to fertile soil.
- Land was farmed collectively; chieftains led community.
- **Hamlets** (small colonies) became large villages and then towns.
- Established trade networks & exchanged food, tools, clothing.
- **New technologies:** beginning of pottery, copper tools, later iron tools & ornaments.
- Basis of early civilisation.

CHAPTER

4

THEME–B
Tapestry of the Past

TIMELINE AND SOURCES OF HISTORY

I. FACTS TO REMEMBER/SUMMARY

HOW DO WE LEARN ABOUT THE PAST?

- The Earth has a very, very long history, of which we humans occupy only a tiny part — the most recent one.
- Many people study the history of the Earth. Some of them are trained to uncover the secrets left beneath the Earth's surface and help us learn about its past – and also our past.

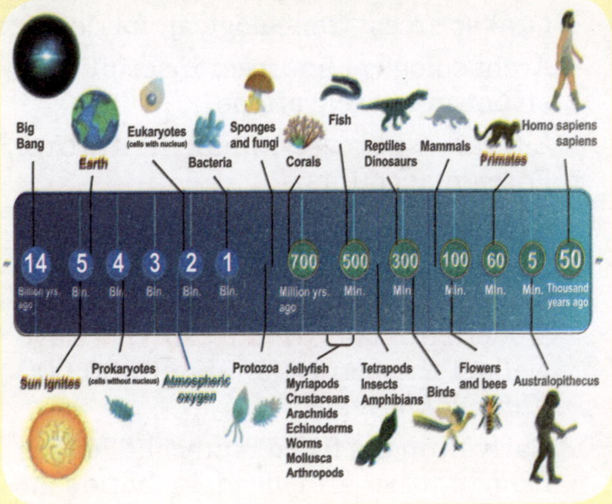

- **Geologists** explore Earth's physical features, such as rocks, soil, stones, hills, mountains, rivers, seas, oceans and other land forms.
- **Palaeontologists** examine fossils of plants, animals and humans from millions of years ago.
- **Anthropologists** explore human societies and cultures from ancient to modern times.
- **Archaeologists** study the past by digging up things left by people, plants and animals, like tools, pottery, beads, figurines, toys, bones and teeth of animals and humans, burnt grains and pieces of buildings.
- **Epigraphists** study ancient inscriptions.

HOW IS TIME MEASURED IN HISTORY?

- Each society and culture has had its own ways of measuring time. Major events, such as the birth of an important person or the start of a ruler's reign, have often marked the beginning of a new era.
- At present, the **Gregorian calendar** is commonly used worldwide; side by side, Hindu, Islamic, Jewish, Chinese and other calendars are also used for calculating the dates of festivals and other auspicious events.
- In the West, the conventional year for **Jesus Christ's** birth has generally been taken to be the starting point for this calendar. Years are counted forward from this point and used to be marked with 'AD' or 'CE' **(Common Era)**.
- The years before the conventional date for the birth of Jesus are counted backward and used to be marked with BC (or **Before Christ**). They are now called **Before Common Era** or BCE.
- **Century:** It is any period of 100 years. In history, specific centuries are counted every 100 years starting from the year 1 CE. For instance, we are currently in the 21st century CE, which runs from 2001 to 2100.

- **Millennium:** It is any period of 1,000 years. In history, specific centuries are counted every 1,000 years from the year 1 CE. For instance, we are currently in the 3rd millennium CE, which began in 2001 CE and will go up to 3000 CE.
- Not only historians, but archaeologists, epigraphists, anthropologists, experts in literature and languages, and many more people contribute to all the sources of history.

WHAT ARE THE SOURCES OF HISTORY?

Sources of history are: Oral sources, Archaeological sources, Literary sources and Artistic sources.

- Oral sources: Genealogical, folklore.
- Archaeological sources: Inscriptions, structures, excavations.
- Literary sources: Indian literature, Foreign accounts.
- Artistic sources: Paintings, sculptures, panels.

THE BEGINNINGS OF HUMAN HISTORY

- Modern humans **(Homo sapiens)** have walked the planet for about 300,000 (*three lakh*) years.
- Early humans faced many challenges from nature and lived in bands or groups to help each other. They were constantly seeking shelter and food, and were mainly hunters and gatherers.

THE FIRST CROPS

- Over long periods, the Earth's climate has undergone many changes. At certain times, it was extremely cold and much of the Earth was covered with ice — this period is known as the **'Ice Age'**.
- The last Ice Age lasted for over 100,000 (one lakh) years and ended around 12,000 years ago.
- As communities grew, so did their social complexity. Leaders or **'chieftains'** were responsible for the well-being of the people, and everyone collectively worked toward the welfare of the community'.

II. DATE LINE

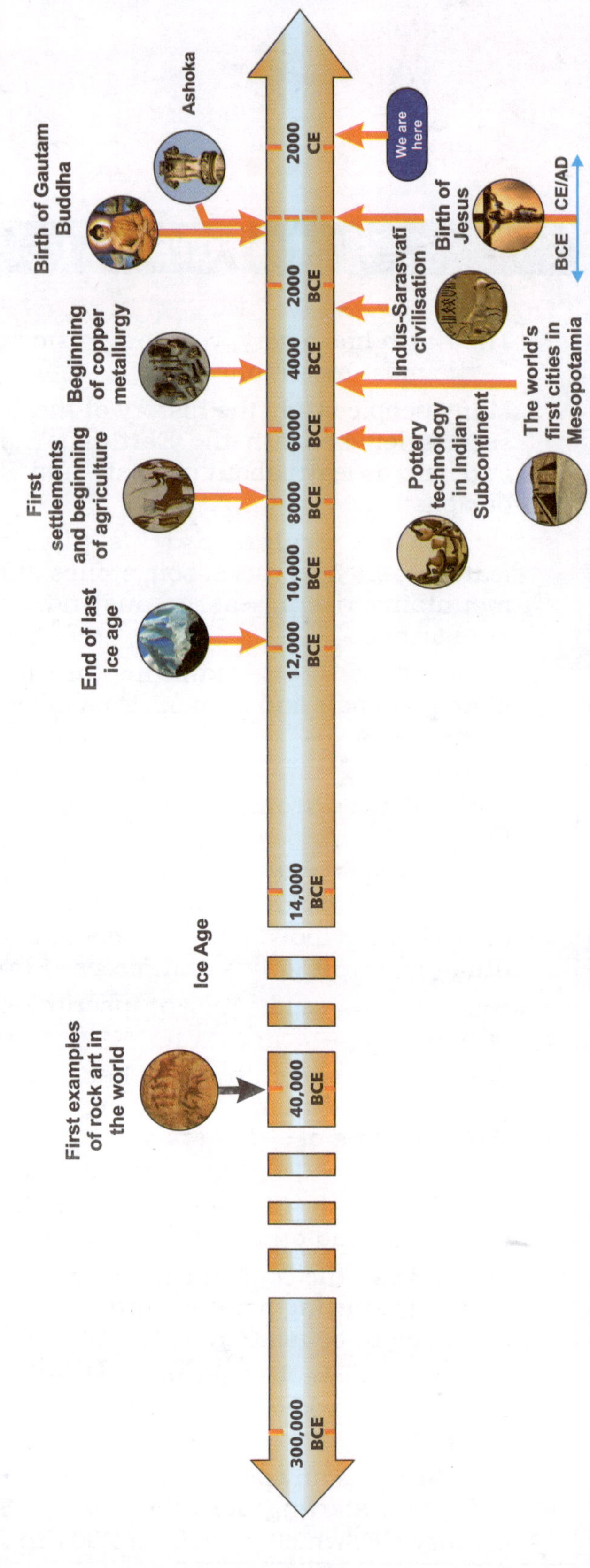

III. TEXTBOOK KEYWORDS/GLOSSARY

1. **Fossils:** Impressions or remains of plants or plant parts or animals that are found preserved within layers of soil or rock.
2. **Era:** A distinct period of time.
3. **Gregorian Calendar:** The calendar now used the world over; it has 12 months adding up to 365 days, and a leap year every four years. However, century years—for example, 1800, 1900, 2000—are leap years only if they are multiples of 400; so in the three centenary years above, only 2000 is a leap year.
4. **Auspicious:** Something favourable or bringing luck; for instance, 'an auspicious beginning'.
5. **Source of History:** A place, person, text or an object from which we gather information about some past event or period.
6. **Historian:** A person who studies and writes about the past.
7. **Genetics:** The branch of biology that studies how, in plants, animals or humans, certain features and characteristics get passed down from one generation to the next.
8. **Afterlife:** A life that begins after death.
9. **Welfare:** Health, prosperity and well-being.
10. **Hamlet:** A small settlement or small village.

IV. THE BIG QUESTIONS *(Page 59)*

Q. 1. ***How do we measure historical time?***

Ans. Historical time is measured in various ways. Major events like the start of a ruler's reign are considered the start of a new era. Various calendars, like the Indian Pañchānga and the Gregorian Calendar help mark significant events.

The Gregorian Calendar begins from the year when Jesus Christ was born. Years after Jesus Christ's birth are counted forward and the term 'AD' is used. This period is also called the Common Era (CE).

The years before Christ's birth are counted backward. Previously marked as 'BC' (Before Christ) they are now known as Before Common Era (BCE).

Q. 2. ***How can various sources help us understand history?***

Ans. Various sources play a crucial role in helping us understand history by providing diverse perspectives, detailed evidence, and contextual insights. Here's how different types of sources contribute to our understanding of history:

1. **Primary Sources:** Original documents or physical objects created during the time under study. *For example*–inscriptions, ancient literature, letters, diaries, official documents, photographs, artifacts, and newspapers.
2. **Secondary Sources:** Works that interpret, analyse, or summarise primary sources. For example: Books, articles, documentaries, and reviews.
3. **Oral Histories:** Recorded interviews and spoken accounts from individuals who experienced or witnessed historical events. *For example:* Interviews, recordings, and transcriptions.

Q. 3. ***How did early humans live?***

Ans. Early humans, also known as Paleolithic humans, lived during the Old Stone Age, which spanned from approximately 2.5 million to 10,000 years ago.

(*a*) **Nomadic Hunter-gatherers:** They travelled in small groups, following animals and seasonal food sources. They hunted animals, gathered fruits, nuts, and plants, and fished.

(*b*) **Shelters:** They constructed simple shelters using natural materials like tree branches, animal hides, and stones.

(*c*) **Tools:** They created stone tools, like flint knives, hand axes, and scrapers, to aid in hunting and processing food.

(*d*) **Clothing:** They generally wore animal hides, furs, and woven fibres for clothing and protection.

V. NCERT INTEXT/TEXTBOOK EXERCISES

LET'S EXPLORE

Q. 1. ***There are a few images of different sources of history given below. Who and what do you think the objects show? Write down in the boxes next to the images any information that you get from these objects.*** *(Page 68)*

Ans.

1. Coins are important sources of history because they provide information about rulers, economies and much more. They tell us about the names, titles and portraits of rulers. The composition of metals in coins indicate the economic conditions of the time. Images on coins can also indicate religious beliefs. Language on coins indicate the languages spoken at the time. The distribution of coins indicate trading activities.
2. This image looks like a sculpture from a temple wall. It provides information regarding the material used and focusses on the religious beliefs and practices of the people.
3. This figure depicts the Lion Capital of Ashoka and is the head of the Sarnath Pillar erected by the Mauryan king Ashoka. It is the finest example of Mauryan sculpture. Now, it is our national emblem.

Q. 2. ***In the picture, look at some activities of early humans in a rock shelter. Which ones can you recognise? Give a brief description for each.*** *(Page 70)*

Ans. Here are some activities of early humans in a rock shelter with brief descriptions for each:

1. **Hunting and Gathering:** Early humans in rock shelters engaged in hunting animals and gathering wild plants for food. Evidence of this activity includes remains of animal bones, tools made from stone and bone, and plant remnants.

2. **Tool Making:** Stone tools, such as hand axes, scrapers, and arrowheads, were crafted by early humans in rock shelters. These tools were essential for hunting, processing food, and other daily tasks. The presence of flakes and cores indicates the tool-making process.
3. **Fire Making and Usage:** Fire played a crucial role in the lives of early humans. It was used for cooking food, providing warmth, and protecting against predators. Charcoal deposits, ash layers, and hearths found in rock shelters are evidence of fire usage.
4. **Art and Symbolism:** Rock shelters often feature prehistoric art, including paintings and carvings on the walls. These artworks depict animals, human figures, and abstract symbols, reflecting early human culture, beliefs, and communication methods.
5. **Shelter and Living Spaces:** Rock shelters served as living spaces, providing protection from harsh weather and predators. Evidence of structured living areas, such as sleeping spots, storage areas, and communal spaces, indicates how early humans organised their living quarters.
6. **Social and Ritual Activities:** Evidence suggests that rock shelters were also used for social and ritual activities. This includes the presence of burial sites, ritualistic objects, and communal spaces where groups of early humans might have gathered for ceremonies or social interactions.
7. **Food Preparation:** Early humans prepared food in rock shelters, as indicated by grinding stones, hearths, and remains of processed plant and animal materials. These activities included cooking, butchering animals, and processing plants for consumption.

Q. 3. ***Observe the scene in the next column. It depicts an agricultural community from a few millenniums ago. List the main activities you can identify.*** *(Page 71)*

Ans. The image depicts an early human settlement, likely from the Neolithic period, where people have adopted agriculture and domestication. The main activities visible in the image include:

1. People are harvesting crops using simple tools.
2. Sheep are being herded, and a dog is present, indicating domestication.
3. A person is seen chopping wood.
4. A woman is cooking food using clay pots.
5. Children can be seen playing.
6. A number of thatched houses can be seen.

NCERT Questions, Activities and Projects
(Page 74)

Q. 1. ***As a project, write the history of your family (or village if you live in one), using sources of history at your disposal. Ask your teacher to guide you.***

Ans. These questions need to be attempted by the students themselves. Here we have provided a sample answer:

We live in a small village called Roshanpur in U.P. Through the Gram Panchayat we came to know various historical facts about the village. The village ancestors first moved in around 1500 years back, i.e., around 500 A.D.

My Paternal Great-Grandfather was Amar Singh, a farmer, born in 1910 in this village. I got this information from family stories and an old photograph.

Q. 2. *Can we compare historians to detectives?* Give reasons for your answers.

Ans. Yes, historians can be compared to detectives for several reasons including their investigative approach, their way of analysing evidence, the way they construct narratives, the manner they give attention to detail and also for their problem-solving skills. We can further detail this as—

S. No	Historians	S. No.	Detectives
1.	Historians examine primary and secondary sources, such as letters, diaries, official records, artifacts, and other documents, to piece together an accurate picture of past events.	1.	Detectives gather evidence, interview witnesses, and analyse crime scenes to solve a case and understand what happened.
2.	Historians critically evaluate the reliability and bias of sources, cross check facts, and place information in its historical context.	2.	Detectives assess the credibility of evidence and testimonies, looking for inconsistencies or corroborative details to determine the truth.
3.	Historians build coherent narratives based on their findings, providing explanations for historical events and the actions of individuals.	3.	Detective reconstruct the sequence of events leading up to and following a crime, creating a logical account that explains how and why the crime occurred.
4.	Historians pay close attention to minor details in documents and artifacts, which can provide crucial insights into the broader historical context.	4.	Detectives notice small clues at a crime scene or in witness statements that can be critical to solving a case.
5.	Historians address gaps in the historical record and reconcile conflicting sources to form a cohesive understanding of the past.	5.	Detective solve puzzles and piece together fragmented information to identify suspects and understand the motive and method of a crime.

Q. 3. *A few Exercises with dates:*

(*a*) Place these dates chronologically on the timeline: 323 CE, 323 BCE, 100 CE, 100 BCE, 1900 BCE, 1090 CE, 2024 CE.

Ans.

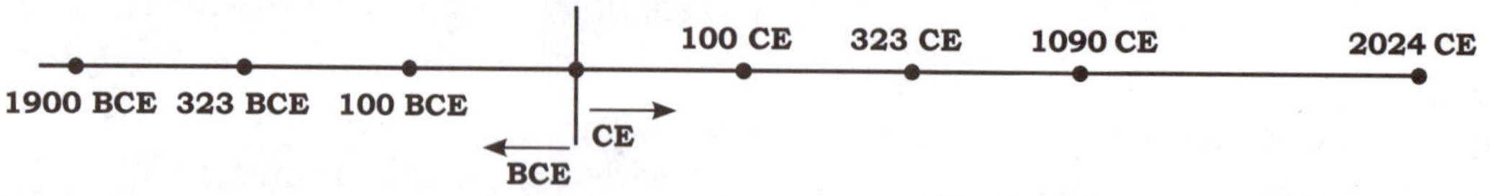

(*b*) If King Chandragupta was born in 320 CE, which century did he belong to? And how many years was that after the Buddha's birth?

Ans. King Chandragupta was born in the 4th century CE.

Given King Chandragupta was born in 320 CE. Buddha was born in 560 BCE.

Hence, 560 + 320 = 880 – 1 = 879 years

That means King Chandragupta was born 879 years after Buddha's birth.

(*c*) Rani of Jhansi was born in 1828. Which century did she belong to? How many years was that before India's Independence?

Ans. Rani of Jhansi was born in the 19th century CE. India gained independence in 1947.

Hence:

1947 – 1828 = 119 years

That means Rani of Jhansi was born 119 years before India's independence.

(*d*) Turn '12,000 years ago' into a date.

Ans. Assuming the current year is 2025 CE, 12,000 years ago would be 12,000 – 2025 = 9975 + 1 = 9976 BCE.

Q.4. ***Plan a visit to a nearby museum: the visit should be prepared with some prior research on the kind of exhibits the museum holds. Keep notes during the visit. Write a brief report afterwards, highlighting what was unexpected/ interesting/fun about the visit and the exhibits.***

Ans. These questions need to be attempted by the students themselves. Here we have provided some sample answers.

Museum Visit Report

- **Preparation:** Before visiting the National Museum, I got in touch with them through their online website and found that it houses artifacts from ancient India. The exhibit featured artifacts such as terracotta figurines, pottery, seals, and jewellery from the various eras of Indian history.
- **During the Visit:** I was keeping and maintaining the notes on the different sections, specifically focusing on the Harappan Gallery, the Mauryan and Gupta Era artifacts, the art section related to Buddhist era, Medieval Indian Art and Sculpture and Textiles and Decorative Arts.
- **Report:** The visit to the National Museum was very enriching. The most interesting was the Harappan pottery, which displayed commendable craftsmanship. The exhibit featured artifacts such as terracotta, pottery, seals, and jewellery from the Harappan civilisation.

  Contemporary Art was another attraction and it housed modern and contemporary artworks by prominent Indian artists which provided a contrast to the historical collections. These works highlighted the dynamic and evolving nature of Indian art in the contemporary era.

Q 5. ***Invite to your school an archaeologist or a historian and ask them to speak on the history of your region and why it's important to know it.***

Ans. Classroom Activity.

VI. EXAM ORIENTED QUESTIONS

A. Very Short Answer Type Questions

Q. 1. ***How is time measured in history?***

Ans. Currently, the Gregorian Calendar is used worldwide to measure current time and historical time line.

Q. 2. ***What is a century?***

Ans. A period of 100 years is known as a century.

Q. 3. ***Define millennium.***

Ans. A period of 1,000 years is known as a millennium.

Q. 4. ***Who studies fossils?***

Ans. Paleontologists study fossils. It is to learn about plants and animals etc., who lived millions of years ago.

Q. 5. ***What do anthropologists study?***

Ans. They study human societies and cultures, from ancient times till present.

Q. 6. ***What do archaeologists study?***

Ans. They study human, animals and plants history through artifacts and physical remains.

Q. 7. ***What were early humans primarily engaged in?***

Ans. The early humans were primarily hunters and gatherers.

Q. 8. ***What is an Ice Age?***

Ans. A period when earth was completely covered with ice is known as Ice Age.

Q. 9. ***What technological advancements did early humans develop?***

Ans. The early humans developed tools such as improved stone axes, blades, and pottery.

Q. 10. ***What sources can historians use to study ancient civilisations?***

Ans. There are many sources such as artifacts, inscriptions, literature, and scientific analyses.

Q. 11. ***How do historians deal with contradictory sources?***

Ans. The historians evaluate the available resources and then cross-verify them to seek their authenticity.

Q. 12. ***How do calendars traditionally work in India?***

Ans. Indian calendars often use astronomical data to predict events like eclipses and festivals.

B. Short Answer Type Questions

Q. 1. ***What is the Gregorian calendar?***

Ans. It is the most widely used calendar today, introduced by Pope Gregory XIII in 1582. It counts years from the birth of Jesus Christ (Anno Domini, A.D. or Common Era, C.E.).

Q. 2. ***How do historians calculate years between BCE and CE dates?***

Ans. Calculating the years between BCE (Before Common Era) and CE (Common Era) dates is straightforward but requires careful attention to detail due to the transition from negative to positive numbering, with no year zero in the traditional Gregorian calendar.

Q. 3. ***What are the sources of history?***

Ans. The sources of history include artifacts, written records, oral sources, literary sources, artistic sources and scientific studies.

Q. 4. ***How old are modern humans estimated to be?***

Ans. It is believed that the modern humans have been on Earth for approximately 300,000 years.

Q. 5. ***How did the development of agriculture change early human societies?***

Ans. As the agriculture led to the growth of settled communities and social complexity, this changed the early human societies in a big way.

Q. 6. ***What are the limitations of historical sources?***

Ans. There are many, such as the historical sources may be incomplete, biased or many times not clear in their meaning.

C. Long Answer Type Questions

Q. 1. ***Why do historians use multiple sources when studying history?***

Ans. When historians study any historical dynasty or monuments they gather information from as many sources they can get. This is to ensure firstly that all possible information is available to them to enable them to come to an accurate conclusion. Further more it also ensures accuracy because if different sources are in accordance with each other the fact is likely to be accurate. If sources contradict each other they need to decide which source is likely to be unbiased and can be trusted. The availability of a plethora of sources makes the task of the historians easier.

Q. 2. ***What changes occurred in the life of early people after the discovery of agriculture?***

Ans. Initially, the Earth was covered with ice and the climate was extremely cold. However, later, the Earth entered a major warming phase leading to the development of agriculture. This brought significant changes in lifestyles and habits.

As people began to grow crops, they had to stay in one place for longer periods. It was no longer possible for them to move frequently as they had done earlier. Therefore humans gave up their nomadic lifestyle and began to live a sedentary life. They started domesticating animals on a large scale providing them with a steady source of meat and dairy products. With more food available people began to settle down near rivers. They lived in thatched huts. Many houses in the same locality formed a village. Villages developed into communities having their own leaders. Later new towns and cities emerged.

Q. 3. ***What are the different sources of history? How do literary sources help in reconstructing the past?***

Ans. There are four main sources of history. These being oral sources, archaeological sources, literary sources and artistic sources.

Oral sources consist of stories and folklore that have been transferred orally from one generation to another. Archaeological sources include the material remains of the past like monuments, mounds, human, animal and plants remains, tools, weapons, figurines and ornaments. Literary sources include Vedas, poems plays, historical texts, collection of stories, travelogues and historical chronicles. Artistic sources include paintings, panels and sculptures.

Literary sources are the written records of history. They include secular and religious literature. The Puranas, Vedas, Upanishads and Tripitakas are examples of religious literature. They shed light on the religious practices followed and the socio-economic conditions of that period. Secular literature focussed on non-religious facts such as dance, music, administration, science and technology of a historical period. Kautilya's Arthashastra gives us information about the Mauryan administration. Accounts of foreign travellers are also an invaluable source of history. Megasthenes's Indica gives us a lot of information about the Mauryan Empire.

D. Assertion and Reasoning Questions

There are two statements marked as Assertion (A) and Reason (R). Mark your answer as per the codes provided below:

1. Assertion (A): Historians can be compared to detectives for several reasons including their investigative approach, their way of analysing evidence.

Reason (R): Historians examine primary and secondary sources, such as letters, diaries, official records, artifacts, and other documents, to piece together an accurate picture of past events.

Codes:

(*a*) Both (A) and (R) are true but (R) is not the correct explanation of (A).
(*b*) Both (A) and (R) are true and (R) is the correct explanation of (A).
(*c*) (A) is true but (R) is false.
(*d*) (A) is false but (R) is true.

2. Assertion (A): Sometimes CE is used instead of AD and BC.

Reason (R): The letters CE stands for 'common era' because Gregorian calendar is now used in most countries.

Codes:

(*a*) Both (A) and (R) are true but (R) is not the correct explanation of (A).
(*b*) Both (A) and (R) are true and (R) is the correct explanation of (A).
(*c*) (A) is true but (R) is false.
(*d*) (A) is false but (R) is true.

3. Assertion (A): Archaeologists contribute to various sources of history.

Reason (R): They study the physical features of the Earth, like the soil, stones, hills, mountains, rivers, seas, oceans and other such parts of the Earth.

Codes:

(*a*) Both (A) and (R) are true but (R) is not the correct explanation of (A).
(*b*) Both (A) and (R) are true and (R) is the correct explanation of (A).
(*c*) (A) is true but (R) is false.
(*d*) (A) is false but (R) is true.

4. Assertion (A): We use the term A.D. after any date to signify the year.

Reason (R): AD refers to the years counted from the birth of Jesus Christ, the founder of Christianity. The Latin term for AD is Anno Domini.

Codes:

(*a*) Both (A) and (R) are true but (R) is not the correct explanation of (A).
(*b*) Both (A) and (R) are true and (R) is the correct explanation of (A).
(*c*) (A) is true but (R) is false.
(*d*) (A) is false but (R) is true.

Ans.

1. → (*b*) **2.** → (*b*) **3.** → (*c*)
4. → (*d*)

E. Case/Source Based Questions

Read the passages given below and answer the questions that follow:

I. Early humans faced many challenges from nature and lived in bands or groups to help each other. They were constantly seeking shelter and food, and were mainly hunters and gatherers; this means that they relied on hunting and collecting edible plants and fruits for their survival. Our early ancestors also had certain beliefs about the natural elements and possibly also some notion of afterlife. These groups lived in temporary camps, rock shelters or caves, and communicated with each other using languages that are now lost. They used fire and started making objects that made their lives easier, like improved stone axes and blades, arrowheads and other tools. Aspects of their life are visible in rock paintings found in hundreds of caves all over the world.

Questions:

(*i*) Why did early humans live in groups?

(*ii*) Why did early humans live a nomadic life?

(*iii*) From where have we got information about their lives?

Ans.

(*i*) Early humans lived and moved in groups to ensure their safety and get protected against wild animals it helped them search for food together and make shelters easily.

(*ii*) Early humans lived a nomadic life because they were constantly seeking food and shelter. So, in search of food they had to move from one place to another. Therefore, they could not settle at one place and lived a nomadic life.

(*iii*) Information about the lives of early humans have been acquired from their rock paintings and artefacts which have been found during excavations. These have been found in caves all around the world. Many paintings depict scenes which give us an idea of the life they led.

II. Who contributes to all these sources of history? Historians themselves, but also archaeologists, epigraphists (who study ancient inscriptions), anthropologists (who study human societies and their cultures), experts in literature and languages, and some more. In addition, in the last 50 years or so, scientific studies have been contributing more and more to the reconstruction of the past. For example, studies of ancient climates, chemical studies of excavated materials and studies of the genetics of ancient people have provided fresh insights, which supplement the more usual sources. And when historians study recent history (which usually means the last two or three centuries), another source is newspapers; for the last few decades, electronic media (television, the internet, etc.) can also be consulted.

Questions:

(*i*) Who contributes to the sources of history?

(*ii*) Why have scientific and historical studies become important?

(*iii*) What sources do historians use while studying recent history?

Ans.

(*i*) Historians, Archaeologists, Epigraphists, Anthropologists and experts in literature and language contribute to the different sources of history.

(*ii*) Scientific studies provide a lot of information to help understand the past. Studies of ancient climates, chemical analysis of excavated materials and genetics of ancient people have provided new information. This supplements our existing sources of information.

(*iii*) Historians use newspapers to study recent history. They also take recourse of electronic media like the television and the internet.

F. Competency Based Questions

Q. 1. ***How is the study of history useful for us?***

Ans. Studying history helps us to understand how events in the past made things the way they are today. We learn how our customs, traditions, festivals and religious beliefs came into being. History helps us to learn from past mistakes and apply these lessons to solve problems. For example it shows how disasters like the changing path of rivers and ignoring climatic changes can destroy civilisation. The Harappan civilisation is believed to have been destroyed in part by such factors. Learning from this, Environmentalists and policy makers have realised that global warming is a serious threat to us. Efforts are underway to provide solutions to this problem.

Q. 2. ***How does the study of coins help historians?***

Ans. Coins give information about the dynastic history of empires. For example, the history of the Gupta Empire has largely been reconstructed from their coins. They also throw light on the trade and foreign relations of empires. Roman coins have been found in South India which indicates trade relations with the Roman Empire. Coins also give information about the religious, cultural and economic conditions of different empires.

Q. 3. ***What role did geographical and climatic factors play in the development of agriculture?***

Ans. Initially the Earth was covered with ice. Man lived as a food gatherer and hunter during this time. But later the climate changed drastically. It became dry and warm providing conditions suitable for the cultivation of crops. Surplus production of food led to population growth and establishment of permanent settlements near rivers. Rivers provided water for agriculture and domestic use. It also helped to make the soil more fertile. Thus, the end of the ice age provided favourable conditions for agriculture to thrive. It provided a stable climate. Rivers provided access to water and the fertile soil.

Q. 4. ***How have inscriptions and monuments helped in understanding our past?***

Ans. Inscriptions provide evidence of significant events and rulers. They tell us about the military achievements of rulers like Samudra Gupta. Some inscriptions tell us about religious policy of rulers. For example, Ashokan inscriptions tell us about his dhamma.*

Buildings of historical importance are called monuments. Monuments reflect the development of architecture and the quality of art of that particular period. They help the historians to know about the social life, religious beliefs and culture of the people.

G. Skill Based Questions

Q. 1. ***"Tools of the stone age tended to change according to man's requirements". Explain the statement.***

Ans. Palaeolithic man or early man needed stone tools to hunt animals, chop meat and cut wood. They also needed stone tools for digging the earth to find edible roots. Therefore, Palaeolithic tools were crude unpolished stone tools made by chipping stone. Examples of tools included choppers, arrowheads and spearheads.

The age when man developed agriculture is known as the Neolithic Age. During this age the tools were completely different. The tools were designed for use in agricultural and other activities. The tools now were well-shaped, polished and had a sharp cutting edge. Axes, sickles, pestles and mortars have been found. Axes were used to clear the land for cultivation. Mortars were used for grinding grains and sickles for harvesting.

---

* Dhamma: Ashoka's Dhamma was an ethical and moral code emphasising non-violence.

Q. 2. ***"Necessity is the mother of invention" Justify this statement with the help of examples from the life of early man. Man has progressed because of the discoveries and inventions he has made. All of which made his life easier.***

Ans. Early man made crude unpolished stone tools so that he could hunt animals, chop meat and cut wood. When man became a farmer, he invented tools like pestles, mortars, axes and sickles which were of use to him. Axes helped to clear more land for cultivation. Sickles were used for harvesting.

A significant discovery made by man was that of fire. Fire helped man to roast food, stay warm, and protect themselves from wild animals.

Lastly the invention of the wheel changed the life of early man forever. It helped them to make bullock and horse carts and move heavy loads faster than before. Gradually improvements made on the wheel enabled them spin cotton, wool and weave them into cloth. The development of potter's wheel improved the art of making pottery.

Q. 3. ***Describe the main differences that existed between Palaeolithic and Neolithic men.***

Ans. Early men were known as Palaeolithic men and were nomads. When men began to lead a settled life they were known as Neolithic men.

Palaeolithic men were hunters and food gatherers while Neolithic Men were herdsmen and farmers.

Palaeolithic men wore clothes made of tree bark and animal skins. Neolithic men wore clothes made of cotton and wool.

The tools of Palaeolithic men included arrowheads and choppers. The tools of Neolithic men included sickles, pestles and mortars.

Palaeolithic man discovered fire while Neolithic men invented the wheel used for transport, spinning and for making pottery.

Palaeolithic men lived in rock shelters and caves while Neolithic men lived in thatched huts.

H. Picture Based Questions

Q. 1. ***Study the pictures given below and answer the questions.***

Fig. Geologists

Fig. Palaeontologists

Fig. Anthropologists

Fig. Archaeologists

(*a*) Why are Geologists important in history?

(*b*) What do Archaeologists study?

(*c*) What do Anthropologists study?

(*d*) What do Palaeontologists study?

Ans. (*a*) Geologists are important in history because they help us to understand Earth's history and process, and the development of life on earth by studying the change in Earth's physical features.

(*b*) Archaeologists study the past by examining tools, pottery, beads, bones, teeth, and remains left by people, plants, and animals.

(*c*) Anthropologists study everything about human beings. They study everything related to societies and cultures around the world and across time.

(*d*) Palaeontologists study the remains of plants, animals and humans.

VII. MAP SKILLS

Q. 1. ***In the given map, locate the major centers of early civilisation in India.***

Ans.

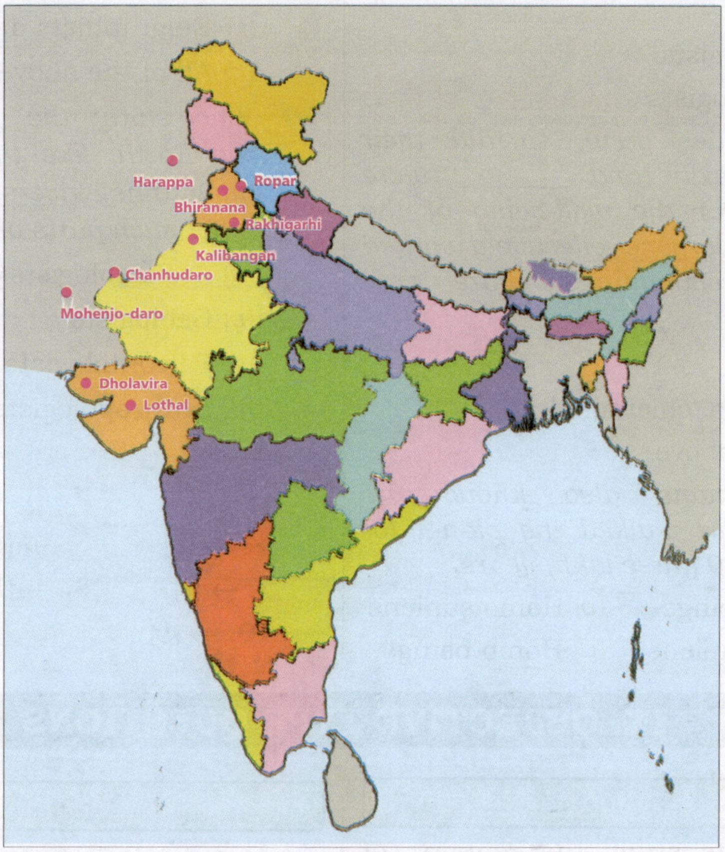

VIII. MULTIPLE CHOICE QUESTIONS

1. *Over long periods, the Earth's climate has gone through many changes. At certain times, it is very cold and much of the Earth was covered with ice, this is called the ______.*

(*a*) Cold age

(*b*) Ice Age

(*c*) Both of the above

(*d*) None of the above.

2. *How is time measured in history?*

(*a*) By counting the number of days.

(*b*) By counting the number of years.

(*c*) By counting the number of hours.

(*d*) By counting the number of minutes.

3. *What is a millennium?*

(*a*) A period of 10 years

(*b*) A period of 100 years

(*c*) A period of 1,000 years

(*d*) A period of 1 million years.

4. *What do anthropologists study?*

(*a*) Physical features of the Earth

(*b*) Human societies and cultures

(*c*) Remains of plants and animals

(*d*) The past by digging up remains

5. *What is a century?*

(*a*) A period of 10 years

(*b*) A period of 100 years

(*c*) A period of 1,000 years

(*d*) A period of 1 million years.

6. *Who studies the remains of plants, animals, and humans from millions of years ago?*
   (*a*) Archaeologists
   (*b*) Geologists
   (*c*) Paleontologists
   (*d*) Anthropologists

7. *As communities grew, so did their social complexity and ________ were responsible for the well-being of the people, and everyone collectively worked towards the community's welfare.*
   (*a*) everyone
   (*b*) no one
   (*c*) leaders and 'chieftains'
   (*d*) all of the above

8. *Modern humans also known as ________ have walked the planet for about 300,000 (three lakh) years.*
   (*a*) Human beings (*b*) Homo sapiens
   (*c*) Human sapiens (*d*) Homo beings.

9. *Who contributes to all the sources of history?*
   (*a*) Historians
   (*b*) Archaeologists
   (*c*) Epigraphists and Anthropologists
   (*d*) All of the above.

10. *Who study the physical features of the Earth, like the soil, stones, hills, mountains, rivers, seas, oceans and other such parts of the Earth?*
    (*a*) Archaeologists
    (*b*) Geologists
    (*c*) Paleontologists
    (*d*) Anthropologists.

Ans.

1. → (*b*) 2. → (*b*) 3. → (*c*)
4. → (*b*) 5. → (*b*) 6. → (*c*)
7. → (*c*) 8. → (*b*) 9. → (*d*)
10. → (*b*)

IX. OBJECTIVE TYPE QUESTIONS

A. True and False

1. Paleontologists study the remains of plants, animals, and humans from millions of years ago.
2. Archaeologists study the physical features of the Earth, like the soil, stones, hills, mountains rivers, seas, oceans and other such parts of the Earth.
3. Anthropologists study the physical features of the Earth.
4. The last Ice Age lasted from over 100,000 years ago to around 12,000 years ago.
5. The Gregorian calendar has a year zero in its timeline.

Ans.

1. True 2. False
3. False 4. True
5. False

B. Fill in the Blanks

1. ____________ is a period of 100 years.
2. The birth of ____________ is used as its starting point by Gregorian calendar.
3. The year 1857 CE can also be written as ____________.
4. Abbreviation of Before Common Era is ____________.
5. The absence of a year zero in the Gregorian calendar means that between 4 BCE and 4 CE, only ____________ years have passed.

Ans.

1. Century 2. Jesus Christ
3. 1857 AD 4. BCE
5. 7

C. Match Column A with Column B

Column A	Column B
1. Anthropologists	(*a*) The conventional year for Jesus Christ's birth has generally been taken to be the starting point for this calendar.
2. Archaeologists	(*b*) They study human societies and cultures from the oldest times to the present
3. Gregorian Calendar	(*c*) Before Common Era
4. BCE	(*d*) 100 years
5. Century	(*e*) They study the past by digging up remains that people, plants and animals left behind, such as tools, pots, beads, figurines, toys, bones and teeth of animals and humans, burnt grains, parts of houses or bricks, among others.

Ans. 1. (*b*) **2.** (*e*) **3.** (*a*) **4.** (*c*) **5.** (*d*)

X. TEST YOUR KNOWLEDGE

A. Multiple Choice Questions

1. .... *is a literary source.*
(*a*) Monuments (*b*) Coins
(*c*) Inscriptions (*d*) Manuscripts

2. *What do Palaeontologists study?*
(*a*) Physical features of the earth
(*b*) Human societies and cultures
(*c*) The remains of the past
(*d*) Fossils

3. *The term 'BCE' is used to indicate*
(*a*) The beginning of the Stone Age
(*b*) The years after Jesus's birth
(*c*) The years before the birth of Jesus Christ
(*d*) The beginning of the Metal Age.

4. *Which of the following is an artistic source of history?*
(*a*) Folklore (*b*) Coins
(*c*) Poems (*d*) Paintings

5. *What is a decade?*
(*a*) A period of 10 years
(*b*) A period of 100 years
(*c*) A period of 1000 years
(*d*) A period of 1 million years.

B. True or False

1. *The first animal to be domesticated was the dog.*
2. *A millennium is a period of 100 years.*
3. *Early Man made tools out of stone.*
4. *Homo sapiens first appeared in Africa.*
5. *Inscriptions are an example of a literary source.*

C. Fill in the Blanks

1. The study of inscriptions is known as ______________.
2. In the ______________ calendar there is no 'zero year'.
3. __________ was an important discovery of this period.
4. Early man had a _________ lifestyle.

D. Very Short Answer Type Questions

1. *How is time measured in history?*
2. *What is CE?*
3. *What is the use of timeline in history?*
4. *What do you understand by the term 'millennium'?*

E. Short Answer Type Questions

1. *Explain BCE.*
2. *Mention a few sources of history.*
3. *Modern humans (Homo sapiens) have walked the planet for about how many years?*
4. *How can sources help us in understanding history better?*

F. Long Answer Type Questions

1. *Early humans faced many challenges from nature and lived in bands or groups to help each other. Explain.*
2. *What do you understand by the term 'Ice Age'?*
3. *How leaders or chieftains played an important role in ancient history of mankind?*
4. *Why is it important to critically analyse sources of history?*

G. Assertion & Reasoning Questions

There are two statements marked as Assertion (A) and Reason (R). Mark your answer as per the codes provided below:

Q. 1. Assertion (A): The Pañchānga precisely predicts solar and lunar eclipses.

Reason (R): It does not provide weather forecasts.

Codes:

(*a*) Both (A) and (R) are true but (R) is not the correct explanation of (A).
(*b*) Both (A) and (R) are true and (R) is the correct explanation of (A).
(*c*) (A) is true but (R) is false.
(*d*) (A) is false but (R) is true.

Q. 2. Assertion (A): A study of history is very important for all societies.

Reason (R): It enables societies to understand how their cultures have evolved over the ages.

Codes:

(*a*) Both (A) and (R) are true but (R) is not the correct explanation of (A).
(*b*) Both (A) and (R) are true and (R) is the correct explanation of (A).
(*c*) (A) is true but (R) is false.
(*d*) (A) is false but (R) is true.

NOTES

NOTES

India, That Is Bharat

1 Introduction

- **India today:** Modern nation with fixed boundaries, state and population.
- In past (500–5,000 years ago): geography & names were very different.
- Present-day **'Indian Subcontinent'** was called by many names.
- **Sources of the past:** Ancient texts, inscriptions, and foreign records/travelogues.

2 How Indians Named India

- **Rig Veda:** the most ancient text of India.
- It mentions northwest region as **Sapta Sindhava** or "land of the seven rivers."
- **Sindhava word:** from **Sindhu** (Indus River/rivers).
- **The Mahabharata:** mentions regions – Kāshmīra, Kurukṣhetra, Vanga, Pragjyotiṣha, Kaccha, Kerala.
- **Names for whole subcontinent: Bharatavarsha** (the country of Bharatas) & **Jambudvipa** (island of jamun/jambul/malabar tree).
- **Bharata:** main Vedic groups of people (Ṛig Veda) & kings named Bharata.
- **Emperor Ashoka (250 BCE):** used **Jambudvipa** for India (India + Pakistan + Bangladesh + Afghanistan).
- **Vishnu Purana:** describes Indian Subcontinent as Bharata.
- **Bharata** gradually became the most accepted name—today's Bharat(North)/ Bharatam (South).
- **Tamil Literature (2000 yrs ago) mentions:**

  India = from **Cape Kumari in the south** to the **Himalayas in the north**, and between the eastern and western oceans.

3 How Foreigners Named India

- Persians (Inhabitants of Iran): first mentioned India.
- **In 6th c. BCE,** Persians conquered Indus region & called it **Hind/Hidu/Hindu.**
- **Greeks:** called it Indoi/Indike and dropped 'h' (not in Greek).
- **Chinese:** called it 'Yintu/Yindu'.
- Chinese also referred it as **'Tianzhu' (heavenly master)**, showing respect for **Buddha land**.
- **Hindustan:** First appeared in Persian inscription ~1800 yrs ago.
- Later invaders called Indian Subcontinent; Hindustan.

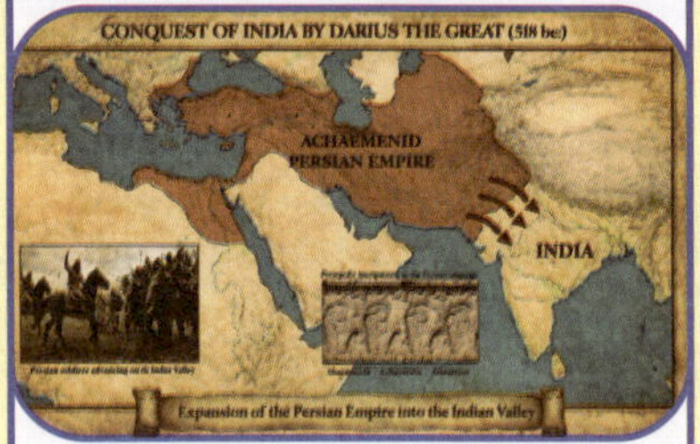

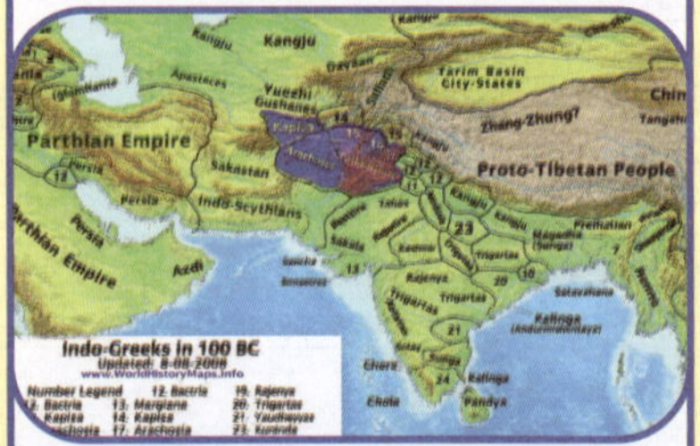

THEME–B
Tapestry of the Past

CHAPTER
5

INDIA, THAT IS BHARAT

I. FACTS TO REMEMBER/SUMMARY

HOW INDIANS NAMED INDIA

- Throughout History India had been called by many names.
- The Mahābhārata refers to the Indian Subcontinent as 'Bhāratavarṣha' and 'Jambudvīpa'.
- Ashoka has used the name '*Jambudvīpa*' to describe the whole of India.
- The ancient text Vishnu Purana refers to the Indian subcontinent as Bharata.
- The Indian Constitution uses the phrase "India, that is Bharat" right at the beginning itself.

HOW FOREIGNERS NAMED INDIA

- The Persians referred India as 'Hind', Hidu or 'Hindu'.
- The Greeks named India, 'Indoi' or 'Indike'.
- The Chinese referred India as 'Yintu' or 'Yindu'.
- Hiuen Tsang was a Chinese traveller who collected many Buddhist texts from India and translated them into Chinese when he returned to China.
- 1800 years ago a Persian inscription referred India as 'Hindustān' for the first time.
- After this, most invaders who came to India began to use the same term to describe the Indian subcontinent.

II. TEXTBOOK KEYWORDS/GLOSSARY

1. **Inhabitants:** People who permanently live in a particular place or region.
2. **Sapta-Sindhava:** The term given to the northwest region of India meaning "land of the Seven Rivers".
3. **Vishnu Purana:** An ancient text which refers to India as 'Bharata'.
4. **Constitution:** The fundamental legal document according to which the government of a country functions.

III. DATE LINE

1. **1500 – 1000 BCE:** Composition of the Rig Veda.
2. **500 BCE – 400 CE:** Composition of the Mahābhārata (*in Sanskrit*).
3. **268 – 232 BCE:** Reign of Ashoka.
4. **629 – 645 CE:** Hiuen Tsang travelled to many parts of India during this period.
5. **1950:** The Constitution of India came into existence.

IV. THE BIG QUESTIONS *(Page 75)*

Q. 1. ***How do we define India ?***

Ans. India can be defined as a country which has a rich cultural and spiritual history that dates back to thousands of years to ancient civilisations like the Indus Valley Civilisation and the Vedic Period.

Q. 2. ***What were the ancient names for India ?***

Ans. The ancient names for India were 'Bhāratavarṣha', 'Jambudvīpa' and 'Bharata'.

V. NCERT INTEXT/TEXTBOOK EXERCISES

THINK ABOUT IT

Q. 1. ***Consider the physical map of the Indian Subcontinent at the start of the chapter. What are its natural boundaries that you can make out?*** *(Page 77)*

Ans. The natural boundaries which can be seen are the Himalayas and Hindukush mountains in the north. The Arabian Sea in the West and Bay of Bengal in the East.

Q. 2. ***Have you identified the 'snowy mountains'? Do you think this brief description of Bhārata is correct?*** *(Page 80)*

Ans. The snowy mountains mentioned in the Vishnu Purana are the Himalayas. This brief description of Bharata is correct as it refers to the natural boundaries of India which has helped to protect India against foreign invaders and made it a well defined unit.

LET'S EXPLORE

Q. 1. ***Do you recognise the names of any regions given in the map (Fig. 5.4) on page 79? List the ones that you have heard of.*** *(Page 78)*

Ans. I have heard of the following:

1. Panchala
2. Kashi
3. Anga
4. Vanga
5. Kosala
6. Chedi
7. Kalinga
8. Cholas
9. Pandavas
10. Matsya

Q. 2. ***In this reproduction of the first page of the original Constitution of India in Fig. 5.5 (page 82), can you make out the phrase 'India, that is Bharat'?*** *(Page 81)*

Ans. The first page of the Constitution clearly states that 'India', that is Bharat shall be a Union of States.

Q. 3. ***Can you complete this table of the many names of India?*** *(Page 83)*

Ans.

Persian	**Hind, Hidu, Hindu**
Greek	**Indoi, Indike**
Latin	**India**
Chinese	**Yintu, Yindu**
Arabic & Persian	**Hind, Hindustan**
English	**India**
French	**Inde**

NCERT Questions, Activities and Projects *(Page 84)*

Q. 1. ***Discuss what could be the meaning of the quotation at the start of the chapter.***

Ans. The quotation indicates that the principles forming the foundations of India's spiritual and cultural unity were established in ancient India itself and have been followed for centuries as a way of life for all.

For example

The Vedas which are India's oldest religious texts have given rise to several schools of thought. The Upanishads and the different schools of Indian philosophy discussed many issues regarding the nature of the ultimate reality. Buddhism and Jainism departed from the authority of the Vedas laying emphasis on different values and practices. But common to all belief systems which helped to unite India spiritually was belief in the need to detach from material things and understand the nature of the ultimate reality.

Similarly, our culture has evolved due to fusion of our various religious beliefs systems which have contributed to our rich heritage of art, sculpture, music, painting etc.

Q. 2. ***True or false?***

(*a*) The Rig Veda describes the entire geography of India.

(*b*) The *Vishnu Purāna* describes the entire Subcontinent.

(*c*) In Aśhoka's time, 'Jambudvīpa' included what is today's India, parts of Afghanistan, Bangladesh and Pakistan.

(*d*) The Mahābhārata lists many regions, including Kashmir, Kutch, and Kerala.

(*e*) The term 'Hindustān' first appeared in a Greek inscription more than 2,000 years ago.

(*f*) In ancient Persian, the word 'Hindu' refers to the Hindu religion.

(*g*) 'Bhārata' is a name given to India by foreign travellers.

Ans.

(*a*) → False (*b*) → True (*c*) → True

(*d*) → True (*e*) → False (*f*) → False

(*g*) → False

Q. 3. ***If you were born some 2,000 years ago and had the chance to name our country, what name or names might you have chosen, and why? Use your imagination!***

Ans. I would have chosen the name 'Bharatavarsha' as the name covers the entire Subcontinent as it existed in ancient times. Moreover this name would include all the people who inhabited the Subcontinent.

Q. 4. ***Why did people travel to India from various parts of the world in ancient times? What could be their motivations in undertaking such long journeys? (Hint: There could be at least four or five motivations)***

Ans. People travelled to India for various reasons: Many people travelled to India for trade purposes. Traders and merchants would travel to sell their goods or exchange them for other products. There was a lot of demand for Indian goods like spices, muslin cloth, silk and indigo. In ancient times, India was famous for it's wealth, culture and philosophy. For traveller's India was a land of wonders. Thus, many people driven by a spirit, of adventure and desire to visit new and exciting places came to India. Some people came as part of an army bent on conquest. For *example* the army of Alexander and the Persian king Cyrus. People also travelled to India in search of knowledge. For example, the Chinese travellers like Fa-Hien, Hiuen Tsang and I-tsing came to India to gain knowledge about Buddhism. Some people like the Shaka tribes were pushed out of their homes in Central Asia, and sought an alternative homeland in India.

VI. EXAM ORIENTED QUESTIONS

A. Very Short Answer Type Questions

Q. 1. ***What is the Rig Veda?***

Ans. The Rig Veda is India's oldest religious text written several thousand years ago.

Q. 2. ***Which area is known as 'Sapta-Sindhava' ?***

Ans. The northwest region of the Subcontinent is known as 'Sapta-Sindhava' or land of the seven rivers.

Q. 3. ***Name any three regions mentioned in the Mahābhārata.***

Ans. Kashmira, Vanga and Kaccha were three regions mentioned in the Mahābhārata.

Q. 4. ***When do we first come across a name for the entire Indian Subcontinent?***

Ans. The first recorded name for the entire Subcontinent appears in the Mahābhārata.

Q. 5. ***What are the two terms used in the Mahābhārata to describe the Indian Subcontinent?***

Ans. The Mahābhārata has used the terms 'Bhāratavarṣha' and 'Jambudvīpa' to describe the Indian Subcontinent.

Q. 6. ***What does the term 'Bhārata-varṣha' mean?***

Ans. The term Bhāratavarṣha means "the country of the Bharatas".

Q. 7. ***What does the term 'Jambudvīpa' mean?***

Ans. The term 'Jambudvīpa' means the island of the fruit of the jamun tree.

Q. 8. ***Which emperor has used the name Jambudvīpa to describe the Indian Subcontinent?***

Ans. The famous Mauryan emperor Ashoka has used the name Jambudvīpa in one of his inscriptions to describe the whole of India.

Q. 9. ***What names did the Persians use to refer India?***

Ans. The Persians referred India as 'Hind', 'Hidu' or 'Hindu' which are adaptations in their language of the term 'Sindhu' which was what the region of the Indus River was called.

Q. 10. ***What names did the ancient Greeks use to refer India?***

Ans. The ancient Greeks named the region 'Indoi' or 'Indike'.

Q. 11. ***What names did the Chinese use to refer India?***

Ans. The Chinese have referred India as 'Yintu' or 'Yindu'.

Q. 12. ***When was the term 'Hindustan' first used to describe India?***

Ans. 1800 years ago, the term Hindustan was used in a Persian Inscription to describe India.

Q. 13. ***The Indian Constitution was first written in which Language?***

Ans. The Indian Constitution was first written in English.

Q. 14. ***What name does it use to describe India ?***

Ans. The Constitution refers India as Bharat.

Q. 15. ***What name does the Hindi version of the Constitution use to describe India ?***

Ans. The Hindi version of the Constitution refers to India as 'Bharat Arthath India'.

B. Short Answer Type Questions

Q. 1. ***What do the two terms 'Bharatavarsha' and "Jambudvīpa" mean?***

Ans. The term "Bhāratavarṣha" means country of the "Bharatas". The name "Bharata" first appears in the Rig Veda referring to one of the main Vedic groups of people.

The term 'Jambudvīpa' 'means' the Island of the fruit of the jamun tree. The Jamun tree native to India is also called 'jambul tree' and 'Malabar' 'plum tree'.

Q. 2. ***How did 'Jambudvīpa' come to mean the Indian Subcontinent?***

Ans. The jamun tree is a common tree to be found throughout the Indian Subcontinent. Consequently Jambudvīpa came to mean the Indian Subcontinent.

The term Jambudvīpa is used by Ashoka to represent his empire in the 3rd century BCE and then repeated in many subsequent inscriptions reinforcing the concept of the Indian Subcontinent being referred to as Jambudvīpa.

Q. 3. ***Who were the first foreigners to mention India? What were the three names they gave India and why?***

Ans. The first foreigners who mentioned India were the Persians. In 535 BCE the Persian emperor Cyrus invaded India and controlled over the northwest region of India known as 'Sindhu' after the Indus River. Therefore, the Persians referred to India as 'Hind', Hidu, or Hindu which are adaptations in their language of the word 'Sindhu'.

Q. 4. ***What is the meaning of the word 'Tianzhu'? From which Indian word has it been derived? What does this word signify?***

Ans. The word 'Tianzhu' means 'heavenly master'. It has been derived from the word 'Sindhu'. It signifies the respect the ancient Chinese had for India.

Q. 5. ***Who was Hiuen Tsang ? When did he come to India ?***

Ans. Hiuen Tsang also known as Xuanzang was a Chinese Buddhist monk who came to India in the 7th century C.E. He collected many Buddhist texts from various parts of the country and returned to China after 17 years.

Q. 6. ***Several Chinese scholars have visited India over the centuries. Name any two of them.***

Ans. Two famous Chinese traveller's who visited India were Xuanzang (Hiuen Tsang), Hsuan Tsang etc. Their accounts are considered to be one of the most authentic sources of history.

C. Long Answer Type Questions

Q. 1. ***In the course of its history, India has been called by many names by its inhabitants. Explain the statement.***

Ans. The Rig Veda referred the northwest region of the Subcontinent as the land of the seven rivers or Sapta-Sindhu. The Indus River was known as 'Sindhu'. Later the Mahābhārata uses the two terms Bharatavarsha and Jambudvīpa to define India. Bhāratavarṣha means the country of the Bharatas. The Bharata were one of the main Vedic tribes of the Rig Vedic Age.

The second term used was Jambudvīpa wherein jambul refers to a species of fruit widely available in the Indian Subcontinent and dvipa means continent.

Ashoka also referred the whole of India as Jambudvīpa.

However, in the course of time Bharata became the name generally used. The Vishnu Purana also mentions the name Bharata in its text. In north India, India is known as Bharat while in South India the word "Bharatam" is used.

Q. 2. ***The many different names that the foreigners have used for India are derived from the word 'Sindhu'. Discuss the above statement.***

Ans. The Persian emperor Cyrus conquered the north west part of India which was known as 'Sindhu' at that time. The Persian equivalent to the word Sindhu was 'Hind', 'Hidu' or Hindu. This was how India was referred to in the earliest Persian records and stone inscriptions. The Greeks dropped the letter 'h' of the Persian words as this letter does not exist in the Greek language. Therefore, the Greeks called India, 'Indoi' or 'Indike'. The Chinese interactions with India led them to refer India as Yintu, or Yindu also derivatives from the word Sindhu.

In recent times, the term Hindustan is being used to refer India. But this term was first mentioned 1800 years ago in a Persian Inscription. Later invaders began to commonly to use this term to describe India.

Q. 3. ***What was India called in Ancient China?***

Ans. In Ancient China, India was called 'Tianzhu' which means 'Heavenly Domain' and 'heavenly master'. It was derived from the Sanskrit word Sindhu which referred to region of the Indus River. The name likely came from the Chinese perception of India as a land of great spiritual significance with a rich tradition of religious and philosophical thought that was seen as closely tied to the heavens.

The Chinese also called India Wutianzhu which literally means 'Five Indias'. This name was used because the Chinese were aware of the five geographical regions of the subcontinent.

Other names for India used by the Chinese were Yintu and Yindu. The Chinese pilgrim Hsuan Tsang was the first to use these names.

He was a Buddhist monk, who travelled to India in the 7th century CE. He visited many parts of India, collected many Buddhist texts which he translated into Chinese when he returned to China.

Q. 4. ***Who were the Chinese pilgrims who visited India?***

Ans. The three most important Chinese pilgrims who visited India are Fa-Hien, Hiuen Tsang and I-tsing. All these Chinese pilgrims travelled to India to visit places associated with the life of Buddha and to study Buddhism. They carried Buddhist textbooks and statues back with them

Fa-Hien visited India during the reign of Chandragupta II. He was the first Chinese monk to travel to India in search of Buddhist scriptures. He wrote a book about his travels which included accounts of early Buddhism .

Hiuen Tsang visited India during the reign of King Harsha. He stayed in India for 15 years studying in Buddhist monasteries like Nalanda. I-tsing visited India in the 7th century .

Q. 5. ***How did the Vishnu Purana define India? What is the importance of its definition?***

Ans. The Vishnu Purana is an ancient Indian scripture which describes India's geographical location in a shloka or verse. It refers to the land north of the ocean (Indian ocean) and south of the snowy mountains (Himalayas) as Bharata.

The shloka also states that this land is home to the descendants of Bharata an ancient Indian king.

This definition highlights the importance of natural features shaping India's identity. The term Bharata in the Vishnu Purana refers to the entire Indian Subcontinent. This shloka has been used to define India's boundaries for centuries and is still an important cultural reference today.

It underscores the importance of geography in shaping the Indian identity. The Vishnu Purana describes India as a blessed land with diverse cultures, great natural resources and holy sages.

D. Assertion & Reasoning Questions

There are two statements marked as Assertion (A) and Reason (R). Mark your answer as per the codes provided below:

1. Assertion (A): The Mauryan king Ashoka used the term Jambudvipa in his inscriptions.

Reason (R): The term was used to represent the extent of his empire.

Codes:

(*a*) Both (A) and (R) are true but (R) is not the correct explanation of (A).

(*b*) Both (A) and (R) are true and (R) is the correct explanation of (A).

(*c*) (A) is true but (R) is false.

(*d*) (A) is false but (R) is true.

2. Assertion (A): Fa-Hien was a famous trader who came to India to buy Indian goods.

Reason (R): There was a lot of demand for Indian goods like spices and muslin cloth.

Codes:

(*a*) Both (A) and (R) are true but (R) is not the correct explanation of (A).

(*b*) Both (A) and (R) are true and (R) is the correct explanation of (A).

(*c*) (A) is true but (R) is false.

(*d*) (A) is false but (R) is true.

3. Assertion (A): The Chinese called India, 'Tianzhu' meaning 'heavenly master'.

Reason (R): This showed the respect they had for India as being the land of the Buddha.

Codes:

(*a*) Both (A) and (R) are true but (R) is not the correct explanation of (A).

(*b*) Both (A) and (R) are true and (R) is the correct explanation of (A).

(*c*) (A) is true but (R) is false.

(*d*) (A) is false but (R) is true.

4. Assertion (A): The term 'Sapta-Sindhava means 'the land of the seven rivers'.

Reason (R): The Rig Veda, refers it to the North-East region of the Subcontinent.

Codes:

(*a*) Both (A) and (R) are true but (R) is not the correct explanation of (A).

(*b*) Both (A) and (R) are true and (R) is the correct explanation of (A).

(*c*) (A) is true but (R) is false.

(*d*) (A) is false but (R) is true.

5. **Assertion (A):** The Greeks modified the name 'Hindu' to call India, Indoi.

Reason (R): They dropped the letter 'H' as it did not exist in their language.

Codes:

(*a*) Both (A) and (R) are true but (R) is not the correct explanation of (A).

(*b*) Both (A) and (R) are true and (R) is the correct explanation of (A).

(*c*) (A) is true but (R) is false.

(*d*) (A) is false but (R) is true.

Ans.

1. → (*c*) **2.** → (*d*) **3.** → (*b*)
4. → (*c*) **5.** → (*b*)

E. Case/Source Based Questions

Read the passages given below and answer the questions that follow:

I. In the course of history, India has been called by many names—both by its **inhabitants** and by visitors from outside. These names come to us from ancient texts, accounts of travellers and pilgrims, and inscriptions.

(*i*) State two names for India which have come to us from ancient texts.

(*ii*) What name for India has been mentioned in inscriptions?

(*iii*) What names for India have come from foreign pilgrims ?

Ans.

(*i*) The term Bharatavarsha has been mentioned in the Mahābhārata and the Vishnu Purana uses the term Bharata to describe the Indian subcontinent.

(*ii*) An Ashokan inscription uses the term 'Jambudvīpa' to describe the whole of India.

(*iii*) The Chinese pilgrims referred to India as Yintu, Yindu, and even Tianzhu.

II. It is interesting to note that different parts of the country adopted a similar definition for India. For instance, a poem of ancient Tamil literature, from about 2,000 years ago, praises a king whose name is known "from [Cape] Kumari in the south, from the great mountain in the north, from the oceans on the east and on the west..." You can now recognise 'the great mountain in the north', and it should not be difficult to identify 'Cape Kumari'. It looks like ancient Indians knew their geography well!

(*i*) Name the great mountain in the north.

(*ii*) Name the oceans mentioned in this extract.

(*iii*) Identify Cape Kumari

(*iv*) What is the importance of this description of India's natural features?

Ans.

(*i*) The great mountain in the north mentioned in this extract are the Himalayas.

(*ii*) The oceans mentioned are the Arabian Sea and the Bay of Bengal.

(*iii*) Cape Kumari can be identified as Kanyakumari.

(*iv*) This description demonstrates that Indians knew their geography well. It highlights the importance of natural features in shaping India's identity. It was the natural boundaries of India which has helped to protect India against foreign invaders and made it a well defined unit.

III. The Mahābhārata is one of India's most famous texts. It lists many regions such as Kashmira (*more or less today's Kashmir*), Pragijyotisha (*roughly today's Assam*) and so on. The Mahābhārata uses the term 'Bhāratavarṣha' and 'Jambudvīpa' to refer to the Indian Subcontinent.

(*i*) What is the importance of the Mahābhārata in India's history ?

(*ii*) Which two regions mentioned in the extract are still part of India today?

(*iii*) Why did the Mahābhārata use the term 'Bhāratavarṣha' to refer to Indian Subcontinent?

(iv) Why did the Mahābhārata refer to India as "Jambudvīpa"?

Ans.

(i) The Mahābhārata is a sacred epic whose central theme is the struggle for power between two warring factions notably the Pandavas and the Kauravas. It is considered as the cornerstone of Indian culture and an important source for understanding Indian ethics and societal values. The text also mentions various regions existing even today which have shaped India's cultural and religious heritage.

(ii) Kashmira corresponds to today's Kashmir and Pragijyotisha corresponds to today's Assam.

Both these regions are mentioned in the Mahābhārata.

(iii) The name 'Bhāratavarṣha' is linked to King Bharata a figure from Indian mythology. His name is mentioned in the Mahābhārata as having conquered the entire Indian Subcontinent making his empire known as Bharatavarsha.

(iv) The term 'jambu' refers to the Indian jamun widely available in the Subcontinent while dvipa means 'island" or 'continent.' Therefore, Jambudvīpa meaning berry island was used in the Mahābhārata as a name for the Indian Subcontinent before 'Bharata' became the official name.

IV. The Rig Veda is India's most ancient text; as we will see in Chapter 7, it is several thousand years old. It gives the northwest region of the Subcontinent the name 'Sapta Sindhava', that is, the 'land of the seven rivers'. The word 'Sindhava' comes from 'Sindhu', which refers to the Indus River, or at times to a river in general.

(i) What is the importance of the Rig Veda?

(ii) What name has it given to the north-western region of India?

(iii) Name the seven rivers found in this region.

(iv) What role did these rivers play in Indian history?

Ans.

(i) The Rig Veda is India's most ancient text and provides knowledge of ancient Indian geography, culture and society. Its hymns and verses have inspired countless generations of Indians shaping their worldview and values.

(ii) It has given this region the name 'Sapta-Sindhava' i.e., the 'land of the seven rivers'.

(iii) The seven rivers of this region are: the Indus, the Sarasvati, the Chenab, the Jhelum, the Ravi, the Sutlej and the Beas.

(iv) These rivers are considered to be the most sacred rivers of India. This region is often known as the cradle of Indian civilisation because the flood plains created by these rivers made the region very fertile. As a result agriculture and trade flourished contributing to the prosperity of this region.

V. "The first foreigners to mention India were the Persians. A Persian Inscription 1800 years ago referred to India as 'Hindusthan'. A Persian emperor in the 6th century BCE gained control of the north-west region of India. The Persians referred to India as 'Hind' 'Hidu' or 'Hindu'.

(i) Who were the first foreigners to mention India ?

(ii) Name the Persian king who invaded India? Which area did he conquer ?

(iii) Who were the first to call India 'Hindusthan' ?

(iv) What did the Persians mean when they called India 'Hindu' ?

Ans.

(i) The first foreigners who mentioned India were the Persians.

(*ii*) The Persian king was Cyrus who invaded India in 535 BCE. He conquered the northwestern region of India known as Sindhu after the Indus River.

(*iii*) The Persians were the first to call India 'Hindusthan' as mentioned in a Persian Inscription 1800 years ago.

(*iv*) For the Persians, the term Hindu was purely a geographical term indicating the north-west region of India. It does not have a religious connotation and does not refer to the Hindu religion.

F. Competency Based Questions

Q. 1. *"The Ancient Indians knew their Geography well." Critically analyse this statement.*

Ans. The ancient texts like the Rig Veda, the Mahābhārata, the Vishnu Purana and ancient Tamil texts have described the boundaries of the different regions of India, the rivers and mountains providing a comprehensive knowledge of the geography of the sub-continent.

The Rig Veda refers to the northwest region of India as "Sapta-Sindhava" or land of the seven rivers thus emphasising the importance of rivers in shaping India's history. These rivers helped to make this region fertile enabling trade and agriculture to flourish.

The Mahābhārata mentions various regions like Kashmira and Vanga which have helped shaped India's rich cultural heritage. The terms 'Bhāratavarṣha' and 'Jambudvīpa' mentioned in the Mahābhārata denoted the entire Subcontinent highlighting its geographical boundaries.

Both the Vishnu Purana and the ancient Tamil texts have referred to the natural boundaries of India. Mention is made of the great mountain of the north as well as the snowy mountains which corresponds to India's northern boundary formed by the Himalayas and the Hindukush mountains. The oceans on the east and the west refer to India's eastern boundary namely the Bay of Bengal and India's western boundary formed by the Arabian Sea. 'Cape Kumari' mentioned in the Tamil text refers to the southernmost part of India namely Kanyakumari. These natural boundaries have helped to protect India against foreign invaders and made it a well defined unit.

Q. 2. *"India is a country which has many names attached to it." State the names which have come from ancient texts, the Greeks and from Indian inscriptions.*

Ans. Three of India's most ancient texts are the Rig Veda, the Mahābhārata and the Vishnu-Purana. The Rig Veda refers to the northwest region of India as 'Sapta-Sindhava' or land of the seven rivers. The Mahābhārata uses the terms Bhāratavarṣha and Jambudvīpa. The Bharatas were a venerable and ancient tribe mentioned in both the Rig Veda and the Mahābhārata whose king Bharata built a vast empire and this empire was called 'Bhāratavarṣha'. The Vishnu Purana also refers Indian Subcontinent as 'Bharata'.

The Greeks basing themselves on the Persian sources referred to India as 'Indoi' or 'Indike'. They dropped the initial letter of 'h' of Hindu because this letter did not exist in the Greek language.

Ashoka used the term 'Jambudvīpa' in his inscriptions to refer to the extent of his empire which included not only present day India but even parts of Bangladesh, Pakistan and Afghanistan. Later, this name has also been used in Kannada inscriptions from the 10th CE.

Q. 3. *"Ashoka used the term 'Jambudvīpa' in his inscriptions." What is the significance of this term for India?*

Ans. The Mauryan king Ashoka who ruled around 250 BCE used the term 'Jambudvīpa' in his inscriptions to describe his vast empire which encompassed the entire Indian Subcontinent including present day India as well as Bangladesh, Pakistan and even parts of Afghanistan. This showed that the concept of a unified area covering the entire Indian Subcontinent existed even in ancient times. His inscriptions spread across his vast empire referring to the Subcontinent as 'Jambudvīpa' highlight the cultural and spiritual significance of this region in Buddhist and Hindu scriptures. It also reflects the emperor's view of his empire as part of a broader interconnected world unified under the principles of the Dhamma which he preached. The term has both a geographic and cultural significance. It emphasises the unity and identity of the region as well as his commitment of spreading Buddhist ideas across his empire during his reign.

Q. 4. ***How did the term 'Hindusthan' come into being ?***

Ans. The term 'Hindusthan' comes from the Persian word 'Hindu'. This word is related to the Sanskrit word Sindhu. Sindhu is another word for the River Indus. The suffix 'stan' was added to the word Hindu to form the word 'Hindusthan' around the first century CE. This term became popular from the 11th century onwards. Most invaders have used this term to describe the Indian Subcontinent. The term 'Hindusthan' was in use simultaneously with 'India' during the British period.

Q. 5. ***When and how did the name 'India' emerge for the Indian Subcontinent?***

Ans. The term 'India' originated from the Sanskrit term 'Sindhu' refers to the Indus River. The ancient Persians referred to India as 'Hind, or 'Hindu'. The omission of the letter 'h' from the word Hindu by the Greeks led to terms like Indoi and Indika.

The transition from Sindhu to Indoi eventually led to the word 'India'. This word was in fact first used by the ancient Greeks around the 5th century BCE with the Greek historian Herodotus being the earliest to mention it. The British used 'India' as the official name of the Indian Subcontinent from the 18th century onwards.

G. Skill Based Questions

Q. 1. ***How has the concept of Bharatavarsha evolved over time ? What is the significance of this concept for India ?***

Ans. The concept of 'Bhāratavarṣha' has evolved over time from referring to the land of the Bharatas to encompass the entire Indian Subcontinent. It has been influenced by geography, culture and politics.

The term 'Bhāratavarṣha' comes from the Vedic word Bharatas. The concept was initially used to describe the land of the Bharatas which was a tribe mentioned in the Rig Veda. Their king conquered many areas and these areas came to be known as Bhāratavarṣha. This concept evolved from the Rig Vedic period throughout history to include the entire Indian Subcontinent. This term symbolises India's unity and diversity. It represents India's rich heritage and the idea of a nation state. It laid the foundation of the Indian Civilisation and has contributed to the cultural and religious identity of India.

Q. 2. ***How does the evolution of the name 'Bharata' reflect the development of an Indian identity ?***

Ans. The term 'Bharata' initially referred to an ancient Rig Vedic tribe whose territory extended to the western part of the Gangetic valley. It later became linked to several legendary kings symbolising leadership. Over the centuries 'Bharata' became the most common term used to describe the Indian Subcontinent. In north India the term Bharat is used while in south India the name Bharatam is used. The Vishnu Purana mentions the land north of the oceans and south of the snowy mountains as Bharata. This description fits the natural geography of India and shows that the name had deep historical roots. Thus, the evolution of this name shows how the Indian identity expanded from a tribal origin to achieve a national identity. The term Bharat holds an important place in India's cultural and linguistic identity and invokes a deep sense of heritage and tradition.

Q. 3. ***Why does the Republic of India have two official names ?***

Ans. The Republic of India has two official names 'India' and 'Bharat'. Both of these are historically significant.

The Persians referred to India as 'Hind' or 'Hindu'.

The Greeks dropped the letter 'h' and used the terms Indoi and Indika to refer India. Ultimately the word 'India' emerged around the 5th century and was widely used by the British from the 18th century onwards. The term 'Bharat' emerged from the word 'Bharatas' which was used in the 'Rig Veda'. It referred initially to a Rig Vedic tribe. Over the centuries, Bharata or Bharat became the most common term for the Indian Subcontinent.

Thus both names reflect India's long history and its connection with the rest of the world. The Indian Constitution acknowledged this dual identity by using the phrase 'India that is Bharat'. This phrase honour's the country's ancient heritage while embracing its modern identity. Over the years, the name India is commonly used internationally while the name 'Bharat' is continues to be used in Hindi and other languages.

VII. MULTIPLE CHOICE QUESTIONS

1. *The northwest region of India was known as*

(*a*) Sapta-Sindhava (*b*) Hindava
(*c*) Aryavarta (*d*) Hindukush

2. *The word Sindhu refers to*

(*a*) the Indus River
(*b*) the Sarasvati River
(*c*) the Ganges River
(*d*) the Sutlej River

3. *The Mauryan emperor who used the name of Jambudvīpa to describe India was*

(*a*) Chandragupta Maurya
(*b*) Ashoka
(*c*) Samudragupta
(*d*) Bindusara

4. *The term Jambudvīpa refers to which tree*

(*a*) jamun tree (*b*) pipal tree
(*c*) mango tree (*d*) coconut tree

5. *The snowy mountains referred in the Vishnu Purana are*

(*a*) The Western Ghats
(*b*) The Himalayas
(*c*) The Aravali mountains
(*d*) The Khasi hills

6. *The Indian Constitution was first written in*

(*a*) English (*b*) French
(*c*) Hindi (*d*) Tamil

7. *The Persian emperor who came to India in the 6th century BCE was*

(*a*) Cyrus (*b*) Darius
(*c*) Alexander (*d*) Megasthenes

8. *The Greek referred to India as*

(*a*) Hind (*b*) Yintu
(*c*) Indoi (*d*) Inde

Ans.

1. → (*a*) **2.** → (*a*) **3.** → (*b*)
4. → (*a*) **5.** → (*b*) **6.** → (*a*)
7. → (*a*) **8.** → (*c*)

VIII. OBJECTIVE TYPE QUESTIONS

A. Fill in the Blanks

1. The word Sindhu refers to the __________ River.

2. __________ was the name of a Rig Vedic tribe.

3. __________ is one of India's most famous epic.

4. In the South, India is known as __________.

5. The Indian Constitution came into force in __________.

6. Persians were the ancient inhabitants of __________.

7. __________ was the Chinese traveller who came to India in the 7th century CE.

8. The French referred to India as ________.

9. ________ was the Chinese scholar who came to India in the 7th century CE.

10. India is an________land.

11. It had________names in the course of its history.

12. Names given by ancient Indians was ________and__________.

13. Foreigners adopted names derived mostly from the_______or the________ River.

14. This led to names like________, and________.

15. Eventually the name________came to be used.

Ans.

1. Indus 2. Bharata
3. Mahābhārata 4. Bharatam
5. 1950 6. Iran
7. Hiuen Tsang 8. Inde
9. Xuanzang, (Hiuen Tsang)
10. Ancient 11. Many
12. Jambudvīpa and Bharata
13. Sindhu or Indus
14. Hindu, Indoi 15. India.

IX. TEST YOUR KNOWLEDGE

A. Fill in the Blanks

1. *The ________ tree is associated with the term Jambudvīpa.*
2. *The name used by the Chinese for India was _______.*
3. *The term 'Sapta-Sindhava' means _____.*
4. *The term 'Hindusthan' was first used in a _______ Inscription.*

B. True or False

1. *The term Bhāratavarṣha means the land of the Kurus.*
2. *The name Bharata first appeared in the Rig Veda.*
3. *The regions listed in the Mahābhārata cover the entire geography of the Sub-continent.*

C. Very Short Answer Type Questions

Q. 1. *In Ashoka's time which regions formed Jambudvīpa?*

Q. 2. *How do we define India?*

Q. 3. *What were the ancient names for India?*

Q. 4. *Name two mountain ranges which protect India from foreign invasions.*

Q. 5. *Kurukshetra is part of which Indian state today?*

D. Short Answer Type Questions

Q. 1. *Why did Jambudvīpa come to refer the Indian Subcontinent?*

Q. 2. *Why did the Persians referred to India as Hind or Hindu?*

Q. 3. *Trace the process by which India came to be known as Yindu by the ancient Chinese.*

E. Long Answer Type Questions

Q. 1. *Trace various names of India that were derived from the word 'Sindhu ' by the foreigners who came to India.*

Q. 2. *What were the various names that ancient Indians called India and why?*

F. Assertion & Reasoning Questions

There are two statements given Assertion (A) and Reason (R) given above. Mark your answer according to the code given below.

1. **Assertion (A):** Bimbisara used the term Jambudvīpa in his inscriptions.

   Reason (R): The term was used to represent the southern extent of his empire.

   Codes:

   (*a*) Both (A) and (R) are true but (R) is not the correct explanation of (A)

   (*b*) Both (A) and (R) are true and (R) is the correct explanation of (A) .

   (*c*) (A) is true but (R) is false.

   (*d*) (A) is false but (R) is true

2. **Assertion (A):** The Hindi version of the Constitution mentions India as 'Bharat, arthath India'.

Reason (R): This indicates 'India' and 'Bharat' are names for the same country.

Codes:

(*a*) Both (A) and (R) are true but (R) is not the correct explanation of (A)

(*b*) Both (A) and (R) are true and (R) is the correct explanation of (A) .

(*c*) (A) is true but (R) is false.

(*d*) (A) is false but (R) is true

G. Match Column A with Column B

	Column A		Column B
(*a*)	Vishnu Purana	(*i*)	north-west India
(*b*)	Sapta-Sindhava	(*ii*)	Today's Assam
(*c*)	Pragjyotisha	(*iii*)	Bharata
(*d*)	Mahābhārata	(*iv*)	Himalayas
(*e*)	Snowy mountains	(*v*)	Jambudvīpa

Notes

The Beginnings of Indian Civilisation

1 What Is a Civilisation?

- **Civilisation:** an advanced stage of human society (well-organised & progressive).
- **Features of civilisation:**
  government & administration to maintain law and order.
  Towns/cities with planned layout, drainage system, water supply.
  Crafts like working with stone, metals, ornaments, and tools.
  Trade (internal & external to exchange goods).
  Writing system for communication & record keeping.
  Cultural ideas (art, architecture, literature, customs) to express life.
  Agriculture, sufficient enough to feed cities/towns.
- Early civilisations—Mesopotamia (~6000 yrs ago), Egypt (slightly later).
- In India: Earliest centre = Harappan (northwest region).

2 From Village to City

- Punjab & Sindh are irrigated by the Indus River and its rivulets (streams).
- Indus & Sarasvati rivers supported early farming.
- Sarasvati flows through Haryana, Punjab, Rajasthan & Gujarat.
- ~3500 BCE: villages grew into towns.
- By 2600 BCE: towns → cities = Indus/Harappan/Indus-Sarasvati civilisation.
- This marked India's first urbanisation.

3 The Sarasvati River

- Many Harappan sites were found on the Sarasvati basin.
- Today, the river is seasonal, called **Ghaggar** (India) & **Hakra** (Pakistan).
- **Rig Veda:** described it as 'flowing from mountains to sea'.
- Later texts mention its drying up and disappearance.

4 Town-Planning

- **Early cities:** Harappa & Mohenjo-daro—Pakistan (1924).
- Other major sites: Dholavira, Rakhigarhi, Ganweriwala, Lothal.
- Smaller sites: Farmana, Kalibangan, Bhirrana, Banawali.
- **Fortification:** A huge wall surrounding the city.
- **City features:**
  Broad streets, aligned with cardinal directions.
  Fortified towns: two parts-upper (elite) & lower (commoners).
  Large storage buildings (warehouses).
  Houses of different sizes, made from bricks.
- **Great Bath (Mohenjo-daro):** 12×7 m, waterproof tank, drains, wells.
  Use: debated (for ritual/royal/common people).

5 Water Management

- **Harappans;** experts in sanitation & water uses.
- Houses had bathing spaces with underground drains.
- **Mohenjo-daro:** hundreds of brick wells.
- **Reservoirs:** large place for water storage (natural/artificial).
- **Elsewhere:** ponds, streams, man-made reservoirs.
- **Dholavira:** 6 big reservoirs (largest 73 m long), linked with drains for rainwater storage.

6 What Did the Harappans Eat?

- Settlements near rivers—fertile fields→supported rich crops.
- **Major crops:** barley, wheat, millet, rice, pulses, vegetables.
- **Harappans;** first in Eurasia to grow cotton→used for cloth.
- **Farming tools:** ploughs (similar to modern).
- Villages supplied food to cities (daily basis).
- **Animals:** domesticated for milk, meat and fishing was common.
- **Evidence:** dairy, turmeric, ginger, bananas, indicating diverse diet.

7 A Brisk Trade

- Harappans active in trade; within civilisation & with distant lands.
- **Exports:** ornaments (beads of carnelian), timber, cotton, gold, food items.
- **Special craft:** carnelian beads (Gujarat), conch shell bangles.
- **Imports:** copper.
- **Trade routes:** land, sea, river.
- **Lothal (Gujarat):** had a huge dockyard (217×36 m), indicating maritime trade.
- **Seals (steatite):** animals + symbols, used for goods & identity (writing uninterpreted).

8 The End or a New Beginning?

- ~1900 BCE: cities slowly abandoned.
- Harappans scattered over hundreds small rural settlements with authority.
- No trace of warfare/invasions, Harappans were peaceful people.
- **Main reasons of decline:**
  Climate change (less rainfall→poor farming)
  Drying of Sarasvati River (Cities; Kalibangan & Banawali disappeared).
- Culture & skills lived on; passed on to the next Indian civilisation.

THEME–B
Tapestry of the Past

CHAPTER
6

THE BEGINNINGS OF INDIAN CIVILISATION

I. FACTS TO REMEMBER/SUMMARY

WHAT IS A CIVILISATION?

- Civilisation in general term, means an advanced stage of human societies.
- A civilisation generally has well planned cities, a form of government and administration, crafts and trade, some form of writing and a productive agriculture.

FROM VILLAGE TO CITY

- This civilisation flourished on the banks of the Indus river and the Sarasvati river. Therefore, this civilisation is known by several different names. It is known as the Indus Valley Civilisation, the Harappan Civilisation and even 'Indus–Sarasvati' or 'Sindhu Sarasvati' Civilisation depending on where a site has been discovered. The inhabitants of this civilisation are known as 'Harappans' because Harappa was the first site to be discovered. In all over a 1000 sites have been discovered. Apart from Harappa, other famous sites include Chanhudaro, and Kot Diji (Pakistan), Kalibangan (Rajasthan), Lothal and Dholavira (Gujarat).

TOWN PLANNING

- Excavations at the various sites indicate that this civilisation was an advanced urban civilisation. The cities were divided into two parts, the Citadel and the lowest town. The only exception to this was Dholavira which was divided into three parts— Citadel, middle and lower town. The citadel contained public buildings, like the Great Bath & granary. The lower town contained residential areas for the people living in the city.

WATER MANAGEMENT

- The Harappans gave a lot of importance to water management and cleanliness. Every house had a well and a bathroom. The houses were provided with covered drains which were connected to the street drains. Roads and streets were laid out in a grid system thus dividing the city into large rectangular blocks or grids.

WHAT DID HARAPPANS EAT?

- Agriculture was one of the main economic activities of the people. Grains found at Harappan sites indicate that wheat, barley, millets and lentils were cultivated.

A BRISK TRADE

- The Harappan people were also engaged in many crafts such as pottery, metal work and ceramics. The Harappans had a flourishing internal and external trade. To conduct the trade they used land routes, rivers and sea for distant destinations.

- Seals are the most distinctive products of the Harappan civilisation. Since the writing on the seals has not been deciphered, the exact purpose of their use is still unknown. Presence of seals in Mesopotamia indicate they were used for trade purposes.
- The Indus script was pictographic but unfortunately has not been deciphered so far. We are also not sure what kind of government they had as no temples or palaces have been found. But the extraordinary uniformity that existed throughout the Civilisation indicates the existence of a centralised authority.

THE END OR A NEW BEGINNING?

- Around 1900 BCE the Harappan Civilisation began to decline. Historians have not been able to find out the exact cause of the decline. Climatic changes, floods, deforestation, natural calamities and invasions may be some of the causes as stated by the historians. But the Indus Valley Civilisation was so vast that no single reason can explain its downfall. Thus, the decline of this civilisation is still shrouded in mystery.

II. TEXTBOOK KEYWORDS/GLOSSARY

1. **Tributary:** A river that flows into a larger river (or lake). For example, the Yamuna is a tributary of the Ganga.
2. **Rig Veda:** It is the oldest and most important of the four Vedas, containing hymns dedicated to various deities in Vedic Sanskrit.
3. **Fortification:** A massive wall surrounding a settlement or city, primarily built for protection.
4. **Elite:** It refers to the higher layers of the society, such as rulers, officials, administrators, and often priests.
5. **Reservoir:** A large natural or artificial place where water is stored.
6. **Pulses:** A category of crops that includes beans, peas and lentils (dal).
7. **Archaeologist:** A person who studies objects made and used in the past.
8. **Metallurgy:** It is a technique to extract metals from nature.

III. DATE LINE

- **4000 BCE:** Beginning of Mesopotamian Civilisation.
- **3000 BCE:** Beginning of the Egyptian Civilisation.
- **2000 BCE:** Indus-Sarasvatī Civilisation.

IV. THE BIG QUESTIONS *(Page 85)*

Q. 1. ***What is a civilisation?***

Ans. A civilisation is a highly developed society with established cities, a well-organised government, social structures, culture and advancement in technology, art and writing.

Q. 2. ***What was the earliest civilisation of the Indian Subcontinent?***

Ans. The earliest known Civilisation of the Indian subcontinent is the Indus Valley Civilisation, also known as the Harappan Civilisation.

Q. 3. ***What were its major achievements?***

Ans. The Harappan Civilisation achieved great things for its time, here are some of their major achievements:

- **Urban Planning:** Well-planned cities with grid layouts, drainage systems, and sanitation facilities.
- **Advanced Architecture:** Use of fired bricks, multi-storied buildings, and impressive granaries.
- **Craft and Technology:** Skilled in metalworking, pottery and seal carving. Developed a system of weights and measures.
- **Trade:** Extensive trade network with Mesopotamia and other regions. Evidence of trade, such as beads and tools.
- **Writing System:** Developed a writing system, though it has not been deciphered as yet.

V. NCERT INTEXT/TEXTBOOK EXERCISES

Think About It

Q. 1. ***Which of the above characteristics do you think is the most fundamental—that is, a characteristic essential to the development of all others?*** *(Page 86)*

Ans. A productive agriculture, urbanism and a system of government are essential for the development of all others.

Q. 2. ***Imagine the large number of workers required to build such a network of reservoirs. Who do you think organised their work and gave them precise instructions? How do you think they were paid for their labour? (Hint: there was no money at that time in the way we have today.) Since the reservoirs needed to be cleaned from time to time, was there some local authority to manage their maintenance? What clues do we get from all this about this city's ruler and municipal administration?. Use your imagination and discuss with your teacher. Archaeologists also discuss these questions, and the answers are not always final!*** *(Page 96)*

Ans. The Harappans had a centralised form of administration who would have been responsible for the construction of these reservoirs. Since there was no money at that time, there must have been some sort of exchange for services. Possibly they were paid by cereals or other goods. There must have been some local administration at every site which would have been responsible for the cleaning of the reservoirs from time to time.

Q. 3. ***Looking at the objects on pages 100 and 101 — or any other pictured in this chapter — can you make out what activities or aspects of life were important for the Harappans?*** *(Page 102)*

Ans. Looking at the objects on page 100-101 it is clear that the Harappans kept themselves busy by playing with games and toys. The stone gamesboard found, resembles with the game of chess as played today. They were fond of jewellery and dressing up. Moreover trade was important to them as the seals depicted in these pages have been used for trade purposes as have stone weights. Pottery and making of sculptures are other activities important to the Harappans. Other pictures like the model of a plough show that agriculture was an important occupation at that time. Pictures of the Great Bath, housing area of Dholavira and streets in Kalibangan indicate that construction of houses, and laying of roads were an important aspect of Harappan life.

Let's Explore

Q. 1. ***For each characteristic in the list above, can you make a list of professions or occupations that might exist in such a society?*** *(Page 87)*

Ans. The list of professions or occupations that might exist in such a society is as follows:

- Farmer
- Fisherman
- Butcher
- Potter
- Weaver
- Stone Carver
- Metalworker
- Jeweller
- Bead Maker

Construction and Engineering

- Mason
- Carpenter
- Architect
- Brick Maker
- Engineer
- Painter

Trade and Commerce

- Merchant
- Trader
- Moneylender
- Warehouse Keeper
- Scribe
- Accountant
- Transporter
- Shipbuilder

Q. 2. *Some of the important cities of this civilisation are marked in the map (Fig. 6.3). As a class activity, can you try to match these cities with the modern states or regions in the table given below?* *(Page 89)*

Ans.

Harappan city	Modern state/region
Dholavira	Gujarat
Harappa	Punjab
Kalibangan	Rajasthan
Mohenjo-daro	Sindh
Rakhigarhi	Haryana

Q. 3. *Have a debate in class about the last two interpretations. Can you think of any others? Remember that in this case, we do not have any other source of history — no inscription, no text, no traveller's account.* *(Page 93)*

Ans. Do it yourself activity under teacher guidance.

Q. 4. *As a class activity, measure the length of your classroom, a school corridor or a playground with the help of any measuring tape. Compare these lengths with the length of the largest reservoir in Dholavira.* *(Page 95)*

Ans. Do it yourself under teacher's guidance.

Q. 5. *Imagine you cook a meal in a Harappan house. What dish or dishes would you prepare, based on the data given above?* *(Page 97)*

Ans. Based on the data given. I would cook some lentils and vegetables and eat my meal with chapatti and curd.

Q. 6. *Looking at these three Harappan seals with some writing signs, what goes through your mind? Would you like to suggest any interpretations? Let your imagination run!* *(Page 99)*

Ans. Looking at these seals, I think that these animals were sacred to the Harappan People. I would also like to suggest that the humped bull might have been worshipped at that point of time, as it is even worshipped by many people in India even today. Possibly this practice may have come down the generations. The seals were used for trade purposes, so possibly the owners names may have been written on the seals.

Q. 7. *Complete the story found on the Lothal pot. How was such a story remembered for more than 4,000 years, in your opinion?* *(Page 102)*

Ans. Story of the Lothal Pot

The thirsty crow finds a pot with some water in it but its level was too low. He then uses his brain, picks up some pebbles and drops them into the pot one by one. The water level rises and the crow is able to drink the water.

This story was probably passed down from generation to generation orally. It is also mentioned in the Aesop fables* written in the 4th century BCE. Aesop must have heard the story from a Greek trader and a traveller who came to India around that time.

Q. 8. *Consider the 'Dancing Girl' figurine. What do you make of the attitude the figurine expresses? Observe her bangles covering an entire arm, a practice still visible in parts of Gujarat and Rajasthan. Where else in this chapter can you spot bangles worn in this manner. What conclusion should we draw from this?* *(Page 102)*

Ans. The Dancing Girl figurine depicts a young woman with a coiled hairstyle and bangles adorning her arms. She props one arm at her waist and the other arm hangs by her side. Her face is tilted upwards and has a confident demeanor. Her body posture seems to indicate a dance posture and signifies that dancing was a means of entertainment at that time.

The large number of bangles represented in the figurine indicates their love for adornments. It also indicates their way of life where wearing a lot of bangles was part of their culture. Fig. 6.1 in this chapter shows a women sitting in the 'Castle' area of Dholavira wearing bangles up to her elbows.

* Aesop's fables are a collection of short moral stories attributed to Aesop, a storyteller from ancient Greece.

NCERT Questions, Activities and Projects
(*Page 104*)

Q. 1. ***Why does the civilisation studied in this chapter have several names? Discuss their significance.***

Ans. The civilisation studied in this chapter has many names based on the area where the sites were discovered. Harappa was the first site to be discovered. so it is known as the Harappan Civilisation. Many sites have also been discovered along the banks of the Indus river and the Sarasvati river. Therefore, this civilisation has also been referred to as Indus Valley Civilisation and even the Indus-Sarasvati Civilisation.

Q. 2. ***Write a brief report (150 to 200 words) summing up some of the achievements of the Indus-Sarasvatī civilisation.***

Ans. The **Indus-Sarasvatī Civilisation**, one of the earliest known in the history of mankind, came up with some remarkable achievements such as–

- The Harappans established well-planned cities with advanced drainage systems, which clearly gives us a glimpse on their emphasis on sanitation and public health.
- The Harappans were very skilled in metallurgy, producing bronze tools and various ornaments.
- The civilisation had a robust trade network extending to Mesopotamia, facilitated by their standardised weights and measures.
- Also, the Harappans excelled in bead-making and pottery, leaving behind intricate artifacts that highlight their artistic prowess.
- Their script, though deciphered, suggests a complex administrative system.

Q. 3. ***Imagine you have to travel from the city of Harappa to Kalibangan. What are your different options? Can you make a rough estimation of the amount of time each option might take?***

Ans. Travelling from Harappa to Kalibangan in ancient times would primarily involve land routes. Utilising the Indus River for the initial part of the journey would be the most efficient as this water route is not only convenient but also safe to start with. Further, followed by land travel using horse, bullock carts or by foot. The total distance is approximately 200 kilometers and hence it might take a few days, depending on the weather conditions and speed of travel.

Q. 4. ***Let us imagine a Harappan man or woman being transported to an average kitchen in today's India. What are the four or five biggest surprises awaiting them?***

Ans. We can imagine how it can be a revelation for a Harappan man or women being transported to an average kitchen in today's India. There will be many surprises for them such as—

- A Harappan will be surprised by the presence of electrical appliances like refrigerators and microwaves.
- They will be amazed to see the variety of processed and packaged milk and foods and the availability of running water through taps.
- They will be further astonished to witness the use of gas or electric stoves instead of traditional firewood.
- Also the presence of modern utensils and cookware made of stainless steel and non-stick materials will be another big surprise for them.

Q. 5. ***Looking at all the pictures in this chapter, make a list of the ornaments / gestures / objects that still feel familiar in our 21st century.***

Ans. Looking at all the pictures in this chapter we can say that – ornaments such as bangles and beads, gestures like the *'namaste'* pose, and objects like mirrors and toys are still familiar in the 21st century.

Q. 6. *What mindset does the system of reservoirs at Dholavira reflect?*

Ans. The system of reservoirs at Dholavira clearly reflects the following–

- **Advanced Planning and Engineering Skills:** The Harappans were able to develop and construct large and interconnected water reservoirs which actually gives us an idea of their smart and well developed engineering and planning skills.
- **Conservation of Water:** The construction of these water reservoirs also demonstrates their understanding towards the importance of water conservation.
- **Social Collaboration and Civic Sense:** Their combined effort to build such huge constructions proves that they had social sense of collaboration and civility.
- **Continuous and Stable Water Supply:** This also proves that how in collaboration they ensured a stable and continuous water supply for the whole society.
- **Sustainability of Resources:** This again highlights their deep understanding for maintaining a sustainable living conditions and to secure resources for the coming future generations.

Q. 7. *In Mohenjo-daro, about 700 wells built with bricks have been counted. They seem to have been regularly maintained and used for several centuries. Discuss the implications.*

Ans. The implications of regularly maintained wells in Mohenjo-daro are as follows:

- **Sophisticated Urban Planning:** The extensive network of 700 wells indicates advanced urban planning and an emphasis on decentralised water supply.
- **A Reliable Water Supply:** Ensuring access to water for all resident's highlights the Harappans' understanding of the necessity of a consistent water source for urban life.
- **Well-Organised Governance:** The regular maintenance of these wells over centuries suggests a stable and efficient administrative system capable of managing public utilities.
- **Commitment to Public Welfare:** The widespread availability of wells demonstrates a strong commitment to public health and welfare, ensuring that all citizens had access to clean water.

Q. 8. *It is often said that the Harappans had a high civic sense. Discuss the significance of this statement. Do you agree with it? Compare with citizens in a large city of India today.*

Ans. The Harappans had the high civic sense. We agree to the statement because of the following points—

- **Meticulous Urban Planning:** The well-planned layout of Harappan cities, with wide streets and a standardised drainage system, indicates a high level of civic sense and concern for urban living conditions.
- **Uniform Quality of Construction:** The consistent quality in building houses, regardless of size, shows a societal commitment to equity and public welfare.
- **Emphasis on Cleanliness:** The extensive and efficient drainage systems reflect a strong emphasis on public health and hygiene.

Comparison with Modern Indian Cities:

- **Similar Challenges:** In contrast modern Indian cities face challenges related to water supply, waste management, and public health.
- **Varying Civic Responsibility:** Issues like pollution and inadequate waste disposal are prevalent due to lack of public awareness and civic duty unlike in the Harappan cities.
- **Historical Benchmark:** The Harappans set a historical benchmark for urban planning and civic responsibility that our modern cities should aspire to sustainable practices.

VI. EXAM ORIENTED QUESTIONS

A. Very Short Answer Type Questions

Q. 1. ***Why are the inhabitants called 'Harappans' in this civilisation?***

Ans. They are called 'Harappans' because of the city Harappa.

Q. 2. ***State four materials used by this civilisation.***

Ans. Copper, Bronze, Clay, and Terracotta were used by this civilisation.

Q. 3. ***Name four cities of the Harappan Civilisation.***

Ans. Mohenjo-daro, Dholavira, Lothal and Kalibangan.

Q. 4. ***Name four Harappan sites which have been excavated in Haryana.***

Ans. Banawali, Karanpura, Bhirrana and Farmana are the sites that were excavated in Haryana.

Q. 5. ***Define the term Civilisation?***

Ans. A civilisation is a highly developed society with established cities, a well-organised government, social structure, culture and advancement in technology, art and writing.

Q. 6. ***When did the civilisation begin?***

Ans. Civilisation began at different times in different parts of the world.

For example, Mesopotamia Civilisation began around 4000 BCE, and Indus Sarasvatī Civilisation began around 2000 BCE.

Q. 7. ***State two main features of the Induas Valley Civilisation.***

Ans. The Indus Valley Civilisation was known for its town planning and drainage system.

Q. 8. ***Why are the Punjab plains so fertile?***

Ans. The Punjab plains — now divided between India and Pakistan — are fertile due to the fact that they are watered by the Indus river and its tributaries.

Q. 9. ***Name the Port City of the Indus Valley Civilisation. Where is it situated ?***

Ans. Lothal is the Port City of the Indus Valley Civilisation. It is situated near the Gulf of Cambay.

Q. 10. ***Where is the Sarasvati river mentioned for the very first time?***

Ans. It is mentioned in the Rig Veda.

Q. 11. ***Name the first two cities to be discovered.***

Ans. Harappa and Mohenjo-daro were the first two cities to be discovered.

Q. 12. ***Name any four objects found by archaeologists.***

Ans. A gamesboard engraved on a stone (from Dholavira), a terracotta whistle (from Karanpura), bronze mirror and chisel (both from Dholavira) have been found by archaeologists.

Q. 13. ***By what names is the Sarasvati River known today?***

Ans. Today, the Sarasvati river is known as the 'Ghaggar', in India and 'Hakra' in Pakistan.

Q. 14. ***What names have archaeologists given to this civilisation?***

Ans. Archaeologists have given this Civilisation many names. The names 'Indus', Harappan', 'Indus - Sarasvati' or 'Sindh Sarasvati', have been used for this civilisation.

Q. 15. ***What is the Great Bath?***

Ans. Found in Mohenjo-daro, the Great Bath is a small but elaborate tank surrounded by small rooms.

Q. 16. ***What did the Harappans eat?***

Ans. Archaeological findings have shown that the Harappans grew cereals like barley, wheat, some millets, and sometimes rice, in addition to pulses and a variety of vegetables.

Q. 17. ***Mention four items which the Harappans exported.***

Ans. They exported ornaments, timber, some objects of daily use probably gold and cotton were also exported.

Q. 18. ***Why is this civilisation also known as the Bronze Age Civilisation?***

Ans. It is also known as the Bronze Age Civilisation because Bronze was the metal used at that time.

B. Short Answer Type Questions

Q. 1. ***Why did the Harappans return to rural settlements?***

Ans. Around 1900 BCE the Harappan Civilisation began to decline. The people abandoned the cities and adopted a rural lifestyle. This was because a rural lifestyle gave them easier access to food and water.

Q. 2. ***State two main causes for the decline of the Harappans?***

Ans. The decline of the Harappans was due to two main factors. Archeologists have suggested that climatic change was first factor. Drought or less rainfall could have reduced the food supply. Second factor was the drying up of the basin of the Sarasvati river which led to migration from cities to villages.

Q. 3. ***How do we know that the Harappans had a flourishing trade?***

Ans. The Harappans had a flourishing internal and external trade. They had trade links with Mesopotamia, Iran, Afghanistan and Oman. Evidence of trade with Mesopotamia can be seen by the fact that many Harappan artefacts have been found here. An ivory Harappan comb has been found in Oman and Harappan Carnelian beads in Susa (*present day in Iran*). The discovery of a dockyard at Lothal further testifies maritime trade. Bullock Carts, boats and ships were used for trade and transport. Many items which the Harappans used came from distant places. For example copper from Rajasthan and gold from Karnataka.

Q. 4. ***What is the importance of the Sarasvati River in ancient Indian history?***

Ans. Many sites of the Indus Valley Civilisation flourished along the banks of the Sarasvati river. The Sarasvati river is first mentioned in the Rig Veda which was an ancient collection of prayers. In this text, Sarasvati is worshipped both as the goddess of learning and as a sacred river. Later texts describe the river as drying up and eventually disappearing.

Q. 5. ***Write a short note on the Harappan Civilisation.***

Ans. The Indus, Harappan or Sindhu-Sarasvatī Civilisation is one of the oldest in the world. Its inhabitants, the Harappans, built planned cities with efficient water management systems, diverse crafts and had a brisk trade. A productive agriculture brought a variety of crops to the cities. The civilisation eventually declined, probably because of climatic and environmental changes and its people returned to a rural lifestyle.

Q. 6. ***What role did agriculture play in the economy of the Harappan Civilisation?***

Ans. Agriculture was one of the main economic activities of the people. Grains found at Harappan sites indicate that wheat, barley, lentils, chickpeas and sesame were among the main crops that were cultivated. Millets have been found at some sites. They were also the first to grow cotton which they used to weave into clothes. They made different types of farming tools including the plough.

Q. 7. ***What was the purpose of the Great Bath?***

Ans. Historians have given different interpretations in this regard. Some have felt that it could have been a public bath for the common people. This interpretation has now been ruled out because in Mohanjo-daro the houses had individual bathrooms. Therefore, there was no need for a public bath. Others Historians felt it could have been a bath for the royal family. But there is no evidence that kings existed at that time. Therefore, it was probably a tank used by the people for ritual bathing on special occasions or for religious ceremonies.

Q. 8. ***What kind of government did the Harappans have?***

Ans. Historians are still not clear what kind of governments existed at this time. The absence of any palace like buildings or temples indicates that neither kings or priests existed.

But the extraordinary uniformity that existed throughout the civilisation be it with regard to their town planning, drainage, or the bricks and seals found indicate the existence of a centralised authority. Possibly the Harappan cities were governed by a committee of rich traders and merchants.

Q. 9. "The Harappan people were engaged in many crafts." ***Critically examine this statement.***

Ans. The Harappan people were engaged in many crafts such as pottery, metal work and ceramics.

The Harappans were excellent potters. They used the potter's wheel to make pots of different shapes and sizes.

C. Long Answer Type Questions

Q.1. ***Describe the main features of Harappan Civilisation.***

Ans. Some of the main features of the Harappan Civilisation are as follows –

- The Harappan cities show a level of sophistication and advancement not seen in any of the other contemporary civilisations. Most cities had similar patterns and were divided into two parts: a upper town and the lower town.
- Most cities had a Great Bath possibly used for bathing on special occasions or religious ceremonies.
- There were also granaries, two-storied houses made of burnt bricks, closed drainage lines, an excellent wastewater management system, weights for measurements, toys, pots, etc. A large number of seals have also been discovered.
- Agriculture was the most important occupation and this was the first civilisation to cultivate cotton. Animals like sheep, goats, and pigs were domesticated. Crops like wheat, barley, cotton, ragi, dates, and peas were cultivated.
- A flourishing trade existed. Metal products of copper, bronze, and tin, were produced. Gold and silver was known to them but not iron.
- A figurine named the 'Dancing Girl' has been found from Mohenjo-daro and is believed to be 4000 years old. A figure of a bearded man has also been found from Mohenjo-daro. This indicates an advanced knowledge of Metallurgy.

Q. 2. ***"The Indus Valley Civilisation is known for its town—Planning." Critically analyse this statement.***

Ans. Excavations at the various sites indicate that the Harappan Civilisation was an Urban Civilisation and its people were skilled engineers.

The cities were properly planned and were according to a set pattern. Signs of planning included the use of bricks which were of a standardised ratio and found at all Harappan settlements. The cities were divided into two parts namely the Citadel and the lower town. The Citadel contained public buildings like the Great Bath and the Granary. The lowest town contained residential areas for the people living in the city.

Houses varied in size from small one roomed houses to more spacious houses. They were built or bricks, lime or gypsum. Roads and streets were laid out in a 'grid' pattern. The main streets were straight and intersected each other at right angles. This divided the streets into large rectangular blocks or grids. This rectangular town planning was a unique feature of the Harappan Civilisation and not known to other civilisations existing at this time.

Q. 3. ***Discuss the possible causes for the decline of the Harappan Civilisation.***

Ans. The decline of the Harappan Civilisation is still shrouded in mystery. It was earlier believed that warfare or invasion might have destroyed the cities but no evidence to support this theory has been found. No weapons of offence have been found and they seem to have been a peace loving people.

Some historians have felt that natural calamities like earthquakes of epidemics might have wiped out this civilisation. There may also have been massive floods which could have led the drainage system to collapse and cause the whole region to be buried in mud.

Climatic changes that occurred world-wide in 2000 BCE led to the reduction in rainfall. This would have affected agricultural production and reduced food supply to the cities.

The drying up of the Sarasvati River in its central basin would have made the land infertile leading to abandonment of cities like Kalibangan and Banawali. However, the Indus Valley Civilisaton was so vast that no single reason can explain its sudden downfall.

Q. 4. ***What are Seals? What were they used for?***

Ans. Seals are the most distinctive products of the Harappan Civilisation. Thousands of seals have been excavated from various sites. These seals were generally made of steatite, a soft stone that was hardened by heating.

They were generally square or rectangular in shape. They generally measured only a few centimetres. They were engraved with figures of animals like the humped bull, horned tiger and an unicorn. They usually had a line of writing at the top.

Since, the writing on seals has not yet been deciphered the exact purpose of their use is unknown. But the presence of seals in Mesopotamia suggest that they were used for trade purposes. Possibly they were used to stamp property or goods as a means of identifying their owners.

Q. 5. ***"What are the major characteristics of a Civilisation? The Harappan Civilisation had a highly advanced drainage system". Explain the statement.***

Ans. Every house had a well, a bathroom and was provided with covered drains. The house drains were connected to the street drains. The drains were covered with stone slabs which could be removed to clean them. There were manholes at regular intervals that could be opened for cleaning and inspection. This shows that the Indus Valley people were very particular about health and sanitation.

D. Assertion & Reasoning Questions

There are two statements marked as Assertion (A) and Reason (R). Mark your answer as per the codes provided below:

Q. 1. Assertion (A): The Harrppan Civilisation is also known as the Bronze Age Civilisation.

Reason (R): They had learnt to produce Bronze, an alloy of copper and tin.

Codes:

(a) Both (A) and (R) are true but R is not the correct explanation of (A).

(b) Both (A) and (R) are true and (R) is the correct explanation of (A).

(c) (A) is true but (R) is false.

(d) (A) is false but (R) is true.

Q. 2. Assertion (A): Harrappa was the first site to be discovered.

Reason (R): This civilisation is known as the Harappan Civilisation.

Codes:

(a) Both (A) and (R) are true but R is not the correct explanation of (A).

(b) Both (A) and (R) are true and (R) is the correct explanation of (A).

(c) (A) is true but (R) is false.

(d) Both (A) and (R) are false

Q. 3. Assertion (A): The Harappan Civilisation had a highly advanced drainage system.

Reason (R): The Harappans were very particular about health and sanitation.

Codes:

(a) Both (A) and (R) are true but R is not the correct explanation of (A).

(b) Both (A) and (R) are true and (R) is the correct explanation of (A).

(c) (A) is true but (R) is false.

(d) Both (A) and (R) are false

Q. 4. Assertion (A): The rulers of the Indus Valley Civilisation were priest.

Reason (R): Remains of temples have been found in many sites.

Codes:

(a) Both (A) and (R) are true but R is not the correct explanation of (A).

(b) Both (A) and (R) are true and (R) is the correct explanation of (A).

(c) (A) is true but (R) is false.

(d) Both (A) and (R) are false

Q. 5. Assertion (A): Beadmaking was an important craft at this time.

Reason (R): Harappan beads have been excavated in Egypt.

Codes:

(a) Both (A) and (R) are true but R is not the correct explanation of (A).

(b) Both (A) and (R) are true and (R) is the correct explanation of (A).

(c) (A) is true but (R) is false.

(d) Both (A) and (R) are false

1. *(b)* **2.** *(b)* **3.** *(b)* **4.** *(d)* **5.** *(c)*

E. Case/Source Based Questions

Read the passages given below and answer the questions that follow:

I. In this whole region, from about 3500 BCE, villages grew into towns, and with increasing trade and other exchanges, those towns further grew into cities. This transition happened around 2600 BCE.

Archaeologists gave this civilisation several names — 'Indus', 'Harappan', 'Indus-Sarasvatī' or 'Sindhu-Sarasvatī' civilisation. We will use all these terms.

Its inhabitants are called 'Harappans'. It is one of the oldest civilisations in the world.

(i) Why are the inhabitants of this Civilisation called 'Harappans'.

(ii) What is the historical significance of the discovery of the Indus Valley Civilisation?

(iii) Why did the villages grew into cities?

Ans.

(i) The inhabitants are called Harappans because Harappa was the first site of this civilisation to be excavated.

(ii) Initially it was believed that Indian history started with the Vedic period. The discovery of the Indus Valley civilisation pushed back the antiquity of Indian history by nearby 2000 years.

(iii) A productive agriculture whereby the villagers could not only meet their requirements but also supply food to the cities is one major reason. This freed people to explore different occupations which provided items for exchange and trade. As a result villages grew into towns and later cities.

II. The Harappans gave much importance to water management and cleanliness. They often had separate areas for bathing in their homes; these were connected to a larger network of drains (Fig. 6.7), which generally ran below the streets and took the waste water away. In Mohenjo-daro, people drew water from hundreds of wells made of bricks. But in other regions, it may have been from ponds, nearby streams or human-made reservoirs. In the case of Dholavira (in the Rann of Kutch in Gujarat), the largest reservoir measured 73 metres in length!

(i) How we do know that the Harappans gave importance to cleanliness?

(ii) How did the Harappans ensure a stable supply of water for their people?

(iii) What were the other sources of water for the people?

Ans.

(i) Every house had a well, a bathroom and was provided with covered drains. These drains were connected to the street drains. The drains were covered with stone slabs. These slabs could be removed so that the drains could be cleaned. They also had manholes at regular intervals to help in cleaning.

(ii) A well constructed network of reservoirs and existence of numerous wells ensured that the people of this civilisation never faced a water shortage. In Mohanjo-daro an extensive network of 700 wells ensured that water shortages did not occur. In Dholavira the Harappans were able to develop and construct large inter-connected reservoirs.

(iii) The people also got water from ponds and nearby streams.

III. The Harappans created many of their settlements along the banks of large or small rivers. This is a logical choice, not just for easy access to water, but also for agriculture, since rivers enrich the soil around them. Archaeological findings have shown that the Harappans grew cereals like barley, wheat, some millets, and sometimes rice, in addition to pulses and a variety of vegetables. They were also the first in Eurasia to grow cotton, which they used to weave into clothes.

(i) *Why were Harappan sites found along the river banks?*

(ii) *What crops did the Harappans cultivate?*

(iii) *Name the item that has been the first to be cultivated in Eurasia. For what was it used?*

Ans.

(i) This was because the rivers provided water for domestic purposes like cooking, washing and for drinking purposes. Rivers provided a constant source of water for agriculture.

The annual flooding of the rivers made the soil fertile. Rivers also provided an easy means of travel by boats and rafts.

(ii) The Harappans grew cereals like wheat and barley, pulses like beans, peas and lentils, rice and millets. They also cultivated a great variety of vegetables.

(iii) The first item to be cultivated in Eurasia was cotton. The cultivation of cotton encouraged the textile industry. The people were expert in weaving and spinning cotton to make clothes.

IV. "Dholavira is one of the largest urban centres of the Indus Valley Civilisation. It is located in the Kachchh district of Gujarat unlike other Harappan cities. Dholavira has been divided into three parts the citadal, middle & lower town. Each part was separated by stone. walls. Many human made reservoirs have been found at Dholavira."

(i) *Where is Dholavira located?*

(ii) *What is Dholavira famous for?*

(iii) *How is Dholavira different from other Harappan sites?*

Ans.

(i) Dholavira is located in the Kachchh district of Gujarat.

(ii) Dholavira is famous for its reservoirs. Dholavira has one of the world's earliest water conservation systems including a rain water harvesting system and numerous reservoirs. At least six large reservoirs were built with stones. These were connected through underground drains for efficient water harvesting and distribution.

(iii) Dholavira unlike other sites was divided into three parts—the citadal, middle and lower town. Also the foundations of most buildings were made of stones not burnt bricks.

F. Competency Based Questions

Q. 1. ***What role have geographical features played in the development of the Harappan Civilisation?***

Ans. The Harappan Civilisation developed along the banks of the Indus and the Sarasvati rivers. The river played a pivotal role. It provided water for both, domestic purposes as well as for agriculture. The annual flooding of the rivers made the soil very fertile. This led to a flourishing agriculture which paved the way for the rise of cities. Furthermore the region's location contributed to a profitable trade with countries like Mesopotamia and Oman.

Q. 2. *"Water management was crucial for the Harappan Civilisation". Explain the statement.*

Ans. An efficient management of water resources is essential for the growth of any civilisation. The Harappans were able to do this by their intricate rainwater harvesting and water storage systems. This included wells—around 700 wells have been found in Mohenjo-daro alone. It also had many reservoirs notably in Dholavira. Moreover the cities had a well-planned drainage system that prevented flooding.

Q. 3. *How do the layouts of the Harappan cities reflect their planning and organisation?*

Ans. The Harappan cities were divided into two areas the citadel and the lower town. The citadel contained the main public buildings while the lower town had residential dwellings. The roads and streets were laid out in a 'grid' pattern. The main streets intersected each other at right angles thus dividing the city into grids. Thus, it is evident that the cities layout was properly planned. Signs of planning include the grid pattern of roads, the uniformity of each city and the use of bricks which were of a standardised ratio throughout all Harappan settlements.

Q. 4. *Why was the discovery of Harappa and Mohenjo-daro regarded as significant?*

Ans. It was earlier believed that Indian history started with the Vedic period. The discovery of Mohenjo-daro and Harappa indicated that a civilisation prior to the Vedic period existed in India. Therefore, the discovery of these two cities pushed back the antiquity of Indian history by nearly 2000 years.

G. Skill Based Questions

Q. 1. *'The Harappan Civilisation offers valuable insights into their hygienic and well planned urban living system.' Elucidate.*

Ans. **Urban Planning:** Harappan cities were well planned which facilitated movement between the cities and allowed for the systematic allocation of residential, commercial and public spaces.

Drainage System: The Harappans had a very well developed and drainage system. The house drains were connected to the street drains. The drains were covered with stone slabs which could be removed to facilitate cleaning.

Water Management: They were adept at managing their water resources which is essential for sustaining urban life. Their system of well and reservoirs ensured that there was no water shortage experienced by the Harappans.

Q. 2. *Why are the main sources for a study of the Harappan Civilisation archaeological in nature?*

Ans. The main sources for an understanding of the Harappan Civilisation are the remains of their cities and the artefacts that they have left behind. All of these are archaeological in nature. This is because even though a script exists it has not been deciphered as yet. The script is largely pictographic and consists of a large number of signs and symbols. These signs probably depict words, objects or ideas but we do not know what they refer to.

Q. 3. *"The Harappan Civilisation still lives on." Analyse the statement.*

Ans. Many beliefs and practices of the Harappan Civilisation continue to be in use today. The universal Indian gesture of welcome – the namaste probably came from a terracotta figurine sitting with hands folded in a 'namaste' mode. The Harappans designed many games and toys. Toys like sliding monkeys, terracotta rattles and whistles are still used in many parts of India especially in the rural areas. Terracotta pots like the one found in Dholavira are used even today to store water. Stone weights and measures used for trading by the Harappans are used even today for weighing vegetables by shopkeepers.

Q. 4. *State two religious customs that can be traced back to the Harappan Civilisation.*

Ans. The Great Bath at Mohenjo-daro was used by the people for ritual bathing on special occasions. Many historians have felt that the practice of taking a holy dip in the River Ganges to wash away one's sins may have originated from here.

On several seals a figure is shown seated cross-legged in a yogic posture and surrounded by animals. This has been regarded as the earliest form of the God Shiva who is widely worshipped in India today.

Q. 5. *What lessons can modern India learn from cities of Harappan Civilisation?*

Ans. The ancient Harappan Civilisation offers valuable insights into hygienic and well-planned urban living. Here are some key lessons we can learn from the Harappans:

- *Urban Planning:* Harappan cities were well planned which facilitated efficient movement within the cities and allowed for the systematic allocation of residential, commercial, and public spaces.
- *Sanitation Systems:* One of the most remarkable features of Harappan cities was their sophisticated sanitation systems.
- *Water Management:* The Harappans were adept at managing water resources, essential for sustaining urban life.
- *Hygienic Practices:* Archaeological excavations have uncovered evidence of public baths highlighting the importance of personal hygiene in Harappan society. Additionally, the presence of well-built toilets in houses suggests a concern for sanitation and cleanliness at the individual household level.
- *Waste Management:* The Harappans practiced waste segregation, with different types of wastes, disposed off at designated areas.
- *Community Living:* The layout of Harappan cities suggests a strong sense of community living, with shared amenities and public spaces.

Therefore, we can learn from the Harappans' urban planning and sanitation and practice them in our modern urban development strategies.

VII. PICTURE BASED QUESTIONS

Q. 1. *Observe the given image below and answer the questions that follow :*

Fig. Housing area in Dholavira, with perpendicular streets, in the middle town (*Dholavira had three distinct zones, not two as in other cities*). Also, in this city, the foundations of most buildings were made with stones.

(a) *What does the above picture depict?*
(b) *How was Dholavira different from other Harappan cities?*
(c) *What mindset does the system of reservoirs at Dholavira reflect?*

Ans.

(a) The picture depicts a housing area in Dholavira. It shows Dholavira's middle town which had streets that intersected each other at right angles.
(b) Dholavira unlike other sites was divided into three parts— the citadel, middle town and lower town. Each part was separated by stone walls and not burnt bricks.
(c) In Dholavira large reservoirs were built with stones and connected through underground drains. This shows that they were aware about the importance of water harvesting. They also provided for an efficient water distribution system.

Q. 2. ***Observe the given image below and answer the questions that follow :***

Fig. The huge dockyard at Lothal

(a) What does the above picture depict?

(b) What activity does the picture indicate?

(c) State two main features of the Lothal dockyard.

Ans.

(a) The above picture depicts a huge dockyard situated in Lothal.

(b) The picture indicates maritime trade. Lothal's massive dockyard was responsible for a flourishing trade with other civilisations of that time namely Mesopotamia and Egypt.

(c) The dockyard was 217 meters in length and 36 metres in width. The dockyard's design shows a thorough understanding of tides. It is considered as one of the world's earliest known dockyard.

VIII. MAP SKILLS

Q. 1. ***In the given map, locate the major centers of the Harappan Civilisation.***

Ans.

1. **Harappa**
2. ____________
3. ____________
4. ____________
5. ____________
6. ____________
7. ____________
8. ____________
9. ____________
10. ____________
11. **Nageshwar**

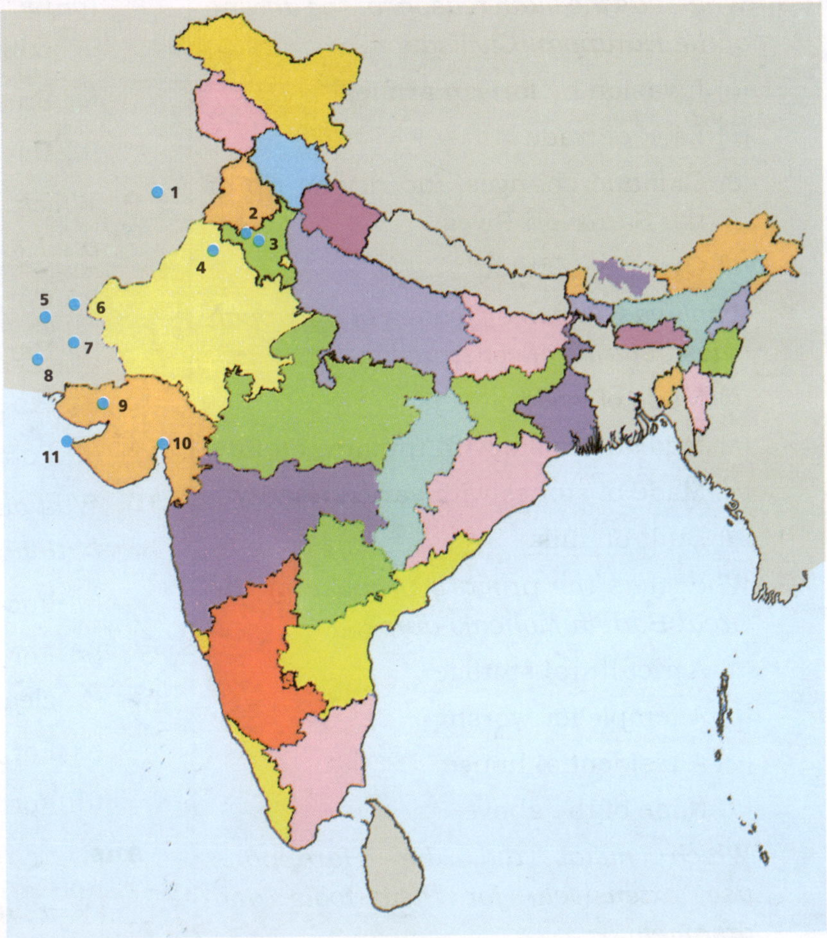

HELP BOX

Mohenjo-daro, Kalibangan, Kot Diji, Chanhundaro, Balakot, Dholavira, Nageshwar, Lothal, Harappa, Banawali, Rakhigarhi.

IX. MULTIPLE CHOICE QUESTIONS

1. *What is the main feature of a civilisation?*
   (*a*) Nomadic lifestyle
   (*b*) Absence of writing
   (*c*) Advanced urban planning
   (*d*) Lack of trade
2. *Why are the inhabitants of the Indus Valley Civilisation called 'Harappans'?*
   (*a*) They lived near the Sarasvati River
   (*b*) The city of Harappa was the first to be excavated
   (*c*) They spoke the Harappan language
   (*d*) They invented the first writing system
3. *What was the main reason for the decline of the Harappan Civilisation?*
   (*a*) Invasion by foreign armies
   (*b*) Lack of trade
   (*c*) Climatic changes and drying up of the Sarasvati River
   (*d*) Over population
4. *What was a common feature of Harappan cities in terms of construction?*
   (*a*) Made of wood
   (*b*) Made of bricks with uniform quality
   (*c*) Made of stones with varied quality
   (*d*) Built on hills
5. *What was the primary purpose of the Great Bath in Mohenjo-daro?*
   (*a*) Agricultural storage
   (*b*) A temple for worship
   (*c*) A residential house
   (*d*) None of the above
6. *Which metal did the Harappans use extensively for their tools and ornaments?*
   (*a*) Iron (*b*) Silver
   (*c*) Bronze (*d*) Platinum
7. *What does the presence of beads of carnelian in Harappan sites suggest about their society?*
   (*a*) They had advanced trade networks
   (*b*) They lacked artistic skills
   (*c*) They did not use metals
   (*d*) They were isolated from other regions
8. *What type of evidence suggests that Harappans were engaged in maritime trade?*
   (*a*) Discovery of airplanes
   (*b*) Large dockyards such as the one at Lothal
   (*c*) Presence of submarines
   (*d*) Use of paper boats
9. *Which crops were commonly grown by the Harappans?*
   (*a*) Corn and tomatoes
   (*b*) Barley and wheat
   (*c*) Pineapples and mangoes
   (*d*) Potatoes and carrots
10. *Why did Harappan cities have separate bathing areas in their homes?*
    (*a*) For religious rituals
    (*b*) For water management and cleanliness
    (*c*) For storing food
    (*d*) For keeping animals

Ans.

1. → (*c*)	2. → (*b*)	3. → (*c*)
4. → (*c*)	5. → (*d*)	6. → (*c*)
7. → (*a*)	8. → (*b*)	9. → (*b*)
10. → (*b*)		

X. OBJECTIVE TYPE QUESTIONS

A. True or False

1. *The Indus valley seals show "Swastika" symbol.*
2. *The Harappans may have imported copper in exchange of other imported materials.*
3. *People of the Indus Valley Civilisation had developed a writing system.*
4. *Harappans did not know how to make ornaments.*
5. *No weapons of offence have been discovered in Indus Valley Civilisation.*
6. *The Indus Valley Civilisation knew the use of iron.*
7. *Almost 700 wells have been found in Mohenjo-daro.*
8. *The Indus Valley Civilisation was ruled by priests as many temples have been found*

Ans.

1. → True 2. → True
3. → True 4. → False
5. → True 6. → False
7. → True 8. → False

B. Fill in the Blanks

1. *The five main tributaries of Indus river are ______, ______, ______, ______ and ______.*
2. *The mature phase of Indus Valley Civilisation (2600–1900 BCE) is known as ________.*
3. *Harappan seals have been found in ____________ Civilisation.*
4. *The Great Bath ruins of the Indus Valley Civilisation are at _____.*
5. *____________ was the first site to be discovered.*
6. *Mohenjo-daro was situated on the ____________ river.*
7. *The Sarasvati River is today known as ________ in Pakistan.*
8. *In Dholavira the foundations of most buildings were made of ________.*

Ans.

1. Jhelum, Sutlej, Beas, Ravi and Chenab.
2. Harappan Civilisation
3. Mesopotamian
4. Mohenjo-daro
5. Harappa
6. Indus
7. Hakra
8. Stone

C. Match Column A with Column B

1.

Column A		Column B	
1.	Terracotta model of plough	(*a*)	Mohenjo-daro
2.	Water reservoirs	(*b*)	Harappa
3.	Great Granary	(*c*)	Susa
4.	Great Bath	(*d*)	Banawali
5.	Carnelian beads	(*e*)	Dholavira

Ans.

1. → (*d*) 2. → (*e*) 3. → (*b*)
4. → (*a*) 5. → (*c*)

2.

Column A		Column B	
1.	Cotton	(*a*)	Gamesboard
2.	Steatite	(*b*)	Dancing girl
3.	Bronze	(*c*)	Whistle
4.	Terracotta	(*d*)	Clothes
5.	Stone	(*e*)	Seals

Ans.

1. → (*d*) 2. → (*e*) 3. → (*b*)
4. → (*c*) 5. → (*a*)

XI. TEST YOUR KNOWLEDGE

A. Multiple Choice Questions

1. *Name one site of the Indus Valley Civilisation found on the Sarasvati River.*
   (*a*) Dholavira (*b*) Lothal
   (*c*) Harappa (*d*) Ganweriwala
2. *Which of the following sites is not found in Haryana?*
   (*a*) Rakhigarhi (*b*) Bhirrana
   (*c*) Banawali (*d*) Lothal
3. *Bronze is an alloy made by mixing*
   (*a*) Copper and tin
   (*b*) Stone and copper
   (*c*) Tin and iron
   (*d*) Iron and copper
4. *The port city of the Harappan Civilisation was:*
   (*a*) Ropar (*b*) Lothal
   (*c*) Kalibangan (*d*) Dholavira
5. *On which of the following rivers was Mohenjo-daro located?*
   (*a*) Indus (*b*) Ravi
   (*c*) Chenab (*d*) Sarasvati

B. Fill in the Blanks

1. *The Great Bath was found in ________.*
2. *The ________ river is known as "Ghaggar" in India.*
3. *The ________ city is found on the Sarasvati River.*

C. True or False

1. *The Harappans knew the use of iron.*
2. *Harappan seals were made of steatite.*
3. *Harappans had a flourishing trade with Oman.*

D. Very Short Answer Type Questions

Q. 1. *Why any form of government is an important characteristic for any civilisation?*

Q. 2. *What do you understand by the term – a productive agriculture?*

Q. 3. *When did Mesopotamia saw the emergence of civilisation?*

Q. 4. *Mention the various cities of the Harappan Civilisation.*

Q. 5. *Name the first two cities where this Civilisation was discovered.*

E. Short Answer Type Questions

Q. 1. *What was the food available to the Harappan Civilisation?*

Q. 2. *Mention any four cities from the Harappan Civilisation and match these with the modern states or regions.*

Q. 3. *Write a short note on any one of the special features of Harappan cities.*

Q. 4. *Make a list of the things that were being exported by the Harappans.*

F. Long Answer Type Questions

Q. 1. *Write a short note on the major characteristics of any civilisation.*

Q. 2. *What do you know about the Sarasvati river?*

Q. 3. *How do you know that the Harappans gave a lot of importance to the water management system?*

Q. 4. *What was the purpose of the structure— the great bath?*

Q. 5. *How the Harappan Civilisation came to an end? Mention the various theories in this regard.*

G. Assertion & Reasoning Questions

There are two statements marked as Assertion (A) and Reason (R). Mark your answer as per the codes provided below:

Q. 1. Assertion (A): The Sarasvati River is now seasonal.

Reason (R): It flows only in the rainy season.

Codes:

(a) Both (A) and (R) are true but R is not the correct explanation of (A).

(b) Both (A) and (R) are true and (R) is the correct explanation of (A).

(c) (A) is true but (R) is false.

(d) (A) is false but (R) is true.

Q. 2. Assertion (A): We know that the diet of the Harappans was very diverse.

Reason (R): Harappan cooking pots contained dairy products and remains of turmeric, ginger and banana have been found.

Codes:

(a) Both (A) and (R) are true but R is not the correct explanation of (A).

(b) Both (A) and (R) are true and (R) is the correct explanation of (A).

(c) (A) is true but (R) is false.

(d) (A) is false but (R) is true.

Q. 3. Assertion (A): India's earliest civilisation is known as the Indus Valley Civilisation.

Reason (R): Several sites were found on the Indus plains.

Codes:

(a) Both (A) and (R) are true but R is not the correct explanation of (A).

(b) Both (A) and (R) are true and (R) is the correct explanation of (A).

(c) (A) is true but (R) is false.

(d) (A) is false but (R) is true.

H. Match Column A with Column B

	Column A		Column B
1.	Harappa	(a)	Terracotta replica of a plough
2.	Dholavira	(b)	Site on the Saras-vati River
3.	Rakhigarhi	(c)	Great Bath
4.	Mohenjo-daro	(d)	Divided into three parts
5.	Banawali	(e)	1st site to be discovered.

NOTES

NOTES

THEME C
OUR CULTURAL HERITAGE AND KNOWLEDGE TRADITIONS

INTERESTING MIND MAP

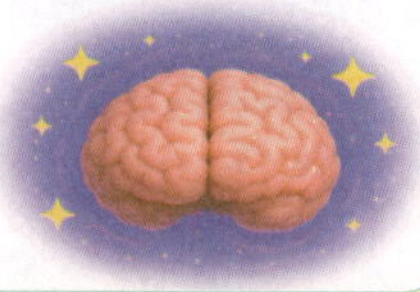

India's Cultural Roots

1 Introduction

- Indian culture: thousands of years old, compared to a tree with roots & branches.
- **Branches of Indian culture:** art, literature, science, medicine, religion, governance, martial arts.
- Schools of thought = groups of seekers/thinkers sharing ideas about life & the world.
- Roots trace back to Indus/Harappan/Sindhu-Sarasvati civilisation & shaped India's cultural identity.

2 The Vedas and Vedic Culture

2(a) What are the Vedas

- 'Veda' = Knowledge (origin from a Sanskrit word *vid*).
- **Four Vedas:** The Rig Veda, Yajur Veda, Sama Veda, and Atharva Veda.
- **Vedas** are among the world's oldest texts.
- Consist 1000 hymns (prayers in forms of songs & poems).
- Preserved orally for 100–200 generations.
- Rig Veda; oldest, composed in Sapta Sindhu (~5th–2nd millennium BCE).
- Created by *rishis* and *rishikas* in early Sanskrit.
- Consists hymns for: Indra, Agni, Varuna, Mitra, Sarasvatl, Ushas.
- Deities seen as forms of one reality – "Ekam Sat Vipra Bahudha Vadanti."
- Core values: Truth; divine & unity of people (seen in last verses of Rig Veda).

2(b) Vedic Society

- Early societies = janas/ clans (large group of people.
- Rig Veda mentions 30 janas (Bharatas, Purus, Kurus, Yadus, Turvashas).
- Each clan linked with specific region in NW India.
- Governance terms: *raja* (king), *sabha* & *samiti* (assemblies).
- **Early professions:** potter, builder, carpenter, healer, farmer, weaver etc.

2(c) Vedic Schools of Thought

- **Rituals:** Yajana (yagya) offered mainly to Agni.
- Upanishads (built upon Vedic concepts): new ideas – karma, rebirth, atman (Self).
- **Vedanta:** a school of thought reveals—brahman (divine essence) includes human & nature life + the universe.
- Stressed interconnectedness – 'Sarve Bhavantu Sukhinah' (May all beings be happy).
- Yoga & other schools arose (1st millennium BCE), seeking realisation of brahman.
- Together these concepts are foundation of Hindu philosophy.

3 Buddhism

- Founded by **Siddhartha Gautama** (Buddha), ~560 BCE, born at Lumbini (Nepal).
- At 29, he saw old age, sickness, death, ascetic → renounced palace life.
- Travelled on foot & met with several hermits and scholars.
- Attained enlightenment at Bodh Gaya (Bihar) under a pipal tree.
- **Realisation:** suffering is caused by ignorance (avidya) & attachment.
- **Teachings:** ahimsa (non-violence), truth, dharma over rituals.
- Formed **Sangha** (monastic community: monks *bhikshus*, later nuns *bhikshunis*).
- Strong influence on India & Asia.

4 Jainism

- Founded by Vardhamana (early 6th century BCE) near Vaishali (Bihar).
- Left palace life at 30, followed ascetic life for 12 yrs. and attained infinite knowledge.
- Titled as 'Mahavira'.
- **Core teachings:** ahimsa (non-violence), anekantavada (truth has many sides) & aparrigraha (detachment from material possessions).
- All lives are interdependent.
- Monks and nuns spread teachings via monasteries & cave dwellings.
- Other schools of thought: 'Charvaka'; preached-no life after death.
- **Common beliefs:** dharma, karma, rebirth, ending ignorance/suffering, moral life.

5 Folk and Tribal Roots

- **Rich oral traditions:** folks (by common people) & tribal traditions (clans/tribes).
- **Tribe:** families/clans with shared descent, culture, language, usually led by a chief.
- No private property; called janas in ancient times.
- Folk & tribal traditions mixed with Hinduism;

  Jagannath (Puri, Odisha)—originally a tribal God.

  Tribal versions of the Mahabharata & Ramayana.
- Worshiping nature was common—trees, plants, rivers, mountains & stones considered sacred.
- **Ex.** For Todas (Nilgiris of Tamil Nadu) 30+ mountain peaks, adobes of gods.

  Arunachal tribes worship Donyipolo (the Sun & the Moon).

  Munda & Santhal worship Singbonga (Creator).
- **Sociologist Andre Beteille:** constant two-way influence between Hinduism & tribal faiths.
- **Folk & tribal traditions:** major contributors to Indian cultural heritage.

THEME C
Our Cultural Heritage and Knowledge Traditions

CHAPTER
7

INDIA'S CULTURAL ROOTS

I. FACTS TO REMEMBER/SUMMARY

INTRODUCTION

- Indian culture is one of the oldest in the world and is considered several millennia old.
- It has several branches such as art, science, literature, medicine, religion, governance, martial arts and many more.

- Many archaeologists and scholars have described about the traditions and the cultural roots which follow the Harappan Civilisation.
- The Vedas, India's earliest texts gave rise to several schools of thought. Vedanta and Yoga are among the best known.

THE VEDAS AND VEDIC CULTURE

- The word 'Veda' is derived from Sanskrit word 'vid', which means knowledge.
- Indian culture traces its roots to the Vedas.

What are the Vedas?

- There are four Vedas: the Rig Veda, the Yajur Veda, the Sama Veda and the Atharva Veda.

- The Vedas depict the songs, lyrics, poems and hymns that the people of that era recited orally.
- The Vedic hymns were composed by Rishis and Rishikas in Sanskrit language.
- They were dedicated to many deities (Gods and Goddesses).

Vedic Society

- The Vedas give us clues through the words like King, Ruler, Dynasty, Sabha etc.
- The Upanishads introduced the concept of atman or self — the divine essence that lives in every human soul but is ultimately the one with the brahman.

Vedic Schools of Thought

- Vedic culture developed many rituals like Yajna and daily prayers.
- Upanishads built upon Vedic concepts introduced new ideas such as rebirth and karma.
- One school of thought, known as vedanta, has the concepts of Brahman and Atman.

Buddhism

- Buddhism, another school of thought did not accept the authority of the Vedas and developed it own system.

- The Buddha started teaching what he realised that inner discipline and non-violence someone leads a peaceful way of life.

Jainism

- Jainism which is said to be more ancient also did not accept the authority of the Vedas.
- Jain teachings include ahimsa, anekantavada and aparigraha.
- Although these schools had different principles and followed different methods, they shared some common goals.

- They also shared some important concepts, as they sought the cause of suffering and the means to eliminate ignorance.

FOLK AND TRIBAL ROOTS

- Tribal belief system had also influenced the society.
- Tribal belief systems regard the land and its features as sacred and have a profound concept of divinity.

II. TEXTBOOK KEYWORDS/GLOSSARY

1. **Anekantavada:** It means not only one aspect or only one perspective. Truth has many aspects and it cannot be explained in a single statement.
2. **Aparigraha:** When someone is advised to detach from materialistic things. Limiting to those things only which are necessary in life.
3. **Archaeology:** The study of human history and pre-history through the excavation of sites and the analysis of artifacts and other physical remains.
4. **Ascetic:** Someone who engages in a rigorous discipline to attain a higher consciousness.
5. **Attachment:** The condition of having a bond with someone or something, usually through sentiment or habit.
6. **Consciousness:** The quality or state of being aware, for instance of something within oneself.
7. **Cosmos:** The world or the universe as an ordered and harmonious system.
8. **Healer:** Someone who uses traditional practices to relieve or heal diseases.
9. **Monk:** A man who, giving up the usual life in the world, dedicates himself to religious or spiritual pursuits. A monk usually takes vows, that is, commits himself to follow strict rules for a disciplined life.
10. **Nun:** The female equivalent of a monk.
11. **Seeker:** Someone who seeks the truths of this world. This could be a sage, a saint, a yogi, a philosopher, etc.
12. **Spiritual:** Concerned with the spirit or soul (*ātman* in Sanskrit and many Indian languages). Spirituality is the search for a deeper or higher dimension beyond our current personality.
13. **Tribes:** A social division in a traditional society consisting of a group of families or clan.
14. **UNESCO:** UNESCO stands for 'United Nations Educational, Scientific and Cultural Organisation'. It promotes dialogue between people and nations through education, science and culture.
15. **Vedas:** The Vedas are a collection of sacred religious texts in Sanskrit, originating in ancient India, and forming the foundation of Hinduism. They were composed during 1500 and 500 BCE.
16. **Worldview:** A certain view or understanding of the world, its origin, or its workings.

III. DATE LINE

- **2500 years ago:** Our civilisation began with Harappan Culture.
- **1500 B.C.:** The Migration of Aryans to India.
- **486 and 468 B.C.:** Rise of Buddhism and Jainism.
- **326 B.C.:** The Invasion of Alexander the Great.

IV. THE BIG QUESTIONS (*Page 105*)

Q. 1. ***What are the Vedas? What is their message?***

Ans. The Vedas are a collection of sacred religious texts in Sanskrit, originating in ancient India, and forming the foundation of Hinduism.

They were composed during 1500 and 500 BCE and are among the most ancient texts in the world.

There are four Vedas: The Rig Veda, the Yajur Veda, the Sama Veda and the Atharva Veda.

The Rig Veda contains the hymns about the mythology.

The Yajur Veda contains the instructions for religious rituals.

The Sama Veda contains mainly the hymns about the religious rituals.

The Atharva Veda contains spells for protection against enemies and diseases.

The main purpose of the divine knowledge contained in the Vedas is to instruct human beings to live a truthful meaningful, progressive, happy and righteous life in the material world and also to plan for the future and final goal of the life.

Q. 2. ***What new schools of thought emerged in India in the 1st millennium BCE? What are their core principles?***

Ans. During the early 1st millennium several new schools of thought emerged from Vedas.

Yoga was one of them which developed methods to achieve one's consciousness.

Vedanta was another school of thought which evolved through Upanishads. Upanishads were group of texts which were built upon Vedic concepts like rebirth and karma.

Vedanta principles hold that everything including human life, nature and the universe is part of one divine essence called Brahman, the supreme existence.

Together these thoughts laid the foundation of Hinduism.

Other schools of thought that emerged and didn't accept Vedas authority were Buddhism, Jainism and Charvaka School.

Their core principle was that God is one, we are the ones giving different names to Him.

The core principles of Buddhism is the idea of ahimsa, which is generally translated as non-violence meaning not causing injury. It also teaches sincere inner discipline.

The core principles of Jain teachings include ahimsa, anekantavada and aparigraha. These ideas, shared to a large extent with Buddhism and the Vedantic school of thought that are central to Indian culture.

The core principles of Charvaka School of thought was that there was no life after death. Charvaka School disappeared with time as its principles could not become popular.

Q. 3. ***What is the contribution of folk and tribal traditions to Indian culture?***

Ans. The folk and tribal traditions provide an invaluable window into the rich heritage of Indian culture.

Many tribes in ancient Bharat believed in the sacredness of natural elements such as rivers, mountains, trees, plants, animals and even stones. This belief stemmed from their understanding that there is a consciousness behind all things.

This belief was also found in Hinduism and continues to this day. Similarly, many tribes worshipped the same deity as others such as Lord Jagannath. Some tribes had their own versions of Hindu epics like the Mahabharata and Ramayana.

All these tribal beliefs along with their folk and cultural traditions merged with Hindu traditions to shape the roots of Indian culture.

V. NCERT INTEXT/TEXTBOOK EXERCISES

Let's Explore

Q. 1. ***Do you know the term for a society where people select their leaders? How do you think people can benefit from such a situation? What could happen if they live under leaders that they did not choose?*** **(Hint: Think back to what you're learning in the theme 'Governance and Democracy'!)** ***Write your thoughts in a paragraph of 100–150 words.***

(Page 109)

Ans.

- As we know throughout the history, one can find evidence of direct democracy in which communities make decisions through popular assembly.
- Today, the dominant form of democracy is a representative democracy, where citizens elect government to govern on their behalf such as Parliamentary or Presidential democracy.

(*i*) **Representation:** People feel that their voices are heard by the leaders they have chosen.

(*ii*) **Accountability:** Elected leaders are accountable to the people who voted for them, which can lead to better government responsiveness to the needs of the population.

(*iii*) **Participation:** Democratic processes encourage civic engagement and participation in decision making leading a more active and informed citizens. Overall, choosing leaders through democratic means can promote equality in the society where the interests of the people are at the forefront of governance.

If they live under leaders that they did not choose. In such case their life could have become quiet worst. They will not be able to lead a comfortable life.

If the leader chosen is without the consent of the people, that is without the democratic process, it is autocratic or a dictatorship.

Kings were known as autocrat, where only family of the king ruled the territory under them. In history, many kings ruled with good governance.

Another example is of Britishers who ruled Indian sub-continent for over two centuries as dictators. Under their rule, Indians were suppressed and looted a lot, thus changing a developed Indian nation, known as Golden Bird (Sone ki Chidiya) into underdeveloped country with severe poverty.

Q. 2. (*a*) ***Discuss the way the Buddha is depicted in the below panel.***

(*b*) ***Can you name some states of India or some other countries where Buddhism is a major religion even today? Try to plot these on a world map.*** (*Page 115*)

Ans. (*a*) This stone panel, which is around 1800 years old, depicts Buddha, teaching his disciples.

His main teachings included non-violence and sincere inner discipline.

(*b*) Buddhism is a major religion of several states in India such as Arunachal Pradesh, Mizoram, Nagaland, Sikkim, Maharashtra, Tripura and Ladakh (a Union Territory).

Buddhism is the official religion of four countries i.e., Bhutan, Cambodia, Myanmar, and Sri Lanka. The religion also holds a special status in two countries, Thailand and Laos.

Buddhism is also followed in China, Japan, Hong Kong and Mongolia.

Map Work: Do it yourself.

Q. 3. ***Observe the below panel (from a Jain temple in New Delhi). What is striking about it? What messages does it carry?*** (*Page 118*)

Ans. The panel depicts a lion and a cow drinking water together from the same vessel. This is striking because they are natural enemies, and yet they are shown co-existing in harmony.

The panel shows that even natural enemies can live together peacefully if they are treated with compassion and respect.

Think About it

Q. 1. ***Have you heard or read any other story that conveyed an important message? What value did it teach you?*** *(Page 110)*

Ans.

- There are many stories and narratives throughout history that have conveyed important messages.
- Yes, I read an interesting story from Panchatantra of, "The Mouse and the Elephant".

  This story taught me that even a small creature like mouse could make a big impact on life of an elephant.

  Similarly, I also read another story from Panchatantra tilted, "The Rabbit and the Lion".

  Moral of this story is that knowledge is more powerful than strength.

  Hence, few stories which I have read have taught me good moral values in life.

NCERT Questions, Activities and Projects
(Page 123)

Q. 1. ***If you were Nachiketa, what questions would you like to ask Yama? Write them down in 100-150 words.***

Ans. I would like to ask Yama, the god of death, following questions, if I was Nachiketa:

(i) What happens after the death of a body?

(ii) What is soul?

(iii) What happens to the soul after death?

(iv) Does the soul also die with the body, if not, where does it go ?

(v) Does the soul take rebirth in the form of another body ?

Q. 2. ***Explain a few central ideas of Buddhism. Briefly comment upon them.***

Ans. Buddhism was started by Siddhartha Gautam (Gautam Buddha). It evolved during 500 BCE and did not accept the concepts and principles of the Vedas.

Buddhism believed that ignorance and attachment are the source of human sufferings. Its teachings sought to remove these two causes of sufferings.

Buddhism preached non-violence and sincere inner discipline to reduce human sufferings.

Q. 3. ***Discuss in class the quotation of the Buddha which begins with "Not by water is one made pure, though many people may bathe here [in sacred rivers]" to make sure that its meaning has been understood by all.***

Ans. Main point of discussion in classroom:

By this quotation Gautam Buddha means that one can not be pure just by having a bath in any sacred river like the Ganges.

One can become pure by following the path of non-violence, inner discipline and by conquering one's inner mind. One can conquer the mind through meditation.

Q. 4. ***Explain a few central ideas of Jainism. Briefly comment upon them.***

Ans. Jainism teaches that the path to enlightenment is through non-violence and not harming living beings (including plants and animals) as far as possible.

- Like Hindus and Buddhists, Jains believe in reincarnation.
- The cycle of birth, death and rebirth is determined by one's karma.
- Jains believe bad karma is caused by harming living beings. To avoid bad karma, one must practice ahimsa, a strict code of non-violence.
- The principle of non-violence includes causing no harm to humans, plants, animals etc.

Q. 5. ***Consider and discuss in class André Béteille's thought (see page 122).***

Ans. André Béteille's is an Indian sociologist.

As per his thoughts, since ancient times, thousands of castes and tribes had great influence on the religious beliefs of Hinduism.

Each tribe follows their own religion influenced by Hinduism. Similarly, as per his views, Hinduism as a religion was also influenced by tribal religions, customs and traditions.

Finally, we could decipher from his views that Hinduism as a religion evolved through believes, customs and traditions of different castes and tribes of ancient India.

Q. 6. ***Make a list of popular gods and goddesses in your region and the festivals they are associated with.***

Ans. Here is a list of popular gods and goddesses with festivals associated with them:

(i) **Lord Rama:** Diwali is celebrated worldwide as on this day Lord Rama returned to Ayodhya after killing the Demon Ravana.

(ii) **Lord Ganesh:** Ganesh Chaturthi is celebrated on his birth anniversary.

(iii) **Lord Shiva:** Shivaratri is celebrated on his birth anniversary.

(iv) **Lord Krishna:** Janmashtami is celebrated on his birth anniversary.

(v) **Goddess Durga:** The deity of strength and motherhood. Durga Pooja festival celebrates the victory of goddess Durga over the demon king Mahishasura.

(vi) **Goddess Laxmi:** The deity of wealth and prosperity is worshipped on Diwali.

(vii) **Lord Hanuman:** Also called 'Bajrang Bali', his birthday is celebrated on 'Hanuman Jayanti'.

Similarly, students can make a list of their regional gods, goddesses and festivals associated with them.

Q. 7. ***As a class activity, list two or three tribal groups from your region or State. Document some of their art and belief systems.***

Ans. Gonds, Bhils, Santhals, Mundas and the Great Andamanese Tribes.

1. The Great Andamanese Tribes are an indigenous people of the Great Andaman Archipelago in the Andaman Islands.

All living things are believed to be endowed with power that affect human beings. The art form depicts culture and tradition.

2. Bhil art is known for its simplicity and use of vibrant colours. The art form is practised on the walls, floors, and clothes.

Similarly, students could give details of tribal groups from their region.

True or False

1. *The Vedic hymns were written on palm-leaf manuscripts.*

2. *The Vedas are India's oldest texts.*

3. *The Vedic statement ekam sat viprā bahudhā vadanti reflects a belief in the unity of cosmic powers.*

4. *Buddhism is older than the Vedas.*

5. *Jainism emerged as a branch of Buddhism.*

6. *Both Buddhism and Jainism advocated for peaceful coexistence and the avoidance of harm to all living beings.*

7. *Tribal belief systems are limited to belief in spirits and minor deities.*

Answers

1. True **2.** True **3.** True **4.** False
5. False **6.** True **7.** False

Class Activity

Q. 1. ***Stage a small play with Yama, god of death, surrounded by several Nachiketas asking him questions about life.***

Ans. Under the guideline of the teacher students will be selected in the class to play the role of different characters.

VI. EXAM ORIENTED QUESTIONS

A. Very Short Answer Type Questions

Q. 1. ***Who founded the Sangha, a community of bhikshus?***

Ans. Sangha, was founded by Gautam Buddha.

Q. 2. ***Who was Rohineya?***

Ans. Rohineya was extra ordinarily skilled burglar during the time of Mahavira, founder of Jainism. He evaded all attempts by others to arrest him.

Later, he confessed all his crimes before Mahavira, returned all the stolen treasures, seeked forgiveness and became a monk.

Q. 3. ***What was the thought of Charvaka School?***

Ans. Charvaka school believed that this material world is the only thing that exists and therefore there can be no life after death.

Q. 4. ***Name one tribal deity.***

Ans. Lord Jagannath.

Q. 5. ***Name two holy books of Hindus.***

Ans. The Mahabharata and the Ramayana.

Q. 6. ***Who wrote Vedas?***

Ans. Veda Vyasa.

B. Short Answer Type Questions

Q. 1. ***Write short notes on India's culture.***

Ans. India's culture is known as the oldest and a very interesting culture in the world.

Citizens of this country belong to different religions, traditions, cultures etc.

Q. 2. ***What is the contribution of folk and tribal traditions to Indian culture?***

Ans.

- Folk and tribal traditions provide a window into the rich heritage of these communities.
- They reflect the beliefs, values and the aspirations of tribal cultures.
- They also tell about the world view and the way of life.

Q. 3. ***What does the term Upanishads mean? What were their two main concepts?***

Ans. The term 'Upanishads' means sitting close to the guru to receive instructions. The Upanishads stressed on two main concepts, Brahman and Atman. The Atman (soul) gains moksha by uniting with the Brahman. To gain moksha one has to have proper knowledge and right belief.

Q. 4. ***How was Vedic society organised? How were they governed?***

Ans. Early Vedic society was organised into different janas or 'clans'. Over 30 janas are listed in the Rig Veda. Examples include the Bharatas, Purus, Kurus etc. Each clan was associated with a particular region of the North West part of India.

The janas were probably ruled by a raja whose function was to protect the Jana from enemies. He was helped in this task by tribal assemblies like the sabha and samiti. The Sabha consisted of a council of select clan members while the Samiti comprised the whole clan.

Q. 5. ***Who composed the Vedic hymns? Who were they addressed to?***

Ans. The Vedic hymns were composed by rishis (male sages) and rishikas (female sages) in Sanskrit. They were sung in poetic forms and addressed to many deities. These deities included gods and goddesses like Indra, Varuna, Saraswati and Agni to name a few. These deities generally symbolised the various forces of nature. For example, Indra was the god of rain and Agni was the god of fire. Furthermore it was believed that all these gods and goddesses were one, not separate entities. Essentially emphasis was on the worship of one god though worshipped in various ways.

C. Long Answer Type Questions

Q. 1. *What were the similarities that existed between Folk, Tribal and Hindu beliefs?*

Ans. Folk, tribal and Hindu beliefs systems have interacted with each other because they share many similar concepts. In all three elements of nature such as mountains, trees, rivers, animals and even some stones are regarded as sacred.

Tribes worship many deities associated with these natural elements. For example, the Toda tribe of the Nilgiris in Tamil Nadu consider the peaks of this mountain range as the residences of gods or goddesses. These peaks are considered sacred to them that they avoid pointing with their fingers towards them.

Many tribes in Hinduism believe in the concept of a highest divinity or a supreme being despite the presence of multiple deities. For example, several tribes of Arunachal Pradesh worship Donyipolo, a combined form of the Sun and the Moon as their Supreme God.

In parts of Central India, the god Khandoba has a similar status. In eastern India, the Munda and Santhal tribes worship Singbonga as their supreme deity responsible for the creation of the universe.

Q. 2. *"There are many definitions for the word 'tribes'." Explain this statement.*

Ans. Anthropologists today consider a tribe to be a group of families sharing a common descent, a common culture and a common language. They live in close knit communities under a chief and hold no private property.

In Ancient India tribes were regarded as simply Janas (groups of people) who lived in forests and mountains.

The Constitution of India uses the 'tribes' and 'tribal communities in English and 'janjati' in Hindi.

In 2011 according to official figures India has 705 tribes across the country amounting to a population of 104 million people. Earlier anthropologists regarded tribes as 'primitive' or 'inferior.' Nowadays such biased judgements have been abandoned. Recent studies have in fact highlighted their rich and complex cultures.

Q. 3. *Explain the main teachings of Buddhism.*

Ans. Buddhism believes in social equality and rejects the authority of the Vedas. It is against animal sacrifices and expensive rituals being performed in the name of religion. It believes that ignorance (avidya) and attachment to worldly desires are the main sources of human sufferings. A disciplined life and meditation are essential to remove the causes of human sufferings. It believes in following a middle path and rejects both extreme luxury and extreme asceticism. Central to its teachings is the stress. It places on Ahimsa or non-violence. It advocates kindness and compassion towards all living beings as a means to reduce sufferings. It believes in the theory of Karma and rebirth. Its aim is for individuals to attain moksha or freedom from the cycle of birth and rebirth.

Q. 4. *Explain the main teachings of Jainism.*

Ans. Jainism believes in social equality and like Buddhism rejects the authority of the Vedas. It believes in the concept of Karma (as you sow, so shall you reap) and rebirth. The main goal of life is to attain moksha (freedom from the cycle of birth and rebirth). The three cardinal principles of Jainism are Ahimsa, Anekantavada and Aparigraha. Jainism believes that everything possesses life. One should avoid causing harm to any living being. Anekantavada means that truth has many aspects. No single perspective can capture the whole truth and different viewpoints should be considered. Aparigraha advocates detachment from material things and limiting one's needs to only what is necessary. Unlike Buddhism which believes in the middle path, Jainism believes in extreme asceticism. It believes that moksha can be achieved through performing austerities based on self-denial, penance and meditation.

D. Assertion and Reasoning Questions

There are two statements Assertion (A) and Reason (R). Mark your answers as per the code given below.

1. **Assertion (A):** Jainism was an easier religion to follow while Buddhism was a more difficult religion to follow.

   Reason (R): Jainism therefore spread to various parts of S.E. Asia while Buddhism was confined to India.

   Codes:

   (*a*) Both (A) and (R) are true but (R) is not the correct explanation of (A).

   (*b*) Both (A) and (R) are true and (R) is the correct explanation of (A).

   (*c*) (A) is true but (R) is false.

   (*d*) Both (A) and (R) are false.

2. **Assertion (A):** Deities, concepts and rituals were freely exchanged in both directions between tribal and Hindu traditions.

   Reason (R): Jagannath worshipped at Puri was originally a tribal deity.

   Codes:

   (*a*) Both (A) and (R) are true but (R) is not the correct explanation of (A).

   (*b*) Both (A) and (R) are true and (R) is the correct explanation of (A).

   (*c*) (A) is true but (R) is false.

   (*d*) Both (A) and (R) are false.

3. **Assertion (A):** The Upanishads consisted of dialogues and debates between the teacher and the student.

   Reason (R): The Upanishads mention the various rituals which are to be followed.

   Codes:

   (*a*) Both (A) and (R) are true but (R) is not the correct explanation of (A).

   (*b*) Both (A) and (R) are true and (R) is the correct explanation of (A).

   (*c*) (A) is true but (R) is false.

   (*d*) Both (A) and (R) are false.

4. **Assertion (A):** Like Hinduism many tribal groups believe in the concept of a supreme being.

   Reason (R): In eastern India the Santhal and Munda tribes worship Singbonga as the supreme deity.

   Codes:

   (*a*) Both (A) and (R) are true but (R) is not the correct explanation of (A).

   (*b*) Both (A) and (R) are true and (R) is the correct explanation of (A).

   (*c*) (A) is true but (R) is false.

   (*d*) Both (A) and (R) are false.

Ans.

1. → (*d*) **2.** → (*b*) **3.** → (*c*)
4. → (*a*)

E. Case/Source Based Questions

Read the passages given and answer the questions that follow.

I. How have such interactions taken place for so long and so naturally? It is, in the end, because folk, tribal and Hindu belief systems have many similar concepts. For instance, in all three, elements of nature such as mountains, rivers, trees, plants and animals, and some stones too, are regarded as sacred, because there is consciousness behind all of them. Indeed, tribes generally worship many deities associated with those natural elements. For the Toda tribals of the Nilgiris of Tamil Nadu, for instance (one of them is pictured in the image on the right), over thirty peaks of this mountain range are residences of a god or a goddess; those peaks are so sacred that the Todas avoid pointing to them with a finger.

(a) ***Why did interactions take place for so long and naturally?***

(b) ***Mention one concept which is common to all three belief systems.***

(c) ***Which tribe worships the mountain peaks of the nilgiri mountains?***

Ans (*a*) This was because all the three-folk, tribal and Hindu belief systems have many concepts in common.

(*b*) In all three belief systems, the elements of nature like mountains, rivers, trees, plants and animals are regarded as sacred and worshipped.

(*c*) The Toda tribals living in the Nilgiri mountains in Tamil Nadu regarded 30 peaks of Nilgiris as sacred. They even avoid pointing a finger towards them.

II. **A Jain story:** Rohineya was an extraordinarily skilled burglar who evaded all attempts to catch him. On his way to a city, he accidentally heard a few sentences from a sermon that Mahāvīra was giving about achieving liberation from the ordinary life of ignorance. Reaching the city, Rohineya was recognised and arrested. He pretended to be a simple farmer. A minister devised a clever plan to force him to confess his identity. But Rohineya, remembering Mahāvīra's words, was able to detect the minister's plan and defeat it.

Feeling remorseful, Rohineya approached Mahāvīra, confessed his crimes, returned the stolen treasures, and asked for forgiveness. He became a monk, realised the illusion he was living in and focused on acquiring higher knowledge.

The story illustrates the importance of right action and right thinking, and also illustrates the fact that everyone should have a second chance.

(a) ***Who was Rohineya?***

(b) ***Why did he return the stolen treasure?***

(c) ***What does this story teach us?***

Ans (*a*) Rohineya was a skilled burglar who could not be caught.

(*b*) He returned the stolen treasure because he was influenced by Mahavira's teachings. He realised the illusion he was living in and focused on acquiring higher knowledge.

(*c*) The story teaches us that right action and right thinking is very important. It also emphasises the fact that everyone deserves a second chance.

III. Once, a man was giving away all his possessions in a ritual. As his son Nachiketa kept asking him which god he would be offered to, the father became angry and answered, "I give you to Yama" — that is, to the god of death. Nachiketa, then, proceeded to Yama's world and, after a long wait, met the mighty god. One question was on his mind — "What happens after the death of the body?" Yama tried to avoid answering, but the boy persisted. Pleased, Yama explained that the ātman, or self, is hidden within all creatures. It is neither born, nor does it die; it is immortal. Having acquired this profound knowledge, Nachiketa returned to his father, who welcomed him joyfully.

(a) ***Who was Nachiketa given to?***

(b) ***What did he ask Yama?***

(c) ***What was Yama's reply?***

Ans (*a*) Nachiketa was given to Yama who is the god of death.

(*b*) He asked Yama what happens after the body dies.

(*c*) Yama told him that inside all of us is the atman or soul. The soul never dies. It is immortal. So when a person dies it is only his physical body that dies, the soul still lives on.

IV. As the story goes, then, Siddhārtha Gautama grew up living a protected life in the palace. One day, at the age of 29, he asked to be driven through the city in a chariot, and for the first time in his life came across an old man, a sick man, and a dead body. He also saw an ascetic, who appeared to be happy and at peace. Following this experience, Siddhārtha decided to give up his palace life, leaving behind his wife and son. Travelling on foot as an ascetic, meeting other ascetics and scholars, he searched for the root cause of suffering in human life. After meditating for many days under a pipal tree at Bodh Gaya (today in Bihar), he attained enlightenment; he realised that avidyā (ignorance) and attachment are the source of human sufferings and conceived a method to remove these two causes.

(a) *What were the four sights that Buddha saw?*

(b) *Where did he gain enlightenment?*

(c) *What did he seek to discover?*

Ans (*a*) When Buddha was driving through the city with his charioteer he saw four sights. He saw an old man, a sick man, a dead body and finally an ascetic. He realised only the ascetic was happy and appeared to be at peace. He therefore gave up his luxurious lifestyle and became an ascetic.

(*b*) He attained enlightenment under a pipal tree at Bodh Gaya. This was after meditating for many days.

(*c*) Buddha wanted to discover the main cause of human sufferings. After attaining enlightenment he realised that avidya (ignorance) and attachment are the causes for human sufferings. He sought to conceive a method to overcome these causes.

F. Competency Based Questions

Q. 1. *How is Buddhism different from the Vedic Religion?*

Ans. Buddhism is a simple religion that does not believe in expensive rituals and sacrifices. It does not believe in Brahmanical supremacy and rejects the caste system. The Vedic texts were written in Sanskrit, a language the common people could not understand whereas, Buddha preached and wrote in Pali, the language of the common man, thus making his teachings easier to follow. Unlike the Vedic religion, which believes in the caste system, Buddhism believes in social equality. The Vedic religion believes in idol worship, rituals and animal sacrifices. Buddhism believes in personal spiritual awakening and is against rituals and animal sacrifice. Ahimsa (*Non-violence*) is one of the cardinal principles of Buddhism.

Q. 2. *What are the main similarities between Buddhism and Jainism?*

Ans. Both Jainism and Buddhism have much in common. Both are simple religions. They do not believe in vedic rituals, animal sacrifices or in expensive rituals. They both believe in social equality and admit people from even the lower castes and women into the Sangha.

Both Buddha and Mahavira preached in the language of the common man, making their teachings easier to follow. Both developed the Sangha or a monastic order which played a major role in spreading these two religions. Finally, both believe in Karma, rebirth and moksha. They believe that the main goal of life is to attain moksha, or freedom from the cycle of birth and rebirth.

Q. 3. *What are the key differences between Buddhism and Jainism?*

Ans. Both Buddhism and Jainism believe in Ahimsa (non-violence) with regard to all living beings–humans and animals. But Jainism takes this principle to an extreme by believing that even all non-living beings have life and should not be hurt.

Buddhism believes in following a middle path, rejecting both extreme luxury and extreme asceticism. But Jainism believes in extreme penance and austerity. To die of starvation is considered a virtue.

Buddhism spreaded beyond India to many countries of S.E. Asia, while Jainism remained confined to certain areas in India itself.

Q. 4. ***What does the term Ahimsa actually mean in Jainism and Buddhism?***

Ans. Ahimsa actually means non-violence. It's cardinal principle is to abstain from physical violence against humans and animals. But in Jainism and Buddhism it also means refraining from violence even in thoughts. That means one should not harbour anger or hatred towards anyone. If any negative thoughts regarding anyone enter our mind we must learn to turn them into positive thoughts. Negative thoughts directed even towards ourselves should be changed into positive thoughts.

G. Skill Based Questions

Q. 1. ***Why is Buddhism still relevant today?***

Ans. Buddhism has taught people how to meditate and improve one's mental and physical health. This helped them to cope with the stress one encounters in daily life. The guiding principles of Buddhism are to respect all life forms and maintain balance and peace in nature. Thus, it encourages social and environmental responsibilities in this age of rapid climatic changes due to environmental degradation the teachings of Buddhism hold great value for us.

Buddha stressed on compassion, peace and non-violence. It is of great relevance in today's world to combat terrorism and end strife among nations.

Q. 2. ***What steps did Buddhism and Jainism took to spread their teachings?***

Ans. Both taught in the language of the people so that the common man could understand and implement their teachings. Moreover, both developed the Sangha or a monastic order which was open to both men and women of all castes. The monks and nuns travelled across the land to spread their respective teachings. Some of them stayed in monasteries while others lived an ascetic life in rock cut caves.

Q. 3. ***State the main traditions, beliefs and way of life of any tribal group in India.***

Ans. The Bhil tribes are generally found in western India including parts of Rajasthan, Madhya Pradesh and also in parts of West Bengal and Tripura.

Their lifestyle is centered on agriculture and is influenced by their culture and lifestyle. They are known for their archery and are skilled sculptures. The Bhils love dancing and music. The Bhils of Gujarat are famous for their Garba dance– a very popular dance form of Gujarat today. In fact the Garba dance is very popular all over India especially during the Navratras, a traditional Hindu festival. This shows the intermingling of tribal and non-tribal groups that have influenced Indian traditions today.

H. Picture Based Questions

I. *Look at the picture given above. Answer the questions that follow.*

(*a*) ***What does the picture depict?***

(*b*) ***Why were rishis so important in the Vedic Period?***

(*c*) ***Who were these hymns dedicated to?***

Ans (*a*) The picture depicts a rishi sitting in meditation. The venue is Hampi in Karnataka.

(*b*) The rishi or male sages were important because they were responsible for composing the Vedic hymns in Sanskrit.

(*c*) These hymns were written in poetic form. They were dedicated to many deities (gods/goddesses) such as Indra, Agni, Mitra, Saraswati and many more.

II. *Look at the pictures, identify them and answer the questions in Column-I and Column-II given below:*

Column-I		Column-II	

1.	Identify and name the person.	1.	Identify and name the person.
2.	When and where was he born?	2.	When and where was he born?
3.	Which religion was founded by him?	3.	Which religion did he preach?
4.	Where did he attain Enlightenment?	4.	Where did he attain Nirvana?
5.	What were his main teachings?	5.	What were his main teachings?

Ans.

Column-I		Column-II	
1.	Gautama Buddha	1.	Vardhamana Mahavira
2.	560 BCE in Lumbini, Nepal	2.	Earlier 6th century BCE in Vaishali, Bihar
3.	Buddhism	3.	Jainism
4.	Bodh Gaya, Bihar	4.	Pawapuri, Bihar
5.	Main teachings of Gautama Buddha were non-violence and inner discipline.	5.	Main teachings of Lord Mahavira were Ahimsa, Anekantavada and Aparigraha.

VII. MULTIPLE CHOICE QUESTIONS

1. ***The vedic hymns were composed by***

(*a*) Saints
(*b*) Rishis and Rishikas
(*c*) Gods
(*d*) None of these.

2. ***Early vedic society was organised in different ______.***

(*a*) Groups
(*b*) Janas or Clans
(*c*) Sub continent
(*d*) None of these.

3. ***Many professions are mentioned in the vedic texts such as***

(*a*) Builder
(*b*) Carpenter
(*c*) Agriculturist
(*d*) All of the above

4. ***_____were built upon vedic concepts and introduced new ones.***

(*a*) Brahman
(*b*) Upanishads
(*c*) Nature
(*d*) None of these

5. ***_____ was born in Lumbini.***

(*a*) Chhandogya Upanishad
(*b*) Siddhartha Gautama
(*c*) Lord Mahavira
(*d*) None of these

6. ***Prince Vardhamana was born into a royal family in the early _____ century B.C.E.***

(*a*) 5th century (*b*) 6th century
(*c*) 7th century (*d*) 8th century

Answers:

1. (*b*) 2. (*b*) 3. (*d*)
4. (*b*) 5. (*b*) 6. (*b*)

VIII. OBJECTIVE TYPE QUESTIONS

Q.1. ***Fill in the blanks with appropriate words.***

(*i*) _______________ gave rise to many schools of thought.
(*ii*) The story of Shvetaketu is to be found in the _______________ Upanishad.
(*iii*) ___________ was originally a tribal deity.
(*iv*) The Munda and Santhal tribes worship ______________________.
(*v*) ________ was an Indian sociologist.

Ans.

(*i*) Vedas (*ii*) Chhandogya
(*iii*) Jagannath (*iv*) Singbonga
(*v*) Andre Beteille

Q.2. ***State whether the given statements are true or false.***

(*i*) The Rigveda was written in Sanskrit.
(*ii*) Jainism emerged as a branch of Hinduism.
(*iii*) Jainism is older than the Vedas.
(*iv*) The story of Nachiketa and his quest is mentioned in Katha Upanishad.
(*v*) Mahavira was born in Vaishali.

Ans.

(*i*) True (*ii*) False
(*iii*) False (*iv*) True
(*v*) True

IX. TEST YOUR KNOWLEDGE

A. Multiple Choice Questions

1. ***Each .... was associated with a particular region of the northwest part of the sub-continent.***
   (*a*) part (*b*) section
   (*c*) clan (*d*) sub-section
2. ***A group of texts known as .... built upon vedic concepts and introduced new ones.***
   (*a*) Coins (*b*) Upanishads
   (*c*) Inscriptions (*d*) Manuscripts
3. ***Siddhartha decided to give up his palace life, leaving behind his .... and ....***
   (*a*) Father and son
   (*b*) Brother and uncle
   (*c*) Son and mother
   (*d*) Wife and son
4. ***Buddha started teaching what he had realised including the ....***
   (*a*) Not-injuring
   (*b*) Not-hurting
   (*c*) Idea of ahimsa
   (*d*) All of the above
5. ***The Buddha founded the Sangha, a Community of .... or .... who dedicated themselves to practising and spreading his teachings.***
   (*a*) Saints
   (*b*) Bhikshus
   (*c*) Bhikshus or monks
   (*d*) Monks
6. ***Jain teachings include ahimsa, ... and aparigraha.***
   (*a*) Anekantavada
   (*b*) Aparigraha
   (*c*) Knowledge
   (*d*) None of these
7. ***Anekantavada means***
   (*a*) Non possession
   (*b*) Not just one
   (*c*) Possession
   (*d*) None of these

B. True or False

1. *The word "Veda" comes from Latin.*
2. *The Vedas consists of thousands of hymns.*
3. *Early Vedic society was organised in different 'janas' or 'clans'.*
4. *The vedic hymns were composed by saints.*
5. *Rigveda reflects unity among the people.*
6. *A.D. stands for Anno Domini.*
7. *Jainism is a school of thought that became wide spread.*
8. *Buddhism and the Vedantic school of thought, are the central to south west Indian culture.*
9. *Rohineya was an extraordinary saint.*
10. *Vedic hymns were composed by Rishis.*

C. Fill in the Blanks

1. *Jainism is another important school of ....*
2. *Prince Vardhamana practised an .... discipline.*
3. *Jain teachings include .... , ... and ....*
4. *The Buddha started teaching about .... and ....*

D. Very Short Answer Type Questions

1. *What is a Tribe?*
2. *Define the term 'culture'.*

3. *What do you mean by Archaeology?*
4. *Write few lines on Buddhism.*
5. *Under which tree Buddha attain enlightenment?*
6. *In which century was Prince Vardhamana born?*
7. *State two teachings of Jainism?*
8. *Who was Rohineya?*

E. Short Answer Type Questions

1. *Explain the central ideas of Jainism.*
2. *What were the primary beliefs of the charvaka school of thought?*
3. *Buddhism is older than the Vedas. Do you agree, how?*
4. *How did the "Four Great Sights" influence Buddha?*
5. *How are Buddhism and Jainism are interlinked with each other?*
6. *What were the rituals that developed in Vedic Culture?*
7. *Why are Hinduism, Buddhism, Jainism and Sikhism referred to as different 'schools of thought' and not as religions?*
8. *How are tribes connected with Hinduism?*

F. Long Answer Type Questions

1. *What are the main differences between Jainism and Buddhism?*
2. *Describe the various schools of thought which collectively formed the foundation of 'Hinduism'.*

NOTES

NOTES

INTERESTING MIND MAP

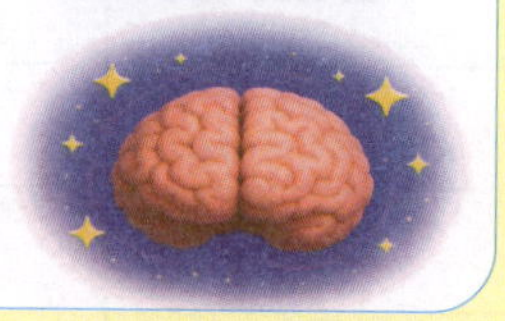

Unity in Diversity, Or 'Many in the One'

1 A Rich Diversity

- India has great diversity in landscapes, languages, scripts, food & clothing.
- India: 1.4 billion people (~18% of the world's population)→natural diversity.
- Anthropological Survey (late 20th century): 'People of India Project' studied 4635 communities, 325 languages & 25 scripts + high migration within the country.
- British Historian Vincent stated 'India is a classic case of unity in diversity'.

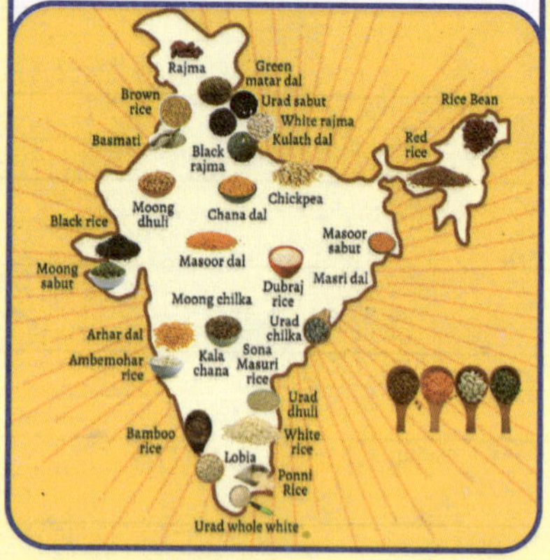

2 Food for All

- Thousands of local dishes across India.
- Staples everywhere
  Cereals: rice, wheat, barley
  Millets: bajra, jowar, ragi
  Pulses: dals, grams
- Common spices: cumin, cardamom, turmeric & ginger.
- Same basic ingredients (unity) cooked differently (diversity) → endless food variety.

3 Textiles and Clothing

- Each region has unique dressing style but sari is common in all traditions.
- Sari: unstitched cloth (silk, synthetic, cotton).
- Famous silks: Banarasi, Kanjivaram, Paithani, Patola, Muga, Mysore.
- Cotton Sarees: several weaving styles.
- Designs: woven or printed; Colours: natural + artificial dyes.
- Sari dates back to BCE (Vaishali stone relief).
- Draping styles differ regionally; new drapes still invented.
- Foreign travellers admired sari for simplicity + versatility.
- Sari also used in daily life for practical purposes.

4 Festivals Galore

- India celebrates numerous festivals.
- Same festivals celebrated across India with different names.
- Ex. Makar Sankranti (harvest festival, 14 Jan. every year.)—celebrated everywhere with different local names.

5 An Epic Spread

- Indian literature; diverse yet connected.
- Panchatantra (Sanskrit, ~2200 years ago): A collection of stories; animals main character.
- Translated into 50+ languages & 200 versions (worldwide→important life lessons).
- Great Epics: the Ramayana & the Mahabharata (~2000 years ago).
- These epics are adopted in folk versions everywhere; Tamil Nadu alone has ~100 versions of the Mahabharata.
- Tribal epics: the Gondas, Bhils & Mundas (northeast Himalayas/ Kashmir); link local languages to Pandavas, Draupadi & Duryodhana.
- Anthropologist K.S. Singh: Folklore shows Pandavas visited almost every part of India.
- These epics spread across Asia→great example of unity in diversity.

6 Conclusion

- Indian classical arts, architecture and traditions balance unity with diversity.
- In India, diversity is seen as enrichment; unity as the bond holding its culture together.

THEME C
Our Cultural Heritage and Knowledge Traditions

CHAPTER
8

UNITY IN DIVERSITY, OR 'MANY IN THE ONE'

I. FACTS TO REMEMBER/SUMMARY

A Rich Diversity

- India is rich in diversity with various types of clothing, food, languages, and scripts. In every region, you will often find people from other parts of India bringing different customs and traditions.
- India has over 140 crore inhabitants, which accounts for about 18 per cent of the world's population contributing to its vast diversity.
- The Anthropological Survey of India, conducted a survey called 'People of India project' of 4,635 communities across all states of the country in the late 20th century.
- The survey recorded 325 languages using 25 scripts, revealing that most people did not reside in their birthplace or among their original community.

Food for All

- India has multiple cuisines numbering in thousands, if not lakhs, that we have tasted.

- Cereals such as rice, wheat and barley, along with millets like pearl millet (*bajra*), sorghum (*jowar*), finger millet (*ragi*), are widely consumed. Various kinds of *dals* and grams are also a part of daily diets across the country.
- Common spices such as turmeric, cumin, cardamom and ginger, are extensively used in Indian cuisine.

Textiles and Clothing

- Every region and community has their own styles of clothing and dress. However, some common features exist in traditional Indian dresses, like saris, regardless of the material used.

  For example:

  Banarasi, Kanjivaram, Paithani, Patan Patola, Muga and Mysore silk saris.
- The sari is an unstitched piece of fabric that comes in hundreds of varieties.

Festivals Galore

- A wide variety of festivals are celebrated across India.
- Makara Sankrānti, marks the beginning of the harvest season and is celebrated across almost all parts of India, under different names around January 14 every year.
- Around same time, Pongal is celebrated in Tamil Nadu, Lohri in Punjab, Uttarayan in Gujarat and Magh Bihu in Assam.

An Epic Spread

- Literature is another significant aspect of unity in diversity. Indian literature is extremely diverse.
- The Pañchatantra, is collection of delightful stories, featuring animals as the main characters. These stories teach essential life skills, and impart good moral values.
- The Rāmāyana and the Mahābhārata — two great epics have been translated and adapted into various regional literatures in India and beyond. Additionally, there are numerous folk versions of these epics, providing another example of unity in diversity.
- Indian culture embraces and celebrates diversity viewing it as an enrichment to unity that further nourishes the cultural diversity.

Map showing how new harvest season is celebrated all over Bharat around January 14th every year.

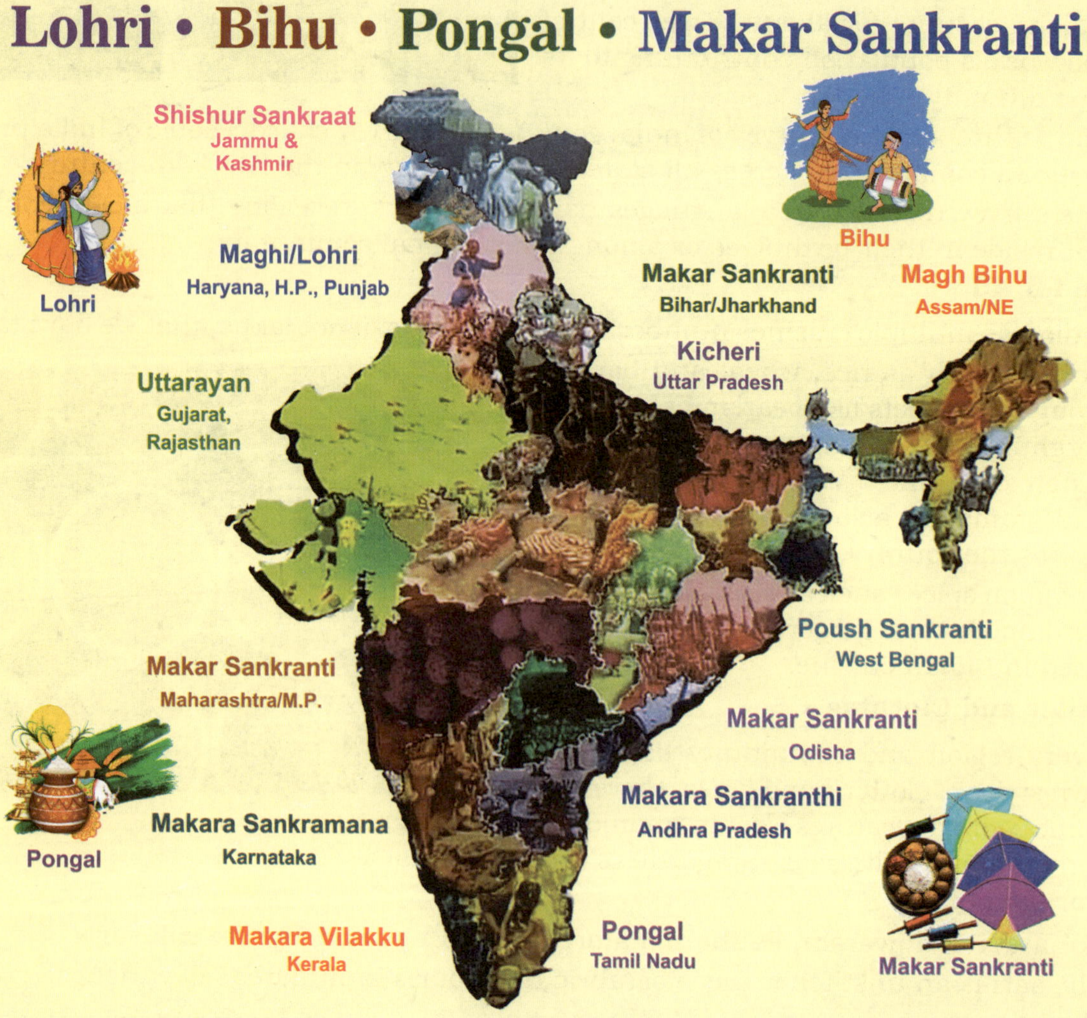

II. TEXTBOOK KEYWORDS/GLOSSARY

1. **Chintz:** Beautiful type of painted or printed cotton cloth from Bharat, with colourful floral patterns, became popular in Europe during 17th and 18th Century.
2. **Diversity:** The existence of social differences of people from different cultural backgrounds, food habits, languages, castes and religions.
3. **Epic:** A long poem or story generally narrating the adventures of heroes and other great figures of the past.
4. **Relief:** A design that is raised out from the surface of a panel (which may be of stone, wood, ceramic or another material).
5. **The Rāmāyana and the Mahābhārata:** India's two grand epics.
6. **Literary Heritage:** Vedas, Upanishads and regional literature.
7. **Migrants:** People who move from one country or region to another for work nowadays or for food (in ancient times).
8. **Panchtantra:** An ancient Indian collection of animal fables* originally written in Sanskrit language, by Vishnu Sharma around 200 BCE, now popular worldwide and being translated into many languages.

III. THE BIG QUESTIONS *(Page 125)*

Q.1. ***What is meant by 'unity in diversity' in the Indian scenario?***

Ans. India has its own and unique sense of unity that keeps its people together. The diversity in India is the result of differences in traditions, languages, festivals, caste, religion and lifestyles, Indians uphold a sense of unity that binds them as one nation.

- This unity comes across various dimensions of Indian life, such as culture, crop pattern, food, clothing, festivals, cricket matches, Bollywood movies and literature.
- A survey by the Anthropological Survey of India, revealed that India has 4,635 communities across all states and has around 325 languages using 25 scripts.
- This diversity has created base for Unity, leading to the concept of Many in One.
- Every household prepares food using different types of spices and oils leading to different taste. However, certain food grains are common to all parts like rice, barley and wheat (cereals); millets and pulses.

Q.2. ***What aspects of India's diversity are the most striking?***

Ans. India's diversity is striking in many aspects. Some of the most notable aspects are as follows:

1. **Languages:** India has 22 officially recognised languages and 325 other languages using 25 scripts.
2. **Major Religions:** India is the birthplace of Hinduism, Buddhism, Jainism, and Sikhism and has significant populations of Muslims, Christians, Jews, Zoroastrians, and others.
3. **Festivals:** There are many festivals like Diwali, Christmas, Eid, Pongal, Baisakhi etc., which are celebrated with great fervor, each showcasing unique cultural practices.
4. **Regional Cuisines:** Indian cuisine varies greatly by region. North Indian food often includes wheat-based breads and rich gravies, while South Indian cuisine is known for its rice dishes and coconut-based preparations.

---

* **Fables:** A short story with a moral, having animals as the main characters, speaking as humans.

5. **Landscapes:** It has diverse geographical features consisting of plains, deserts mountains like Snow-Capped Himalayas. The Thar Desert, the fertile plains of the Ganges etc.

Q. 3. ***How do we make out the unity underlying the diversity?***

Ans. The unity underlying India's diversity can be understood through several factors that bind the nation together.

The idea of "Unity in Diversity" within the context of India means that people live peacefully and harmoniously despite their differences. Diversity means difference. This diversity arises because of 1.4 billion inhabitants known for their vast cultural, linguistic, and geographical differences.

There are some food grains which are common to all parts like rice, barley and wheat (cereals); millets and pulses.

Clothes also represents diversity based on tradition and local environment. At the same time there are some dresses that are common like Sari, Kurta-Pyjamas, Dhoti and Lungi.

There are different festivals in different part of India but gives equal happiness and joy. One common festival is Makara Sankrānti which has different names in different parts of the country all associated with harvest season.

The political unity arises from the Constitution and the rule of law.

1. The Indian Constitution establishes a uniform legal framework for everyone.
2. **National Symbols**
   - **Flag and Anthem:** The Indian flag, national anthem (*"Jana Gana Mana"*), and national symbols like the national bird (*peacock*) and animal (*tiger*) are respected and celebrated across the country, fostering a sense of national pride.
   - **Emblems and Mottos:** Symbols like the Ashoka Chakra and the national motto "Satyameva Jayate" (Truth Alone Triumphs) are important unifying elements.
   - **Many Festivals** are celebrated by people from across the states like Diwali, Christmas, Holi and Eid etc.

IV. NCERT INTEXT/TEXTBOOK EXERCISES

Let's Explore

Q.1. ***As a class activity, make lists of (1) the birthplaces of at least 5 classmates and the birthplaces of their parents; (2) the students' mother tongues and other languages known to them. Discuss the results in terms of diversity.*** (*Page 126*)

Ans. Students to do research by talking to their friends and write the value points:

Tentative answers (as in many small towns, villages we may have children from similar background).

1. **Birthplaces of Classmates and Their Parents**

Classmate Name	Classmate's Birthplace	Father's Birthplace	Mother's Birthplace
Classmate 1	Kochi- Kerala	Thiruvananthapuram, Kerala	Thiruvananthapuram, Kerala
Classmate II	Shillong-Meghalaya	Shillong-Meghalaya,	Shillong-Meghalaya,
Classmate III	Srinagar-Jammu & Kashmir	Pahalgam-Jammu & Kashmir	Dachigam-Jammu & Kashmir
Classmate IV	Delhi- Delhi	Nirsha-Jharkhand	Madhubani-Bihar
Classmate V	Ahmedabad, Gujarat	Ahmedabad, Gujarat	Porbandar-Gujarat

2. Students' Mother Tongues and Other Languages Known

Classmate Name	Mother Tongue	Other Languages Known
Classmate 1	Malayalam	Tamil, English
Classmate II	Khasi	English, Hindi
Classmate III	Kashmiri	Hindi, English
Classmate IV	Maithili	English, Hindi
Classmate V	Gujarati	English, Hindi, Marathi

The above research-based discussion led to the conclusion that, classroom itself has multiple diversity.

Many students in fact belong to different states. Most students know two or more languages, reflecting strong linguistic knowledge and better communication skills.

Q.2. ***As a class activity, make a list of ingredients (grains, spices, etc.) that are used in your home.*** (*Page 128*)

Ans. Grains-STAPLE: Rice, Wheat, Multi-grain wheat, Millet (*bajra, jowar, ragi*).

Pulses: Toor (*arhar*) dal , moong dal, chana dal, masoor dal, and rajma.

Spices: Turmeric (*haldi*), Ginger, Garlic, Cumin (*jeera*), Coriander (*dhaniya*), Mustard seeds (*sarson*), Red chilli powder, Black pepper, Garam masala, Cinnamon (dalchini), Cloves, etc.

Other Ingredients used: Salt, Green Vegetables, Oil, Ghee.

Q.3. ***Take any one vegetable and think of the number of different dishes you can prepare with it.*** (*Page 128*)

Ans. Students may take any vegetable.

Let's take palak (*spinach*) as the vegetable and see the variety of dishes that can be prepared with it:

1. Palak-Plain palak (*spinach*) sabzi
2. Paneer Palak
3. Potato Palak
4. Palak Paratha
5. Palak Soup
6. Palak Dal
7. Palak Pakora
8. Mixed vegetables with Palak

Q. 4. ***Explain how the example of the sari reflects both unity and diversity (in 100-150 words).*** (*Page 129*)

Ans. The sari exemplifies unity through its presence as a single dress worn across India, despite the diverse ways of draping it in different regions and communities. It showcases diversity through using different materials and various styles of weaving, designing, and colours used in its creation. The sari's long history and adaptability reflect both unity in its essence as a single garment and diversity in the multiple ways it can be worn and styled, making it a symbol of India's rich cultural heritage.

Some typical examples of Silk Sari are Banarasi, Kanjivaram, Paithani, Patan Patola, Muga or Mysore. Sari has many variations in colour and style to be worn. Historically, sari's one of the earliest references comes from stone relief from Vaishali (today in Bihar) from few centuries BCE ago. There are multiple uses of sari and various style to wear it at all important occasions.

Q. 5. ***In the pictures, can you recognise what a sari has been used for?*** (*Page 130*)

Picture 1

Picture 2

Picture 3

Picture 4

Picture 5

Picture 6

Ans. In the pictures, a sari has been used for various creative purposes beyond just being worn as a dress. The six pictures illustrate some of these innovative uses of the sari, showcasing its versatility and adaptability in different contexts.

Picture 1. Sari has been used as a swing for kids when their mothers work in fields.

Picture 2. Sari has been used as a fishing net to catch fish.

Picture 3. Some women make a small cushion from a sari to carry water pots on their head.

Picture 4. Sari has been used as a cloth bag to carry grain, fruits or vegetables.

Picture 5. Sari is used as a shed to get protection from the sunlight/dust etc.

Picture 6. Sari has been used as a pillow or a head rest while sleeping.

Q. 6. ***Are you aware of, or can you imagine, more uses for the sari?***

(*Page 130*)

Ans. Some other possible uses for the sari are:

It can be used as a curtain.

It can be used as a wrapping cloth.

It can also be used as a blanket or a shawl for warmth in cool weather.

Q. 7. ***Following the example of the sari, make a list of different styles you have seen for the dhoti — both as regards the fabric and the uses the dhoti can be put to. What conclusion can you draw?***

(*Page 131*)

Ans. Dhoti is a long cloth mostly made of cotton, silk or synthetic yarn and traditionally worn all over Bharat.

The Dhoti, a traditional garment worn by men in India, varies significantly in style, fabric, and usage across different regions. Dhoti is worn in most of the states in Bharat with different styles for casual daily use wear.

Some Styles of Dhoti are: In many parts of north India Dhoti is a traditional dress, generally worn by men which is tied around the waist, along with a kurta.

In many south Indian states, dhoti is draped differently, sometimes left open at the back, wore along angavastram.

Lungi: Dhoti worn as Lungi, is universal in India.

Dhotar in Maharashtra shorter style with pleats in front and back.

It is also worn on festivals and during traditional dances, specially in southern states of Bharat.

Names of dhoti in different states are: Mekhela in Assam, Mundu in Kerala and Veshti in South India.

In conclusion, the dhoti is adaptable to various occasions, from daily wear to formal events and religious ceremonies. The choice of fabric (cotton, silk) and the style of wearing the dhoti differ across regions, reflecting local customs, climate, and cultural preferences. This diversity highlights the rich cultural tapestry of India, where traditional attire continues to play a vital role in everyday life and special occasions.

Q. 8. ***What is your favourite festival and how is it celebrated in your region? Do you know whether it is celebrated in any other part of India, may be under a different name?*** (*Page 132*)

Ans. My favourite festival is Durga Puja which is dedicated to worship Goddess Durga. It is celebrated at a grand level in West Bengal, Bihar, Assam, Odisha, Tripura and other parts of India.

During the celebration of Durga Puja beautiful pandals are set up, where idols of Goddess Durga and idols of other God and Goddesses are kept such as Lakshmi, Saraswati, Kartikeya, and Ganesha.

The festival spans over 10 days starting with Mahalaya, marking the arrival of the Goddess. Prayers, and aarti (*devotional songs*) are offered during the festival period.

Various Cultural Programs are also organised after the daily puja.

Special community rasoi is organised to offer bhog and dish like khichuri and sweets, such as sandesh and rosogolla.

On the 10th day that is on Vijayadashami the idols are immersed in a nearby pond or river with grand fervour and celebrations.

This festival has different names in different parts of India:

- In UP and other parts of North India it celebrated as Navratri,
- In Karnataka- Mysuru Dasara,
- In Gujarat, it is celebrated as Navratri,
- In Maharashtra, it is also celebrated as Navratri festival,
- In Himachal Pradesh, it is celebrated as Kullu Dussehra.

Q. 9. ***During October–November, many major festivals take place in India. Make a list of the few main ones and their various names in different parts of the country.*** (*Page 133*)

Ans. October-November is a vibrant period in India, marked by several major festivals celebrated across the country. Here are a few main ones and their various names in different regions:

1. Diwali (Deepavali)

- **North India:** Diwali
- **South India:** Deepavali
- **West India (Maharashtra):** Divali
- **East India (Bengal):** Kali Puja/Shyama Puja
- **West India:** Lakshmi Puja

2. Dussehra (Vijayadashami)

- **North India:** Dussehra
- **South India (Karnataka):** Dasara
- **West Bengal:** Durga Puja

- **Andhra Pradesh and Telangana:** Vijaya Dashami
- **Maharashtra:** Dasara

3. **Bhai Dooj (Bhaiya Dooj)**
   - **North India:** Bhai Dooj/ Bhaiya Dooj
   - **West Bengal:** Bhai Phonta
   - **Maharashtra:** Bhau Beej
   - **Gujarat:** Bhai Beej
4. **Chhath Puja**
   - **Bihar and Jharkhand:** Chhath Puja
   - **Uttar Pradesh:** Surya Shashti

In conclusion, the festival season in India during October—November showcases the country's rich cultural diversity. Each festival has its unique customs, rituals, and regional variations. Despite these differences, the essence of joy, devotion, and community bonding remains a unifying thread across the celebrations. Again showing our unity in diversity.

Q. 10. ***In a class discussion, try to identify the episode depicted in the painting shown in Fig. 8.6 below and important details associated with it.*** *(Page 134)*

Fig. A painting depicting a major episode from the Ramāyana (18th century, Himachal Pradesh)

Ans. The given above painting is of 18th-century from Himachal Pradesh, showing incidents from the Holy Book Ramayana.

The Scene

The painting depicts the moment when demon Ravana, King of Lanka, abducts Devi Sita, the wife of God Rama.

Ravana is shown forcefully taking Devi Sita away in a chariot.

Some important other details:

- The figure in orange is Lakshman who is signified as protector of Devi Sita before abduction.
- There is a large divine vulture 'Jatayu', who is seen trying to rescue, Mata Sita by attacking Ravana's chariot. However, he gets injured in this process.

Importance of the scene

This episode is considered as a turning point in the Ramayana. The abduction of the Devi Sita by demon Ravana leads to Ram's quest to rescue her. In the epic battle, God Ram defeats Demon Ravana, signifying victory of good over evil, victory of rightness.

NCERT Questions, Activities and Projects
(Page 136)

Q. 1. ***Conduct a class discussion on the two quotations at the start of the chapter.***

I. *Oh, grant me my prayer, that I may never lose the bliss of the touch of the one in the play of the many.*

— Rabindranath Tagore

Ans. This quote is from Rabindranath Tagore's "Gitanjali". It is a prayer reflecting about the connection to a universal presence of "the one" even with multiple diversity of life.

Key points about the quote:

- "The One": Here it is a higher power, a unifying force that connects all things.
- "The Play of the Many": Refers to the diversity and multiple dimensions of the world, the different individuals and experiences that make up life.
- "Bliss of the Touch": Describes the ultimate joy and happiness that comes from feeling connected to this universal presence.

II. *The principle of unity in diversity which has always been normal to [India] and its fulfilment the fundamental course of her being and its very nature, the Many in the One, would place her on the sure foundation of her Swabhava and Swadharma.*

— Sri Aurobindo

Ans. Sri Aurobindo's words highlight India's own strength in respecting its unity in diversity as a most important principle of its existence. His idea reflects India's true nature (Swabhava) and duty (Swadharma) lie in bringing many diverse elements within a unified whole.

The idea of "the Many in the One" reflects that diversity does not lead to division instead, it strengthens the nation by fostering inclusivity and collective progress.

Q. 2. ***Read the National Anthem and its translation in the preliminary pages of this textbook. Where do you see the diversity? And where the unity? Write two or three paragraphs on this.***

Ans. The national anthem, "Jana Gana Mana," beautifully embodies the spirit of "unity in diversity" that defines India. The lyrics themselves are written in Bengali, by Rabindranath Tagore.

Celebrating Diversity: The anthem showcase India's vibrant diversity. Phrases like "Punjab Sindh Gujarat Maratha" and "Dravida Utkal Banga" mentions different diverse regions and languages coexist. It mentions the majestic Himalayas, the life-giving rivers like the Ganga and the Yamuna, and the Indian Ocean, highlighting the geographical diversity. This celebration of diversity creates a sense of shared identity amongst all Indians, regardless of their background.

Unifying Threads: The anthem emphasises a sense of national unity. Words like "Sindhu-sagar" (sea of Sindhu-Indus) and "Himachal-Dravida" (Himalayas and Dravidian lands) create a sense of geographical and cultural integration.

The anthem addresses India as "Bharat bhumi" (land of Bharat), a unifying term for the nation. Phrases like "jaya he" (victory to thee) and "jana-gana-mangal" (welfare of the whole people) evoke a collective spirit of patriotism and a shared aspiration for the nation's progress.

The national anthem serves as a powerful symbol of India's "unity in diversity." The anthem serves as a reminder that India's diversity is not a weakness, but a beautiful melody that creates a symphony of unity and national pride.

Q. 3. ***Select a few stories from the Pañchatantra and discuss how their message is still valid today. Do you know of any similar stories from your region?***

Ans. Panchatantra stories are of timeless wisdom. Here are a few stories that remain relevant today:

The Lion and the Jackal: This story highlights the importance of wit and intelligence over brute strength.

Even a weak jackal can outsmart a powerful lion through cunningness. This translates well to modern life, **where strategy and problem-solving often trump brute force.**

The Crow and the Pitcher: This tale teaches us perseverance and resourcefulness. The thirsty crow repeatedly drops pebbles into the pitcher to raise the water level so he can drink. We can apply this lesson in our own struggles, reminding us not to give up easily.

The Foolish Lion and the Clever Rabbit: The story teaches us that intelligence and wisdom can overcome strength and power. The clever rabbit outsmarts the foolish lion, showing that quick thinking and strategy are more valuable than brute force. It also highlights the importance of patience, presence of mind, and problem-solving skills in difficult times.

While these stories come from different cultures and eras, they share a common thread of universal wisdom for navigating life's challenges.

Q. 4. ***Collect a few folk tales from your region and discuss their message.***

Ans. Tentative answer: Students to collect folk tales from their region. We have taken a few folk tales from Maharashtra with their messages:

1. The Greedy Weaver (Vidarbha Region):

Story: This tale from the Vidarbha region tells the story of a weaver who gets progressively greedier. Initially happy with his simple life, he wishes for more wealth. As his wishes are granted, he becomes increasingly dissatisfied, ultimately losing everything due to his greed.

Message: This folk tale warns against the dangers of greed and the importance of appreciating what you have. It encourages contentment and living within your means.

2. Savitri and Satyavan (Satara District):

Story: This folk tale, popular in the Satara district, revolves around Savitri, a woman renowned for her devotion to her husband Satyavan. When Yama, the god of death, comes to claim Satyavan's life, Savitri follows him, pleading for her husband's return. Impressed by her love and courage, Yama grants Satyavan's life back.

Message: This story celebrates true love, devotion, and the power of unwavering determination. It highlights the importance of fighting for what you believe in.

Q. 5. ***Is there any ancient story that you have seen being depicted through a form of art? It could be a sculpture, a painting, a dance performance, a movie ... Discuss with your classmates.***

Ans. The Panchatantra stories have been a rich source of inspiration for artists for centuries. Here's an example:

Story: The Lion and the Mouse

Art Form: Sculpture

India is known for depiction of tradition through different art form. Most of the important events from the Ramayana, have been represented and depicted in paintings, short dance, art, sculptures, theatre, and in film etc.

Some of the examples are as follows:

Paintings: The famous Madhubani painting from Bihar have depicted many Ramayana's stories.

Sculpture: An interesting battle scene between Ram with Ravana has been depicted in the Ellora and Ajanta Caves in Maharashtra.

There are countless examples of fables and stories being depicted in art across different cultures.

Q. 6. ***Discuss in class the following quotation by India's first prime minister, Jawaharlal Nehru, when he travelled to many parts of India before Independence:***

"Everywhere I found a cultural background which had exerted a powerful influence on their lives. ... The old epics of India, the Ramayana and the Mahabharata and other books, in popular translations and paraphrases, were widely known among the masses, and every incident and story and moral in them was engraved on the popular mind and gave a richness and content to it. Illiterate villagers would know hundreds of verses by heart and their conversation would be full of references to them or to some story with a moral, enshrined in some old classic."

Ans. This quote comes from his travels across India before independence.

Nehru emphasises that India's cultural background significantly influenced the lives of people across the nation. This influence transcended social classes and locations.

He mentions the Ramayana and Mahabharata, highlighting their popularity even in "illiterate villages." These epics weren't just stories; they were moral compasses with lessons deeply ingrained in people's minds.

Nehru suggests that these epics provided "richness and content" to people's lives, shaping their values and sense of identity.

V. EXAM ORIENTED QUESTIONS

A. Very Short Answer Type Questions

Q.1. ***What is India famous for in terms of diversity?***

Ans. India is famous for its rich diversity in religion, language, culture, food, festivals, and geographical features.

Q.2. ***What kind of variety do we find in Indian food?***

Ans. Indian food offers a wide variety of flavours, spices, and ingredients. From vegetarian curries in the south to rich butter curries in the north, there's something for everyone.

Q.3. ***How does the staple food differ across various regions in India?***

Ans. Rice is a staple food in many southern and eastern regions, while wheat dominates the north and west. Roti, chapati, and paratha are different types of flatbreads made from wheat that are popular in various regions.

Q.4. ***How does clothing in India differ based on climate?***

Ans. In hotter regions, people wear lighter clothes made from cotton or light material. In colder regions, people wear warmer clothes made from wool or silk.

Q.5. ***Write the geographical spread of India.***

Ans. India has a vast geographical spread, from the snow-capped Himalayas in the north to the tropical beaches in the south.

Q.6. ***Why is Indian food so diverse?***

Ans. Different regions have their own cuisines based on local crops, spices, and cooking styles.

Q.7. **Give some elements of diversity in India.**

Ans. India is a diverse country with multiple elements of diversity, including:

- Linguistic diversity with 22 officially and over 1,600 dialects .
- Religious diversity with important religions like Hinduism, Islam, Christianity, Sikhism, Buddhism, Jainism, and others.

Geographical diversity with diverse landscapes, from the Himalayas in the north to the coastal regions in the south, deserts in the west and huge green cover in north-east.

Q.8. ***Give any two reasons for the diversity in Indian food.***

Ans. Two main reasons for the diversity in Indian food are:

(*a*) Climatic differences spreading with high rainfall to dry-desert, plain areas to mountainous areas.

(*b*) India is the birthplace of some important religions like Hinduism, Sikhism, Jainism, Buddhism, and is home to Islam, Christianity and many more.

Q.9. ***Why does India celebrate so many festivals throughout the year?***

Ans. Each religion and region has its own festivals, reflecting the diverse beliefs and traditions.

Q.10. ***How do these festivals promote unity?***

Ans. People from different backgrounds participate in each other's festivals, fostering a sense of togetherness and respecting each other's customs.

Q.11. ***Besides regional variations, what are some common threads that bind Indian clothing?***

Ans. Vibrant colours and intricate designs are hallmarks of Indian textiles. Traditional clothing like sarees and kurtas are worn across the country, albeit with regional variations in style and fabric.

Q.12. ***Give the central idea of the Panchatantra.***

Ans. The central idea of the Panchatantra is to impart wisdom, moral values, and practical knowledge through engaging stories. It teaches lessons about life, politics, human nature, and relationships using fables where animals often act like humans.

B. Short Answer Type Questions

Q. 1. ***Can you name two festivals celebrated in different parts of India, highlighting their cultural significance?***

Ans. Diwali and Makar Sankranti are two major festivals which are celebrated all over India.

Makar Sankranti signifies beginning of new harvest year as due to Earth's revolution around Sun. Sun begins its movement from Southern to Northern hemisphere.

At around same time, Lohri is celebrated in Punjab, Pongal in Tamil Nadu and Bihu in Assam.

Diwali is celebrated as Lord Rama came back to his home town Ayodhya after defeating the demon Ravana. It is celebrated as victory of good over evil.

Both the above festivals show deep cultural roots in Bharat since ancient times.

Q. 2. ***India is known for its incredible diversity. Can you name some ways this diversity is reflected in our society?***

Ans. India's diversity is evident in the various languages spoken, religions practiced, and customs followed across the country. We have people from different ethnicities and backgrounds, each adding their unique flavour to the national unity in diversity.

Q. 3. ***How does Indian food differs and reflect the idea of unity in diversity?***

Ans. Indian food differs and reflect the idea of unity in diversity:

- Indian food varies from region to region due to differences in climate, availability of ingredients, and cultural influences.
- For example, North Indian cuisine includes wheat-based dishes like chapati and paratha, while South Indian cuisine is rice-based, featuring dishes like dosa and idli.
- Despite these differences, common ingredients like rice, wheat, pulses, and spices such as turmeric and cumin are used throughout the country, reflecting unity in diversity.

Q. 4. ***How does the project of Anthropological Survey of India's People of India highlight India's diversity?***

Ans. The *People of India* project was conducted by the Anthropological Survey of India.

- It found 4,635 communities across the country, identifying 325 languages and 25 different scripts.
- It highlighted the vast linguistic, cultural, and ethnic diversity of India and showed that migration has played a key role in shaping India's multicultural identity.
- The project reinforced the idea that despite this diversity, India maintains a shared cultural heritage.

Q. 5. ***Every region and community in India has developed its own styles of clothing and dresses. Elaborate the statement with suitable examples.***

Ans. India's clothing traditions vary and are based on geography, climate, and culture.

- For example, in North India, women wear Banarasi or Phulkari sarees, while in South India, Kanjivaram and Kasavu sarees are popular.
- Men in Punjab often wear kurta-pyjama, whereas dhoti is commonly worn in Tamil Nadu and West Bengal.
- Despite these differences, unstitched garments like sarees and dhotis symbolise a shared cultural tradition, reflecting unity in diversity.

Q. 6. ***Highlight the multiple uses of sari.***

Ans. The sari, apart from being a traditional dress, has several practical uses in Indian households. Some of them include:

- Being used as a cradle to rock infants.
- Acting as a headscarf or protection against heat and dust.
- Serving as a makeshift basket to carry grains or vegetables.
- Used as a curtain or bedsheet in rural homes.
- Used as a religious offering or prayer cloth in temples.

Q. 7. ***What are various staple food grains commonly consumed across India?***

Ans. India's staple food grains include:

- **Rice** is mostly consumed widely in East and South India.
- **Wheat** is consumed in almost whole part of India but widely used as a staple food in North and Central India.
- **Millets** like Bajra, Jowar, and Ragi are popular in Rajasthan, Maharashtra, and Karnataka.
- **Pulses** like Moong dal, Arhar dal, Chana dal, and Masoor are used across the country.

Q. 8. ***Write the central theme of The Ramayana.***

Ans. The *Ramayana* is an ancient Indian epic that narrates the journey of Prince Rama, who embarks on a mission to rescue his wife, Sita, from the demon king Ravana. The central theme of the epic revolves around the values of dharma (righteousness), devotion, loyalty, and the triumph of good over evil. It teaches moral lessons about duty, respect, and sacrifice, making it an integral part of Indian cultural heritage.

Q. 9. ***Why is India known as the land of festivals?***

Ans. India is known as the land of festivals because there are numerous festivals that are celebrated throughout the year, reflecting the diversity of religions and cultures.

Diwali, Holi, Dussehra, Makar Sankranti, Pongal, Lohri, Christmas, Onam, and Durga Puja are some of the major festivals celebrated in India.

Q. 10. ***India is renowned for its diverse textiles and clothing styles. How does climate and geography influence these variations?***

Ans. People in hot and humid regions like the south often wear lightweight cotton clothes, while those in colder northern areas like Kashmir wear woolen garments for warmth. This demonstrates how textiles adapt to the specific needs of the local environment.

C. Long Answer Type Questions

Q.1. ***How does geographical variation contribute to India's diversity? Despite regional variations, what unites Indians in terms of food?***

Ans. From the snow-capped mountains of the Himalayas to the tropical beaches of Kerala, India's diverse landscapes influence the way people live, dress, and even the food they eat.

Despite diverse cuisines, a sense of community and sharing is central to Indian food culture. We often share meals with family and friends, celebrating festivals and occasions together.

Q.2. ***How do these festivals showcase unity in diversity? Can you give an example of a festival that transcends religious or regional boundaries?***

Ans. We celebrate various festivals throughout the year, the underlying message of togetherness, joy, and community spirit remains constant.

- We share sweets, participate in rituals, and celebrate each other's cultures, fostering a sense of national unity.
- Diwali, the festival of lights, is a prime example.
- It is celebrated by people of different faiths across the country, symbolising the victory of good over evil.
- This shared celebration exemplifies our unity despite our diverse backgrounds.

Q.3. ***Imagine you are organising a national event showcasing India's epic spread. How would you highlight the diverse agricultural products from different regions?***

Ans. Our national event, "Flavours of India," would be a vibrant tapestry celebrating the diversity of our agricultural bounty!

We will create regional pavilions showcasing each region's unique products.

- Live cooking demonstrations by local chefs with regional specialties, from Kashmiri pulao to appams and Kerala curries.

- Interactive booths would display agricultural products like mangoes from Maharashtra, golden pineapples from Meghalaya, and fragrant spices from Kerala.

This multi-sensory experience would leave visitors with a deeper appreciation for India's incredible agricultural diversity.

Q.4. *How does geographical variation contribute to India's diversity ?*

Ans. India's geographical features have played a major role in shaping diversity. The country has varied physical features like plains, mountains, plateaus, desert, islands and coastal regions.

- The Himalayan region has cold climates, leading to warm clothing, sturdy houses, and cuisines based on barley and dairy.
- The Gangetic plains have fertile lands, supporting agriculture and a diet rich in wheat and rice.
- The coastal areas rely on seafood and coconut-based dishes, while their clothing is lightweight due to the humid climate.
- The desert regions of Rajasthan have adapted to arid conditions with structures like stepwells and foods that require minimal water, such as bajra roti and buttermilk.

These regional variations contribute to India's rich diversity in culture, food, clothing, and traditions.

Q.5. *Explain the central theme and importance of the Panchatantra.*

Ans. The Panchatantra is a collection of ancient Indian fables, primarily written to impart wisdom and life lessons through animal-based stories.

Central Theme: This collection of delightful stories, with animals as the main characters, teaches us important life skills. The original Sanskrit text is at least 2,200 years old, but its stories have been adapted in almost every Indian language.

Importance:

- It teaches valuable life skills such as diplomacy, leadership, and problem-solving.
- It promotes ethical values and critical thinking in children, making it an essential part of Indian literature and education.

Q.6. *Literature offers us another fine illustration of unity in diversity. Justify the given statement.*

Ans. Indian literatures are extremely diverse and offer basics and have generated the ideals to unify Indians. Some examples are as follows:

- The Pañchatantra: This contains collection of delightful stories, with animals as the main characters. This teaches important life skills and have been translated into all local languages.
- The most striking case, however, is that of India's two **epics** — the Rāmāyana and the Mahābhārata
- The Rāmāyana is an ancient Indian epic that narrates the journey of Prince Rama, who embarks on a mission to rescue his wife, Sita, from the demon king Ravana.
- In **Mahābhārata**, the Pāndavas, with the help of Lord Krishna, fight their own cousins, the Kauravas, to reclaim their kingdom.

These stories contain many short stories that focus on values, and constantly ask questions about what is right and what is wrong.

D. Assertion and Reasoning Questions

There are two statements marked as Assertion (A) and Reason (R). Mark your answer as per the codes provided below:

Q. 1. Assertion (A): India has around 4,635 communities across all states of the country. and 325 languages using 25 scripts.

Reason (R): The People of India Project documented the linguistic diversity of the country.

Codes:

(*a*) Both (A) and (R) are true but (R) is not the correct explanation of (A).

(*b*) Both (A) and (R) are true and (R) is the correct explanation of (A).

(*c*) (A) is true but (R) is false.

(*d*) (A) is false but (R) is true.

Q. 2. Assertion (A): Indian harvest festivals like Pedda Panduya are celebrated in different part.

Reason (R): Festivals in India are influenced by local cultures , traditions and methods of celebration.

Codes:

(*a*) Both (A) and (R) are true but (R) is not the correct explanation of (A).

(*b*) Both (A) and (R) are true and (R) is the correct explanation of (A).

(*c*) (A) is true but (R) is false.

(*d*) (A) is false but (R) is true.

Q. 3. Assertion (A): The epics like the Mahābhārata and the Ramayana exist in many versions throughout India.

Reason (R): Ancient Indian literature and traditions are preserved without any adaptations.

Codes:

(*a*) Both (A) and (R) are true but (R) is not the correct explanation of (A).

(*b*) Both (A) and (R) are true and (R) is the correct explanation of (A).

(*c*) (A) is true but (R) is false.

(*d*) (A) is false but (R) is true.

Q. 4. Assertion (A): Indian textiles have been highly valued in European markets.

Reason (R): European countries banned certain Indian fabrics like chintz to protect their own industries.

Codes:

(*a*) Both (A) and (R) are true but (R) is not the correct explanation of (A).

(*b*) Both (A) and (R) are true and (R) is the correct explanation of (A).

(*c*) (A) is true but (R) is false.

(*d*) (A) is false but (R) is true.

Q. 5. Assertion (A): The Panchatantra stories were originally written in Pali.

Reason (R): The Panchatantra was written to teach moral lessons in a simple language to people.

Codes:

(*a*) Both (A) and (R) are true but (R) is not the correct explanation of (A).

(*b*) Both (A) and (R) are true and (R) is the correct explanation of (A).

(*c*) (A) is true but (R) is false.

(*d*) (A) is false but (R) is true.

Ans.

1. (*a*) **2.** (*a*) **3.** (*c*) **4.** (*a*) **5.** (*d*)

E. Case/Source Based Questions

Read the passages given below and answer the questions that follow:

Food for All

I. Some of you will have eaten food from different regions of India. The number of different dishes and preparations you can taste in India must be in their thousands, if not lakhs! Yet certain food grains are common to almost every part of the country — cereals such as rice, barley and wheat; millets such as pearl millet (bajra), sorghum (jowar), finger millet (ragi); and pulses such as various kinds of dals and grams. All these are called 'staple grains' because they are the basic food for most Indians.

(*i*) What do you mean by staple grains?

(*ii*) Identify any two staple grains and spices which are commonly used across India and mentioned in the above paragraph.

(*iii*) Why do different regions have their own styles of food preparation?

(*iv*) How do you think Indian food reflect the idea of "unity in diversity"?

Ans.

(*i*) Staple grains are the primary and important food crops people eat on a daily basis. Some important examples are: rice, wheat, and bajra.

(*ii*) - Staple Grains: Rice, Wheat
- Spices: Turmeric, Cumin

(*iii*) Different regions have their own styles of food preparation due to variations in spices, way of making food, local ingredients, and cultural influences and climate.

(*iv*) Despite regional differences, staple grains like rice, wheat and pulses and common spices like cinnamon, coriander, turmeric are used across length and breadth of the country.

II. Every region and community in India has developed its own styles of clothing and dresses. Yet, we notice a commonality in some traditional Indian dresses, irrespective of the material used. An obvious example is the plain length of cloth called the sari, a type of clothing worn in most parts of India and made from different fabrics — mostly cotton or silk, but nowadays synthetic fabrics too. Banarasi, Kanjivaram, Paithani, Patan Patola, Muga or Mysore are some of the famous types of silk saris.

(*i*) Name the most commonly worn traditional dress by Indian women.

(*ii*) Identify any two special variety of sari mentioned in the above paragraph.

(*iii*) Which two cities are famous for origin of sari ?

(*iv*) Why do draping styles of the sari vary across different states?

(*v*) What does India's diverse clothing tradition tell us about its cultural heritage?

Ans.

(*i*) The most commonly worn traditional dress by Indian women is the **sari**.

(*ii*) Two special varieties of saris mentioned in the paragraph are **Banarasi and Kanjeevaram silk saris.**

(*iii*) Two cities famous for the origin of the sari are **Varanasi (for Banarasi silk) and Kanchipuram (for Kanjeevaram silk).**

(*iv*) The draping styles of the sari vary across different states due to **regional customs, climate, and cultural influences.** Different communities have developed unique ways of wearing the sari over centuries.

(*v*) India's diverse clothing tradition reflects its rich cultural heritage and regional diversity, showcasing the variety of fabrics, weaving techniques, and traditional craftsmanship passed down through generations.

III. For more than two millenniums, these two epics have been translated or adapted into regional literatures in India and beyond. In addition, there are countless folk versions of them. A few years ago, a scholar conducted a survey in Tamil Nadu alone and counted "about a hundred versions [of the Mahābhārata] that have come down to us in folklore forms." Imagine what the number might be for the whole of India!

In fact, many communities have their own versions of the Rāmāyana and the Mahābhārata. They have also preserved legends connecting their own history with these epics

(*i*) Identify the two important epics mentioned in the passage.

(*ii*) Why do tribal communities have their own versions of these stories?

(*iii*) Which epic tells the story of Rama's journey to rescue Sita?

(*iv*) What does the adaptation of these epics tell us about Indian cultural diversity?

(*v*) Highlight the moral values derived from the mentioned epics.

Ans.

(*i*) The Rāmāyana and the Mahābhārata.

(*ii*) Tribal communities have their own versions of these stories because they adapt them to their local traditions, beliefs, and cultural contexts. These adaptations reflect their unique perspectives, values, and oral storytelling traditions, making the epics more relatable and meaningful to their communities.

(*iii*) The Rāmāyana

(*iv*) The adaptation of these epics highlights the rich cultural and traditional diversity of India.

(*v*) Both epics lays the importance of sacrifice, politeness, cooperation, and family integrity standing up for what is right and importance of actions (karma).

F. Competency Based Questions

Q. 1. ***If you were to create a new school project showcasing Unity in Diversity in India, what three aspects (e.g., food, clothing, literature) would you include, and why?***

Ans. Tentative answer.

Food: Different regions have different food like -South India- Dosa, Idli, Uttapam etc.

North India: Roti, Dal, Butter Chicken, Bajra Roti.

East India Litti Chokha, Khichdi.

Clothing: According to climatic conditions-Dhoti, Kurta, Trousers, Lungi, Sari, etc.

Q. 2. ***The People of India Project found that many Indians live away from their birthplace. How has migration contributed to India's cultural diversity?***

Ans. Migration has played a significant role in shaping India's cultural diversity by bringing people together from different regions, languages, traditions, and lifestyles.

- It has created linguistic diversity -Multilingual cities.
- Tasty and variety of foods.
- Celebration of different festivals in different areas.
- Variations in art, music and dance.

Q. 3. ***Imagine you are travelling across India. Give two examples how food and clothing change from one region to another while still showing unity in diversity.***

Ans. As I travelled across India, I saw men wearing dhotis in West Bengal, while lungis were common in Kerala. In Rajasthan, women wore vibrant ghagras, whereas in Punjab salwar kameez dominated. Despite regional variations, the rich colours and traditional fabrics reflected India's unity in diversity.

G. Skill Based Questions

Q. 1. ***The Ramayana and Mahabharata have been adapted in multiple regional versions across India.***

(*a*) Select any important episode and narrate in the class.

(*b*) Prepare a short skit on any important episode from any of the epics.

Ans. (*a*) Some examples are:

- Sita's Swayamvara (*Ramayana*)
- Lakshmana Rekha (*Ramayana*)
- Hanuman ji's travel to Lanka
- God Ram vs Ravana fight
- Krishna and Arjuna on the Battlefield (Mahabharata)
- Abhimanyu and the Chakravyuha (Mahabharata)
- War between Pandavas and Kauravas.

(*b*) Do a research and prepare a detailed skit.

- Select an episode that allows for multiple characters and some dialogues.
- Assign roles like Rama, Sita, Hanuman, Arjuna, Krishna, etc.
- Keep the dialogues simple but meaningful.
- Use basic props like bows, crowns, or scarves for costumes.

VI. PICTURE BASED QUESTIONS

1. ***Observe the given image and answer the questions that follow:***

Q. 1. ***What is Magh Bihu?***

Ans. Magh Bihu is a harvest festival celebrated in Assam, marking the end of the harvesting season in mid-January.

Q. 2. ***Which state is primarily associated with it ?***

Ans. Assam

Q. 3. ***How this festival creates unity?***

Ans. Magh Bihu fosters unity by bringing people together for feasts, bonfires and traditional games. Communities, regardless of background, celebrate with shared meals and cultural events, strengthening bonds and reinforcing Assam's rich heritage of togetherness.

VII. MULTIPLE CHOICE QUESTIONS

1. *Which of the following contributes to India's diverse population?*
   (*a*) Different languages spoken across regions.
   (*b*) Wide range of climates from mountains to deserts.
   (*c*) Cultural practices influenced by historical rulers.
   (*d*) All of the above.

2. *What are examples of a cultural practice that unites India?*
   (*a*) Importance placed on family values.
   (*b*) Celebration of major festivals like Diwali.
   (*c*) Tradition of wearing Sari and Dhoti.
   (*d*) All of the above.

3. *The following is the most important staple food consumed in most parts of India:*
   (*a*) Meat (*b*) Rice
   (*c*) Maize (*d*) Sugarcane
4. *The use of spices contribute to India's food diversity. Identify the correct option:*
   (*a*) It limits the variety of flavours available.
   (*b*) It creates a uniform taste across all dishes.
   (*c*) It allows for regional variations in food preparation.
   (*d*) It discourages the use of fresh ingredients.
5. *What is a characteristic feature of traditional Indian clothing?*
   (*a*) Use of imported yarn thread.
   (*b*) Use of bright and vibrant colours and patterns.
   (*c*) Preference for loose and comfortable styles.
   (*d*) Made entirely from synthetic materials.
6. *How does the climate of a region influence clothing choices in India?*
   (*a*) It has no significant impact.
   (*b*) Warmer regions favour lighter and more breathable fabrics.
   (*c*) Colder regions require light and thin clothing year-round.
   (*d*) All regions prefer the same type of clothing.
7. *The primary reason for celebrating a variety of festivals in India is:*
   (*a*) To have more national holidays.
   (*b*) To showcase the dominance of one particular religion.
   (*c*) To express the cultural heritage of different communities.
   (*d*) To create a sense of competition between regions.
8. *What is an example of a harvest festival celebrated in some parts of India?*
   (*a*) Holi (*b*) Pongal
   (*c*) Dussehra (*d*) Eid-ul-Fitr
9. *Select the main reasons for India's rich diversity.*
   (*a*) Its location at the crossroads of trade routes.
   (*b*) Its vast geographical features.
   (*c*) Its long history of different rulers.
   (*d*) All of the above.
10. *What is a traditional Indian garment worn by women across many regions, but with variations in style and fabric?*
    (*a*) Dhoti (*b*) Kurta
    (*c*) Sari (*d*) Sherwani
11. *The main idea behind the concept of "unity in diversity".*
    (*a*) Everyone in India must wear the same clothes.
    (*b*) All Indians must eat the same food.
    (*c*) Despite differences, India remains one nation.
    (*d*) People from different regions cannot celebrate together.
12. *Which of the following is NOT a common staple food found across most regions of India?*
    (*a*) Rice (*b*) Wheat
    (*c*) Pulses (Dals) (*d*) Sugarcane

Ans. 1. → (*d*) 2. → (*d*)
3. → (*b*) 4. → (*c*)
5. → (*b*) 6. → (*b*)
7. → (*c*) 8. → (*b*)
9. → (*d*) 10. → (*c*)
11. → (*c*) 12. → (*b*)

VIII. OBJECTIVE TYPE QUESTIONS

A. True and False

1. India's rich diversity, and it is usually the first thing that strikes visitors to our country.
2. The Archaeological Survey of India, a national organisation, conducted a massive survey called 'People of India project'.
3. Cereals such as rice, barley and wheat; millets such as pearl millet (bajra), and pulses are called 'staple grains'.
4. A stone relief of a woman in a sari from Sarnath (today in Bihar) has been found.
5. One beautiful type of printed cotton called 'chintz' became so popular in 17th-century in Europe that the sale of some European dresses dropped sharply.

Ans.

1. → True 2. → False 3. → True
4. → False 5. → True

B. Fill in the Blanks

1. India is a land of immense ________ (diversity/poverty).
2. The diverse food habits in India reflect our __________ (unity/differences).
3. Spicy curries are a common feature in ________ (North/South) Indian cuisine.
4. The _______ (Sari/Dhoti) is a traditional Indian garment worn by women.
5. _______ (Diwali/Dussehra) is the festival of lights, celebrated across India.
6. __________ (Bihu/Onam) is a harvest festival celebrated in Kerala.
7. We celebrate festivals with great ________ (joy/sadness) and enthusiasm.
8. Each region in India contributes its own unique ________ (flavour/cost) to the national identity.
9. One beautiful type of printed cotton cloth called ________ became so popular in 17th-century Europe that the sale of some European dresses dropped sharply. (phulkari, chintz)
10. The two most famous ________ of India are the Rāmāyana and the Mahābhārata. (epics/stories)

Ans.

1. diversity 2. unity 3. North
4. Sari 5. Diwali 6. Onam
7. joy 8. flavour 9. chintz
10. epics

C. Match Column A with Column B

Column A		Column B
(*a*) Silk	(*i*)	A natural fibre to make soft clothes.
(*b*) Leather	(*ii*)	A luxurious fabric used for elegant clothing.
(*c*) Jute	(*iii*)	A material used for making warm winter clothes and shoes.
(*d*) Cotton	(*iv*)	A natural fibre used for making bags and other accessories.

Ans. (*a*) → (*ii*), (*b*) → (*iii*), (*c*) → (*iv*), (*d*) → (*i*)

IX. TEST YOUR KNOWLEDGE

A. Multiple Choice Questions

1. *How does India's geographical location contribute to its diversity?*
   (*a*) It helps to access trade routes.
   (*b*) It provides a variety of landscapes for different cultures.
   (*c*) It restricts the movement of people between regions.
   (*d*) It provides resources for diverse populations.
2. *How does migration of people contribute to diversity?*
   (*a*) It leads to a homogenous society.
   (*b*) It introduces new customs and traditions.
   (*c*) It reduces the number of languages spoken.
   (*d*) It creates barriers between different communities.
3. *What is the term used for various types of lentils and legumes consumed in India?*
   (*a*) Spices (*b*) Pulses (Dals)
   (*c*) Grains (*d*) Vegetables
4. *What is a traditional Indian garment worn by men, often made from cotton or silk?*
   (*a*) Sari
   (*b*) Dhoti
   (*c*) Lehenga
   (*d*) Salwar-Kameez
5. *How has India's textile industry contributed to its cultural diversity?*
   (*a*) It promotes mass production of uniform clothing styles.
   (*b*) It showcases the artistic traditions of different regions.
   (*c*) It discourages the use of traditional weaving techniques.
   (*d*) It limits the availability of clothing choices for people.
6. *How do festivals like Diwali or Holi promote unity in diversity?*
   (*a*) People from different religions are forbidden to participate.
   (*b*) They celebrate the achievements of specific historical figures.
   (*c*) They bring together people from various backgrounds to share joy.
   (*d*) They focus on the differences between religious practices.
7. *What is one of the main reasons for India's rich diversity?*
   (*a*) Its location at the crossroads of trade routes
   (*b*) Its vast geographical features
   (*c*) Its long history of different rulers
   (*d*) All of the above

B. True or False

1. *India is a secular country.*
2. *All Indians speak the same language.*
3. *Diversity is harmful to a country.*
4. *India has a rich cultural heritage.*
5. *People of different religions cannot live peacefully together in India.*
6. *Majority of the festivals are celebrated during June-July in India.*
7. *The Pañchatantra has travelled well beyond India, all the way to Southeast Asia, the Arab world and Europe, inspiring new collections of stories on the way.*

C. Fill in the Blanks

1. The Anthropological Survey of India recognised ...... languages using 25 ....
2. Banarasi, Patan Patola, Muga are some famous types of ......
3. The sari has a long history, a stone relief from .....(today in Bihar) which goes back a few centuries BCE has been found.

4. To protect their own products, England and France decided to ban the import of ....from India.
5. the Pañchatantra exist in more than ..... languages.

D. One Word Questions

1. *The feeling of belongingness to one's country.*
2. *The variety of cultures, languages, and religions in India.*
3. *The most widely spoken language in India.*
4. *The festival of lights.*
5. *The spirit of togetherness among people.*

E. Very Short Answer Type Questions

1. *Name two important epics of India.*
2. *Who was the author of Panchantatra?*
3. *What is the main reason for diversity in India?*
4. *What is the official language of India?*
5. *How many states and union territories are there in India?*

F. Short Answer Type Questions

1. *How can diversity be a strength for India?*
2. *Explain the importance of respecting different cultures and religions.*
3. *What steps can be taken to promote unity in diversity in India?*

G. Long Answer Type Questions

1. *Discuss the various factors that contribute to the diversity of India.*
2. *How can we celebrate India's diversity while maintaining national unity?*

H. Assertion & Reasoning Questions

There are two statements marked as Assertion (A) and Reason (R). Mark your answer as per the codes provided below:

Q. 1. Assertion (A): Epic is a long poem generally narrating the adventures of heroes and other great figures of the past.

Reason (R): The Rāmāyana and the Mahābhārata together might fill some 7,000 pages in their original versions, narrate the stories of heroes who fight to re-establish dharma.

Codes:

(*a*) Both (A) and (R) are true but (R) is not the correct explanation of (A).
(*b*) Both (A) and (R) are true and (R) is the correct explanation of (A).
(*c*) (A) is true but (R) is false.
(*d*) (A) is false but (R) is true.

Q. 2. Assertion (A): There is an immense variety of festivals in India.

Reason (R): Makara Sankrānti, which marks the beginning of the harvest season in many regions.

Codes:

(*a*) Both (A) and (R) are true but (R) is not the correct explanation of (A).
(*b*) Both (A) and (R) are true and (R) is the correct explanation of (A).
(*c*) (A) is true but (R) is false.
(*d*) (A) is false but (R) is true.

Match Column A with Column B

I.

	Column A		Column B
1.	Traditional Indian dress	(*a*)	Mahabharata
2.	Indian Epic	(*b*)	Khichdi Parv
3.	Harvest Festival	(*c*)	Panchatantra
4.	Ancient Story Collection	(*d*)	Sari

II.

	Column A (Festivals)		Column B (States)
1.	Bihu	(*a*)	Punjab
2.	Pongal	(*b*)	Assam
3.	Lohri	(*c*)	Tamil Nadu
4.	Makar Sankranti	(*d*)	Maharashtra
5.	Makara Vilakku	(*e*)	Kerala

THEME D
GOVERNANCE AND DEMOCRACY

INTERESTING MIND MAP

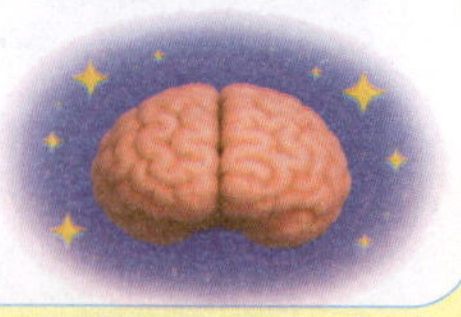

Family and Community

1 Family

- Family is the **basic unit of society**
- Two types: joint and nuclear
- Indian languages have many names for relatives
- Cousins are also our brothers and sisters

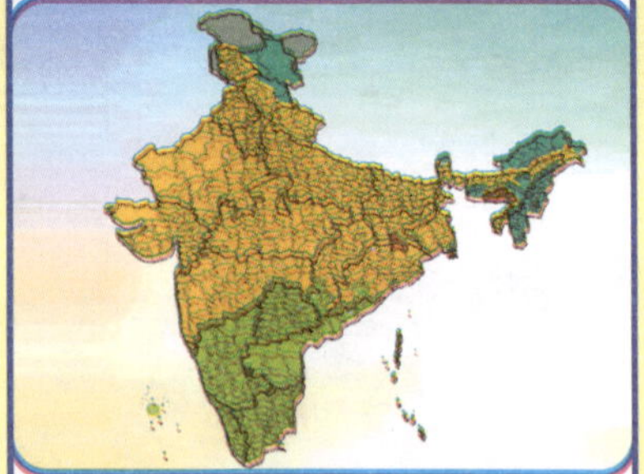

2 Roles and Responsibilities

- Family relationships are based on love, care, **cooperation,** and **interdependence**
- Each member has roles and responsibilities towards others
- Parents raise children, children help at home and learn family traditions
- **Family is a school** where children learn values like giving (*dana*), *ahimsa*, service (*seva*), and sacrifice (*tyaga*) in the family
- Members sometimes sacrifice their own needs for the family

3 Community

- **Community** is a group of connected families and people
- They come together for festivals, events, farming, and shared resources
- Communities make rules and members have duties
- They exist in rural and urban areas
- **Residents' Welfare Associations** are an example of urban communities
- People in communities are interdependent on each other
- **Types of Communities:** Jāti, religion, region, occupation, interest, etc.
  Examples: Mumbai's Parsi community, Kerala's scientific community, our school's art community
- **School Communities:** Class, sports, NSS (National Service Scheme), NCC (National Cadet Corps), science or drama clubs, etc.
- **Real-life example:** **Kamal Parmar** in Ahmedabad taught street children, with volunteers helping and learning
- Bhil community practiced **halma** by planting trees and building water structures as duty towards community and environment
- During **Chennai floods 2015**, groups helped people with food and aid

THEME D
Governance and Democracy

CHAPTER 9

FAMILY AND COMMUNITY

I. FACTS TO REMEMBER/SUMMARY

FAMILY

There are different types of families:

- **Nuclear Family:** Consists of parents and their children.
- **Joint Family:** Includes extended family members that live together like grand parents, *Chacha, Chachi, Tauji, Taiji* and their children.
- **Single-Parent Family:** One parent raising children due to various circumstances.

ROLES AND RESPONSIBILITIES

- Understanding the different roles that family members play.
- Sharing responsibilities among family members.
- Emphasising the importance of cooperation and support within the family.
- Cultural values and traditions play a vital role in shaping family life and relationships.
- Traditions are passed down through generations, preserving heritage and strengthening identity.
- Festivals and rituals bring family members together, fostering unity and strengthening family bonds.
- Urbanisation and distant employment opportunities are changing family structures.
- Migration has also impacted family systems.

COMMUNITY

- Different types of communities exist in both rural and urban areas.
- In a family system, the community plays a crucial role in providing support and resources.
- It also helps maintain cooperation and unity in society.
- Families and communities support each other and are interdependent.
- Communities also play a crucial role in providing services for family welfare.

These themes **aim** to provide students a comprehensive understanding of different family structures, their functions, and the importance of community in individual and collective well-being.

II. TEXTBOOK KEYWORDS/GLOSSARY

1. **Joint Family:** A family that consists of grandparents, parents and their children, uncle, aunts and cousins.
2. **Nuclear Family:** A family consisting of parents and their children.
3. **Relationships:** The way people or family members live and communicate.
4. **Dharma:** Duty.
5. **Ahimsa:** Non-violence.
6. **Dana:** Giving, The act of charity
7. **Seva:** Service.
8. **Tyaga:** Sacrifice.
9. **Interdependence:** It is the state of being dependent upon one another: mutual dependence.
10. **Social Values:** Understanding the relative importance that people place on changes to their well being and using the insights we gain from this understanding to make better decisions.

III. THE BIG QUESTIONS (*Page 137*)

Q. 1. ***Why is the family unit important?***

Ans. The family unit is important as it plays a crucial role in the development of individuals and the well-being of society as a whole. Here are some reasons why families are important:

(*a*) Nurturing and emotional support– Families provide love, care and emotional security.

(*b*) Socialisation and values– They teach social norms, values and ethics.

(*c*) Identity and self-esteem– Families shape personal identity and self-worth.

(*d*) Practical support– They provide financial and daily life assistance.

(*e*) Community building– Families contribute to forming larger social network.

(*f*) Resilience– They help members overcome life's challenges.

Q.2. ***What is a community and what is its role?***

Ans. A community is a group of people living in a specific area and sharing common characteristics or interests. It can be defined by geography (*a village, town, or city*), by social ties (religious groups, sports teams, online communities), or by shared experiences (people who have gone through a similar life events).

Key roles of a community:

(*a*) Shared Resources and Services: Schools, hospitals, parks, and transportation systems contribute to the well-being of members.

(*b*) Problem-Solving and Collaboration: Communities work together to address common challenges like environmental protection, crime prevention, and cleanliness.

(*c*) Preserving Culture and Traditions: They help pass down traditions and provide spaces to celebrate cultural practices.

IV. NCERT INTEXT/TEXTBOOK EXERCISES

LET'S EXPLORE

Q. 1. ***What types of families do you see in your neighbourhood? List the type with the number of households for each type.*** (*Page 138*)

Ans. There are a few different family structures found in many societies in my neighbourhood:

(*a*) **Nuclear Family:** This is the most common type in many societies, A nuclear family consists of parents and their children. There are around 40–50 nuclear families in our society.

(*b*) **Joint Family:** In a joint family multiple generations live together, including parents, children, grand-parents, uncles, aunts and cousins. There are around 10–15 such families in our society.

(*c*) **Single-parent Family:** A house-hold with a single parent and their children. There are around 4–5 such families in our society.

(*d*) **Childless Family:** It is a family where a couple live and do not have kids. There are around 10–18 such families in our society.

Q. 2. ***What types are more frequent? Why do you think this is so?*** (*Page 138*)

Ans. Nuclear families are more frequent due to urbanisation, economic factors, and changing lifestyles. People prefer smaller families for independence, convenience and better financial management. Additionally, migration for jobs and education encourages nuclear family structures over joint families.

Q. 3. ***As a class activity, compare with your classmates, findings and discuss.*** (*Page 138*)

Ans. On comparing it was found that more nuclear families live in urban areas than rural areas.

Q. 4. ***Make a list of all the members of your family you can think of, including a few distant relatives. List their terms in your mother tongue or regional language and try to find the equivalent in English. Two examples are below for Hindi.*** (*Page 139*)

Ans. Here's a sample list of family members with their terms in Hindi and their English equivalents:

Name	Term in Hindi	Description / Term in English
Rani	बहन	Sister / Mother's brother's daughter (Cousin)
Sameer	चाचा	Father's younger brother (Uncle)
Roshni	माँ	Mother
Amar	पिताजी	Father
Sony	बुआ	Father's sister (Aunt)
Mithun	ताऊ	Father's elder brother (Uncle)
Susheela	ताई	Father's elder brother's wife (Aunt)
Rohan	मामा	Mother's brother (Maternal Uncle)
Sonia	मामी	Mother's brother's wife (Maternal Aunt)
Jyoti	मौसी	Mother's sister (Aunt)
Ritesh	मौसा	Mother's sister's husband (Uncle)
Raghu	दादा	Grandfather
Mohini	दादी	Grandmother
Sohan	नाना	Maternal Grandfather
Geeta	नानी	Maternal Grandmother

Q. 5. ***Answer these questions and compare your answers with your classmates:*** (*Page 140*)

(*a*) ***Who in your family decides what is to be bought from the market?***

Ans. In my home , both parents-mother and father make decisions together.

(b) Who cooks food in your home?

Ans. My mother cooks food in our home. Other family members help her in odd jobs like cutting and peeling vegetables etc.

(c) Who is the oldest person in your family?

Ans. My grandmother is the oldest person in my family.

(d) Who cleans the floor in your house?

Ans. Our maid cleans the floor in our house.

(e) Who washes utensils in your house?

Ans. Our maid washes the utensils in our house.

(f) Who helps you to do your homework?

Ans. My parents.

Q. 6. ***Draw a simple tree of this family of seven members.*** *(Page 141)*

Ans.

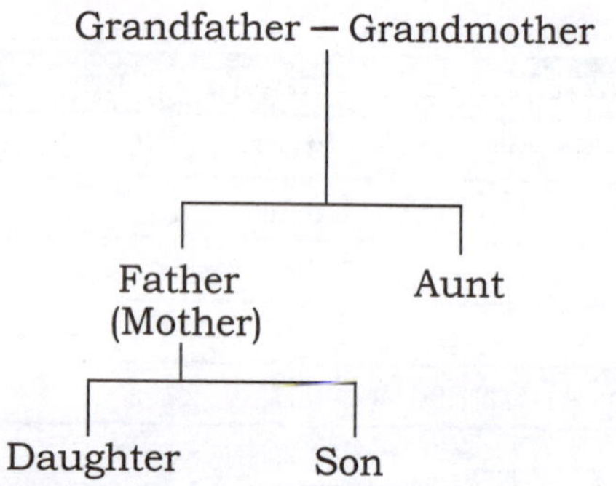

Q. 7. ***Why do you think Shalini's parents bought clothes for everyone?*** *(Page 141)*

Ans. Family relations are based on love, care, and affection. Each member of the family has a role and responsibility towards other members. Shalini's parents bought clothes for everyone to show their love and support for her uncle and aunt.

Q. 8. ***What would you have done if you were in Shalini's place?*** *(Page 141)*

Ans. If I were in Shalini's place, I would be happy that everyone in my family get some new clothes for the festival of Onam. Even if I had to settle for a cotton cloth, instead of a silk cloth, I would have been happy as family members support each other.

Moreover, it is good to see everyone happy in the family.

Q. 9. ***Create a story of a family somewhere in India, where we see some family values practised. Share it with your class either through writing or drawing.*** *(Page 143)*

Ans. The Wisdom of the Emperor Ashoka

In the heart of Bihar, in a small village near Pataliputra, lived young Prayan with his parents and grandparents. His grandfather, Baba, often told him stories from history, especially about Emperor Ashoka. Prayan loved listening to how Ashoka, once a unkind king who believed in harsh policies, became a kind and just ruler after the deadly and inhuman Battle of Kalinga(Odisha) .

One evening, under the old **mango tree**, Baba shared a story that left a deep imprint on young Prayan.

"Ashoka, after witnessing the pain of war, death and suffering decided to give up war. He adopted the policy of compassion, peace, love and just rule. This was his Dhamma. He treated everyone as his own family, whether rich or poor, Hindu or Buddhist. He built hospitals, planted trees, and helped people live in harmony."

During **Chhath Puja**, the whole family gathered at the riverbank to offer prayers to the Sun God. Prayan noticed how people helped each other, sharing sweets and guiding elders carefully. It reminded him of Ashoka's lesson of love, care and respect.

Family values derived from the story :

- Respect
- Love
- Cooperation
- Sympathy

Q. 10. ***In the stories of Shalini and Tenzing, we see examples of joint families. What do you think are the aspects of modern living that make some couples opt for a nuclear family (i.e., living apart from older generations or other relatives)? What could be some advantages as well as disadvantages of the two kinds of families?*** *(Page 143)*

Ans. In modern day, many people choose to live in nuclear families:
The reasons are :

- Better career opportunities and growth in far away places.
- More individual freedom and better decision making process.
- Better social infrastructure like schools and hospitals.

Family system	Advantages	Disadvantages
Joint Family	Responsibilities are shared Support system in time of crisis	Less privacy Chance of constant conflict
Nuclear Family	More independence and freedom Less expenditure	No support system during crisis Lack of traditional value system to younger generation

Q. 11. ***Make a list of all people outside your family that are supporting you through their work in one way or another.*** *(Page 147)*

Ans. People who support us beyond our family through their work include:

- Teachers
- Medical professionals like Doctors, Nurses and pharmacists
- Farmers
- Police and security guards
- Sanitation staff
- Online delivery personnel – Bringing you food, parcels, and essentials.
- Professionals like electricians & plumbers.

Q. 12. ***What types of communities are you part of?*** *(Page 148)*

Ans. Do it yourself.

Q. 13. ***Is there a club that you are a part of in school? How does it function?*** *(Page 148)*

Ans. Yes, I am a part of Debating Club, NCC, and Sports Club.

THINK ABOUT IT

Q. 1. ***Why does Tenzing's father consult his wife for special expends?*** *(Page 142)*

Ans. Tenzing's father consult his wife for special expenses because they try to save some money for any unexpected needs that may arise in the future.

Q. 2. ***How do you feel about his participation in household chores?*** *(Page 142)*

Ans. Tenzing's father actively doing in household chores, such as cleaning and gardening, shows responsibility and equality. His involvement breaks traditional gender roles and ensuring a balanced home environment.

Q. 3. ***What roles do the grandparents fulfil?***

Ans. • Tenzing's grandmother plays an important role by sharing stories with humour and wisdom, that teaches life lessons.

• His grandfather helps him with his homework, takes him to the school bus stop, and engages in social work, and organises community aid during crises.

INTEXT QUESTIONS

Q. 1. ***Discuss this story in your class. What kind of attitude towards the community does it reveal?*** *(Page 146)*

Ans. The story reflects a sense of being responsible towards society, having empathy, kindness and working for collective well-being.

Q. 2. ***What values get reflected in Kamal Parmar's initiative?*** *(Page 146)*

Ans. Kamal Parmar's initiative reflects being responsible towards society, especially for poor children. He shows compassion and empathy and gives back what he got from society, in terms of teaching poor and left out children.

Q. 3. ***Think about those under-privileged children. Do you think society has been unfair to them?*** *(Page 146)*

Ans. Yes, society is unfair to these underprivileged children. Many children lack access to education, medical facilities and means of life.

Q. 4. ***What should society do to make sure that all children get access to education?*** *(Page 147)*

Ans. Society should create free and easy access to education.

- It should ensure proper mid-day meal system to these children.
- Free uniforms, textbooks, and stationery.
- If possible, free lodging should be provided.

NCERT Questions, Activities and Projects
(Page 148)

Q. 1. ***What are some of the rules you follow in your family and neighbourhood? Why are they important?***

Ans. Some general rules in my family and neighbourhood are as follows:

I. In the Family

(a) **Respectful Communication:** This might involve using kind words, listening attentively, and resolving conflicts peacefully.

(b) **Chores and Responsibilities:** Contributing to household tasks teaches responsibility, time management, and life skills.

(c) **Curfews and Screen Time Limits:** These rules promote healthy sleep habits, a balance between screen time and other activities, and personal safety (especially for nighttime curfews).

(d) **Honesty and Truthfulness:** Building trust is essential within a family. Honesty allows parents to provide guidance and support when needed.

II. In the Neighbourhood

Property Respect: This involves not damaging other people's property, being mindful of noise levels, and keeping the neighbourhood clean.

By following these rules, I have learnt valuable life skills and have become a responsible member of my family and neighbourhood.

Q. 2. ***Do you think some rules are unfair to a few people in the family or community? Why?***

Ans. Some rules are unfair for a few reasons:

- **Unequal Application:** Sometimes, children might feel like the rules are enforced inconsistently. For example, a younger sibling might get away with something an older sibling gets in trouble for. This can lead to feelings of resentment and a belief that the rules are unfair.
- **Lack of Understanding:** If the reasons behind a rule aren't explained clearly, people might not understand the purpose. This can make them feel like the rule is arbitrary and unfair. For instance, a teen might not understand why there is a time limit of returning home if their parents haven't explained the importance of sleep or safety concerns.

- **Favouritism:** If one perceives that certain family member or neighbour is favoured and get away with breaking rules, one may feel it is unfair.

Here's how parents and communities can address these issues:

- **Open Communication:** Explain the reasons behind the rules and have open conversations about expectations.
- **Fair and Consistent Enforcement:** Apply the rules fairly to everyone, regardless of age or relationship.
- **Consider Age and Maturity:** Adjust rules as students grow and demonstrate responsibility.

By working together, parents, students, and communities can create a set of rules that are fair, understandable, and beneficial for everyone.

Q. 3. ***Describe several situations that you have observed where community support makes a difference. You can draw or write about these.***

Ans. Here are some situations where community support makes a difference:

1. **Natural Disasters:** Recently after a hurricane, community members came together to provide food, shelter, and emotional support to affected families.
2. **Neighbourhood Watch:** A community organised a neighbourhood watch program, reducing crime and increasing safety through collective vigilance.
3. **Fundraising for Medical Treatment:** Community members raised funds for a neighbour's medical treatment, showing financial and emotional support.
4. **Volunteer Cleanup Initiatives:** Community volunteers cleaned up local parks and waterways, promoting environmental responsibility.
5. **Disability Support:** Community members rallied around a family with a disabled child, providing resources and inclusivity.
6. **Food Banks and Pantries:** Community-run food banks and pantries ensured no one went hungry, especially during economic downturns.
7. **Community Celebrations:** Cultural events and festivals brought the community together, fostering connection and belonging.

V. EXAM ORIENTED QUESTIONS

A. Very Short Answer Type Questions

Q. 1. ***What is the basic unit of society?***

Ans. Family.

Q. 2. ***What type of family has parents and children living together?***

Ans. Nuclear family.

Q. 3. ***Give example of the values we should practice within our family.***

Ans. Respect, sharing, love and affection.

Q. 4. ***What is one responsibility you might have within your family?***

Ans. Helping with household chores.

Q. 5. ***What is the foundation of strong families?***

Ans. Love and respect (both are important).

Q. 6. ***What is a group of people living in the same area with common interests called?***

Ans. Neighbourhood.

Q. 7. ***Give few examples of elements found in a community.***

Ans. A community consists of people, culture (schools, hospitals), economy (businesses, jobs), infrastructure (roads, electricity), environment (parks) and social services (Police, NGOs).

Q. 8. ***How can you participate in your community?***

Ans. By volunteering in cleanliness drive, I can help the community.

Q. 9. ***Give few examples of responsibilities we might have towards our community.***

Ans. Helping a neighbour and keeping our surroundings clean.

Q. 10. ***How are strong families and strong communities related?***

Ans. Interdependence (they rely on each other).

B. Short Answer Type Questions

Q. 1. ***Explain the importance of family in society.***

Ans. Families provide love, care, and support, which are essential for a child's healthy development.

Families are the primary agents of socialisation, teaching children social skills, communication, and how to interact with others.

Families transmit values, beliefs, and morals to the next generation, shaping their understanding of the world.

Families provide for basic needs like food, shelter, and clothing.

Strong families contribute to strong communities by raising responsible and caring individuals.

Q. 2. ***Describe two different types of families.***

Ans. **Nuclear Family:** A family with parents and children living together.

Joint Family: A family that includes parents, children, grandparents, aunts, uncles, and cousins living together.

Q. 3. ***What are some responsibilities that family members might have towards each other?***

Ans.

(*a*) Helping with household chores.

(*b*) Respecting each other's opinions and feelings.

(*c*) Taking care of younger or elderly family members.

(*d*) Communicating openly and honestly.

(*e*) Supporting each other through difficult times.

C. Long Answer Type Questions

Q. 1. ***How does a strong family system benefit a community?***

Ans. A strong family system contributes to communities in several ways:

- **Raise Responsible Citizens:** Families that instill positive values like respect, cooperation, and social responsibility contribute to a more positive community environment.
- **Active Participation:** Family members who value community involvement are more likely to participate in community activities and contribute their time and skills.
- **Support Systems:** Strong families provide a foundation of support for individuals, which can help them cope with challenges and contribute more effectively to the community.
- **Positive Role Models:** Strong families can serve as positive role models for other families within the community.

Q. 2. ***Imagine you and your classmates want to plant a tree in the schoolyard. How can you get your community involved in this project?***

Ans. Here are some ways to get our community involved in planting a tree in the schoolyard:

- **Make Posters and Flyers:** Announce the project and invite community members to participate.

- **Contact Local Organisations:** Environmental groups or gardening clubs might be interested in helping.
- **Spread the Word Online or through Social Media:** Increase awareness and encourage community participation.
- **Hold a Planting Event:** Organise a specific day for the project where everyone can contribute.

Q. 3. ***Describe the different roles that family members play in a healthy and supportive family environment.***

Ans. A healthy and supportive family environment relies on all members fulfilling different roles that contribute to the overall well-being of the family members.

Parents: Provide love, care, and security for their children.

Parents are also responsible for meeting their children's basic needs for food, education, clothing, and healthcare.

Children: Respect their parents and contribute to the family environment in age-appropriate ways.

Siblings: Learn to share, cooperate, and resolve conflicts peacefully.

Siblings can also provide companionship and support to one another.

Q. 4. ***Explain how strong family values can help children develop into well-rounded individuals.***

Ans. Strong family values play a crucial role in shaping children's development and helping them become well-rounded individuals.

Emotional Security: A loving and supportive family environment provides a sense of security and belonging, which is essential for healthy emotional development.

Children feel safe to explore, learn, and take risks knowing they have a secure base to return to.

Positive Values: Families instill values like respect, responsibility, honesty, andcompassion. These values guide children's behaviour and shape their moral compass as they navigate the world.

Social Skills: Families provide opportunities for children to learn and practice social skills like communication, cooperation, conflict resolution, and empathy.

Through interactions with family members, children develop the ability to build healthy relationships.

This self-esteem allows them to face challenges and pursue their goals.

Identity: Families play a role in shaping children's sense of identity. Cultural traditions, family history, and shared experiences contribute to how children see themselves and their place in the world.

Q. 5. ***Describe the concept of community and explain how different elements contribute to a strong community.***

Ans. A community is a social unit of people living in the same area and sharing common interests, culture and history. It can be defined geographically (a neighbourhood, town, city) or by social ties (religious groups, sports teams, online communities). Different elements that contribute to a strong community are:

Public Places and Services: Educational institutes hospitals, recreational centres, transportation systems, and infrastructure that improve the quality of life for community members.

Commercial establishments: Shops, restaurants, banks, and other business houses that create jobs, offer goods and services, and contribute to the economic vitality of the community.

Social Organisations: Clubs, sports teams, religious groups, and community centres provide opportunities for social interaction, shared interests, and a sense of belonging.

Civic responsibilities: Residents who participate in community activities, volunteer their time, and take responsibility for their surroundings contribute to a more vibrant and positive community environment.

Q. 6. *Explain roles and responsibilities of family members.*

Ans. Family is an important unit of society and plays very important role in life of an individual. It helps in :

- Living in a family generates lot of values and responsibilities.
- Different family members get their responsibilities and shares at it best.
- Relationships among family members are based on love, care, cooperation and interdependence.
- Over a period of time, children learn different values like ahimsa, *dāna* (giving), *sevā* (service) and *tyāga* (sacrifice) which helps them face real life problems later in life.

Q. 7. *Examine some family values which we can be practised in day to day life.*

Ans. Some important family values that can be practised in our daily life include:

(*a*) **Cooperation:** This is important as family members cooperate each other in all types of inside and outside work.

(*b*) **Respect:** Another aspect of family is respecting and treating them with empathy.

(*c*) Being polite to elders and younger ones.

(*d*) Being responsible towards task assigned

(*e*) Having patience in terms of crisis.

(*f*) Feeling of gratitude towards family members.

D. Assertion and Reasoning Questions

There are two statements Assertion (A) and Reason (R). Mark your answers as per the code given below.

1. **Assertion (A):** Nuclear families are becoming less common in modern society.

   Reason (R): New cities and job opportunities encourage nuclear families.

   Codes:

   (*a*) Both (A) and (R) are true, but (R) is not the correct explanation of (A).

   (*b*) Both (A) and (R) are true, and (R) is the correct explanation of (A).

   (*c*) (A) is true, but (R) is false.

   (*d*) (A) is false, but (R) is true.

2. **Assertion (A):** In Indian tradition and culture, brothers and sisters are considered cousins.

   Reason (R): Most Indian languages have a separate word for 'cousin.'

   Codes:

   (*a*) Both (A) and (R) are true, but (R) is not the correct explanation of (A).

   (*b*) Both (A) and (R) are true, and (R) is the correct explanation of (A).

   (*c*) (A) is true, but (R) is false.

   (*d*) (A) is false, but (R) is true.

3. **Assertion (A):** The members of community support each other during crises.

   Reason (R): A community is formed based on mutual cooperation and interdependence.

   Codes:

   (*a*) Both (A) and (R) are true, but (R) is not the correct explanation of (A).

   (*b*) Both (A) and (R) are true, and (R) is the correct explanation of (A).

   (*c*) (A) is true, but (R) is false.

   (*d*) (A) is false, but (R) is true.

4. **Assertion (A):** The Bhil community planted trees and dug trenches to solve their water crisis.

   Reason (R): The Bhil people of Maharashtra followed the tradition of halma, where everyone cook food for poor people.

Codes:

(*a*) Both (A) and (R) are true, but (R) is not the correct explanation of (A).

(*b*) Both (A) and (R) are true, and (R) is the correct explanation of (A).

(*c*) (A) is true, but (R) is false.

(*d*) (A) is false, but (R) is true.

5. **Assertion (A):** Kamal Parmar provided free education to underprivileged children.

Reason (R): He believed that education should be also given to those who cannot afford it.

Codes:

(*a*) Both (A) and (R) are true, but (R) is not the correct explanation of (A).

(*b*) Both (A) and (R) are true, and (R) is the correct explanation of (A).

(*c*) (A) is true, but (R) is false.

(*d*) (A) is false, but (R) is true.

Ans.

1. → (*d*) 2. → (*d*) 3. → (*b*)
4. → (*c*) 5. → (*b*)

E. Case/Source Based Questions

Read the passages given and answer the questions that follow.

I. More than 20 years ago, in an area of Ahmedabad (Gujarat), Kamal Parmar, owner of a small auto-fabrication workshop, noticed a group of underprivileged children on the street. Some had dropped out of school, while others had never been to school. Kamal started giving them tuition from 5:30 to 9:30 pm every day, after his regular work hours. He also provided the kids with a free dinner. Soon, 150 children were attending those classes regularly and were deeply interested in the lessons!

(*a*) ***Who was Kamal Parmar?***

(*b*) ***Give his contribution to society.***

(*c*) ***Mention any two values from the above passage.***

Ans. (*a*) Kamal Parmar was the owner of a small auto-fabrication workshop, who helped the underprivileged children.

(*b*) He taught the underprivileged children and provided free meal to them.

(*c*) Empathy and Selflessness.

II. New types of communities have also emerged in the last 30 or 40 years. Residents' Welfare Associations in many urban areas are examples of communities that make their own rules and regulations. Those could be rules about waste management, cleanliness of common areas, taking care of pets, and so on. People living in the community participate in making such rules and regulations.

(*a*) ***Give features of a community.***

(*b*) ***Why is a community important ?***

(*c*) ***Mention importance of Residents' Welfare Associations (RWA).***

Ans. (*a*) A community is a group of people who are connected by common interests, geography, or shared values. Some key features of a community include:

- Sense of being one
- Cooperation
- Financial and emotional support to members.

(*b*) Communities play an important role:

- Emotional and social support to its members.
- Provide security and safety to its members.

(*c*) RWAs ensure waste management and cleanliness in residential areas.

- They organise cultural programs, health check-ups, and social events.
- Many RWAs help in collection of garbage.

F. Competency Based Questions

I. Mausami lives in a nuclear family far away from her village with her parents and younger brother. Both her parents are software engineers and work full-time. She often notices that her mother struggles to complete all the household work.

Q. ***What should Mausami do to support her family, and why is sharing responsibilities important in a family?***

Ans. Mausami should help her mother in household chores

- She should take charge of some household work, like cleaning, dusting, watering plant.
- She should along with her father to take lead in taking care of the house.
- Sharing household work is important for the family members as it reduces the burden on one particular person.
- House become home, with a sense of equal sharing.

II. Prayan wanted to buy a new cricket bat, but he noticed that a girl Sheesh in nearby area needed a new school bag because her old one was torn. Her parents could not afford to buy bag this month. He volunteered and convinced his father to buy bag of the Sheesh.

Q. ***Suppose you were Prayan, what decision would you have taken? Justify your decision based on family values that you have inherited.***

Ans.

- Just like Prayan, I also would have convince my parents to come forward to purchase a bag for Sheesh.
- I have been told on a regular basis by my parents and elders, to share whenever possible, to empathise with needy people and become more responsible towards society.

G. Skill Based Questions

I. A Residents' Welfare Association (RWA) of DDA Housing Society, HASTSAL finds that many young children in their society spend too much time on mobile phones. They do not engage in any kind of outdoor activities. The RWA wants to motivate and encourage young minds to participate in community events and physical activities.

Q. ***As an active member of RWA-student group propose an action plan to reduce screen time and promote sports activity among children in the community.***

Ans. Organise outdoor sports events, set screen free hours, conduct fitness challenges and encourage parent-child games. Collaborate with schools and RWAs for awareness programs and better playground access.

II. There is a village which has been witnessing drought for last two years and people are facing a severe water shortage. The local school , plays a role of problem solver. The villages involve students and have requested the school to come up with creative ways to save and manage water.

Q. ***Suggest some creative ways and methods to manage water shortage.***

Ans. Install rainwater harvesting, reuse water for gardening, fix leaks, promote drip irrigation, and run awareness campaigns. Encourage water efficient appliances and community driven conservation projects.

H. Picture Based Questions

I. **Observe the given picture and answer the questions that follow:**

Q. 1. ***Identify the personality associated with Shivganga movement.***

Ans. Shri Mahesh Sharma

Q. 2. ***Which award was given to him?***

Ans. Padma Shri.

II. Observe the given picture of *HALMA* tradition and answer the questions that follow :

Q. 1. ***What is halma tradition ?***

Ans. The people of Bhil community came together to support any individual or family in times of crisis, the Bhil community decided to plant thousands of trees in hundreds of villages.

Q. 2. ***Which state is associated with it ?***

Ans. Madhya Pradesh.

Q. 3. ***State advantages of halma tradition.***

Ans. Community Cooperation – It brings people together to work for a common cause, strengthening unity and cooperation.

Environmental Conservation – The practice helps in water conservation, afforestation, and soil preservation.

VI. MULTIPLE CHOICE QUESTIONS

Instructions: Choose the most appropriate answer for each question.

1. *The basic unit of society is the:*
(a) School (b) Playground
(c) Family (d) Market

2. *A family with parents and children is called a:*
(a) Joint family
(b) Nuclear family
(c) Big family
(d) Extended family

3. *Which of the following is NOT a value we should practice within our family?*
(a) Cooperation
(b) Respect
(c) Sharing
(d) Arguing constantly

4. *A group of people living in the same place and sharing common interests is called a:*
(a) Neighbourhood
(b) Playground
(c) Team
(d) Classroom

5. *Which of the following is the element of a community?*
(a) Park (b) Dispensary
(c) Home (d) All of these

6. *It is important to participate in community activities because:*
(a) It's mandatory
(b) It helps us make friends only
(c) It contributes to the well-being of the community
(d) It gets us out of chores

7. *An example of a responsibility we might have towards our community is:*
(a) Doing our homework
(b) Helping a neighbour in need
(c) Watching TV all day
(d) Littering in the park

8. *Strong families and strong communities are:*
(a) Independent of each other
(b) Interdependent
(c) Completely separate
(d) Always in competition

9. *The message of this chapter is to:*
(*a*) Focus only on your family
(*b*) Value family, community, and social responsibility
(*c*) Ignore your neighbours
(*d*) Be selfish

10. *Which of the following is a value we should practice within our family?*
(*a*) Sharing
(*b*) Arguing constantly
(*c*) Ignoring each other
(*d*) Being disrespectful

11. *Responsibilities within a family can include:*
(*a*) Helping with household chores
(*b*) Watching TV all day
(*c*) Arguing with siblings
(*d*) Disobeying parents

12. *Strong families are built on the foundation of:*
(*a*) Competition
(*b*) Love and respect
(*c*) Disagreement
(*d*) Ignoring each other's needs

13. *The two main parts of a chapter are:*
(*a*) Playground and classroom
(*b*) Family and community
(*c*) School and library
(*d*) Market and hospital

14. *A value we should practice within our family is:*
(*a*) Respect
(*b*) Arguing constantly
(*c*) Ignoring each other
(*d*) Being bossy

15. *A place where we can buy groceries is an example of a:*
(*a*) School (*b*) Market
(*c*) Hospital (*d*) Playground

16. *Helping a neighbour in need is an example of:*
(*a*) Family responsibility
(*b*) Community responsibility
(*c*) School responsibility
(*d*) Playground responsibility

17. *John lives with his parents and younger sister. What type of family does John have?*
(*a*) Extended family
(*b*) Nuclear family
(*c*) Big family
(*d*) Joint family

18. *Sarah helps her mother with chores like laying the table and cleaning her room. What value is Sarah demonstrating?*
(*a*) Respect
(*b*) Laziness
(*c*) Sharing responsibilities
(*d*) Selfishness

19. *The local park is overgrown with weeds. What can you do to help your community?*
(*a*) Ignore the problem
(*b*) Organise a neighbourhood clean-up day
(*c*) Vandalise the park equipment
(*d*) Complain to everyone but take no action

20. *Ms. Lopez notices her elderly neighbour struggling to carry groceries home. What is the most responsible course of action?*
(*a*) Pretend you didn't see anything
(*b*) Offer help to Ms. Lopez carry the groceries
(*c*) Make fun of Ms. Lopez for having too many groceries
(*d*) Tell everyone in the neighbourhood about Ms. Lopez's struggles

21. *Strong families and strong communities benefit each other in many ways. How can a strong family contribute to a strong community?*

(*a*) By isolating themselves from their neighbours

(*b*) By raising responsible and caring individuals

(*c*) By competing with other families in the community

(*d*) By gossiping about their neighbours

22. *Imagine you and your classmates want to plant a tree in the schoolyard. How can you get your community involved in this project?*

(*a*) Keep it a secret and surprise everyone.

(*b*) Ask your classmates for help only.

(*c*) Put up posters around the neighbourhood inviting everyone to participate

(*d*) Ask your teacher to handle everything.

ANSWERS

1. → (*c*)	**2.** → (*b*)	**3.** → (*d*)
4. → (*a*)	**5.** → (*a*)	**6.** → (*c*)
7. → (*b*)	**8.** → (*b*)	**9.** → (*b*)
10. → (*a*)	**11.** → (*a*)	**12.** → (*b*)
13.→ (*b*)	**14.**→ (*a*)	**15.** → (*b*)
16.→ (*b*)	**17.** → (*b*)	**18.**→ (*a*)
19.→ (*b*)	**20.** → (*b*)	**21.**→ (*b*)
22.→ (*c*)		

VII. OBJECTIVE TYPE QUESTIONS

1. One Word Questions

1. *The basic unit of society:*

2. *A family with parents and children:*

3. *A value to practice in family:*

4. *Responsibility within a family:*

5. *Foundation of strong families:*

6. *A group of people in the same area with common interests:*

7. *Places like schools and hospitals are elements of:*

8. *Participating in community activities:*

9. *Responsibility towards the community:*

10. *Relationship between strong families and communities:*

Answers

1. Family.
2. Nuclear.
3. Respect/Sharing Love (any acceptable value).
4. Chores/Helping.
5. Love and Respect.
6. Neighbourhood.
7. Community.
8. Cleaning/Helping.
9. Helping neighbours.
10. Interdependent.

2. Fill in the blanks

Q.1. ***Fill in the blanks with appropriate words.***

(*i*) Shalini's family was preparing for ....

(*ii*) Shalini's parents bought clothes for their relatives as they believed in the value of ....

(*iii*) Tenzing's .... helped him with his homework and also participated in social work.

(*iv*) The Bhil community in .... followed the tradition of .... to help with water conservation.

(*v*) During Chennai floods of 2015 ....group provided foods and other help.

(*vi*) A jāti, is also example of.............

Ans.

(*i*) Onam
(*ii*) sharing
(*iii*) grandfather
(*iv*) Madhya Pradesh, halma
(*v*) spiritual and religious organisation
(*vi*) community

3. True or False

Q. 1. ***State whether the given statements are true or false.***

(*i*) The first school of children is their family.

(*ii*) Shalini was sad that she got a simpler dress.

(*iii*) Community exists in rural areas only and not in urban areas.

(*iv*) Communities are ultimately interdependent.

Ans.

(*i*) True (*ii*) False
(*iii*) False (*iv*) True

VIII. TEST YOUR KNOWLEDGE

A. Multiple Choice Questions (MCQs)

1. *The word "dharma" refers to :*

(*a*) Being religious
(*b*) Doing one's duty
(*c*) Worshipping regularly
(*d*) Spreading religious ideas

2. *In the story of Shalini, why did her parents buy clothes for the whole family ?*

(*a*) They had surplus money
(*b*) Shalini did not like silk dresses
(*c*) They wanted to share
(*d*) They wanted to save money for a festival

3. *Identify the incorrect statement/s:*

(*i*) Kamal Parmar belongs to Ahmedabad .

(*ii*) He started giving tuition to privileged students.

(*iii*) He also provided the kids with free dinner.

(*iv*) A few teachers from a local school noticed the classes and joined the teaching for a while.

Option :

(*a*) only iv
(*b*) i.ii and iii
(*c*) only ii.
(*d*) i, , iii and iv

4. *Year after year, the region around the town of Jhabua, in Madhya Pradesh, suffered from an acute water crisis. How did the Bhil community resolve their water crisis?*

(*a*) By making canal and joining them with the Narmada river
(*b*) They dug many trenches to conserve rainwater
(*c*) They took support from government for water supply
(*d*) Purchasing water from nearby village

B. Fill in the Blanks

1. In most Indian languages, elder brother / sister or younger brother / sister. are often referred ....

2. Tenzing belongs to ....

3. A .... family consists of several generations living together.

4. A nuclear family includes only .... and their children.

5. The concept of .... means working together and supporting each other in the family.

C. True or False

1. Residents' Welfare Associations, depend on the trading community for supplies and also on municipal workers to handle waste.
2. Grandparents are part of a nuclear family and pass down traditions, stories, and values to the younger generation.
3. The family is also a 'school' where children learn important values such as ahimsa, *dāna* (giving), *sevā* (service) and *tyāga* (sacrifice).
4. Communities often disagrees upon some practices on the use of shared natural wealth.

D. Very Short Answer Type Questions

Q. 1. *Give an example of a value to practice within your family.*

Q. 2. *What kind of place can you find in a community where you could get treated for a wound?*

Q. 3. *Helping a neighbour in need is an example of what kind of responsibility?*

Q. 4. *How can strong families contribute to strong communities?*

Q. 5. *Sunny lives with his parents and younger sister. What type of family does Sunny have?*

Q. 6. *Priyanka helps her mother with chores like laying the table and cleaning her room. What value is Priyanka demonstrating?*

Q. 7. *The local park is overgrown with weeds. What can you do to help your community?*

Q. 8. *Ms. Lalita notices her elderly neighbour struggling to carry groceries home. What is the most responsible course of action?*

Q. 9. *Strong families and strong communities benefit each other in many ways. How can a strong family contribute to a positive community environment?*

Q. 10. *Give two features of community.*

Q. 11. *What is the fundamental unit of society?*

Q. 12. *Mention the different types of family system.*

Q. 13. *Give two important features of 'halma' tradition.*

Q. 14. *Write the purposes of Residents' Welfare Associations?*

Q. 15. *Which state is associated with Tenzing's family?*

E. Short Answer Type Questions

Q. 1. *Imagine you are arguing with your sibling over a toy. How can you use family values to resolve the situation peacefully?*

Q. 2. *What are some elements that make up a community?*

Q. 3. *Explain why participating in community activities is important.*

Q. 4. *Describe how a community can benefit from strong family system.*

Q. 5. *What are the primary advantages and disadvantages of living in a joint family compared to a nuclear family?*

Q. 6. *In what ways do family roles and responsibilities differ between joint and nuclear families?*

Q. 7. *What are the key differences between joint families and nuclear families?*

Q. 8. *Enumerate the value system reflected in Kamal Parmar's effort.*

Q. 9. *Explain the role of community.*

Q. 10. *The family is also a 'school'. Elaborate the statement.*

Q. 11. *Give the role of society in ensuring that underprivileged children get access to education.*

F. Long Answer Type Questions

Q. 1. *How can community support systems impact the well-being of families in various structures?*

Q. 2. *How does the concept of extended family play a role in both joint and nuclear family systems?*

Q. 3. *What role do government policies and social services play in supporting different family structures?*

Q. 4. *How do personal and economic factors influence the choice between living in a joint family versus a nuclear family?*

Q. 5. *Elaborate the main differences between a joint family and a nuclear family.*

Q. 6. *The family is the fundamental and most ancient unit of any society. Give reasons.*

Q. 7. *Indian languages have many terms to describe family relationships. Explain the statement with suitable examples.*

Q. 8. *Relationships among family members are based on love, care, cooperation and interdependence. Do you agree ? Give reasons to support your answer.*

G. Skill Based Questions

1. Stage a small drama with all your classmates around two or three families. The play you write could include some challenging situations that the families faced, and show how they are resolved.

NOTES

NOTES

Grassroots Democracy– Part 1: Governance

1 Introduction

- Living in communities can lead to disorder, so rules are necessary
- Rules operate at home, school, roads, exams, and workplaces
- **Governance** is the process of making and enforcing rules
- **Government** makes these rules, some of which are **laws**
- Rules and laws can be changed with citizen participation

2 Three Organs of Government

- Digital technology has changed society and created cybercrime
- Government has passed laws to deal with cybercrime
- Criminals are punished by courts
- **Legislature** makes and changes laws
- **Executive** implements laws and maintains order
- **Judiciary** decides guilt, punishment, and reviews laws and decisions
- **Separation of powers** ensures checks and balances

3 Three Levels of Government

- **Government operates at three levels: local, state, and national**
- Each level deals with different matters
- **Local handles** small issues at village/town level
- **State government** handles health, education, agriculture, irrigation, and local administration at state level
- **Central government** handles defence, foreign affairs, and national policies at national level

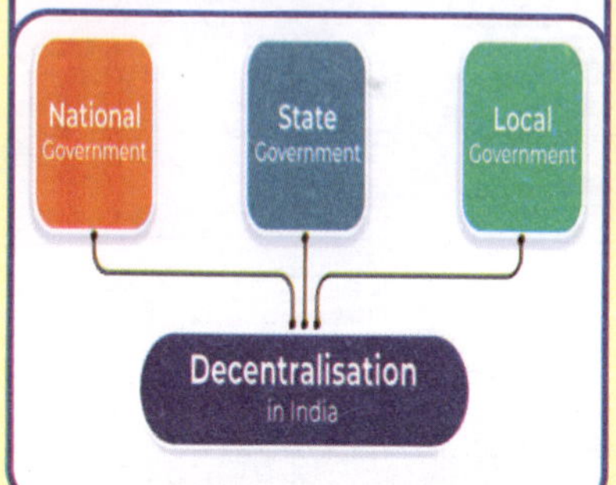

4 Democracy

- **Democracy** means rule of the people
- People cannot rule directly, so they elect representatives
- State representatives = MLAs; National representatives = MPs
- Representatives discuss laws and problems in assemblies
- India is a **representative democracy** and the world's largest democracy
- All citizens aged 18 and above can vote
- **Direct democracy** lets people vote themselves
- **Grassroots democracy** allows citizen participation

THEME D
Governance and Democracy

CHAPTER
10

GRASSROOTS DEMOCRACY– PART 1: GOVERNANCE

I. FACTS TO REMEMBER/SUMMARY

INTRODUCTION

- All countries require government for proper governance, welfare and security of the people.
- Human being lives in communities and form diverse group.
- The diversity and large number of people in any community is bound to create differences and conflict.
- In case of disagreements and conflicts rules are applied to create peace, respect and generate trust for orderly society.
- Rules help to avoid chaos and mismanagement in society.
- For example, different traffic lights like red, green and yellow are used for better and smooth traffic flow and to avoid accidents.
- Every institution like our family, schools, colleges, sports, classrooms, hospitals, malls, parking areas, cinema halls etc. requires some basic rules and laws.
- Rules and laws are made by the government and different authorities.
- 21st century and information technology revolution created new standard of living and plenty of opportunities to earn money.
- This also paved way for new age technological driven criminals to steal money.
- New laws and methods to arrest these type of criminals are required.

THREE ORGANS OF GOVERNMENT

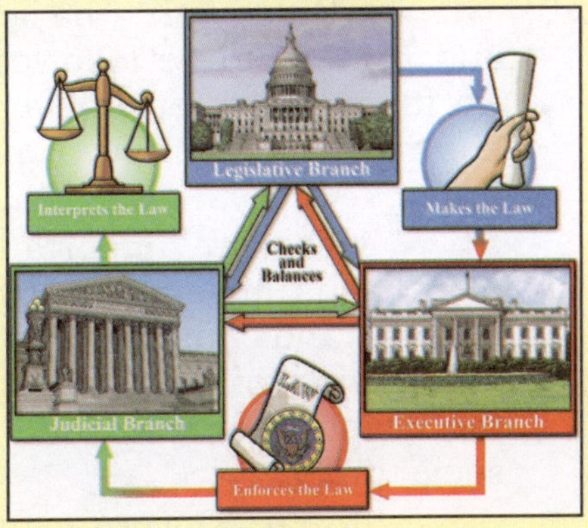

- Government plays an important role to check unlawful activities. It has three organs to uphold the sanctity of society.
- Three organs are:
  - **Legislature:** Make laws (The Parliament).
  - **Executive:** To implement rules and laws (Civil servants like IAS and IPS officers).
  - **Judiciary:** To uphold the constitutional laws and solve disputes. (High Courts, Supreme Court).
  - All the three organs of the government works together for smooth functioning of the society.
  - They also keep a check on each other.

THREE LEVELS OF GOVERNMENT

- India, that is Bharat is a huge and diverse country. For efficient management, easy delivery of services and practical democracy, we have three levels of the government.
  - **Central/Union Government:** It manages the affairs at the National (whole country) level.
  - **State Government:** State governments manage state affairs such as states like Sikkim, Manipur, Karnataka, Madhya Pradesh, etc.
  - **Local Government:** Government at village and urban areas (Panchayati Raj/ Municipal Corporation), they manage the affairs of their particular areas.

DEMOCRACY

- The constitution has defined India as a democratic country. All citizens above 18 years have a right to vote and they elect their representatives every 5 years.
- These representatives at national and state levels form the governments. The form of government is termed as representative government.
  - It is physically not possible for more than 970 millions (97 crores) of people (voters) to take decisions on day-to-day basis and hence we have empowered our representatives to take these decisions.
- Representatives are called **'Members of Legislative Assembly'** (MLAs) at the state level, and **'Members of Parliament'** (MPs) at the national level.
- At grassroot level democracy exists in the form of Panchayati Raj (in villages) and Municipal Corporations/Municipalities (in cities and towns).

II. TEXTBOOK KEYWORDS/GLOSSARY

1. **Community:** Community is associated with people having and sharing common interest and lives in a specific areas.
2. **Governance:** Governance is the process of managing the affairs of the society for the betterment of people through institutions like elected leaders, police, civil servants, army and others.
3. **Rules:** Rules are basic guidelines and process to be followed for normal working of society. (Even classroom has rules like proper uniform, shoes, timings etc.)
4. **Laws:** Laws are important rules and regulations implemented by government bodies and institutions for better functioning of the society, preventing the violation of rules and maintaining social order.
5. **Government:** Government is a set of different institutions (along with the group of individuals) that operates for welfare and security of the people. It makes and implements laws.
6. **Public Service:** Public service(s) are those services which are provided by the government to people at a low price or free of cost like water supply, security, schools, hospitals etc.
7. **Digital Technology:** The use of various technologies like smartphones, emails, computers to transmit, store and process the data. Payment of money through Net-Banking, UPI, watching movies through OTT etc.
8. **Constitution:** A constitution is a document that contains the fundamental laws for governing the nation. It outlines the type of government, and its rights and duties towards people.
9. **Legislature:** An organ of the government that makes laws. At union level it is called the Parliament (Sansad) and at state level it is known as State Legislative Assembly (Vidhan Sabha).
10. **Executive:** An organ of the government that implements the laws made by the legislature.

11. **Judiciary:** An organ of the government that upholds the constitutional laws and solves the disputes.
12. **Money Order:** Money order is a process of sending money through post office, where the recipient receives money in cash.
13. **Demand Draft:** A demand draft also known as DD is a banker's cheque.
14. **Cyber Crime:** Cyber crime is an illegal activity that is committed using technologies like computer, smartphones, internet , voice over etc. to cheat people. In cyber crime, criminals fraudulently transfer victims money from their bank accounts to their own bank accounts.
15. **Harmony:** Harmony is a situation in which different people live together peacefully.
16. **MLA:** MLA stands for Member of the Legislative Assembly. An MLA is an elected leader and representative to the legislative assembly of a state.
17. **MP:** MP stands for Member of Parliament, is an elected representative to either the Lok Sabha (house of the people) or the Rajya Sabha (council of states).
18. **Representative Democracy:** Representative democracy is a form of democratic government in which people take decisions through their elected representatives.
19. **Direct Democracy:** A country like Switzerland where people take major decisions directly.

III. THE BIG QUESTIONS *(Page 149)*

Q. 1. *What is the meaning of 'governance'?*

Ans.

- Governance is the process of managing the affairs of society.
- It is done for betterment of people through institutions like elected leaders, police, civil servants, army, etc.
- Different sets of rules, regulations and laws are made by the government and authorities for an organised social order.
- One of the basic principles of a democracy is better and honest governance for the welfare of people.

Q. 2. *Why do we need a government?*

Ans. Government is the most important institution in maintaining a peaceful society. Here are some key functions:

(i) **Maintaining law and order:** The primary task of a government is to make laws for proper social order and avoid conflict in the society.

(ii) **Providing public services:** It has another important role in providing basic and essential services like hospitals (AIIMS), education (government schools, colleges, IITs, IIMs), etc.

(iii) Taking care of people by providing foodgrains, medical services, education at an affordable price etc.

(iv) Protecting environment, forests, animals, birds and other species.

(v) Providing security to country from foreign enemy attacks and against terrorism.

Q. 3. *What is the meaning of 'democracy'? Why is it important?*

Ans. Democracy is a system of government in which people choose their own rulers. The word 'democracy' comes from two Greek words—dēmos meaning 'people', and kratos meaning 'rule' or 'power'; so 'democracy' literally means the 'rule of the people'.

Importance of Democracy:

- Democracy ensures that all are treated equally and no one is discriminated.
- Every people have an equal chance to attain the highest post like the Prime Minister, the President, the Chief Justice and Army Chief.
- Every one has freedom, right to, express their opinion, choose their religion, etc.
- Democracy gives power to people to choose, change and criticise their own government.

IV. NCERT INTEXT/TEXTBOOK EXERCISES

Let's Explore

Q.1. ***Describe the two pictures given in Fig. 10.1 on page 151 — what differences do you see between them?*** *(Page 150)*

Ans. The two pictures in Fig 10.1 on page 151 describes two **traffic scenes** on a busy road in urban place (City). However both the pictures are contrasting in nature in which Picture 1 depicts **smooth flow** of vehicles and Picture 2 reflects **complete breakdown**, chaos, with no rules and regulations.

Let us see the differences between Picture 1 and Picture 2.

	Picture 1	Picture 2
Vehicles	Cars, cycle and bikes (Limited number)	Cars, cycles, bikes, (Large numbers).
Rules and Regulations	Proper rules and regulations are followed	Chaos, disorder and violation of all traffic rules.
Comfort in driving	Provides better experience of driving	May lead to stress and frequent accidents.

Q. 2. *How do you connect this with our discussion on rules?* *(Page 150)*

Ans. Rules are essential for social order and better life. Rules made once can be changed for betterment. In school and home also we have rules.

Q. 3. *What are some of the rules in your school? Who made them?* *(Page 150)*

Ans. Every school has some rules and regulation for students, teaching staff and non-teaching staff. These are made for safe, better and productive learning environment.

Common School Rules

- **Attendance:** It is mandatory for students to attend school regularly.
- **Discipline:** Students are expected to follow certain discipline for orderly functioning of the classes.
- **Uniform:** Students are expected to wear a neat school uniform and maintain proper hygiene.
- **Classroom Behaviour:** There are certain conduct of conduct in classroom for better learning process.
  - No use of electronic devices like mobiles and laptops.
  - Bullying, teasing, commenting, and discriminating others are strictly not allowed.

Who Make the School Rules?

Ans. The school rules are made by the school administration including the Principal and Vice-Principals, along with the suggestions from parents and teachers.

Q. 4. *Can you identify the categories of public service or other activities that are represented in the ten pictures in Fig. 10.2 on page 152?* *(Page 153)*

Ans. Picture 1: Road Construction

Picture 2: Transport service (*Rail transport*)

Picture 3: Security and safety services (*Soldiers protecting boundaries*)

Picture 4: Healthcare services

Picture 5: Disaster management and relief services.

Picture 6: Road traffic safety (*Traffic Police*)

Picture 7: Judicial services (*The Supreme Court order*)

Picture 8: Educational services (*Classroom*)

Picture 9: Postal services (*Postman*)

Picture 10: Banking services (*Bank*)

Q. 5. *What role do you think the government plays in each of these activities?* *(Page 153)*

Ans. Government is directly involved in providing all kind of public service. It ensures that these services are provided to all people with minimum hindrance and on time. It creates adequate infrastructure, employs trained manpower and ensures free flow of service.

Q. 6. *Can you think of other aspects of your daily life where the government plays an important role?* *(Page 153)*

Ans. There are other areas of our daily lives where the government plays an important role, for example:

(*i*) Checking and ensuring quality and prices of food articles, milk etc.

(ii) Helping to preserve forest cover, environment and reduction of pollution.

(iii) Ensuring regular supply of water and electricity.

(iv) Maintenance of parks, cleaning of roads, providing, streets lamps etc.

(v) Providing health and education services.

Q. 7. *Explain how the three government organs are at work in the case of the cybercriminals described above. How do they intervene?* *(Page 154)*

Ans. Digital technologies have eased the life of people and at the same time created a new class of criminals who, find digital ways of stealing people's money.

- To prevent cybercrime government (legislative) has passed new laws in order to fight such criminal activities.
- Many criminals, who have been involved in robbing innocent people of their hard-earned money, have been arrested (executive) police and convicted by court (judiciary).
- They are usually fined as well as jailed for some years.

Q. 8. *As a class activity, can you imagine the sort of disorder we might witness if all three organs were under the control of the same group of people? Can you describe any such real-life situation you may have heard of?* *(Page 155)*

Ans. If all three organs of the government—executive, legislative, and judicial were under the control of the same group of people, then it will create imbalances in social order and society.

It will lead to discrimination and rise of injustice to common people.

This may lead to corruption and inefficient administration.

A news system of undemocratic government may come in place of people's rule.

Real-life situation

(i) Saudi Arabia— Monarchical Rule

(ii) North Korea— Military Rule

(iii) Germany— Under Adolf Hitler

- For instance, **Germany during 1933–1942** was under Nazi rule led by the military dictator Adolf Hitler.
- He took all the decisions regarding the running of the government.
- All the organs of the government were under military rule. He had special forces, security services and specialised military team to create fear and havoc.
- Hitler and his supporters, just to enhance their personal ego killed many people in gas chambers.
- They also created conditions that led to World War II affecting and killing millions of people worldwide.

Q. 9. *Observe the table (Fig. 10.5). Highlight the functions and responsibilities that affect your life the most.* *(Page 156)*

Ans. The functions and responsibilities that affect our life the most are as follows:

Central Government

1. Defence
2. Currency
3. Education
4. Communications: railways, roadways.

State Government

1. Police, law and order
2. Public health
3. Education
4. Agriculture
5. Local government

Q. 10. *Ask two or three adults about their connection or interaction with the government—at what levels does it take place and for what purpose?* *(Page 156)*

Ans. PRAYAN (aged 9 years was helped by his father): Interaction with **local government-Municipalities** – Purpose to get the park and playing area clean and free of garbage.

Saanvi (aged 10 years helped by her father): Making of passport – Saanvi was suppose to go to USA along with her father. She applied for Passport. **This interaction started with central government** – who is authorised to make and issue passport. The verification was done by local police (which comes under state government). After few weeks of formalities she received her passport through registered post (Central government).

Neighbour: Police and Advocate—Theft of bike **(Interaction with State government).**

There was a theft of a bike in our locality. The bike belonged to our neighbour Antony. He registered an FIR and approached police along with his advocate at the nearby police station. After two months of intense search police was able to trace the bike, 70 km from our residential area. The police handed over the bike to uncle Antony after all formalities.

NCERT Questions, Activities and Projects

(Page 161)

Q.1. *Test yourself — What is the meaning of democracy? What is the difference between direct democracy and representative democracy?*

Ans. Democracy is a system of government in which people choose their representatives. These representatives forms government **'democracy' means** the **'rule of the people'.**

Direct and representative are part of democratic government and they mainly differ in the process of decision making.

	Direct Democracy	Representative Democracy
Definition	In a direct democracy, common people participate directly in the decision-making process.	In a representative democracy, common people elect their representatives through election. In turn the elected representatives take decisions on behalf of the people.
Suitability	Generally it is suitable in small countries with less diversity.	Suitable in all countries but preferred in large countries.
Examples	Switzerland.	India, USA, UK, Germany etc.

Q. 2. *Recall the three organs of government. What are their different roles?*

Ans. The three organs of government are:

– Legislature, Executive and Judiciary.

Their different roles are:

– **Legislature:** Make laws for running of the government and country or state. (The Parliament).

– **Executive:** Implements rules and laws (Civil servants like IAS and IPS officers)

– **Judiciary:** Upholds the constitutional laws and solve disputes. (District Courts, High Courts and the Supreme Court).

– All the three organs of the government work together for smooth functioning of the society.

– They also keep check and balance on one another.

Q. 3. *Why do we need three tiers of government?*

Ans. India has three tiers of government to manage its vast and diverse population spreading across length and breadth. It enhances the efficiency of government and delivery of services, as each tier has different set of roles and responsibilities.

Central Government: The central government take decisions which are important at national level like foreign affairs, defence, management of railways. This requires huge resources and expertise, may not be possible for state government.

State Government: The state government looks after the state's specific needs like law and order through police.

Local Government: Whereas the local government takes care of local issues like garbage and sanitation, primary health etc.

- It encourages participation of people and strengthens the democracy at grassroot level.

Q. 4. *Project: Many of you will remember the lockdown that took place during the COVID-19 pandemic. Make a list of all the actions that were taken at that time? Which tiers of government were involved in managing the situation? What was the role of each of the organs of government?*

Ans. COVID-19 was a pandemic which affected almost entire section of the society and created havoc on lives of millions of people not only in India but across the globe.

It was the first major pandemic for people and government with almost no experience to deal with the new VIRUS. All the three tiers of government were actively involved in dealing with this crisis.

Some important actions taken by the Central Government were:

Lockdown: The central government declared nationwide lock down to control the spread of virus.

Quarantine and isolation: The people who were affected by the virus were quarantined and isolated to minimise the spread of virus.

Testing facilities: At government hospitals, free testing of virus was provided to detect the symptoms.

Research and vaccine: Parallelly government started to do research on large scale on the virus symptoms, mode of infection, transmission and methods to control its spread.

Upgradation of Hospitals, Clinics, Availability of medicines: Government took special care to upgrade the existing health infrastructure:

Providing vaccination

Closing down of schools and other educational infrastructure.

By the State Government: State government in coordination with central government provided new infrastructure, equipment, medicines, gloves, masks, sanitizers etc. to hospitals to check and control covid. They also developed new makeshift hospitals on priority.

Local Government: Local government made sure that lockdown is followed strictly. Local government also did a great effort in co-ordination with the Central and State Governments to make sure that all their policies are implemented at the ground level.

The role of the organs of the government

Each organ of the government made tireless efforts to fight against the COVID-19 pandemics. Examples:

Legislature: At central level laws were made to give emergency powers to executive to deal with the crisis.

Executive: Police, Doctors, Nurses, Teachers, Defence personnel etc., played important role in implementing the laws and helped in vaccination drive.

Judiciary: The Supreme and other courts too played an important role in ensuring justice and upholding the Indian vaccine as safe.

V. EXAM ORIENTED QUESTIONS

A. Very Short Answer Type Questions

Q. 1. *What would happen if no one follows rules?*

Ans. If no one follow rules, then there will be lot of problems and chaos. People will do whatever they feel is correct and that will lead to frequent misunderstandings and fights. Society will not be able to live in peace and trust people.

Q. 2. *Who makes the rules?*

Ans. Government makes rules.

Q. 3. *Give some examples of the executive wing of government at the central level.*

Ans. The President, the Prime Minister, the Governor, IAS, IPS officers.

Q. 4. *Give the full form of:*

(*a*) F.A.I.L.

(*b*) E.N.D.

(*c*) N.O.

Ans. (*a*) 'First Attempt In Learning'.

(*b*) 'Effort Never Dies'.

(*c*) 'Next Opportunity'.

Q. 5. *Name the three organs of the government.*

Ans. The three organs of the government are the Legislature, the Executive and the Judiciary.

Q. 6. *Give the function of the executive.*

Ans. The executive implements the laws made by the legislature.

Q. 7. *Which institution is involved in making and amending laws ?*

Ans. The central government through Parliament and the state governments through State Legislative Assemblies, make and amend laws for the country and their respective states respectively.

Q. 8. *What do you mean by the term separation of power?*

Ans. As per the constitution, the three organs of the government that is the legislature, the executive and the judiciary have defined role to perform. They do not exceed or interfere with the functions of the other branches of the government.

Q. 9. *Mention the three levels of the government.*

Ans. Three levels of government are:

1. Central (Union) Government
2. State Governments
3. Local Government (Municipalities & Panchayats)

Q. 10. *What is grassroot-democracy ?*

Ans. Grassroot democracy refers to the system where governance begins at the local level, allowing people to participate directly in decision-making. In India, it includes Panchayati Raj institutions and local self-governments.

Q. 11. *What is the motto of the government of India ? Also give its meaning.*

Ans. The motto of Government of India is Satyameva Jayate. Its meaning is Truth Alone Triumphs. (It is taken from the Mundaka Upanishad and signifies the power of truth.)

Q. 12. *Who is the highest executive in India ?*

Ans. The highest executive in India is the President of India.

B. Short Answer Type Questions

Q. 1. *Why rules are required in society?*

Ans.

- Human being lives in communities and form diverse groups.
- This diversity in communities is bound to create differences and conflict. In case of disagreements and conflicts rules are applied to create peace, respect and generate trust in the society.
- Rules help in avoiding chaos and mismanagement in society.

Q. 2. *How are rules made?*

Ans.

- Rules are generally made by legislative wing of the government.
- These are first discussed by cabinets (senior) and important ministers in form of draft. Then it is discussed in the legislature (the Parliament/State legislature) by the members.
- Once the members vote in favour of the bill (draft of rule/law), then it goes to the President/Governor for the signature.
- As and when the President/Governor signs the draft, it becomes new rule or law.

Q. 3. *How do cybercriminals operate?*

Ans.

- Digital technologies have created new group of criminals.

- The use of digital ways like internet, smartphones, WhatsApp call, Telegram, artificial intelligence etc, for stealing people's money.
- They deceive and threaten people into giving up their money.

Q. 4. *What will happen if there is no checks and balances at the government level?*

Ans.

- In the absence of checks and balances at the government level, the branches will not function according to the constitution and may act in their own self-interest.
- Tendency may develop of any branch to overpower other branch of the government.
- There may be permanent conflict leading to bad, delayed and inefficient decisions.

Q. 5. *Who are MLAs and MPs? Elaborate their role.*

Ans. MLA: MLA stands for Member of the Legislative Assembly. An MLA is an elected leader and representative of the legislative assembly of a state.

MP: MP stands for Member of Parliament, is an elected representative to either house of parliament i.e., the Lok Sabha (House of the People) or the Rajya Sabha (Council of States).

They work for the welfare of their area. They are part of legislature and participate in discussion which helps in making of laws.

Q. 6. *Enumerate some important features of representative government.*

Ans. In a large country like India, people choose their representatives who form a government on their behalf.

- It is better and organised form of government for large, less educated population.
- Most often the government takes decision with lot of deliberation and discussion, which often brings people welfare at centre of all decision.

Q. 7. *Who are new class of criminals? How do they operate?*

Ans. The digital technology has created a new class of criminals who, without even leaving their desks, find digital ways of stealing people's money.

They operate by using new generation technology like internet, telephone, smartphone, UPI, internet banking system to cheat people.

These criminals exploit technology, loopholes in the law, and global networks to operate on a large scale while remaining undetected for long periods.

C. Long Answer Type Questions

Q. 1. *Analyse the importance of 'separation of powers'.*

Ans.

- In democratic system of governance, and as per the constitution the three organs legislature, executive and judiciary are kept separate.
- They interact with each other and work together.
- The system of separation of power of the government check what the other is doing and restore balance if one organ acts beyond its expected role.

Q. 2. *How does judiciary strengthen the democratic structure of the country?*

Ans.

- The judiciary is the system of different levels of courts–with district courts, high courts and the supreme court on the top.
- They decide whether the accused has broken the law or not. It also pronounces punishment if necessary when a law is broken.
- At times it also examines whether a decision taken by the executive is right, or whether a law passed by the legislature is as per the constitution and fair to all.

Q. 3. *Mention the three levels of the government. Enlist any two functions of each tier.*

Ans. In India we have **three levels** of the government, Central/Union Government, State Government and Local Government. Their two functions are:

(*i*) **Central/Union Government:** It manages the affairs at the National (whole country) level. Defence, Foreign Affairs, Atomic Energy and Communication.

(*ii*) **State Government:** At the state level, the state government manages departments like:
Police, law and order, Public health, Education and Agriculture.

(*iii*) **Local Government:** Government at village and urban areas (Panchayati Raj & Municipal Corporation) garbage collection, sanitation, water supply etc.

Q. 4. *Why does India have representative democracy? Give reasons to support your answer.*

Ans.

- India has a representative democracy because it has more than 1.4 billion population and it is practically not possible for more than 970 million (97 crores) voters to take part in decision making process on day-to-day basis.
- At the same time a large section of society may not be politically and technically aware about the issues around India, economics etc.
- Many people might not be interested in taking part, hence we elect our leaders who take decisions on our behalf.

Q. 5. *Elaborate some important features of democratic government.*

1. Important Features of a Democratic Government are:

Ans. It is a government formed by elected representatives.

- There are regular, free and fair elections that take place every five years.
- Constitution is supreme and everyone is equal before the law.
- Citizens have fundamental rights.
- There is an independent Judiciary system to ensure justice and fairness to people.

Q. 6. *All over the world, digital technologies have transformed the lives of people. Justify the statement.*

Ans. Digital technologies have significantly transformed lives worldwide in multiple ways. People can connect through voice and videos in one go from any part of world. (***Example***: WhatsApp calls, Internet based calls).

- With AI (Artificial Intelligence) health care and education is and will further get boost.
- Internet banking and UPI payments have made financial inclusion of all people.
- Airways, Railways and road transport have made travel easy, faster and comfortable.

Q. 7. *No country can run without governance and government. Do you agree?*

Ans. Yes, we agree that no country can run without governance and government. Governance is an important tool for the welfare for people. The task to bring happiness on the face of people is of government.

- The primary task of government is to maintain law and order.
- Government create job opportunities for people.
- Government provides free education and healthcare to all.
- Simultaneously it ensures security to people both inside and outside country.

D. Assertion & Reasoning Questions

There are two statements marked as Assertion (A) and Reason (R). Mark your answer as per the codes provided below:

1. **Assertion (A):** Dr. A.P.J. Abdul Kalam was a renowned scientist, nicknamed the 'Rocket Scientist of India'.

   Reason (R): He had crucial role in the development of India's space programme, missile programme and nuclear capabilities.

   Codes:

   (*a*) Both (A) and (R) are true but (R) is not the correct explanation of (A).

   (*b*) Both (A) and (R) are true and (R) is the correct explanation of (A).

   (*c*) (A) is true but (R) is false.

   (*d*) (A) is false but (R) is true.

2. **Assertion (A):** India is a representative democracy.

   Reason (R): It has 970 million voters in 2024.

   Codes:

   (*a*) Both (A) and (R) are true but (R) is not the correct explanation of (A).

   (*b*) Both (A) and (R) are true and (R) is the correct explanation of (A).

   (*c*) (A) is true but (R) is false.

   (*d*) (A) is false but (R) is true.

3. **Assertion (A):** Governance is important for success of democracy.

   Reason (R): India is a secular and republic country.

   Codes:

   (*a*) Both (A) and (R) are true but (R) is not the correct explanation of (A).

   (*b*) Both (A) and (R) are true and (R) is the correct explanation of (A).

   (*c*) (A) is true but (R) is false.

   (*d*) (A) is false but (R) is true.

4. **Assertion (A):** In India, the President of India and the Governor of a State are not the actual executive heads.

   Reason (R): They do have certain powers under special circumstances, but normally do not interfere in the affairs of the Central or State government.

   Codes:

   (*a*) Both (A) and (R) are true but (R) is not the correct explanation of (A).

   (*b*) Both (A) and (R) are true and (R) is the correct explanation of (A).

   (*c*) (A) is true but (R) is false.

   (*d*) (A) is false but (R) is true.

Ans. **1.** → (*d*) **2.** → (*a*) **3.** → (*a*) **4.** → (*b*)

E. Case/Source Based Questions

Read the passages given below and answer the questions that follow:

Jodhpur

I. A neurosurgeon from Jodhpur lost Rs 62.8 lakh to cyber criminals who lured him with promises of high returns on stock market investments, the police said.

The fraudsters managed to siphon off the amount within just one-and-a-half days.

Realising he had been scammed, the doctor filed an FIR at nearest police station.

(*i*) What is cybercrime?

(*ii*) What is role of police in such case?

(*iii*) Which institution makes law on cybercrime?

Ans.

(*i*) Cybercrime is the use of technology to commit fraud, theft or other illegal activities, often by manipulating people's greed or fear.

(*ii*) The police investigate cybercrimes, enforce laws, prevent online fraud, assist victims, and raise awareness. They also collaborate with other agencies to track cybercriminals and ensure digital security.

(*iii*) Legislature-the Parliament.

II. "There is no peace without justice;

- no justice without equality;
- no equality without development;

- no democracy without respect to the identity and dignity of cultures and peoples."

(*i*) Which organ is associated with delivering justice to people?

(*ii*) No democracy without respect to the identity and dignity of cultures and peoples. Explain the statement.

(*iii*) How do democracy ensures equality?

Ans.

(*i*) The Judiciary.

(*ii*) Democracy cannot succeed without creating condition for equal treatment to people. Democracy respects and treats people from all cultural background. It gives ample reservation to people from all background in education and jobs.

(*iii*) Democracy ensure people have right to vote and stand in election. It treats everyone equally with dignity.

F. Competency Based Questions

Q. 1. *Why is the legislature important in a democratic system? How does it ensure that laws benefit the people?*

Ans. The legislature is important because it makes laws that govern the country. It ensures laws benefit people by:

1. Debating issues in Parliament before passing laws.
2. Representing citizens' needs through elected members.
3. Holding the government accountable for its actions.

Q. 2. *What is the role of the executive in implementing laws? Give two examples of how it affects people's daily lives.*

Ans. The executive enforces laws and runs the government. Its role includes:

1. Maintaining law and order through the police.
2. Providing public services like education, healthcare, and transport.

Examples: The police ensure safety by enforcing traffic laws.

The municipal corporation manages waste collection and sanitation.

Q. 3. *How does the judiciary protect citizens' rights? Why is an independent judiciary important?*

Ans. The judiciary protects citizens' rights by ensuring fair trials and interpreting the law. An independent judiciary is important because:

1. It prevents government misuse of power.
2. It ensures everyone is treated equally under the law.

Example: If a law is unfair, the Supreme Court can declare it unconstitutional.

G. Picture Based Questions

Q. 1. *Observe the given image below and answer the questions that follow:*

(*a*) Identify the picture.

(*b*) In which city is it located ?

(*c*) Which institutions are associated with it?

(*d*) Give its role in strengthening democracy.

Ans.

(*a*) The given image is of the Parliament of India (New Building).

(*b*) It is located in NEW DELHI.

(*c*) The institution associated with it are the President, the Lok Sabha and the Rajya Sabha.

(*d*) Parliament makes and modifies laws to protect citizens' rights.

- It is the highest forum of discussion and debate for the citizens' welfare.
- The two houses, the Lok Sabha and the Rajya Sabha will give platform for the representation from all walks of life.
- It also controls the executive.

VI. MULTIPLE CHOICE QUESTIONS

1. *The group of individuals or the system that make the rules and laws is:*
(a) Legislature (b) Judiciary
(c) Executive (d) Police

2. *Dr. Abdul Kalam served as the President of India from ....*
(a) 11th, 2002 to 2007
(b) 11th, 2004 to 2009
(c) 10th, 2009 to 2014
(d) 13th, 2014 to 2019

3. *Which tier of government has power to deal with interstate commerce and education?*
(a) Gram Panchayat
(b) State
(c) Municipal Corporation
(d) Central.

4. *Supreme Court of India is situated in:*
(a) Mumbai (b) New Delhi
(c) Kolkata (d) Chennai

5. *Members of Parliament are elected to:*
(a) Only for Lok Sabha
(b) Only for Rajya Sabha
(c) Both Lok Sabha and Rajya Sabha
(d) State Legislative Assembly

6. *.................. and .... are the executive head of the state government:*
(a) The Governor and the Prime Minister
(b) The Governor and the Chief Minister
(c) Governor and Chief Justice of high court
(d) The Governor and the President.

7. *Satyameva Jayate is the motto of:*
(a) Supreme Court
(b) Indian Army
(c) Government of India
(d) State Assembly.

8. *Identify the incorrect statements about representative democracy:*
I. It allows people to rule directly
II. It helps elect leaders to take decisions on behalf of citizens
III. It ensures that only a few people have power
IV. It eliminates the need for laws
(a) only I (b) II and III
(c) only II (d) I , III and IV

9. *In a country if there is no governance, it will lead to:*
(a) organised traffic system
(b) lawlessness, mismanagement and chaos
(c) peaceful existence of the society
(d) smooth running of malls and schools

10. *The organ of the government which decides if a law is constitutional or not ......*
(a) Police (b) Judiciary
(c) Legislature (d) Army

Ans.

1. → (a) 2. → (a) 3. → (d)
4. → (b) 5. → (c) 6. → (d)
7. → (c) 8. → (d) 9. → (b)
10. → (b)

VII. OBJECTIVE TYPE QUESTIONS

A. True or False

1. Public services are provided by private sector at free of cost.
2. Money order is issued by Reserve Bank of India.
3. All States have a single assembly.
4. The word 'democracy' comes from two latin words — 'dēmos' meaning 'people', and 'kratos' meaning 'power to rule'.

5. 'Members of Legislative Assembly' (MLAs) are at the National level, and 'Members of Parliament' (MPs) are at the state level.
6. Rules and laws once made are set once and for all and cannot be changed.
7. Digital technologies have been transforming the way societies function since time immemorial.
8. The President of India has real power to administer the country.
9. Dr. A.P.J. Abdul Kalam was a renowned scientist, nicknamed the 'Missile Man of India'.
10. Dr. Abdul Kalam served as the 11th President of India from 2002 to 2007.

Ans. 1. False 2. False 3. False 4. True 5. False 6. False 7. False 8. False 9. True 10. True

B. Fill in the Blanks

1. Human beings have been living in .... for a long time.
2. "The ruler protects dharma and dharma protects those who protect it." Is from ....
3. In India, all Indian citizens above the age of .... have the right to participate in the elections.
4. .... was born in a humble family in Rameswaram, Tamil Nadu, in 1931 and became the 11th President of India.
5. .... government has power to deal with Atomic energy in India.
6. The Supreme Court's motto is...........

Ans.
1. Communities
2. The Mahābhārata
3. 18 years
4. Dr. A.P.J. Abdul Kalam
5. Central
6. 'Yato Dharmastato Jayah'

C. Match Column A with Column B

(a)

	Column A		Column B
1.	Central Government	A	A. Town or village level
2.	State Government	B	B. National level
3.	Local Government	C	C. State level

(b)

	Column A		Column B
1.	High Court	A	Formulates state laws
2.	Prime Minister	B	Formulates national laws
3.	Lok Sabha	C	Judiciary
4.	Vidhan Sabha	D	Executive

Ans.
(a) 1. → (B) 2. → (C) 3. → (A)
(b) 1. → (C) 2. → (D) 3. → (B) 4. → (A)

VIII. TEST YOUR KNOWLEDGE

A. Multiple Choice Questions

1. The three tiers of government in India consist of :
   (a) MPs, MLAs and Central Government
   (b) Legislative, Executive, and Judiciary
   (c) Local, State, and National
   (d) UTs, National and State
2. Give the correct meaning of democracy:
   (a) Rule by an elected King
   (b) Rule by religious leaders
   (c) Rule by elected representatives
   (d) Rule by military officials

3. Identify function/s of the legislature for its state:
   (i) To make laws
   (ii) To execute laws
   (iii) To interpret laws
   (iv) To modify laws

   Option :
   (a) only (iv)
   (b) (i), (ii), (iii) and (iv)
   (c) (i) and (iv)
   (d) (iii) and (iv)
4. Who is the Supreme Commander of the Indian Armed Forces?
   (a) The President
   (b) Chief of the Defence Staff
   (c) Defence Minister
   (d) Defence Secretary
5. Who has the nominal powers ?
   (i) The Governor
   (ii) The President
   (iii) The Prime Minister
   (iv) The Council of Ministers

   Option :
   (a) only (ii)
   (b) (i), (ii), (iii) and (iv)
   (c) (ii) and (iv)
   (d) (i) and (ii)

B. Fill in the Blanks

1. The ______ is the system of courts which decides whether someone has broken the law and, if so, what course of action should be taken.
2. The word democracy comes from ______ language.
3. Two houses ______ and _____ formulates and modifies new national laws at the Union level.
4. State Level Government governs the particular and is headed by the ______.

C. True or False

1. Grassroots democracy enables and encourages the participation of only rich people.
2. A modern government has three organs — legislative, executive and judiciary — which may not work together.
3. Dream is not that which you see while sleeping; it is something that does not let you sleep.- Dr. A.P.J. Abdul Kalam
4. State government manages police, law and order .

D. Very Short Answer Type Questions

Q. 1. *Distinguish between rules and laws.*

Q. 2. *Why is judiciary an important organ of the government?*

Q. 3. *Elaborate the importance of grass-roots democracy.*

Q. 4. *Define the following terms:*
   (a) Governance
   (b) Money order
   (c) Cyber criminals
   (d) Judiciary
   (e) Checks and balances.

Q. 5. *What is the motto of the Supreme Court of India ? Also give its meaning.*

Q. 6. *Who is the real executive head in India?*

Q. 7. *Give the meaning of separation of power.*

Q. 8. *Mention two features of representative democracy.*

E. Short Answer Type Questions

Q. 1. *Can democratic system have only one tier of government? Explain by giving suitable arguments.*

Q. 2. *Explain the importance of direct democracy.*

F. Long Answer Type Questions

Q. 1. *Three organs of government must be kept separate. Explain the statement.*

Q. 2. *Describe the composition and functions of the executive and the judiciary.*

G. Competency Based Questions

Q. 1. *Suppose you become CM of your state for a week. What changes you will bring about and how will you implement it.*

NOTES

INTERESTING MIND MAP

Grassroots Democracy–Part 2: Local Government in Rural Areas

1 Introduction

- Local government works in villages so people can take part in decisions and solve their problems
- India has more than 6 lakh villages, and about two-thirds of our population lives in rural areas
- So, local government is important to manage village life properly

2 Panchayati Raj System

- A local government called Panchayat is the Village: council; Panchayati Raj is a system of self-government
- Brings governance closer to people and allows participation in decisions
- Panchayats address local issues, promote development, and implement government schemes
- Works at three levels:
  Village (Gram Panchayat)
  Block (Panchayat Samiti)
  District (Zila Parishad)
- Manages agriculture, roads, water, education, health, welfare, and culture

3 Gram Panchayat

- Gram Panchayat is the local body closest to the people
- Members are elected by the Gram Sabha, a group of adult villagers
- Gram Sabha discusses and decides local matters
- Head of Gram Panchayat is called Sarpanch or Pradhan; more women are becoming Sarpanchs
- Panchayat Secretary and Patwari maintain records, hold meetings, and link the Gram Panchayat to district authorities
- Some Patwaris also keep old maps of the village

4 Exemplary Sarpanchs

- Dnyaneshwar Kamble: Transgender Sarpanch of Tarangfal (2017); believes serving the village is serving the people
- Vandana Bahadur Maida: First female Sarpanch of Khankhandvi; promoted women's participation, education, and sanitation
- Popatrao Baguji Pawar: Sarpanch of Hiware Bazar, Maharashtra; used rainwater harvesting and tree planting to prosper the village; awarded Padma Shri in 2020

5 Child-Friendly Panchayat Initiative

- Bal Panchayats let children aged 8 to 14 share their views and influence decisions
- Maharashtra: Bal Panchayats worked to end child labour and child marriage, and brought children back to school
- Sikkim: Sangkhu Radhu Khandu Gram Panchayat made schools safer and built kitchens
- Rajasthan: Children's Parliament teaches democracy and addresses education, sanitation, and equality
- Initiatives have won awards in 2001 for promoting child participation

6 Panchayat Samiti and Zila Parishad

- Panchayat Samiti links Gram Panchayat with Zila Parishad
- Members are elected locally; include Sarpanchs and State Assembly members
- Panchayat Samitis coordinate development plans and fund allocation and government schemes like Pradhan Mantri Gram Sadak Yojana for rural roads across villages
- One-third of seats reserved for women
- Seats also reserved for disadvantaged groups
- Structure varies by State; goal is active local participation
- Kauṭilya's Arthaśhāstra: village to provincial administration

THEME D
Governance and Democracy

CHAPTER 11

GRASSROOTS DEMOCRACY – PART 2: LOCAL GOVERNMENT IN RURAL AREAS

I. FACTS TO REMEMBER/SUMMARY

INTRODUCTION

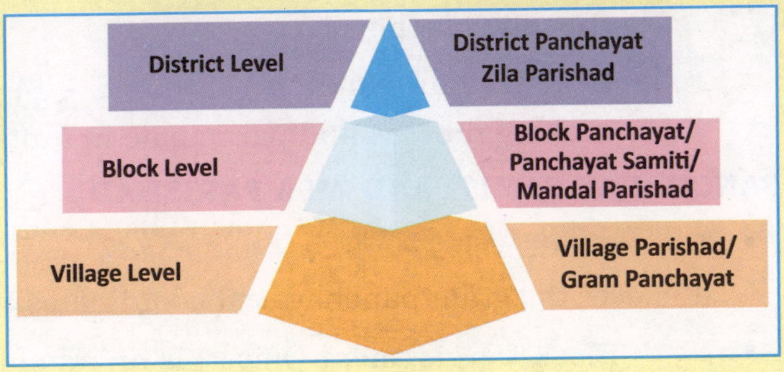

- Local government exist in rural areas to cater the need of the people through their participation.
- India is a vast country having more than 6 lakh villages, eight thousand towns and over four thousand cities. Around two-thirds of total population out of 140 crore lives in rural areas.
- Such a vast population requires effective governance and involvement of local population in solving their day-to-day problems.

PANCHAYATI RAJ SYSTEM

- Panchayati Raj System is a three-tier system as per the constitution, which involves local people in solving their local problems.
- It is a **three – tier/level** structure institutional body consisting of: **Gram Panchayat**-at village level, then **Block Panchayat** at the block level and **Zila Parishad**-at district level.
- It plays an important role in solving local issues and ensuring development. They also bring the state and central governments welfare schemes and other policies to common people.

GRAM PANCHAYAT

- Gram Panchayat is a local governing body that represents the interest of a village.
- The members of a Gram Panchayat are elected by the **Gram Sabha**. The election are held every five years.
- Gram Sabha is a group of adults in the village.
- Gram Sabha overall supervises the functioning of the Gram Panchayat. It meets at least twice a year.
- In recent times due to one-third reservation for women, the participation of elected and non-elected women in a Panchayat has increased.
- **Panchayat Secretary** and **Patwari** are two important officials who help in maintaining records, coordinating the meeting and forms the link between Gram Panchayat and district officials. Few Patwaris also keep old maps of the village.

CHILD-FRIENDLY PANCHAYAT INITIATIVE

- In many states Gram Panchayat has opened doors for children to participate in functioning, organising and solving disputes.
- Some noteworthy examples are:
  - In Maharashtra–these children have brought many children back to school and helped to tackle child labour.
  - In north-east state of Sikkim–Sangkhu Radhu Khandu Gram Panchayat has taken lot of efforts to make it a child-friendly Panchayat.
  - In Rajasthan children between 8 – 14 years are directly involved in decision making process and participate in functioning of Parliament-like institutes.

PANCHAYAT SAMITI AND ZILA PARISHAD

- The second level is **Panchayat Samiti/Mandal Parishad** that functions at block level. It is over the gram panchayat. It coordinates Panchayats with the zila parishad.
- **BDO** (Block Development Officer) is an administrative officer appointed by the state government to help the gram panchayats with zila parishad.
- District level-District Panchayat/ Zila Parishad works at the district level and is the highest level institution in the local level of the government.

  –They are responsible for the overall development of the Panchayats.

  –Zila Parishad is headed by an **IAS (Indian Administrative Service)** officer or state level officers appointed by the state government.
- Funds allocated by the state or central government for the benefit of villagers are facilitated through district panchayat and then through the block panchayat to the gram panchayat.
- **One-third** of the seats are **reserved for women** at the local level—including the gram panchayat, block and zila parishad.

II. TEXTBOOK KEYWORDS/GLOSSARY

1. **Panchayati Raj System:** Panchayati Raj System is a local self-governing body at rural areas aimed at solving local problems through people's participation. It consists of three tiers/levels—the village, the block and the district.
2. **Gram Panchayat/Gram Sabha:** The Gram Sabha consists of all adult residents of 18 years and above in age in a village or a group of villages within a Gram Panchayat who are eligible to vote in Panchayat elections.

3. **Sarpanch/Pradhan:** She/He is the elected head of Gram Panchayat elected by the members of the Gram Panchayat.
4. **Panchayat Secretary:** Panchayat secretary is an official appointed by the government and acts as a link between the Gram Panchayat and the government. He calls meeting, keeps and maintains records of the Panchayat.
5. **Patwari:** Patwari is an official at the Panchayat level who helps the Panchayat secretary in maintaining land records and maps.
6. **Block Panchayat:** Block panchayat is the second level of institution which coordinates a group of panchayat with Zila Parishad. They are above gram panchayat.
7. **Mandal Parishad:** Mandal Parishad is another name of block panchayat and is known by different names in different states.
8. **Zila Parishad:** A Zila Parishad, is a local government body at the district level, which is above the block panchayat/ mandal parishad.

III. THE BIG QUESTIONS *(Page 163)*

Q. 1. *What are Panchayati Raj institutions?*

Ans. Panchayati Raj institutions are local-self democratic government bodies at the rural/village level. Their aim is to address problems at village level and enhance the local people's participation in the democratic process. The Panchayati Raj institutions function at three tiers/levels:

(*i*) Gram Panchayat—at village level

(*ii*) Block Panchayat—at the block level

(*iii*) Zila Parishad—at district level.

Q. 2. *What are their functions?*

Ans. Panchayats take democracy to the local level by addressing local challenges and encouraging the participation of people. Collectively, these institutions manage a wide range of responsibilities within the district, including agriculture, housing, road maintenance, water resource management, education, healthcare, social welfare, and cultural activities.

Q. 3. *Why are they important in governance and democracy?*

Ans. Panchayats are vital to governance and democracy because they bring democracy to local level addressing local challenges and encouraging the participation of people. Panchayati Raj institutions are essential for tackling these challenges, fostering development, and ensuring that government programs and welfare schemes benefit communities at the grassroots level. They have opened doors to large scale women's participation and strengthened grassroot democracy.

IV. NCERT INTEXT/TEXTBOOK EXERCISES

Think About It

Q. 1. *How do you think can these old maps be helpful for us? Can they tell us something about the past and the present?* *(Page 167)*

Ans. Old maps can help us understand how places have changed over time. They depict some important historical events, migration and movement of people. They can also be useful for comparing the nature of soil, rivers, population size and density. Moreover, if there is a dispute between villagers over land ownership, these maps can be quite useful in resolving the dispute.

Q. 2. *Why do you think it is important for the government to pay more attention to the needs and problems of the disadvantaged sections of society?* *(Page 170)*

Ans. The government should pay more attention to the needs and problems of the disadvantaged sections of society because the basic philosophy of the government is to ensure that everyone lives a decent life. The poorer sections have less resources, less education, less skills and do not get an equal chance to earn and succeed in life. The disadvantaged sections are not able to pursue even basic education and do not get proper healthcare for themselves and their children which further aggregates their problems.

Under such scenario it becomes the moral duty of the government to take care of these people and uplift them from poverty. Government should also create conditions for their prosperity, only then India can succeed and develop.

Let's Explore

Q. 1. ***As a class activity, let four or five students form a Bal Panchayat and the rest of the class imagine they are the villagers. (a) What issues will the Gram Sabha discuss? (b) What challenges could it encounter? (c) What solutions will it propose?*** *(Page 169)*

Ans. *(a)* Some important issues for discussion could be regarding:

- Dropout of children from school especially girls.
- Evening educational classes for senior citizens.
- Cleanliness of village and proper disposal of garbage.
- Depletion of pastureland for animals.
- Drought and floods.

(b) The main challenges villagers could encounter are:

- Absence of support from villagers for girl child education, due to poverty and other reasons.
- Absence of motivation and hesitancy among senior citizens.
- Limited resources and man-power.
- Lack of knowledge.
- Absence of support from local authorities.

(c) Possible solutions could be as follows:

- Resource mobilisation from villagers and awareness raising.
- Informing villagers about benefits of education.
- Regular meetings of elders of the village.
- Making a small expert group consisting of elders, children and women.
- Involving and taking support from local authorities.

Q. 2. ***What similarities and differences do you notice between the governance system at the Central level and at the Panchayat level? (Hint: refer back to Chapter 10 if required.)*** *(Page 170)*

Ans. Similarities between the governance system at the Central level and at the Panchayat level.

1. The members at the both levels are elected every five years. Everyone gets a chance to contest election.
2. Both the governments work for the welfare of people. They are responsible for providing all kind of services to people, like education, basic and primary healthcare, drinking water etc.
3. They make policies for the betterment of poor and disadvantaged section of the societies.

The main difference between them are:

1. Central government make policies for the entire nation, while Panchayat make policies for one particular panchayat or group of villages only.
2. Central government has huge resources at their disposal and deals with foreign affairs and security of the entire nation. Panchayat has limited resources.

Q. 3. ***If you get an opportunity to meet a few Panchayat members, what questions would you like to ask them? Discuss in small groups to create a questionnaire. Meet some Gram Panchayat members or invite them to your school. Ask them the questions in your questionnaire and write a short report.*** *(Page 170)*

Ans. Questionnaire for Panchayat members could be:

1. Who are the members of the Gram panchayat?
2. What are the roles and functions of panchayat members?

3. How are the resources collected for development process?
4. Give any recent project completed by the panchayat.
5. What challenges were faced in executing the project?
6. What are the roles of women members?
7. What are the future programmes and policies of the panchayat?
8. How are local people are involved in working with the panchayat?
9. Who coordinates with government officials?
10. How can we become a part of the panchayat?

NCERT Questions, Activities and Projects (*Page 171*)

Q. 1. *Test yourself—without looking at the text above, can you name the three tiers of the Panchayati Raj system? What are the key functions of each of the three tiers?*

Ans. The three tiers of the Panchayati Raj system are:

(*a*) Gram Panchayat— at village level

(*b*) Block Panchayat/Panchayat Samiti/ Mandal Parishad— at the block level

(*c*) Zila Parishad— at district level.

The Key Functions of the Panchayati Raj System are:

(*a*) **The Gram Panchayat:**

(*i*) Running of primary schools and primary healthcare system.

(*ii*) Providing clean water, collection and disposable of garbage and maintaining sanitation in the village.

(*b*) **Block Panchayat/Panchayat Samiti/ Mandal Parishad:** They prepare developmental plans, collect details from Gram Panchayats and present them together to the District or State levels respectively. This facilitates them to get funds for development.

(*c*) **Zila Parishad:** It overall makes development plans for the entire district.

Ensures that they get the fund from state or central government, depending on the project.

Q. 2. *Write a letter to the Sarpanch regarding the issue of plastic bags lying on the roadside in the village.*

Ans. To,

The Sarpanch,

Sapta Village

Madhya Pradesh

Subject: ***Request to look into the issue of plastic bags lying on the roadside in the village.***

Respected Sarpanch Ji,

I hope this letter finds you in great health and happiness. I am writing this letter to highlight the increasing number of plastic bags lying on the roadside.

The number of plastic bags lying on the roadside has been increasing day by day. It has become a serious threat to the health of both people and animals, as well as to the environment. They can block the drainage system. It is important that gram panchayat takes up the issue on urgent basis and finds a better solution of disposal such as, replacing the plastic bags with eco-friendly cotton and jute bags.

I have full faith in your leadership, and I am confident that you, along with the other members, will resolve these issues at the earliest and make our village neat and clean. This will set an example for other villages.

Thank you for your time and attention.

Yours sincerely,

Prayan

Q. 3. *In your view, what type of person should be a Gram Panchayat member?*

Ans. The Gram Panchayat member should be honest, hardworking, a good listener, a problem solver, visionary and should have leadership qualities.

Q. 4. ***Let us suppose that you study in a village school. The school is located next to a highway and students find it difficult to cross the road when they come to school or leave at the end of the day. What are the options to solve this issue? Which institutions in the Panchayati Raj can help you? What can the students do?***

Ans. There are several options for solving the issue of crossing the highway:

1. Construction of speed breakers and zebra crossing.
2. Appoint guard to help children cross the road.
3. Halting traffic for 10 minutes for children to cross the highway.
4. Making of pedestrian subway or footover bridge.

Since the matter is concerned with Highway (State or National Highway), the Sarpanch of Gram Panchayat along with the Principal of the school can forward this issue to BDO-at the Block level. The BDO can take up this issue to DM-the administrative head of the Zila parishad who can coordinate with state government to solve this issue.

Students can raise this issue through school authorities by making a poster, writing a letter and raising awareness.

V. EXAM ORIENTED QUESTIONS

A. Very Short Answer Type Questions

Q. 1. ***What is a system of local government in village?***

Ans. The system of local government in village is called Panchayat.

Q. 2. ***Which institution is known as a village council?***

Ans. A system of local government called 'Panchayat', is also known as village council.

Q. 3. ***Who elects the members of the Gram Panchayat?***

Ans. Gram Sabha.

Q. 4. ***What is the tenure/period of members of the Gram Panchayat?***

Ans. Five years.

Q. 5. ***Who is the head of the Gram Panchayat?***

Ans. Sarpanch is the head of the Gram Panchayat.

Q. 6. ***Where is Sangkhu Radhu Khandu Gram Panchayat?***

Ans. Sangkhu Radhu Khandu Gram Panchayat is located in west Sikkim.

Q. 7. ***What is a Zila Parishad?***

Ans. A Zila Parishad, is a local government body at the district level.

B. Short Answer Type Questions

Q. 1. ***Give a brief description about village Lakshmanpur.***

Ans. Lakshmanpur is a small village in the foothills of the Himalayas.

- It has a population of about 700 and most of them are farmers.
- They also rear cows and goats.
- Some have relatives serving in the armed forces.
- Few of them have migrated to the city in search of jobs.

Q. 2. ***Elaborate the role of the Panchayati Raj System.***

Ans. Panchayats play an important role in addressing local issues, promoting development and ensuring that the benefits of government schemes reach the grassroots level.

Q. 3. ***Describe the responsibilities of the Panchayati Raj System.***

Ans. The responsibilities of the Panchayati Raj System cover almost all aspects of life in the district, from agriculture, housing, maintenance of roads, management of water resources, education, health care and social welfare to cultural activities.

Q. 4. *Give the composition of the Gram Sabha.*

Ans. The Gram Sabha consists of all adult residents of 18 years or above of age of a village or a group of villages within a Gram Panchayat who vote in Panchayat election.

Q. 5. *Explain the functions of the Gram Sabha.*

Ans. The functions of the Gram Sabha are as follows:

- Gram sabha elects the members of the gram panchayat.
- The members discuss all matters related to their area and take decisions.
- Keeps an eye on the functioning of the Gram Panchayat.

Q. 6. *Who is a Panchayat Secretary?*

Ans. Panchayat Secretary is an official appointed by the government, who acts as a link between the Gram Panchayat and the government. He calls meeting, keeps and maintains record of the Panchayat.

Q. 7. *Explain the efforts of the Bal Panchayat in Maharashtra.*

Ans. Some of the efforts of the Bal Panchayat in Maharashtra are as follows:

They have worked to eliminate child labour and child marriages in many areas of Maharashtra.

They have brought many children back to school.

They have also convinced parents for delayed arranged marriages of their girl child and to support their studies.

Q. 8. *How have Sangkhu Radhu Khandu Gram Panchayat helped children?*

Ans. The Panchayat has built compound walls for schools to make them safer for children. To ensure that students get hygienically cooked midday meals, the Gram Panchayat has constructed kitchens in the schools.

Q. 9. *What is a Children's Parliament' in Rajasthan?*

Ans. Children's Parliament' is an offshoot of Bunker Roy's 'Barefoot College', in Rajasthan. It took an initiative to help underprivileged children in rural areas through education and democratic participation.

Q. 10. *What is Panchayat samiti?*

Ans. Block panchayat is the second level of institution which coordinates a group of panchayat with Zila Parishad. They are above Gram Panchayat.

Q. 11. *Explain the importance of the Panchayat Samiti.*

Ans. It is over the gram panchayat. It co-ordinates the group of villages with the zila parishad. BDO (block development officer) is the administrative officer appointed by the state government to help the gram panchayats with zila parishad.

C. Long Answer Type Questions

Q. 1. *What is a Child-Friendly Initiative of the Panchayat?*

Ans. The Child-Friendly Initiative of the Panchayat in various states creates opportunities for children to be a part and express their ideas and opinions on matters related to their interest. Several steps are being taken in many states to encourage their participation in Bal Sabhas and Bal Panchayats. The village elders help them find solutions for their concerns.

Q. 2. *Enumerate the importance of the Zila Parishad.*

Ans. Zila Parishad works at the district level and is the highest level institution in the local level of the government.

- It is responsible for the overall development of the Panchayats.
- It is responsible for planning, coordinating and helping in all kind of activities of the Panchayat Samitis and gram panchayats.

Q. 3. *Describe the composition of the Gram Panchayat.*

Ans. Every village Panchayat is divided into wards, i.e., the smaller areas.

Each ward elects a representative who is known as the Ward Member (Panch).

Members of the Gram Sabha elect a Sarpanch who is the Panchayat President.

The Ward Panchs and the Sarpanch form the Gram Panchayat.

The Gram Panchayat is elected for five years.

The Gram Panchayat has a Secretary who is also the Secretary of the Gram Sabha. This person is not an elected person but is appointed by the government. He is responsible for calling the meeting of the Gram Sabha and Gram Panchayat. He also keeps record of the proceedings.

Q. 4. *Enumerate the works of Gram Panchayats. What are the sources of funds of Gram Panchayats?*

Ans. The works of Gram Panchayats are as follows:

(*i*) Construction and maintenance of water sources, roads, drainage, school buildings and other common property resources.

(*ii*) Levying and collecting local taxes.

(*iii*) Executing government schemes related to generating employment in the village.

Sources of funds for the Panchayat are as follows:

(*i*) Collection of taxes on houses, market places etc.

(*ii*) Government scheme funds received through various departments of the government—through the Janpad and Zila Panchayats.

(*iii*) Donations for community works etc.

D. Assertion & Reasoning Questions

There are two statements marked as Assertion (A) and Reason (R). Mark your answer as per the codes provided below:

Q. 1. Assertion (A): Like every village in India, the Lakshmanpur people have a system of local government called 'Panchayat'.

Reason (R): Panchayats bring governance closer to the people, making it possible for them to actively participate in decision-making processes.

Codes:

(*a*) Both (A) and (R) are true but (R) is not the correct explanation of (A).

(*b*) Both (A) and (R) are true and (R) is the correct explanation of (A).

(*c*) (A) is true but (R) is false.

(*d*) (A) is false but (R) is true.

Q. 2. Assertion (A): The structure and functions of the Panchayati Raj institutions differ a little across States.

Reason (R): The Central government has authority over those institutions.

Codes:

(*a*) Both (A) and (R) are true but (R) is not the correct explanation of (A).

(*b*) Both (A) and (R) are true and (R) is the correct explanation of (A).

(*c*) (A) is true but (R) is false.

(*d*) (A) is false but (R) is true.

Q. 3. Assertion (A): In recent years, more and more women have become Sarpanch.

Reason (R): Two-third seats are reserved for women at Panchayat level.

Codes:

(*a*) Both (A) and (R) are true but (R) is not the correct explanation of (A).

(*b*) Both (A) and (R) are true and (R) is the correct explanation of (A).

(*c*) (A) is true but (R) is false.

(*d*) (A) is false but (R) is true.

Q. 4. Assertion (A): The Gram Panchayat is assisted by a Panchayat Secretary who performs administrative functions.

Reason (R): Most Gram Panchayats are also assisted by an officer called 'Patwari' who maintains the villagers' lands records.

Codes:

(*a*) Both (A) and (R) are true but (R) is not the correct explanation of (A).

(*b*) Both (A) and (R) are true and (R) is the correct explanation of (A).

(*c*) (A) is true but (R) is false.

(*d*) (A) is false but (R) is true.

Q. 5. Assertion (A): At all the three levels, special rules have been made so that disadvantaged sections of the population can make their needs and problems heard.

Reason (R): Panchayati Raj System has a provision for reserving one-third of the seats for women.

Codes:

(*a*) Both (A) and (R) are true but (R) is not the correct explanation of (A).

(*b*) Both (A) and (R) are true and (R) is the correct explanation of (A).

(*c*) (A) is true but (R) is false.

(*d*) (A) is false but (R) is true.

Ans.

1. (*b*) **2.** (*a*) **3.** (*b*) **4.** (*a*) **5.** (*a*)

E. Case/Source Based Questions

Read the passage given below and answer the questions that follow:

I. The *Arthaśhāstra* is an ancient text of governance written by Kautilya (later also known as Chānakya) some 2,300 years ago. Among other things, it describes how a state should be structured and run, how the economy can be made prosperous, what the duties of the ruler are and how to conduct war. Kautilya, an expert in statecraft, also explains how a whole administrative structure should be put in place from the village to the regional capital. *(Page 170)*

(*i*) Who was the author of the *Arthaśhāstra*?

(*ii*) Give the main theme of the Arthaśhāstra.

(*iii*) How does the *Arthaśhāstra* reflects the current scenario?

Ans.

(*i*) Chanakya wrote the *Arthaśhāstra.*

(*ii*) The *Arthaśhāstra* is an ancient text of governance.

(*iii*) The *Arthaśhāstra* remains relevant today as its most of the concern are related with governance, tact, economic policies that relate to present day. Concepts like welfare, governance, financial planning, foreign policy, and strategic defence are still applied by governments.

F. Competency Based Questions

Q. 1. ***The village of Saraswatipuram has been facing frequent power cuts and low voltage, affecting farming, poultry farming and irrigation. The villagers are upset about it and want to resolve the issue.***

(*a*) *What is the role of local representatives in solving the issue?*

(*b*) *Suggest two steps the Panchayat and people can take to resolve an issue.*

Ans. (*a*) Local leaders can take up the matter to concern authorities to solve the issue and ensures that there are no power cuts in the near future.

(*b*) Two steps the Panchayat and people can take to resolve an issue are:

- Writing a letter to local authorities.
- Protests and dharna.
- Interaction with local media and highlighting the issue.

Q. 2. ***In many of Panchayats, elected women leaders may not get support from male members. Suggest ways and means to promote women's leadership in Panchayati Raj institutions.***

Ans.

- Raising awareness and breaking away the taboos.
- Inviting women leaders and convincing the rural elders to support women.
- Regular workshops and seminars.
- Identify women leaders and encourage them to come forward.

Q. 3. ***Find out some Panchayati raj leaders who have become MLA or MP and paste their picture in your notebook.***

Ans. Students do it themselves with the help of the teacher.

G. Skill Based Questions

Analyze the following scenario and answer the question below:

A village has a local governing body called the Gram Panchayat. The members of the Panchayat hold regular meetings to discuss issues like water supply, road repairs, and waste management. However, some villagers feel that their concerns are not being heard.

Q. 1. ***Imagine you are a villager attending a Gram Panchayat meeting. How would you use communication and problem-solving skills to ensure that your concerns are addressed effectively?***

Ans. To ensure concerns are addressed, I would speak clearly and respectfully, presenting specific problems with evidence. I would suggest practical solutions and involve others who share similar issues. If ignored, I would request a follow-up meeting or seek help from higher authorities.

VI. MULTIPLE CHOICE QUESTIONS

1. *The real India lives in its villages. The statement was given by:*

(*a*) Dr. B.R. Ambedkar
(*b*) Jyotiba Phule
(*c*) Mahatma Gandhi
(*d*) Vivekanand.

2. *Which of the following statements about village Lakshmanpur are correct ?*

A. Lakshmanpur, a large village is located in the foothills of the Himalayas.

B. It has 200 houses and a population of about 700, most of whom are farmers.

C. Some have relatives serving in the armed forces.

D. A few younger villagers have migrated to the city for higher studies in IITs and IIMs.

(*a*) A and B (*b*) C and D
(*c*) B and C (*d*) A, B and D

3. *Which of the following statements about Vandana Bahadur Maida, are correct?*

A. Vandana Bahadur Maida, is a member of the Bhil community from the village of Khankhandvi in Madhya Pradesh.

B. She defied matriarchal norms to become the first female Sarpanch of her village.

C. She convinced women in the village to attend the Sabha meetings and addressed critical issues like education and sanitation.

D. Vandana's journey shows how women can play a leading role in transforming rural India.

(*a*) A and B (*b*) A and D
(*c*) A and C (*d*) A, C and D

4. *The members of the gram panchayat are generally elected for a term of:*

(*a*) 1 year (*b*) 3 years
(*c*) 5 years (*d*) 4 years

5. *The .... is an ancient text written by Kautilya.*

(*a*) Ramayana (*b*) Gita
(*c*) Young India (*d*) Arthaśhāstra

Ans.

1. → (c) **2.** → (c)
3. → (d) **4.** → (c)
5. → (d)

VII. OBJECTIVE TYPE QUESTIONS

A. True or False

1. Panchayati Raj system works at two levels — from bottom up — the village, and the district.
2. The members of the Zila parishad are directly elected by the Gram Sabha.
3. Dnyaneshwar Kamble is a transgender person who was elected Sarpanch of Tarangfal village.
4. The head of the Panchayat is called Patwari.
5. There is a reservation of one third Seats for women in Panchayat.

Ans.

1. → False
2. → False
3. → True
4. → False
5. → True

B. Fill in the Blanks

1. Panchayats bring ________ closer to the people, making it possible for them to actively participate in the ____________ processes.
2. After______became ______ he started applying Anna Hazare's model of rainwater harvesting, watershed conservation and massive tree planting of lakhs of trees.
3. There is a reservation of______ seats for women in Panchayat.
4. The head of the Panchayat is called______ .
5. Dnyaneshwar Kamble is an elected Sarpanch whose motto is __________.
6. Pradhan is an elected head of_________.

Ans.

1. Governance, decision
2. Popatrao Baguji Pawar, Sarpanch
3. One-third
4. Sarpanch
5. lok seva, gram seva
6. Gram Panchayat

C. Match Column A with Column B

1

Column A	Column B
1. Panchayat Secretary	A. Consists of all adult residents of 18 years and above of age of a village or a group of villages within a Gram Panchayat who vote in Panchayat election.
2. Patwari	B. An official appointed by the government, acts as a link between the Gram Panchayat and the government.
3. Sarpanch	C. The elected head of the Gram Panchayat.
4. Gram Sabha	D. Is an official at the Panchayat level who helps the Panchayat secretary in maintaining records and maps.

Ans. 1—B, 2—D, 3—C, 4—A

2.

Column A		Column B	
1.	Works at the block level	(a)	Gram Panchayat
2.	The lowest level of Panchayati Raj	(b)	Sarpanch
3.	Functions at the district level	(c)	Zila Parishad
4.	Head of the Gram Panchayat	(d)	Panchayat Samiti

(a) 1 – (a) 2 – (b) 3 – (c) 4 – (d)
(b) 1 – (c) 2 – (b) 3 – (a) 4 – (d)
(c) 1 – (d) 2 – (a) 3 – (c) 4 – (b)
(d) 1 – (b) 2 – (d) 3 – (c) 4 – (a)

Ans.
(c) 1 – (d) 2 – (a) 3 – (c) 4 – (b)

3.

Column A		Column B	
1.	Three-tier system of local governance in rural areas	(a)	Gram Sabha
2.	Children's participation in governance	(b)	Patwari
3.	Maintains land records	(c)	Bal Panchayat
4.	Group of adult voters in a village	(d)	Panchayati Raj

(a) 1 – (a) 2 – (b) 3 – (c) 4 – (d)
(b) 1 – (c) 2 – (b) 3 – (a) 4 – (d)
(c) 1 – (d) 2 – (c) 3 – (b) 4 – (a)
(d) 1 – (b) 2 – (d) 3 – (c) 4 – (a)

Ans.
(c) 1 – (d) 2 – (c) 3 – (b) 4 – (a)

VIII. TEST YOUR KNOWLEDGE

A. Multiple Choice Question

1. *The elected head of a Gram Panchayat in rural area is:*
(a) Sarpanch
(b) District Commissioner
(c) Parishad
(d) Member of Legislative Assembly

2. .... *percentage of seats are reserved in Panchayati Raj institutions and urban local bodies for women.*
(a) 49% (b) 33.5%
(c) 33% (d) 50%

3. *Identify the incorrect statement about the Gram Panchayat.*
I. The Gram Panchayat, is closest to the people in rural areas
II. Its members are elected indirectly by the Gram Sabha,
III. In recent years, more and more women have become Sarpanchs
IV. Each Gram Panchayat elects a head or president who is always MLA
(a) I only (b) I & II
(c) II & IV (d) I , II & IV

4. *The primary function of the Panchayat Samiti is/are:*
I. to help the gram panchayat.
II. to serve as a link between the Gram Panchayat and the Zila Parishad.
III. to coordinate the group of villages with the zila parishad.
IV. Enforcing law and order
(a) I & II (b) only II
(c) II & IV (d) I , II & III

5. *Identify the given women leader below :*

(a) Dnyaneshwar Kamble
(b) Vandana Sethi
(c) Vandana Bahadur Maida
(d) Baguji Pawar

B. True or False

1. *The Panchayat system, also known as Panchayati Raj, is a form of self-government at Urban area.*

2. *Sangkhu Radhu Khandu Gram Panchayat, in West Bengal, has given a lot of importance to children's needs and rights.*

3. *The 'India Parliament', an offshoot of Bunker Roy's 'Barefoot College empowered underprivileged children in Sikkim's rural areas.*

4. *Mahabharata is an ancient text of governance.*

5. *Shri Popatrao Pawar was awarded the Padma Shri in 2020 because of his effort to transform Hiware Bazar, a village in Ahmednagar district as prosperous village.*

C. Fill in the Blanks

1. ____________, a member of the ________ community from the village of Khankhandvi in Madhya Pradesh, became the first female Sarpanch of her village.

2. ________ became its Sarpanch, he started applying Anna Hazare's model of rainwater harvesting, watershed conservation and massive tree planting of lakhs of trees.

3. The Gram Panchayat is assisted by a ________ who performs administrative functions.

4. The ________ at the block level is the link between the Gram Panchayat and the Zila Parishad at the district level.

D. Complete the given figure

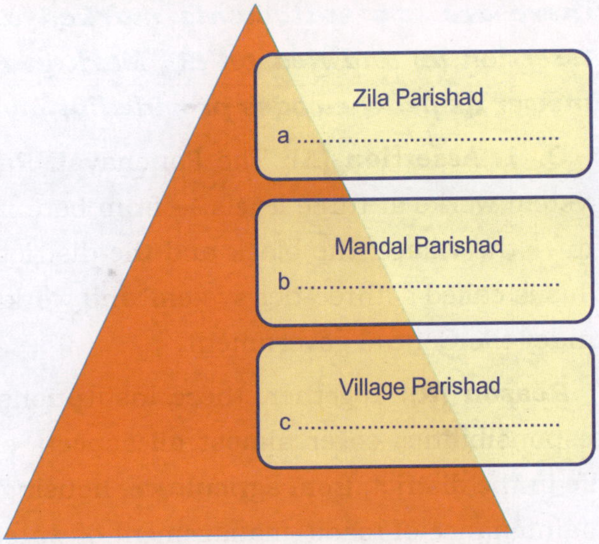

E. Short Answer Type Questions

Q. 1. *How is Panchayati Raj a form of self-governance?*

Q. 2. *Enlist the three-tier structure of the Panchayati Raj System.*

Q. 3. *Who is a Pradhan?*

Q. 4. *Write a short note on the Gram Panchayat.*

Q. 5. *Explain the important roles of the Panchayat Secretary and Patwari.*

F. Long Answer Type Questions

Q. 1. *Why is the Gram Sabha an important institution of the Panchayati Raj System?*

Q. 2. *What are Bal Panchayats?*

Q. 3. *Give some examples of the Bal Panchayats.*

Q. 4. *Why is Sangkhu Radhu Khandu Gram Panchayat been declared a child-friendly Gram Panchayat?*

Q. 5. *Mention the structure and composition of Zila Parishad. Give its two functions.*

Q. 6. *Explain the advantages of Village Panchayat.*

Q. 7. *How have Bal Panchayat extended the basic idea of democracy ?*

G. Assertion & Reasoning Questions

There are two statements marked as Assertion (A) and Reason (R). Mark your answer as per the codes provided below:

Q. 1. Assertion (A): The Panchayati Raj system works at three levels — from bottom up — the village, the block and the district. This is called a 'three-tier system' and works under the Central government.

Reason (R): Together, these institutions' responsibilities cover almost all aspects of life in the district, from agriculture, housing, maintenance of roads, management of water resources.

Codes:

(*a*) Both (A) and (R) are true but (R) is not the correct explanation of (A).

(*b*) Both (A) and (R) are true and (R) is the correct explanation of (A).

(*c*) (A) is true but (R) is false.

(*d*) (A) is false but (R) is true.

Q. 2. Assertion (A): Dnyaneshwar Kamble is a transgender person who was elected Sarpanch of Tarangfal village in the Solapur district of Maharashtra in 2017.

Reason (R): Kamble defeated four other candidates to become the Sarpanch.

Codes:

(*a*) Both (A) and (R) are true but (R) is not the correct explanation of (A).

(*b*) Both (A) and (R) are true and (R) is the correct explanation of (A).

(*c*) (A) is true but (R) is false.

(*d*) (A) is false but (R) is true.

NOTES

NOTES

1 Introduction

- Participatory democracy empowers citizens at all levels
- Urban governance is complex but follows basic principles
- Indian governance is a pyramid: local at base, national at top

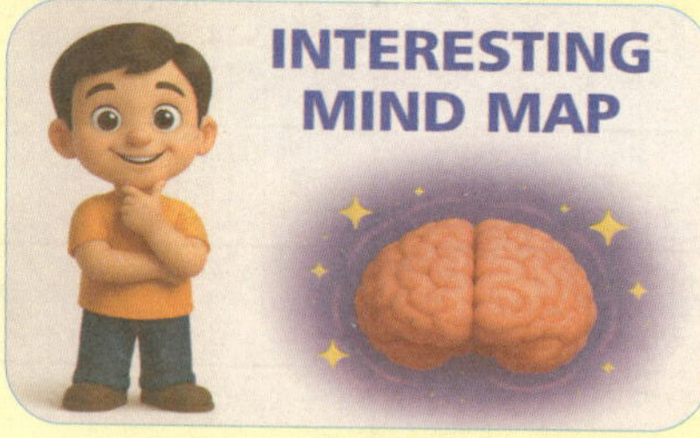

Grassroots Democracy– Part 3: Local Government in Urban Areas

2 Urban Local Bodies

- Urban area have local governing institutions known as urban local bodies
- Urban local bodies let citizens take part in decision making
- Cities and towns are split into smaller sections called wards; committees handle local issues like health, water, roads, and public welfare
- They manage infrastructure, garbage, taxes, schemes, and local development
- Citizens must take responsibility to help the system work
- Madras Corporation, established in 1688, is India's oldest municipal body
- Municipal Corporations (Mahanagar Nigam): For cities with more than 10 lakh people
- Municipal Councils (Nagar Palika): For towns with 1-10 lakh people
- Nagar Panchayats: For towns with less than 1 lakh people
- Cities are busy and crowded; people are more independent
- Villages are quiet and people help each other
- Both have local governments with elected representatives
- Citizens, including children in villages, can participate in decisions making

THEME D
Governance and Democracy

CHAPTER 12

GRASSROOTS DEMOCRACY – PART 3: LOCAL GOVERNMENT IN URBAN AREAS

I. FACTS TO REMEMBER/SUMMARY

INTRODUCTION

- Local government aims at participatory democracy, encouraging citizens to be part of decision-making process. This is achieved by involving people in local administration, both in urban local bodies and panchayati raj system.

- Urban areas are more complex in nature due to diverse population and large number of people living in these areas.
- Therefore, urban administration is more complex, with a wide range of functions and responsibilities.

URBAN LOCAL BODIES

- Urban local bodies are a decentralised form of government.
- Local communities have a direct say on how their areas are managed and the issues they face.
- Cities and towns are divided into smaller units called 'wards'. The ward committees organise health camps, campaign against single-use of plastics and many more.
- Urban local bodies maintain parks, water supply, garbage disposal. They are also responsible of issuing birth and death certificates, giving permission for cultural activities, etc.
- They also manage schools and primary healthcare system.
- Indore is the cleanest municipal area because of world class services provided by them and equally well responsible citizens.

S.No.	Population	Urban Local Bodies
1.	Less than 1 lakh	Nagar Panchayat
2.	Population between 1 and 10 lakhs	Municipal Council (Nagar Palika)
3.	Population more than 10 lakhs	Municipal Corporation (Mahanagar Nigam)

II. TEXTBOOK KEYWORDS/GLOSSARY

1. **Ward:** For smooth functioning, a city or town is divided into smaller units called wards.
2. **Municipal Corporation:** Cities with a population above 10 lakhs have a Municipal Corporation. They are also known as 'Mahanagar Nigam'.
3. **Municipal Council:** Cities with population between 1 and 10 lakhs, have a Municipal Council. They are also called 'Nagar Palika'.
4. **Nagar Panchayat:** Towns with population below 1 lakh have Nagar Panchayat.

III. THE BIG QUESTIONS *(Page 173)*

Q. 1. ***What are urban local bodies and what are their functions?***

Ans. As per the Constitution we have local government structures in urban areas called 'urban local bodies'. According to the size and population of the cities we have:

- **Municipal Corporation:** Cities with a population above 10 lakhs have a Municipal Corporation. They are also known as 'Mahanagar Nigam'.
- **Municipal Council:** Cities with population between 1 and 10 lakhs, have a Municipal Council. They are also called 'Nagar Palika'.
- **Nagar Panchayat:** Towns with population below 1 lakh have Nagar Panchayat.

The functions of the Urban bodies includes the construction and maintenance of infrastructure, burial ground, garbage collection and disposal, water supply, running of primary schools and healthcare system, collecting local taxes and fines and many other essential services.

Q. 2. ***Why are they important in governance and democracy?***

Ans. Urban local bodies are a form of local government in urban areas that take care of daily needs like water supply, garbage disposable, maintenance of parks, burial cremation grounds among other things. These works are collectively taken with the participation of local people of the same areas. With the one-third reservation of women in urban bodies, it has widened the concept of participatory democracy. Their existence has made the burden of central and state government lighter and more effective.

IV. NCERT INTEXT/TEXTBOOK EXERCISES

Let's Explore

Q. 1. ***Why is a city like Kolkata, Chennai or Mumbai more complex and diverse than a village or a town?*** *(Page 174)*

Ans. City like Kolkata, Chennai or Mumbai are more complex and diverse than a village or a town because it has huge and diverse population coming from different states, different religion, caste, economic background. These are the places with huge job opportunities, better infrastructure such as local bus service, local trains and Metro. Diverse people stay together and share their respective culture, food habits, festivals, clothing and traditional life styles. These features make cities like Kolkata and Mumbai more diverse and complex.

Q. 2. ***With your classmates, make a list of diverse communities residing in any city that you are familiar with. How many were you able to list? What else do you observe in the list?*** *(Page 174)*

Ans. Hint Based: The response will vary depending on the city, town and villages.

Taking the example of Delhi, the capital of India it is home to people from diverse region such as Tamil Nadu, Kerala, Rajasthan, Sikkim, Manipur, Tripura, Jammu and Kashmir, Punjab, Bihar and Uttar Pradesh.

Additionaly individuals from foreign countries like Nepal, Bangladesh, Kenya, Britain, France also reside in Delhi.

Observation: Delhi is a cosmopolitan city with immense diversity, where people of different castes, genders, religions, regions and economic backgrounds coexist peacefully. This makes it a culturally vibrant and rich city.

Q. 3. ***In Fig. 12.2 (See NCERT textbook page 175), what similarities and differences do you notice between the Panchayati Raj system and the urban local government?*** (Page 175)

Ans. Similarities:

- **Governance:** Both the panchayati raj system and urban local governments are forms of decentralised local areas like villages and cities respectively. They are responsible for taking care of people's needs and ensuring basic services to the people in their areas.
- Members are chosen through elections held every five years.
- One-third seats are reserved for women in both the set ups.

Differences: Panchayati raj is a three-tier system looking at the needs of people in rural areas, whereas urban local bodies are either single or two-tiered structures for managing the administration of urban areas.

The panchayati bodies have fewer resources as compared to urban bodies.

Q. 4. ***Can you think of four or five more actions that responsible citizens might take to help their area of the city?*** (Page 177)

Ans. Responsible citizens can take following actions to improve their city:

- Planting trees and ensuring their upkeep.
- Opting public transportation to reduce pollution.
- Using eco-friendly cotton and jute bags instead of plastic bags.
- Spreading awareness by educating children and other community members.
- Switching to LED lighting and promoting the use of Solar Energy.
- Recycling water wasted by RO systems for uses like watering plants, cleaning utensils, washing clothes and cleaning vehicles.

Q. 5. ***Select a few cities, from your State and from a few neighbouring States. These may include the city you live in or the city nearest to your town or village. How will you find out if they have a Nagar Panchayat, Municipal Council or Municipal Corporation? Draw a table with the names of the cities and the type of urban local body each of them has.*** (Page 179)

Ans. Hint based-Suggestive.

State-I: Sikkim

City	Type of local Bodies
Gangtok	Municipal Corporation.
Namchi	Municipal Council.
Mangan	Nagar Panchayat.

State-II: Karnataka

City	Type of local Bodies
Bengaluru	Municipal Corporation.
Belgavi	Municipal Council.
Shimoga	Nagar Panchayat.

Q. 6. ***How do urban local bodies fund their activities? (Hint: Look carefully at the pictures of the functions performed by Indore Municipal Corporation in Figure 12.4 on page 178.) Are some of them paid services?*** (Page 179)

Ans. Urban local bodies fund their activities through sources such as Property Taxes, Water Charges, Waste Management Fees, Trade Licences and grants received from the State government.

Some paid services they offer are Water tankers, Auditorium Rentals, Septic tank cleaning and more.

THINK ABOUT IT

Q. 1. ***Indore in Madhya Pradesh has been awarded the cleanest city in India under the Swachh Survekshan government scheme for seven years in a row. What could have been the role of Indore citizens in this achievement?*** (Page 179)

Ans. All governments work for the welfare and happiness of their citizens. Indore's local bodies have been providing the best services and its citizens have actively participated in maintaining the city's cleanliness. Residents of Indore have strictly followed rules regarding garbage collection and disposal. They have taken proactive steps such as avoiding littering, minimising the use of plastics and using public transport systems. Additionally, regular campaigns have encouraged people to take ownership of their cities welfare, contributing significantly to this achievement.

NCERT Questions, Activities and Projects
(*Pages 181–182*)

Q. 1. ***On your way to school, you and your friends notice that a water pipe is leaking. A lot of water is being wasted on account of the leak. What would you and your friends do in such a situation?***

Ans. Steps that, we shall take after noticing a leaking water pipe are as follows:

1. Immediately report the issue to local elders, teachers, or school authorities.
2. Contact local authorities using helpline numbers.
3. Encourage nearby residents to collect and use the leaking water.
4. Take the help of nearby residents to click the image of the leaking pipeline and share with local leaders through WhatsApp etc.
5. Will try to fix the leaking pipeline in best possible way.

Q. 2. ***Invite a member of an urban local body near you to your class. Discuss with them their role and responsibilities. Prepare a set of questions to ask them so that the meeting is fruitful.***

Ans. Local Councillor Ms. Rakhi has been invited to share her experience, role, duties and vision for her area:

Questionnaire

- Could you please introduce yourself?
- What is your specific role in the Urban Local Body?
- Can you highlight your key duties and responsibilities.?
- What aspects of your role do you enjoy the most?
- What challenges do you face while performing your duties?
- What are your plans to make your ward the best area?
- How do you involve local citizens in participatory government?
- Kindly advice how to involve students in Municipals work.
- How to stop littering on roads?
- What are the future plans in politics?
- How to motivate children to join clean politics?

Q. 3. ***Discuss with adult members of your family and neighbourhood, and make a list of their expectations from the urban local bodies.***

Ans. Hint based-Suggestive Answer

Some expectations as shared by my uncle and neighbour are as follows:

1. Regular supply of clean drinking water.
2. Well maintained green parks and walking areas.
3. Better and trained staff to clear up the hanging wires.
4. Regular collection and disposable of garbage. Separation of dry and wet garbage.
5. Clean roads and pavements.
6. Check on stray animals.
7. Some cultural activities on important event days.
8. Various cultural and sports activities for children.
9. Regular medical check-up camps.

Q. 4. ***Make a list of characteristics of a good urban local body.***

Ans. A good urban local body is which listens to citizens adheres to its duties and does its task on time. Some important characteristics of a good urban local body are as follows:

1. Citizen friendly.
2. Responsive to the need of people.
3. Should have citizen charters showing its duties and responsibilities.
4. Should have mobile APP and be technology friendly.
5. Should have strict, proper, quick grievance redressal mechanism.
6. It should create conditions for common people to be a part of the local body.

Q. 5. ***What are the similarities and differences between the Panchayati Raj system in rural areas and the urban local bodies?***

Ans. Refer to Question no. 3 LET'S EXPLORE on page 209 of this book.

V. EXAM ORIENTED QUESTIONS

A. Very Short Answer Type Questions

Q. 1. ***What are urban local bodies?***

Ans. Self governing local government structures in urban areas are called 'urban local bodies'. *For example*, Municipal corporation, Municipal council.

Q. 2. ***What is the smallest unit of local urban bodies?***

Ans. Ward is the smallest unit of local urban bodies.

Q. 3. ***What do you mean by the term 'Ward'?***

Ans. For smooth functioning, a city or town is divided into smaller units called wards.

Q. 4. ***Enlist any two aim of good governance.***

Ans. Good governance aims to empower the citizens so that they can actively participate in their country's functioning and become a responsible and critical citizen.

Q. 5. ***Give the main functions of urban local bodies.***

Ans. Urban local bodies are responsible for a range of functions — helping, taking care of the infrastructure, maintaining the burial grounds, garbage collection and its disposal. Issuing birth and death certificates, licencing commercial establishments. Collection of house tax, property tax and toll tax.

Q. 6. ***Name the highest urban local body in a city with a population above 10 lakhs.***

Ans. Municipal Corporations.

Q. 7. ***Name the most cleanest city of India. In which state is it located ?***

Ans. Indore (Madhya Pradesh).

Q. 8. ***When was the Bombay Municipal Corporation established ?***

Ans. The Bombay Municipal Corporation was established in 1865.

Q. 9. ***When was the Madras Corporation (now Greater Chennai Corporation) established?***

Ans. The Madras Corporation was established in 29 September 1688.

Q. 10. ***Mention any one reason for uniqueness about the Indore Municipal Corporation.***

Ans. Active participations of citizens and taking up the responsibilities to maintain and clean the city.

Q. 11. ***How do urban local bodies fund their activities?***

Ans. Urban local bodies fund their activities through taxes (property tax, water tax) and government grants.

B. Short Answer Type Questions

Q. 1. *What do you understand by the concept of participatory democracy ?*

Ans. The purpose of good governance is to motivate the citizens to actively participate in their country's functioning, at the rural, regional, urban, state or national level. In participatory democracy, people should perform their duties and obey law and order.

Q. 2. *Why do you think that Local government is also a decentralised form of government?*

Ans. Local government is part of decentralisation of power because central and state governments delegate some power and areas of function to local authorities. The common people are encouraged to participate in decision-making process through elections. They are decentralised, which means that instead of operating under a central authority at the top, the local communities have a direct say on how their areas are managed or the issues they face.

Q. 3. *Enumerate the functions of the ward committees.*

Ans. The ward committees help in conducting various activities like health camps, campaign against the use of single-use plastics, cleanliness of the area and so on. They also maintain a list for water pipe leak, a blocked drain, a damaged road, etc. and report such problems to the authorities.

Q. 4. *Give two importance of participatory democracy.*

Ans. Two importance of participatory democracy are as follows :

- It encourages common people to participate in decision making process.
- It enhances the dignity of people.
- It strengthen democracy through people taking active part in election process.

Q. 5. *Write the role of a ward committee in urban governance.*

Ans. The ward committees facilitate activities such as conducting health camps, organising a campaign against the use of single-use plastics, and so on.

They also keep an eye on anything that might go wrong — a water leak, a blocked drain, a damaged road, etc. — and report such problems to the authorities.

Q. 6. *How does a Municipal Corporation differ from a Municipal Council and a Nagar Panchayat?*

Ans. Municipal Corporations are established in larger cities like Delhi, Pune, Kochi, Chennai with populations more than 10 lakhs.

- They have a more complex administrative structure and more sources of fund.
- More challenges and task

In comparison, Municipal Councils cater to smaller urban areas with a between 1 and 10 lakhs in population.

They have simpler structures and less responsibilities.

Nagar Panchayats, meanwhile, cater to smaller urban settlements or transitional areas with population less than 1 lakh.

Their governance structure is more basic and focused on providing essential civic amenities.

Q. 7. *How does a municipal corporation generate funds for its activities?*

Ans. Municipal Corporations have variety of sources of funds including government grants.

The most important source being taxes like property tax, trade licenses, and water and sewage charges, tolls etc.

They even collect fines for violations of laws.

Q. 8. *What are some key services provided by urban local bodies?*

Ans. Some important services include water supply and sanitation, garbage collection, road cleaning and street lighting.

- They provide primary health services, and education.
- At the same time these bodies issue trade licenses, oversee local markets, and implement various government schemes of state and central government.

C. Long Answer Type Questions

Q. 1. ***Elaborate the responsibilities of the urban local bodies.***

Ans. Urban local bodies are urban self government that look after the interests of residents of their area.

The functions of the urban bodies are as follows:

- Construction and maintenance of infrastructure like roads.
- Taking care of cremation and burial grounds, garbage collection and its disposal.
- Ensuring regular water supply.
- Running of primary schools and healthcare system.
- Collecting house tax, tolls and fines.

Q. 2. ***List the roles of common people in supporting the duties and responsibilities of the urban local bodies.***

Ans. To ensure the efficient functioning of the urban local bodies, city residents must fulfil their duties and responsibilities sincerly and honestly. They should dispose garbage at designated places, pay house tax on time and avoid littering. Citizens should also conserve water and take proper care of their pets. This demonstrates their care and concern for the community.

Q. 3. ***Why do cities have Municipal corporation ?***

Ans. Large metropolitan cities like Chennai, New Delhi, Kolkata etc. have Municipal Corporations.

- They provide a structured system of governance to the diverse urban populations.

In large urban areas the local challenges and requirement cannot be easily and efficiently managed directly by central and state government.

Issues such as infrastructure, sanitation, water supply, pollution and urban planning requires direct involvement of local people.

MunicipalCorporationsbeingdecentralised, take care of the above aspiration of people and strengthens democracy.

Q. 4. ***Compare the Panchayati Raj system with urban local bodies.***

Ans. The Panchayati Raj system and urban local bodies both are part of decentralised governance and serve in different challenges:

Panchayati Raj System:

- At rural areas(village)

It consists of a three-tier system—Gram Panchayat at the village level, Panchayat Samiti at the block level, and Zila Parishad at the district level.

Target: To cater the need of villagers, promoting agricultural development, primary health and education, child vaccination and rural welfare.

Head of the gram panchayat is Sarpanch.

Urban Local Bodies:

Presence in cities, towns and semi-urban areas.

According to population size—Nagar Panchayats for small towns, Municipal Councils (Nagar Palikas) for medium-sized cities, and Municipal Corporations for large cities.

Functions: Helps to sort out complex urban issues and solves local issues like, sanitation, water supply, pollution and urban planning requires direct involvement of local people.

Q. 5. ***Highlight the role of citizens to make their local bodies efficient and responsible.***

Ans. The success of local urban bodies depends upon the participation of citizens.

- Active participation in electing leaders and criticising them, when they are not working.
- Keeping a check on issues such as water leaks, pollution, road damage, traffic and reporting issues to the appropriate authorities.
- Paying taxes on time and following rules and regulations.

D. Assertion and Reasoning Questions

There are two statements marked as Assertion (A) and Reason (R). Mark your answer as per the codes provided below:

Q. 1. Assertion (A): Good governance aims to empower the citizens so they can actively participate in country's functioning.

Reason (R): In participatory democracy, all are not required to be part of governance

Codes:

(*a*) Both A and R are true but R is not the correct explanation of A.

(*b*) Both A and R are true and R is the correct explanation of A.

(*c*) A is true but R is false.

(*d*) A is false but R is true.

Q. 2. Assertion (A): Chennai and Indore have a Municipal Corporation at the top of their urban bodies.

Reason (R): They have population above 10 lakhs.

Codes:

(*a*) Both A and R are true but R is not the correct explanation of A.

(*b*) Both A and R are true and R is the correct explanation of A.

(*c*) A is true but R is false.

(*d*) A is false but R is true.

Q. 3. Assertion (A): Urban local bodies are part of decentralised institution and allow local decision-making.

Reason (R): It helps urban areas function independently.

Codes:

(*a*) Both A and R are true but R is not the correct explanation of A.

(*b*) Both A and R are true and R is the correct explanation of A.

(*c*) A is true but R is false.

(*d*) A is false but R is true.

Q. 4. Assertion (A): Cities and towns are divided into smaller units called 'wards'.

Reason (R): Ward activities facilitate activities such as conducting health camps, organising a campaign against the use of single-use plastics.

Codes:

(*a*) Both A and R are true but R is not the correct explanation of A.

(*b*) Both A and R are true and R is the correct explanation of A.

(*c*) A is true but R is false.

(*d*) A is false but R is true.

Ans.

1. (*c*) **2.** (*b*) **3.** (*b*) **4.** (*b*)

E. Case/Source Based Questions

Q. 1. ***Read the passage given below and answer the questions that follow:***

Sameer: The other day a few kids noticed that an electricity wire was hanging dangerously low, almost touching the roof of a building. Not only did we report it, but we explained to one of our Gram Sabha members that an electric post should be shifted a little. And it was done!

Anita: Great! I suppose that's how democracy should work. It seems more complicated in the city, but the idea is the same — everyone's voice matters.

Sameer: Yes, it does! Sorry, I must make a move. My mother needs my help for a little shopping. Thanks for telling me about the city.

Anita: And thanks for telling me about your village! I am definitely going to look around.

Questions:

(*i*) What is Gram Sabha ? How does it differs from ward committee ?

(*ii*) Why is the urban local bodies system different from the Panchayati Raj system?

(*iii*) Give any two role of elected representatives in urban local body.

(*iv*) Why is citizen participation crucial in both urban and rural governance?

(*v*) Mention any two ways to improve the effectiveness of elected representatives.

Ans. (*i*) The Gram Sabha is a body consisting of all adult members (*18 years and above*) of a village or group of villages in a Gram Panchayat.

Feature	Gram Sabha	Ward Committee
Location	Rural areas	Urban areas
Members	All adult voters of the village	Ward councillor and selected members
Function	Discusses and approves rural development plans	Addresses urban local issues

(*ii*) Urban areas has multiple challenges, with complex problems and huge diverse problems. Whereas the Panchayati raj which is associated with rural areas have less challenges and requirements are basic.

(*iii*) Elected representatives, such as ward councillors along with other members, participate in making policies, designing activities for economic development of local areas.

- They monitor the development programmes of the government.

(*iv*) Citizen participation is crucial in both urban and rural governance, as their participation is critical for success of local government.

They keep a check on the functioning of the elected representatives.

They ensure that local problems are solved and sorted.

(*v*) Two ways are :

- regular feedback and critical evaluation
- training and upgradation of skills of leaders (*Any other*)

Q. 2. ***Read the passage given below and answer the questions that follow:***

The Madras Corporation (now Greater Chennai Corporation), established on 29 September 1688, is the oldest municipal institution in India. The East India Company issued a charter the previous year constituting the town of 'Fort St. George' and all territories within 16 km from the Fort into a corporation. A Parliamentary Act of 1792 gave the Madras Corporation power to levy municipal taxes in the city, which is when the municipal administration properly began. (*Page 177*)

Questions:

(*i*) When was the Madras Corporation established?

(*ii*) Give any two initial functions of the Madras Corporation.

(*iii*) Mention two challenges faced by the Municipal corporations.

Ans.

(*i*) The Madras Corporation (now Greater Chennai Corporation), established on 29 September 1688.

(*ii*) Maintaining cleanliness and sanitation in the city. Collection of taxes to provide basic civic amenities.

(*iii*) Lack of funds for development and maintenance of city infrastructure.

F. Competency Based Questions

Q. 1. ***As a responsible child, what steps would you take to improve waste management and cleaning in your city?***

Ans.

(*i*) Create awareness among citizens.

(*ii*) Report dump garbage to local authorities.

(*iii*) Create a list of volunteers who will look into the cleanliness process and report in case of violation.

(*iv*) Have some cultural events to promote a sense of civic alertness among local residents.

(*v*) Involve elders to guide and motivate people to be more sensitive towards cleanliness and sanitation.

Q. 2. ***How can you become part of Municipal Corporation and ensure it works efficiently ?***

Ans. To be a part of Corporation one need to be minimum of 18 years, however a student can become volunteer.

One can participate in awareness programs and campaigns like cleanliness drives, tree plantation, and anti-plastic campaigns.

Be a responsible child by following civic rules and to report problems like garbage, potholes, and broken streetlights.

Join school and community projects.

One can start Community club in school and call members of Municipal corporation to interact with them.

G. Skill Based Questions

Q. 1. ***How does the model of governance change when one move from rural to urban areas ? Highlight some of the challenges.***

Ans. Changes in the model of governance:

- **Rural Areas:** Administrative management under by Panchayati Raj System— Gram Panchayat, Panchayat Samiti, and Zila Parishad.
- **Urban Areas:** Administrative management by Municipalities—Municipal Corporations in large cities, Municipal Councils in smaller towns.

Challenges:

1. Towns and cities have huge population size , leading to multiple challeneges.
2. Huge population leads to shortage of essential services like drinking water, garbage selection.
3. Pollution and traffic problems.

Q. 2. ***Suppose you are a member of a Municipal bodies, and you notice an increase in water wastage and garbage dump in your neighbourhood on a regular basis. What steps would you take to ensure the problem is resolved effectively and permanently?***

Ans.

- To organise a regular awareness campaigns of being an ethical and sensitive citizen.
- Organise community awareness programs to educate residents on the importance of water conservation and proper waste disposal.
- Use posters, social media, and public announcements to spread awareness.
- Making eco-friendly policies and laws.
- Implementing laws seriously.
- Imposing fines and penalty. (*Any other*)

Q. 3. ***Create a banner or poster to encourage citizens in your area to make your ward the most clean and to participate in Swachh Survekshan program.***

Ans. Students' Activity to be done by students with the help of Teachers and Parents.

Hints:-

- Make a meaningful posture.
- Give creative slogan.
- Make small pictures.

VI. MULTIPLE CHOICE QUESTIONS

1. *The Municipal Corporation of Greater Mumbai was created in:*

   (*a*) 1865 (*b*) 1965
   (*c*) 1866 (*d*) 1951

2. *Where does the election for Urban Bodies take place?*

   (*a*) Vidhan Sabha
   (*b*) Lok Sabha
   (*c*) Municipal Corporation
   (*d*) Nagar Panchayat

3. *Participatory democracy involves participation of:*
   (*a*) women
   (*b*) children
   (*c*) old age people
   (*d*) all of the above.

4. *Which is the oldest Municipal Corporation in India?*
   (*a*) Municipal Corporation of Delhi.
   (*b*) Bombay Municipal Corporation.
   (*c*) Kolkata Municipal Corporation.
   (*d*) Greater Chennai Corporation.

5. *Identify the state in which the following Municipal Corporation is located?*

   (*a*) Kerala (*b*) Tamil Nadu
   (*c*) West Bengal (*d*) Maharashtra

6. *Identify the given Municipal Corporation located in financial capital city of India.*

   (*a*) Kolkata (*b*) Chennai
   (*c*) Delhi (*d*) Mumbai

7. *How much population should a city have to have a municipal corporation?*
   (*a*) Between 1 to 10 lakhs
   (*b*) More than 10 lakhs
   (*c*) Less than 1 lakh
   (*d*) None of these

8. *Why large city like Kolkata, Noida or Mumbai have municipal corporation?*
   (*a*) Foreigner people live here
   (*b*) It has population of more than 10 lakhs
   (*c*) Because they are Metro Cities
   (*d*) Because complex, diverse and large population live in these cities.

9. *Identify the incorrect statement about participatory democracy :*
   (*i*) Good governance
   (*ii*) Aims to empower the citizens
   (*iii*) Encourages actively participation of common people.
   (*iv*) Promotes corruption and encourages inefficiency

   Options:
   (*a*) only (*iv*) (*b*) (*i*), (*ii*) and (*iii*)
   (*c*) (*ii*) and (*iii*) (*d*) (*iii*) and (*iv*)

10. *The main function of urban local bodies is*
   (*a*) Helping rural agriculture
   (*b*) Managing and providing services in urban areas
   (*c*) Managing urban law and order
   (*d*) Conducting elections

11. .... *has been awarded the cleanest city in India under the Swachh Survekshan .*
   (*a*) Jamshedpur (*b*) Bengaluru
   (*c*) Indore (*d*) Kochi

12. *Identity sources of revenue for urban local bodies:*
   (*i*) Property tax
   (*ii*) Local taxes and service charges
   (*iii*) Water Charges
   (*iv*) Donations from private companies

   Options:
   (*a*) only (*iv*) (*b*) (*i*), (*ii*) and (*iii*)
   (*c*) (*ii*) and (*iii*) (*d*) (*iii*) and (*iv*)

13. *Cities with a population less than 10 lakhs have ....*
   (*a*) Nagar Palika
   (*b*) Municipal Corporation
   (*c*) Gram Panchayat
   (*d*) Zila Parishad

14. *Cities and towns are divided into smaller units called......*
   (*a*) Nagar Panchayat
   (*b*) Municipal Corporation
   (*c*) Wards
   (*d*) Zila Parishad

Ans.

1. → (*a*) 2. → (*c*) 3. → (*d*)
4. → (*d*) 5. → (*b*) 6. → (*d*)
7. → (*b*) 8. → (*b*) 9. → (*a*)
10. → (*b*) 11. → (*c*) 12. → (*b*)
13. → (*a*) 14. → (*c*)

VII. OBJECTIVE TYPE QUESTIONS

A. True and False

1. Bombay Municipal Corporation was renamed the Mumbai Municipal Corporation.
2. 'Urban local bodies' operate under a central authority.
3. Urban local bodies take care of rural areas.
4. A Nagar Panchayat manages towns with a population of more than one million.
5. The Swachh Survekshan survey ranks cities based on cleanliness and has ranked Gangtok as the cleanest city.
6. Local governance helps in decentralisation and better administration.
7. Greater Mumbai Corporation is the oldest municipal institution in India.
8. The most important source of revenue for urban local bodies is taxes collected from private companies.
9. The success of urban local bodies depend on the active participation of citizens in urban governance.

Ans.

1. → False 2. → False 3. → False
4. → False 5. → False 6. → True
7. → False 8. → False 9. → True

B. Fill in the Blanks

1. *Complete the given figure of Urban local bodies:*

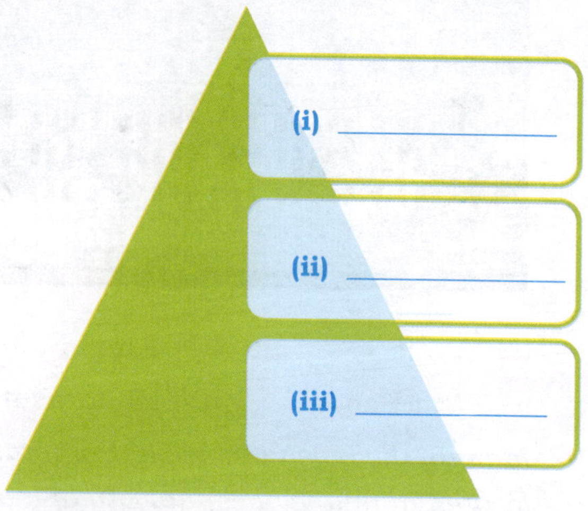

2. *Complete the given figure with respect to Tiers/Levels of government in India.*

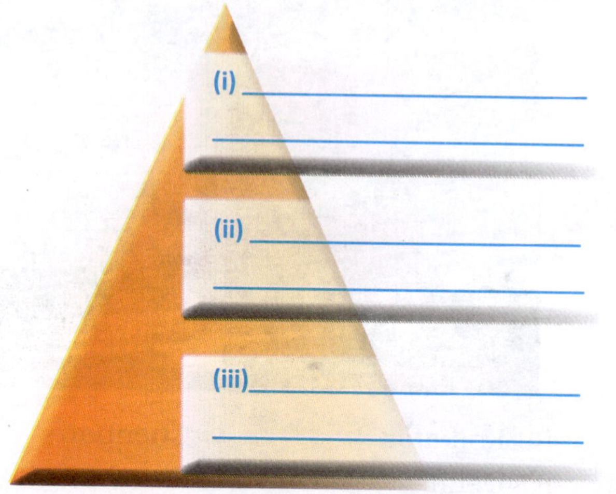

3. *A .... governs city with a population of more than 10 lakhs.*

4. *Urban local governance is based on ________ system, meaning local participation and decisions taken at the local level.*

5. *The correct sequence of government in India is ______, State and __________.*

6. *The ____________ Corporation, is the oldest municipal institution in India.*

7. *Under __________ water tanker, debris clearance are provided by Indore Municipal Corporations.*

Ans.

1. (*i*) Municipal Corporation
   (*ii*) Ward Committee
   (*iii*) People of the Ward
2. (*i*) Central Government
   (*ii*) State Government
   (*iii*) Local Government
3. Municipal Corporation
4. decentralised
5. Central Government, Local Government
6. Madras
7. **CRM:** Citizen Relationship Management

C. Match Column A with Column B

1.

Column A	Column B
1. More than 10 lakh	(*a*) Municipal Council
2. Between 1 to 10 lakh	(*b*) Municipal Corporation
3. Less than 1 lakh	(*c*) Indore
4. Cleanest city	(*d*) Nagar Panchayat

(*a*) 1 – (*a*) 2 – (*b*) 3 – (*c*) 4 – (*d*)
(*b*) 1 – (*b*) 2 – (*a*) 3 – (*d*) 4 – (*c*)
(*c*) 1 – (*a*) 2 – (*c*) 3 – (*d*) 4 – (*b*)
(*d*) 1 – (*b*) 2 – (*a*) 3 – (*c*) 4 – (*d*)

Ans.
(*b*) 1 – (*b*) 2 – (*a*) 3 – (*d*) 4 – (*c*)

VIII. TEST YOUR KNOWLEDGE

A. Multiple Choice Questions

1. *Which among the following is the oldest municipal corporation in India ?*
   (*a*) Indore Municipal Corporation
   (*b*) Municipal Corporation of Greater Mumbai
   (*c*) Greater Chennai Corporation
   (*d*) Municipal Corporation of Delhi

2. *Identify the basis of urban governance in India ::*
   (*i*) Regular interference of central government
   (*ii*) Managing local issues
   (*iii*) Decentralised decision making
   (*iv*) People participation

   Option :
   (*a*) only (*iv*)
   (*b*) (*i*), (*ii*), (*iii*) and (*iv*)
   (*c*) (*ii*) and (*iii*)
   (*d*) (*iii*) and (*iv*)

3. *What does a municipal corporation primarily oversee?*
   (*a*) Rural administration
   (*b*) Large urban areas
   (*c*) National governance
   (*d*) Military operations

4. *In India, local government is divided into:*
   (*a*) Urban and rural bodies
   (*b*) State and central bodies
   (*c*) Private and public bodies
   (*d*) Industrial and residential bodies

5. The urban local body which is responsible for towns with a population between 1 and 10 lakhs is.....
   (a) Nagar Panchayat
   (b) Municipal Council (Nagar Palika)
   (c) Taluka
   (d) Nagar Nigam

B. Fill in the Blanks

1. Cities with population between ________ and _______ have Municipal Council.
2. Election for urban local bodies take place after ________ years.
3. _________ governs towns with smaller populations below 1 lakh.
4. Urban areas are divided into ________ managed by ________, which handle local issues like health camps, campaigns, and infrastructure maintenance.
5. Indore in Madhya Pradesh has been awarded the cleanest city in India under the ___________ government.
6. Local government structures in urban areas are called ___________ .

C. True or False

1. The Madras Corporation (now Greater Chennai Corporation), was established on 29 September, 1988.
2. Pune in Maharashtra has been awarded the cleanest city in India under the *Swachh Survekshan* government scheme for seven years in a row.
3. Cities and towns with smaller populations have a Nagar Palika.
4. The large metropolitan cities has a Municipal Corporation as a local urban body.
5. Indore a city in Maharashtra has been ranked the cleanest city in India for seven consecutive years.
6. Urban local bodies are responsible for garbage collection, sanitation services, primary schools and health.
7. Election takes place at ward, in which candidate getting maximum votes are declared as a winner
8. The urban local bodies are named according to the quality and skills of population.

D. Very Short Answer Type Questions

1. *Given any two functions of ward committee.*
2. *Name the place where election take place in urban areas and after how many years.*

E. Short Answer Type Questions

1. *What are the different structures of urban local bodies?*
2. *Explain the need of Urban Local Bodies.*
3. *Examine the cause of inefficiency in the functioning of Urban Local Bodies.*
4. *Enumerate the importance of Ward committee.*
5. *Enlist the sources of revenue of Urban Local bodies.*
6. *How can sources of revenue of local bodies be enhanced?*
7. *Enumerate elements of participatory democracy.*
8. *How is different urban bodies different ?*
9. *What makes Indore the most clean Municipal corporation ?*

F. Long Answer Type Questions

1. *Explain the role of urban local bodies .*
2. *How does Urban local bodies differ from Panchayati Raj.*

G. Assertion & Reasoning Questions

Q. 1. Assertion (A): Good governance aims to empower the citizens so they may actively participate in their country's functioning.

Reason (R): In participatory democracy, all are not required to be a part of governance.

Codes:

(*a*) Both A and R are true but R is not the correct explanation of A.

(*b*) Both A and R are true and R is the correct explanation of A.

(*c*) A is true but R is false.

(*d*) A is false but R is true.

Q. 2. Assertion (A): There is three tier system of government.

Reason (R): India has a large, diverse and complex population.

Codes:

(*a*) Both A and R are true but R is not the correct explanation of A.

(*b*) Both A and R are true and R is the correct explanation of A.

(*c*) A is true but R is false.

(*d*) A is false but R is true.

Q. 3. Assertion (A): Cities and towns are divided into smaller units called wards and have ward committee.

Reason (R): They keep an eye on anything that might go wrong — a water leak, a blocked drain, a damaged road, and report such problems to the authorities.

Codes:

(*a*) Both A and R are true but R is not the correct explanation of A.

(*b*) Both A and R are true and R is the correct explanation of A.

(*c*) A is true but R is false.

(*d*) A is false but R is true.

Q. 4. Assertion (A): Indore in Madhya Pradesh has been awarded the cleanest city in India.

Reason (R): Under Citizen Relationship Management, they get various services like Septic Tanker, Funeral Van etc.

Codes:

(*a*) Both A and R are true but R is not the correct explanation of A.

(*b*) Both A and R are true and R is the correct explanation of A.

(*c*) A is true but R is false.

(*d*) A is false but R is true.

NOTES

NOTES

THEME E
ECONOMIC LIFE AROUND US

The Value of Work

1 Introduction

- **Human activities:** economic & non-economic.
- **Economic activities:** involve money.
- **Ex.** Buying/selling goods, farming for sale, lawyer charging fees, factory worker making cars.
- **Market:** a place where people buy or sell goods or services or sometimes exchange goods/services for other goods/services.
- **Non-economic activities:** done out of respect, love, care or responsibility; no money involved.
- **Ex.** Caring for grandparents/parents, parents cooking for their children, family repairing house together.
- **Story example:**

  Geeta Aunty (Air Force pilot, salary) → Economic.

  Rohan (software job, salary) → Economic.

  Rohan (volunteer computer teacher, no pay) → Non-economic.

2 Types of Economic Activities

People earn by doing economic activities in the following ways:

- **Salary:** a fixed regular payment (usually paid monthly), made by an employer to an employee for work performed.

  Examples:
  - Kavya's uncle – bulldozer operator → receives a monthly salary
  - Kavya's aunt – post office job → receives a monthly salary
- **Fees:** Money paid for a service, like tuition or classes
- **Wage:** Money earned by a worker for their efforts or work, usually on a daily basis

  Example: Sahil, a farm labourer, works with a tractor and earns a daily wage
- **Payment in kind:** Receiving goods instead of money (of equal value)

  Example: Sahil receives mangoes of equal value as his payment
- **Value addition:** goods become more valuable at each stage of production
- **Monetary value:** The extra value of a product that comes from a person's time, skill, and effort

  Example: Rajesh (carpenter) → buys wood for ₹600 → makes a chair→ adds ₹400 for his skill and effort → sells it at ₹1,000

3 The Importance of Non-Economic Activities

- Non-economic activities do not bring money but add value to our lives.
- These activities strengthen our **family, society & culture.**

3(a) Seva: selfless service

- **Seva:** At gurudwaras, mosques, temples & churches.
- **Ex.** Langars/community kitchens at gurudwaras.
- **Langars:** free meals for all.

3(b) The strength of community participation

- **Swachh Bharat Abhiyan:** Collective cleanliness drive; all citizens help to keep our surroundings clean.
- **Van Mahotsav:** Citizens come up together for tree planting & forest care.
- Such community efforts build **gratitude, unity & shared responsibility in community.**

THEME-E
Economic Life
Around Us

CHAPTER
13

THE VALUE OF WORK

I. FACTS TO REMEMBER/SUMMARY

INTRODUCTION

- All individuals engage in various activities daily.
- Some activities are undertaken to earn money for livelihood while others are to serve oneself, family, or community.
- Activities that involve money or are performed in exchange for money are called Economic activities. These activities are done to earn a livelihood.

TYPES OF ECONOMIC ACTIVITIES

- Money can be earned by producing goods and services and exchanging them in the market. Employers hire workers to produce goods and services.
- When a worker is hired temporarily (daily or weekly) on a non-contractual basis, they are paid WAGES.
- When a worker is hired permanently on a contractual basis they are paid a SALARY.
- The FEE is paid to the worker for doing a specific service.
- Payment for work can be made in cash or kind.
- Value addition occurs when economic activities add value at each stage of transforming things into another form.

THE IMPORTANCE OF NON-ECONOMIC ACTIVITIES

- Activities that do not generate any income or wealth but are done out of love and care are called non-economic activities.
- Non-economic activities do not involve money but they contribute to social welfare, personal well-being and improving the overall quality of life.
- Community service activities add value to society by engaging in welfare programs like Swachh Bharat Abhiyan and Van Mahotsav.

II. TEXTBOOK KEYWORDS/GLOSSARY

1. **Activity:** An activity is something you do or simply the state of doing.
2. **Economic Activities:** Activities that involve money or are performed in exchange for money or its equivalent for the parties involved are called Economic activities.
3. **Value Addition:** It implies adding value at each stage of the process of transforming something into another form.
4. **Non-Economic Activities:** Activities that do not generate income or wealth but are done out of feelings like love, care, gratitude and respect.
5. **Market:** A place where people engage in the exchange of goods and services.

6. **Money's Worth:** The monetary value that a person places on an object based on the benefit that they derive from it.
7. **Fee:** A payment made to a person or organisation in exchange for professional advice or services.
8. **Salary:** A fixed regular payment generally paid monthly by an employer to an employee.
9. **Wage:** A payment made by the employer to the worker for a specific period of time.
10. **Payment in Kind:** A non-cash payment that is received for the work performed.

III. THE BIG QUESTIONS *(Page 183)*

Q. 1. ***What are the different types of activities that people engage in?***

Ans. There are two types of activities that people are engaged in. These are—

Economic Activities

An economic activity is an activity that involves money or is performed in exchange for money.

Examples: Pilot, Teacher, Actor, Journalist and Fashion Designer.

Non-Economic Activities

An activity that is done out of feeling of gratitude, love and care without any involvement of money is called a non-economic activity.

Examples: Cooking food, serving at temple or Gurudwara, doing voluntary services of taking care of the elderly in old age homes, etc.

Q. 2. ***What is their contribution to our everyday lives?***

Ans. Economic activities enable people to earn their livelihood by producing goods and services which are needed in an economy. Farmers by cultivating grains satisfy food requirements whereas a police officer by enforcing laws protects lives and properties of people.

Non-Economic activities are essential in our everyday lives. They foster love, care, gratitude, respect and patriotism amongst the citizens in the country.

IV. NCERT INTEXT/TEXTBOOK EXERCISES

LET'S EXPLORE

Q. 1. ***What activities did the people in Anu's and Kabir's story engage in? Mention them in the table given below:*** *(Page 185)*

Q. 2. ***In the table given on page 185, did you notice the third empty column? Label this column 'economic / non-economic activity'. Now classify them according to the nature of activity.*** *(Page 187)*

Ans. 1 and 2

Character in the story	Activities they are engaged in	Economic/Non-economic Activity
Geeta Aunty	1. Pilot in the Indian Air Force	1. Economic
Kabir's Grandfather	1. Retired from BSF 2. Teaches kids in the neighbourhood, looks after vegetable garden, runs errands for home	1. Economic 2. Non-economic activities
Anu's parents	1. Sell uniforms and other readymade garments. 2. Mother voluntarily teaches knitting to community women.	1. Economic 2. Non-economic
Anu's brother Rohan	1. Software Engineer in a computer company 2. Voluntarily teaches computer skills to youth in the college	1. Economic 2. Non-economic

Q. 3. ***Put a ✓ against those activities/professions that you think create monetary value. Can you add two activities and examples of money related value creation to the empty rows at the end?*** (*Page 191*)

Ans.

Activity /profession (create monetary value)	Examples of money-related value creation
1. Baker ✓	1. Converting flour into bread/biscuits, cupcakes. 2. Making hampers of baked items to sell during festivals.
2. Tailor ✓	1. Converting cloth into dresses like shirts, trousers etc. 2. Adding embroidery to the cloth while stitching.
3. Farmers repairing their tractor	Non-economic
4. Doctor	1. Diagnosing a patient's medical condition. 2. Treating a medical problem by administering medicine.
5. Parents cooking dinner in their family	Non-economic
6. Scientist	1. Explains various natural phenomena by conducting experiments. 2. Data Scientists analyse past data.
7. A person taking care of his sick grandfather	Non-economic.
8. Driver	Drives car and earns.
9. Gardener	Earns by taking care of plants in the garden.

THINK ABOUT IT

Q. 1. ***When Kabir's grandfather voluntarily teaches the neighbourhood kids for free, is that an economic activity or a non-economic activity? How is it different from your teachers teaching you at school? Discuss with your classmates.*** (Page 187)

Ans. When Kabir's grandfather voluntarily teaches the neighborhood kids for free, it's a non-economic activity as this activity does not involve money. Grandfather wishes to contribute to the community by teaching kids in his free time. He is not earning income from this activity.

When a teacher teaches us at school, they are paid a salary for the service rendered by them. Thus, teaching at school involves an exchange of service for money. Therefore, it is an economic activity.

Q. 2. ***What are some non-economic activities that are important to you and your family? Why are they valuable?*** (Page 187)

Ans. Many non-economic activities are important in a family. Some of these are parents cooking nutritious meals at home, washing clothes, and maintaining hygiene at home by keeping it clean. Most importantly looking after the physiological and psychological needs of the young and the old in the family.

These activities are very valuable to the family as well as the society. These activities contribute to personal well-being, social cohesion, cultural development, and overall quality of life.

Q. 3. ***On your way from home to school today, can you recall the various economic activities that people are engaged in? In what ways do you think those people are paid?*** (Page 189)

Ans. Way from home to school, lots of economic and non-economic activities can be seen:

1. Traffic policeman regulating traffic. (Paid salary by the Government; therefore, it is an economic activity.)
2. Labour working at the construction site. (Paid daily wages; therefore, it is an economic activity.)
3. Hawker selling vegetables. (Earns money in cash or through online payment from the buyer; therefore, it is an economic activity.)
4. Vendor selling ice-cream. (Earns money in cash or through online payment from the buyer; therefore, it is an economic activity.)
5. People cleaning a temple premise. (They do not earn any money from this service as it is done voluntarily; therefore, it is a non-economic activity.)

Q. 4. ***Many communities in India have similar practices that involve community participation. Can you identify a few from your area?*** (Page 193)

Ans. Community participation activities: Meditation or yoga in a park, celebration of a birthday or a wedding, attending religious functions, community kitchens or langars at Gurudwaras, volunteering for or donating to local schools, resident welfare associations etc.

Q. 5. ***We celebrate many festivals in India. During these festivals, people gather to organise all the various activities. They decorate the place together and share the food that they cook. Are these non-economic activities? Why do you think they still hold value?*** (Page 193)

Ans. Celebrating festivals is a non-economic activity as it is not done with the motive to earn money. Sharing food, decorating places, and organising various activities during festivals foster the feeling of oneness, unity, love, respect, and care among people living in a country.

Q. 6. ***Can you identify community programmes that have been undertaken by your school or in your locality? What did you observe during these programmes?*** (Page 193)

Ans. My school has undertaken various community programmes:

The Environment Club: The environment club organises cleanliness drives in surrounding areas. Students are taken to clean nearby localities, gardens, beaches, rivers, etc.

The Interact Club: The interact club teaches students about empathy, compassion and selflessness. It urges students to work beyond themselves for society at large and the country as a whole.

NCERT Questions, Activities and Projects (*Page 193*)

Q. 1. ***How are economic activities different from non-economic activities?***

Ans. Differentiation between economic and non-economic activities are:

Economic Activities

(*a*) Economic activities are those activities that are undertaken to earn a livelihood.

(*b*) The main aim of these activities is to earn income (Wage, salary, profits).

(*c*) *Example:* Business, lawyer, teacher, doctor.

Non-Economic Activities

(*a*) Non-economic activities are those activities that are undertaken out of love, care and sympathy.

(*b*) The main aim of these activities is self-satisfaction.

(*c*) *Example:* Father teaching his child, mother cooking at home.

Q. 2. ***What kind of economic activities do people engage in? Illustrate with examples.***

Ans. People engage in different types of economic activities to earn their livelihood—Farming, fishing, poultry farming and mining. Some workers engage in manufacturing activities like the production of cars, cement, steel, clothes and shoes.

People also engage in services, such as Doctors, Architects, Lawyers, Journalists, etc.

Q. 3. ***There is great value attached to people who are engaged in community service activities. Comment on this statement.***

Ans. People engage in various community service activities in the form of Sewa which can be seen in temples, gurudwaras, churches and mosques. Langars at Gurudwaras serve food to every visitor for free. These practices foster a sense of satisfaction and gratitude for what we have, and they are also a way of contributing to society without expecting anything in return.

Q. 4. ***What are the various ways in which people are compensated for various economic activities? Give some examples.***

Ans. People are compensated in different ways while performing an economic activity. These are:

(*a*) **Wages:** A type of cash payment made to workers for working for a short period of time.

(*b*) **Salaries:** A type of payment made to permanent workers on monthly basis is called Salary.

(*c*) **Fee:** A type of payment made to an individual or an organisation in exchange of professional advice or service. For example: fee charged by a tutor, a doctor or a lawyer.

(*d*) **Payment in Kind** is a non-cash payment given for a small work. For example giving part of farm output to the labourer working on the farm.

(*e*) **Profits:** Big companies earn profits from running a business.

(*f*) **Rent:** Landowners earn rent on the land owned by them.

V. EXAM ORIENTED QUESTIONS

A. Very Short Answer Type Questions

Q. 1. ***What is an activity?***

Ans. An activity is something you do or simply the state of doing.

Q. 2. ***What are the different types of activities?***

Ans. There are two types of activities—Economic and Non-economic.

Q. 3. ***What is an economic activity?***

Ans. Economic activity is an activity that involves money or is performed in exchange for money or payment in kind.

Q. 4. ***What is a non-economic activity?***

Ans. An activity that is done out of feeling of gratitude, love and care without any involvement of money is called a non-economic activity.

Q. 5. ***Is the father dropping a son to school, economic or non-economic activity? Give reason.***

Ans. It's a non-economic activity as a father has no intention to earn money through this activity.

Q. 6. ***Name the different types of payments an employer can pay to an employee.***

Ans. Different types of payments are—wages and salaries in cash or some part of payment in kind.

Q. 7. ***What is value addition?***

Ans. Addition to the value of raw materials at each stage of transforming something into another form is called value addition.

Q. 8. ***Does value addition takes place in non-economic activities? Support your answer with an example.***

Ans. Yes, value addition can take place in non-economic activity also. For example, mother while cooking adds value to the raw materials (vegetables).

Q. 9. ***What do we pay to an e-rickshaw driver when we take their services?***

Ans. We pay fee to the e-rickshaw driver when we take their services.

Q. 10. ***What do we pay to a permanent worker; Wage or a Salary?***

Ans. We pay salaries to permanent employees on a monthly basis.

Q. 11. ***Define Fee.***

Ans. A payment made to a person or an organisation in exchange of a professional advice or service.

Q. 12. ***Give one example each of payment in cash and payment in kind.***

Ans. Payment made in cash to a worker of a paddy field is payment in cash. Giving 5 kg of paddy to the worker is payment in kind.

Q. 13. ***What are community service activities? Give few examples.***

Ans. Activities that are done by an individual or by a group of people to serve the interest of a community are called community service activities. Examples are—Teaching less privileged children in free time by retired people, distributing food or medicines to the underprivileged, and participating in cleanliness drives in the locality.

Q. 14. ***Why do people work?***

Ans. People work either to earn their livelihood, contribute to society and gain a sense of purpose and self-worth.

Q. 15. ***Which activities (economic or non-economic) involve the use of money?***

Ans. Economic Activity.

Q. 16. ***A musician playing music for the audience in a show. Is it an economic or a non-economic Activity?***

Ans. Economic Activity.

Q. 17. ***A cobbler repairing shoes of his own son. Is it an economic or a non-economic activity?***

Ans. Non-economic activity.

B. Short Answer Type Questions

Q. 1. ***There are lots of non-economic activities that are done by our parents which add value to our lives. Give two examples of the same.***

Ans. Many activities are done by parents at home like the father packing lunch for kids, the mother dropping children at school, Parents looking after grandparents. All these activities foster feelings of love, care, respect within the family. These can lead to healthy families in the society which results in overall better quality of life.

Q. 2. ***A company gives free ration to its employees. Is it an economic or a non-economic activity?***

Ans. A company giving free ration to its employees is an economic activity. Free ration is a payment in kind to the employee for the services rendered by them.

Q. 3. ***Give two examples of Community Participation.***

Ans. (*a*) **Swachh Bharat Abhiyan:** It is based on the collective effort of all the citizens of the country. People come together to clean up the roads, parks, markets and surroundings.

(*b*) **Van Mahotsav:** This initiative brings together members of the community for tree plantation drives. It's very important to conserve our forests for a cleaner environment in the future. Collective community participation will bring more awareness about the value of trees.

Q. 4. ***Mukesh is a carpenter who buys wood from a nearby market for ₹500 to make furniture. He uses special tools and other materials to make a chair. Mukesh sells the chair for ₹1100 in the market. How much is the value added by him?***

Ans. Value added is ₹1100 – ₹500 = ₹600. It's the monetary value of Mukesh's skill, time and effort that went into making the chair.

Q. 5. ***Students cleaning beaches during the cleanliness campaign initiated by school is a non-economic activity. Do you agree with this statement? Give reason for your answer.***

Ans. Yes, I agree with this statement beacuse students are providing their services without any monetary gain.

C. Long Answer Type Questions

Q. 1. ***Akshay is an associate in a law firm and is paid a salary for it. In his free time he goes to an old age home to look after the sick and elderly people. Identify economic and non-economic activities of Akshay. Give reason for your answer.***

Ans. Akshay working in a law firm is an economic activity as he is compensated in salary (*monetary value of his service*). When he goes to an old age home it's a non-economic activity as there is no money involved in it. He does out of compassion and sympathy for elderly people.

D. Assertion and Reasoning Questions

1. *There are two statements marked as Assertion (A) and Reason (R). Mark your answer as per the codes provided below.*

   Assertion (A): Business is a non-economic activity.
   Reason (R): Business is undertaken with the aim of earning money.

   Codes:

   (*a*) Both (A) & (R) are true but (R) is not the correct explanation of (A).

   (*b*) Both (A) & (R) are true and (R) is the correct explanation of (A).

   (*c*) (A) is true but (R) is false.

   (*d*) (A) is false but (R) is true.

2. **Assertion (A):** Agriculture is an economic activity.

   Reason (R): Agriculture is undertaken to satisfy consumption needs of people.

Codes:

(*a*) Both (A) & (R) are true but (R) is not the correct explanation of (A).

(*b*) Both (A) & (R) are true and (R) is the correct explanation of (A).

(*c*) (A) is true but (R) is false.

(*d*) (A) is false but (R) is true.

3. **Assertion (A):** Salaries are paid in kind while wages are paid in cash.

Reason (R): Farm labourers can be paid in form of cash or kind in crops.

Codes:

(*a*) Both (A) & (R) are true but (R) is not the correct explanation of (A).

(*b*) Both (A) & (R) are true and (R) is the correct explanation of (A).

(*c*) (A) is true but (R) is false.

(*d*) (A) is false but (R) is true.

Ans.

1. → (*d*) 2. → (*a*) 3. → (*d*)

E. Case/Source Based Study Questions

Read the passage given below and answer the following questions.

"Life of a Doctor"

Scenario: A highly professional doctor Mr. Arora, spends his week days treating patients at a private clinic for a salary, and on weekends he volunteers at a local community center to provide free treatment to poor families.

Q. (*i*) ***Identify the economic and non-economic activities performed by the doctor.***

Q. (*ii*) ***What is the basis of classifying an activity into an economic and a non-economic activity?***

Q. (*iii*) ***Give two differences between economic and non-economic activities.***

Ans (*i*) The activity performed by the doctor at a private clinic is an economic activity because he receives salary for it. While the services he provides at the community centre is a non-economic activity because there is no monetary remuneration in it.

Ans (*ii*) The basis of defining an activity whether it is an economic activity and a non-economic activity is monetary remuneration. If a person is monetarily benefitted than it is an economic activity otherwise it is a non-economic activity.

Ans (*iii*) Economic activities are performed to earn income or profit, whereas non-economic activities are done for personal satisfaction, social service or leisure. Economic activities involve financial transactions and contribute to the economy, while non-economic activities do not generate monetary income.

F. Competency Based Questions

Q. 1. ***If Suhana goes with her mother to distribute free meals to the underprivileged children of the community, what kind of activity is she performing?***

Ans. Suhana is performing a non-economic activity as she is not doing it with the motive to earn profit.

Q. 2. ***Give two examples of economic activities which add value at each stage of transformation.***

Ans. (*a*) A baker adds value to flour by converting it into bread and selling it in the market.

(*b*) A carpenter adds value to the wood by converting it into chair.

Q. 3. ***'Non-economic activities are not important in our lives as they do not involve money.' True or False. Justify your answer.***

Ans. Non-economic activities do not involve money but they foster a feeling of oneness, love, care and brotherhood in the community. Parents taking care of their children leads to a healthy emotional and mental up-bringing of children.

Community participation help in achieving social goals like cleanliness of roads, parks, neighbourhood society and country.

Q. 4. ***What are the various ways in which a school teacher can earn income?***

Ans. When a teacher works in a school, she is paid a monthly salary which is paid to her in cash.

She can be paid in kind also in the form of facility of free conveyance given to her for coming to school.

She can also help some students by taking online classes and charging fee for her services.

G. Skill Based Questions

1. ***Discuss as to how economic and non-economic activities play an important role in the society.***

Ans. Economic activities provide a source of livelihood to the members of a society. All individuals need to earn income to satisfy their and family wants.

Alongwith material prosperity, society also needs emotional and social well-being. Non-economic activities like helping underprivileged members, maintaining cleanliness, celebrating festivals foster the feeling of brotherhood amongst the members.

VI. MULTIPLE CHOICE QUESTIONS

1. *Which of these is an economic activity?*

(*a*) Religious (*b*) Social

(*c*) Patriotic (*d*) Profession

2. *Which of these is a non-economic activity?*

(*a*) Business (*b*) Parental

(*c*) Employment (*d*) Profession

3. *What is the meaning of an economic activity?*

(*a*) To help someone

(*b*) To donate

(*c*) To earn a living by doing some work

(*d*) To work for something without expecting any monetary reward.

4. *Which of these is an example of payment in kind?*

(*a*) Wage in cash

(*b*) Free lodging to labour

(*c*) Salary in cash

(*d*) Fee

5. A baker buys flour and other raw materials for ₹40, makes bread and sells it to a consumer for ₹50.

A sandwich seller buys bread for ₹50 and sells sandwich at ₹70.

How much will be value added by each of them?

(*a*) 10, 20 (*b*) 20, 10

(*c*) 20, 20 (*d*) 10, 10

Ans.

1. → (*d*) **2.** → (*b*) **3.** → (*c*)

4. → (*b*) **5.** → (*a*)

VII. OBJECTIVE TYPE QUESTIONS

Q.1. ***Fill in the blanks with appropriate words.***

(*i*) Market is a place where people engage in the exchange of ______ and ________.

(*ii*) Wages can be paid either in_____ or in _____.

(*iii*) Economic activities add ______ at each stage of the process of transforming something into another.

(*iv*) Doctor treating a patient is an ________ activity whereas, a doctor treating his own wife is a ____________activity.

(*v*) Salary is a fixed regular payment generally paid ________ by an employer to an employee.

Ans.

(*i*) goods, services
(*ii*) cash, kind
(*iii*) value
(*iv*) economic, non-economic
(*v*) monthly

Q.2. ***State whether the given statements are true or false.***

(*i*) Non-economic activities are performed to earn livelihood.
(*ii*) Wages can be paid in cash only.
(*iii*) Salary cannot be paid in kind.
(*iv*) A baker adds value to the flour while manufacturing bread.
(*v*) Non-economic activities are those that generate income.

Ans.

(*i*) False (*ii*) False
(*iii*) False (*iv*) True
(*v*) False

Q.3. ***Match column A with column B.***

	Column A		Column B
1.	Fee	(*a*)	Compensation given to an electrical engineer in a firm
2.	Wages in kind	(*b*)	Bringing awareness of polio vaccination in the locality
3.	Salary	(*c*)	Free meals to workers
4.	Value addition	(*d*)	Payment to a lawyer for his advice
5.	Community participation	(*e*)	Converting raw materials into finished good

Ans.

1. → (*d*) **2.** → (*c*) **3.** → (*a*) **4.** → (*e*) **5.** → (*b*)

VIII. TEST YOUR KNOWLEDGE

A. Multiple Choice Questions (MCQs)

1. *What is a payment made to a person in exchange of professional service called_____.*

(*a*) Salary (*b*) Rent
(*c*) Wage (*d*) Fee

2. *Which of these is an example of payment in cash?*

(*a*) Free ration to labourers
(*b*) Monetary wages
(*c*) Free transportation to workers
(*d*) Free uniform to workers

3. *A duty of protection of law and order in Delhi by a policeman is an_______.*

(*a*) Economic activity
(*b*) Non-economic activity
(*c*) Both economic and non-economic
(*d*) Neither economic nor non-economic

4. *Market can exist________.*

(*a*) in a physical area only
(*b*) only for goods
(*c*) online and offline for both goods and services
(*d*) only for services.

B. Very Short Answer Type Questions

Q. 1. *Is farmers repairing their tools an economic or non-economic activity?*

Q. 2. *Give two examples of payment in kind.*

Q. 3. *Why people engage in Sewa though it does not result in any monetary benefit?*

Q. 4. *Why are activities done by parents at home are important though there is no economic value attached to them?*

C. Short Answer Type Questions

Q. 1. *Define the following terms:*

(*a*) Wages (*b*) Salary (*c*) Fee

Q. 2. *What is value addition? Give one example of value addition.*

Q. 3. *People engage in economic activities in three sectors. Name these three sectors.*

Q. 4. *Discuss some economic and non-economic activities performed by each member in your household.*

Q. 5. *Mention some of the non-economic activities that you can engage in either in school or at home.*

Q. 6. *Is playing a game in your free time an economic or a non-economic activity? Give reason for your answer.*

D. Long Answer Type Questions

Q. 1. *'People engaged in community service activities add great value to the society.' Explain the statement with examples.*

Q. 2. *Explain the various ways in which people are compensated for various economic activities.*

E. Assertion and Reasoning Questions

There are two statements marked as Assertion (A) and Reason (R). Mark your answer as per the codes provided below.

1. Assertion (A): Schools charge education fee from the students for imparting education to them.

Reason (R): Fee is a payment made to a firm or organisation in exchange for professional service.

Codes:

(*a*) Both (A) & (R) are true but (R) is not the correct explanation of (A).

(*b*) Both (A) & (R) are true and (R) is the correct explanation of (A).

(*c*) (A) is true but (R) is false.

(*d*) (A) is false but (R) is true.

2. Assertion (A): Community services are non-economic activities.

Reason (R): Community services are not done to earn money. They are undertaken to foster the spirit of unity, oneness, love and respect amongst people.

Codes:

(*a*) Both (A) & (R) are true but (R) is not the correct explanation of (A).

(*b*) Both (A) & (R) are true and (R) is the correct explanation of (A).

(*c*) (A) is true but (R) is false.

(*d*) (A) is false but (R) is true.

Economic Activities Around Us

1 Introduction

- **Human activities:** economic & non-economic.
- Early activities: weaving, tool-making, cattle farming, agriculture, pottery etc.
- Today: new jobs→ banking, teaching, IT, transport, tailoring, manufacturing.

The Classification of Economic Activities into Economic Sectors

- **Economic sectors:** Grouping of activities with similar features.
- Three main sectors; primary, secondary & tertiary.

2(a) Primary Activities

- Depend directly on nature for goods.
- **Activities:** farming, fishing, coal mining, raising cattle, forestry.

2(b) Secondary Activities

- Dependent on the output of primary sector.
- **Convert raw materials** into usable products.
- Also includes construction (roads, buildings) & utilities (electricity, water, solar power).
- **Examples:**

  Wheat → flour.

  Cotton → clothes.

  Iron ore → steel → automobiles.

  Wood → furniture, paper.

  Groundnut → oil.

2(c) Tertiary activities

- Provides services to support primary & secondary sectors.
- Sometimes invisible yet vital in production.
- Examples:

  Transport & trade (truck drivers, vendors).

  Education (teachers).

  Healthcare (doctors, nurses).

  Communication & IT (internet, software).

  Repair & maintenance (mechanics, electricians).

  Tourism, hotels, warehouses.

3 Interdependence Among Sectors

- All three sectors work together for a successful production.
- They help in converting natural raw materials into finished products (ready for consumption).
- Each sector depends on the other for completing the process.

4 Dairy Cooperative: From Farm to Plate (A Case Study)

- Gujarat farmers sold milk to local buyers, facing spoilage & low price.
- **1940s:** farmers sought help from Sardar Vallabhbhai Patel.
- 1946: Tribhuvandas Patel & Varghese Kurein started **Amul**.
- Farmers controlled production, processing & sales.
- Expansion: Factories set up → butter, cheese, ghee, milk powder.
- Today: Amul = many plants, products sold in India & abroad.
- **Activities:**

  Primary: milking cows.

  Secondary: making butter, cheese, ghee, milk powder.

  Tertiary: transporting, trading & retailing milk products.

THEME-E Economic Life Around Us

CHAPTER 14

ECONOMIC ACTIVITIES AROUND US

I. FACTS TO REMEMBER/SUMMARY

INTRODUCTION

Activities that create monetary value are called economic activities.

As societies progressed, the number of activities through which people could earn their livelihoods increased vastly.

THE CLASSIFICATION OF ECONOMIC ACTIVITIES INTO ECONOMIC SECTORS

Some economic activities share similar characteristics and are based on this, they can be grouped or classified into broader groups called economic sectors.

The three main sectors are:

A. Primary Sector B. Secondary Sector C. Tertiary Sector.

A. Primary Activities

Economic activities in which people are directly dependent on nature to produce goods and services are known as primary activities or primary sector economic activities.

Examples of Primary Activities are: agriculture, mining, fishing, raising livestock, forestry etc.

B. Secondary Activities

Economic activities in which people are dependent on outputs of the primary sector and transform them to produce goods are known as Secondary activities or Secondary sector economic activities.

Examples of secondary activities are: Manufacturing, Construction, Electricity, gas, and water supply.

C. Tertiary Activities

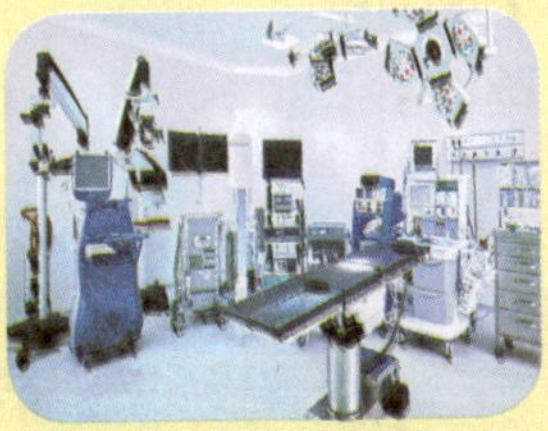

Economic activities that provide support to people involved in primary and secondary activities are called Tertiary activities or Tertiary sector economic activities.

Examples of tertiary sector economic activities are: Communication services, and services provided by hotels, banks, schools, airports etc. This sector is also called service sector.

INTERDEPENDENCE AMONG SECTORS

All the three sectors are interdependent. The secondary sector depends on primary sector for its raw materials and the tertiary sector to transport and sell its finished products. The tertiary sector depends on the primary and secondary sectors for a product to sell and for income from business.

II. TEXTBOOK KEYWORDS/GLOSSARY

1. **Monetary Value:** Value of something that can be measured in terms of money.
2. **Economic Sectors:** Broad groups that include various activities that help with the economic prosperity of the nation.
3. **Primary Sector:** The group of activities that involves extraction of raw materials directly from nature such as farming, fishing, forestry etc.
4. **Secondary Sector:** The group of activities that involves the processing of raw materials derived from the primary sector into products for sale or consumption.
5. **Tertiary Sector:** The group of activities that involves the provision of services that complement both primary and secondary sectors such as transportation, banking, and management of business.
6. **Warehouses:** Large buildings used for storing products before they are sold.
7. **Dairy:** A place where milk is collected and stored.
8. **Cooperative:** A group of people who voluntarily come together to meet their economic and social needs in a formal way. They own the cooperative and decisions are taken by the members collectively.
9. **Middlemen:** Persons who buy goods from producers and sell them to wholesalers or retailers. They charge a fee for the services.
10. **Pasteurisation:** A process by which milk is preserved through heating to a specific temperature to kill harmful bacteria.
11. **Factory:** Building or group of buildings where goods are manufactured or various components are put together to make a final product.
12. **Retail:** The sale of goods in small quantities for use by the end consumer rather than for resale.
13. **Export:** Goods and services that are produced in one country and sold to buyers and consumers in another country.
14. **Import:** Goods and services that are produced in other countries and sold to buyers and consumers in the home country.
15. **Wholesale:** Buying and selling goods in large quantities especially in order to sell them again and make a profit.

III. THE BIG QUESTIONS *(Page 195)*

Q. 1. *How are economic activities classified?*

Ans. Economic activities are classified based on their characteristics. Some activities depend on nature, some activities transform raw materials into final products and some others provide services to all producers in an economy.

Q. 2. *What differentiates these activities to be grouped into sectors?*

Ans. All those economic activities which are directly dependent on nature to produce goods are grouped into Primary sector.

All those activities in which people transform output of primary sector into other goods are grouped under Secondary Sector.

All those activities that provide services to primary and secondary sector are grouped under Tertiary Sector.

Q. 3. *How are the three sectors interconnected?*

Ans. All three sectors are interdependent. The secondary sector depends on the primary sector for its raw materials and the tertiary sector to transport and sell its finished products. The tertiary sector depends on the primary and secondary sectors for a product to sell and for income from business. The primary sector depends on the secondary sector for its inputs and on the tertiary sector to transport its final output.

IV. NCERT INTEXT/TEXTBOOK EXERCISES

Let's Explore

Q. 1. *Now that we have seen some examples of secondary sector activities, can you name two more economic activities in the secondary sector?* *(Page 200)*

Ans.

1. Food industry — converting fruits or vegetables into jams, sauces, pickles etc.
2. Chemical industry — converts raw materials such as oil, natural gas, air, water, metals and minerals into useful products to be used by industries and consumers.

Q. 2. *Label the pictures in the illustration shown in Fig. 14.1 on page 206 as:* *(Page 207)*

1. Primary sector
2. Secondary sector
3. Tertiary sector

Ans. 1. Primary
2. Primary
3. Tertiary
4. Tertiary
5. Secondary
6. Tertiary
7. Secondary
8. Tertiary

NCERT Questions, Activities and Projects *(Page 208)*

Q. 1. *What is the primary sector? How is it different from the secondary sector? Give two examples.*

Ans. The primary sector includes all those activities that directly depend on natural resources.: agriculture, mining, forestry, fishing etc.

The secondary sector companies are those that are involved in manufacturing, construction and processing. These companies produce goods that use the resources obtained from companies within the primary sector: Manufacturing of steel, cement, automobiles, readymade garments, etc.

For example, production of cotton from cotton seeds by a farmer is a primary activity whereas production of cloth from cotton mills is a secondary activity.

Similarly, the cultivation/farming of sugarcane is a primary activity whereas the production of sugar from sugarcane is a secondary activity.

Q. 2. *How does the secondary sector depend on the tertiary sector? Illustrate with a few examples.*

Ans. Secondary sector needs transport to procure raw materials and supply finished goods to the market.

For example, AMUL uses trucks, railway, air and shipping services to transport its milk products.

Retail stores are set up by the secondary sector to sell their output. Amul set up retail stores and supplies milk and milk products to other shops in towns, cities, and villages across India. Here, transportation, trading and retail are tertiary activities.

Q.3. *Give an example of interdependence between primary, secondary, and tertiary sectors. Show it using a flow diagram.*

Ans.

AMUL, AS AN EXAMPLE

Primary Activity		Secondary Activity		Tertiary Activity
Farmers milking Cows and collecting milk	→	Processing of milk into milk powder, ghee, cheese, butter etc.	→	Products transported through lorries, trucks, air, ships etc. Setting up retail stores to sell

V. EXAM ORIENTED QUESTIONS

A. Very Short Answer Type Questions

Q. 1. *What do you mean by Economic sectors?*

Ans. Economic sectors classify economic activities into categories based on their nature. The three main sectors are: Primary (raw material), Secondary (manufacturing) and Tertiary (services).

Q. 2. *Extracting coal from mines is a primary activity. True or false. Give reason.*

Ans. True, as coal is a natural product in the form of a fossil fuel.

Q. 3. *Mention few most common primary activities.*

Ans. Agriculture, mining, raising livestock, forestry etc.

Q. 4. *What is meant by secondary sector?*

Ans. The group of activities that involves processing of raw material derived from primary sector into products for sale or consumption.

Q. 5. *Give a few examples of secondary sector.*

Ans. Processing of grains into flour, extraction of oil from groundnut, processing tea leaves to derive tea, to manufacture sugar from sugarcane are few examples of secondary sector.

Q. 6. *What is a tertiary sector?*

Ans. The group of activities that involves the provision of services that complement both primary and secondary sectors such as transportation, banking, and management of business. This is also known as service sector.

Q. 7. *When and under whose leadership was AMUL set up?*

Ans. AMUL was set up in 1946 under the leadership of Tribhuvandas Patel (*lawyer and freedom fighter*) and Dr. Varghese Kurien (an engineer who was working at a dairy factory in Mumbai), Amul was setup on the advise of Sardar Vallabhbhai Patel, a famous national leader. Amul is well known for leading white revolution in India.

B. Short Answer Type Questions

Q. 1. *"Over the decades, the number of activities has increased tremendously." Illustrate this statement with examples.*

Ans. Over the decades needs have multiplied so does the activities. Earlier, most people were engaged in agriculture, livestock, production of tools, pottery and weaving cloth.

With economic development and progress many new diverse economic activities have emerged such as mobile phones, drones, manufacturing computers, washing machines, refrigerators. There is a greater demand for services too such as transportation, banking, software development, data analysis and interpretation etc.

Q. 2. *How do we classify economic activities into three sectors? Explain with example.*

Ans. We classify economic activities in three sectors namely, primary, secondary and tertiary.

The primary sector includes all those activities that are directly dependent on natural resources: agriculture, mining, forestry, fishing, etc.

The secondary sector companies are those that are involved in manufacturing, construction, and processing. These companies produce goods that use the resources obtained from companies within the primary sector: Manufacturing of steel, cement, automobiles, readymade garments etc.

All those economic activities that provide support to people involved in primary and secondary activities are called tertiary activities or tertiary sector economic activities.

Q. 3. *What was the problem faced by farmers in AMUL in 1940s?*

Ans. Farmers would have to cycle or walk to nearby villages to sell the milk under scorching heat. Milk got spoiled or curdled in hot weather. The farmers had to sell the milk before it could got spoil. In fear of milk being wasted, they would sell it to middlemen. Middlemen would buy at meagre prices and sell it at higher price in the market.

Q. 4. *Who solved the problem of farmers selling milk to middlemen in Gujarat and how?*

Ans. Sardar Vallabhbhai Patel, a prominent leader solved the problem of farmers by suggesting them to form a cooperative. As a cooperative, the farmers would be able to buy and sell milk as a group, taking care of the entire operation of milk collection, processing and distribution themselves.

C. Long Answer Type Questions

Q. 1. *Explain how three sectors are interdependent on each other.*

Ans. Primary sector provides raw materials to the secondary sector *e.g.* cotton is needed to make shirts in a factory, sugarcane is needed to make sugar, and wood is needed to make furniture.

Similarly, fertilisers, chemicals, electricity, water supply and machinery is required by the primary sector which is provided by the secondary sector.

Tertiary sector comprises of services like transportation, banking, trade, retail which is essential for both primary and tertiary sector.

Q. 2. *'All three sectors must grow simultaneously for economic growth of an economy.' Explain the statement.*

Ans. All three sectors, *i.e.*, primary, secondary and tertiary sector are interdependent on each other if one sector witnesses slow growth other sectors get affected. Slow growth of agriculture will result in shortage of raw materials for the industries. Also slow growth of agricultural incomes will reduce the demand of industrial goods.

Slow growth in industrial sector would reduce the demand of raw materials and also the demand of food items.

Slowdown in primary and secondary sector will reduce the demand for transportation services and banking services.

D. Assertion and Reasoning Questions

There are two statements Assertion (A) and Reason (R). Mark your answer according to the code given below.

1. **Assertion (A):** The primary sector is essential for a country's economy.

   Reason (R): It includes activities like farming, fishing and mining, which provide raw materials for other sectors.

Codes:

(*a*) Both (A) and (R) are true but (R) is not the correct explanation of (A).

(*b*) Both (A) and (R) are true and (R) is the correct explanation of (A).

(*c*) (A) is true but (R) is false.

(*d*) (A) is false but (R) is true.

2. **Assertion (A):** The secondary sector does not depend on the primary sector.

   Reason (R): The secondary sector involves manufacturing and processing of raw materials into finished goods.

Codes:

(*a*) Both (A) and (R) are true but (R) is not the correct explanation of (A).

(*b*) Both (A) and (R) are true and (R) is the correct explanation of (A).

(c) (A) is true but (R) is false.

(d) (A) is false but (R) is true.

3. **Assertion (A):** The tertiary sector helps in the growth of both primary and secondary sectors.

Reason (R): The sector provides services like banking, transport, and communication, which support other economic activities.

Codes

(a) Both (A) and (R) are true but (R) is not the correct explanation of (A).

(b) Both (A) and (R) are true and (R) is the correct explanation of (A).

(c) (A) is true but (R) is false.

(d) (A) is false but (R) is true.

Ans.

1. → (b) 2. → (d) 3. → (b)

E. Competency Based Questions

1. *Arrange the following activities in the correct sequence*

(i) Transporting cloth to the workshops

(ii) Sale in shops and showrooms

(iii) Spinning the yarn

(iv) Weaving the fabric

Select the correct answer

(a) (iii) - (iv) - (i) - (ii)
(b) (i) - (iv) - (iii) - (ii)
(c) (iii) - (iv) - (ii) - (i)
(d) (iv) - (i) - (ii) - (iii)

2. *Which of the following statement is true for primary sector?*

(a) Primary sector comprise of transportation, banking and trade.

(b) Primary sector comprise of agriculture, mining, construction and electricity.

(c) Primary sector comprise of manufacturing, mining and construction.

(d) Primary sector comprise of agriculture, mining, fishing and forestry.

3. *Which of the following statement is correct about 'AMUL' cooperative?*

(a) AMUL was set-up in 1950.

(b) Farmers collectively approached J.L. Nehru with their problem.

(c) AMUL was set-up in 1946 under the leadership of Tribhuvandas Patel and Dr. Varghese Kurien.

(d) AMUL is a private limited company with an aim to maximise profits.

Ans.

1. → (a) 2. → (d) 3. → (c)

F. Case/Source Based Questions

Read the following paragraph and answer the following questions.

I. The fruit or vegetable vendors sell the farm produce to household consumers. Similarly, doctors, nurses, teachers, lawyers and pilots provide their services to those who need them. There are technicians who repair and service electronic items including mobile phones and televisions, mechanics who repair vehicles like cars and tractors, and electricians who ensure regular supply of electricity. Their services make our lives easier.

(i) Which sector is being referred to in the above paragraph?

(ii) How do this sector make our life easier? Give two examples.

(iii) *'Primary and secondary sector can't grow without the development of this sector.'* Explain the statement.

Ans.

(i) Tertiary sector is being referred in this paragraph.

(ii) The tertiary sector provides essential services like banking, transportation and communication, which support other sectors.

It includes healthcare and education improving the quality of life and human development.

(iii) The primary (*agriculture, mining*) and secondary (*manufacturing, industry*) sectors rely on tertiary sector for essential services like transportation, banking, communication and marketing. Without these services, raw materials cannot be distributed, goods cannot reach markets and financial transactions cannot occur efficiently. Thus, the growth of primary and secondary sectors depends on a well-developed tertiary sector.

G. Skill Based Questions

Q. 1. *Analyse the role of AMUL cooperative in the development of rural economy of Gujarat.*

Ans. AMUL cooperative helped the economy in following ways –

(*a*) It reduced the dependence of farmers on middlemen.

(*b*) It increased their decision-making power and led to strengthening of the group.

(*c*) It increased incomes of the farmers. They could sell at a higher price.

Q. 2. *My grandfather was a forest contractor. My father works as an accountant in Maruti Udyog limited and my mother is a nurse in Apollo hospitals. Identify the sectors in which they are working.*

Ans. Grandfather – Primary sector

Father – Secondary sector

Mother – Tertiary sector

Q. 3. *How does the growth of primary, secondary and tertiary sectors affect the lives of citizens of a country?*

Ans. Since all the three sectors are interdependent on each other, growth of these sectors will lead to growth of the country.

Growth will result in increase in incomes of people in the country.

Rise in incomes will improve the standard of living, better access to education and health facilities, overall better well-being of citizens of a county.

VI. MULTIPLE CHOICE QUESTIONS

1. *Which of these is a tertiary activity?*
(*a*) Manufacturing of computers
(*b*) Fisherman catching fish
(*c*) Construction of a house
(*d*) Repairing of computers.

2. *What is the full form of AMUL?*
(*a*) Anand Milk Union Limited
(*b*) Amar Milk Union Limited
(*c*) Amul Milkcake Union Limited
(*d*) Amar Mangoes Union Limited.

3. *Goods and services that are produced in one country and sold to buyers in another country are called:*
(*a*) Imports
(*b*) Non-economic goods
(*c*) Exports
(*d*) Non-economic services.

4. *Hotel, restaurants, schools, hospitals, banks, airports, shops are a part of:*
(*a*) primary sector
(*b*) secondary sector
(*c*) tertiary sector
(*d*) both primary and secondary sector.

5. *Extracting pulp from the trees is a:*
(*a*) primary sector
(*b*) secondary sector
(*c*) tertiary sector
(*d*) both primary and secondary sector

6. *As e-commerce activities are on the rise in this digital age: they fall under which sector?*
(*a*) primary sector
(*b*) secondary sector
(*c*) tertiary sector
(*d*) both secondary and tertiary sector

Ans.

1. → (*d*) **2.** → (*a*) **3.** → (*c*)
4. → (*c*) **5.** → (*a*) **6.** → (*c*)

VII. OBJECTIVE TYPE QUESTIONS

A. *Fill in the blanks with appropriate words:*

1. Construction of a hospital will belong to __________sector.
2. Economic activities in which people are dependent on outputs of the _____ sector and transform them to produce goods are known as ______ activities.
3. Large buildings used for storing products before they are sold, used or rented out to shops are called _______.
4. ________ is a group of people who voluntarily come together to meet their economic and social needs formally.
5. The sale of goods in small quantities for use by the end consumer rather than for resale is called _______.

Ans.

1. secondary
2. primary, secondary
3. warehouses
4. cooperative
5. retail

B. *State whether the given statements are true or false.*

1. All primary activities depend on natural resources.
2. Secondary sector is the only sector that depends on tertiary sector.
3. With the formation of Cooperatives Amul farmers could not make their own decisions on all matters relating to production and sale.
4. All three sectors are interdependent on each other.
5. AMUL products are not sold in other countries as it is a cooperative.

Ans.

1. → True 2. → False 3. → False
4. → True 5. → False

C. *Match Column A with Column B:*

	Column A		Column B
1.	Primary activity	(a)	Mobile manufacturing
2.	Secondary activity	(b)	Milk, curd, ice-cream
3.	Tertiary activity	(c)	Nature dependent activities
4.	AMUL products	(d)	Preservation through heating
5.	Pasteurisation	(e)	Mobile repairing

Ans.

1. → (c) 2. → (a) 3. → (e)
4. → (b) 5. → (d)

VIII. TEST YOUR KNOWLEDGE

A. Multiple Choice Questions

1. *Which of the following is a primary sector activity?*
   (a) Banking
   (b) Farming
   (c) Teaching
   (d) Construction
2. *The secondary sector is mainly involved in*
   (a) Extracting natural resources
   (b) Providing healthcare services
   (c) Manufacturing and processing goods
   (d) Transporting people and goods

3. *Which sector includes activities like transport, communication and trade?*
   (*a*) Quaternary sector
   (*b*) Primary sector
   (*c*) Secondary sector
   (*d*) Tertiary sector
4. *Which of the following is an example of a secondary sector activity?*
   (*a*) Fishing
   (*b*) Making furniture
   (*c*) Selling clothes
   (*d*) Courier services
5. *Why is tertiary sector important for economic growth?*
   (*a*) It provides raw materials for industries
   (*b*) It supports other sectors by providing services
   (*c*) It is involved in direct production of goods
   (*d*) It does not contribute to the economic

B. Fill in the Blanks

1. *The .... sector involves extracting natural resources like farming, fishing and mining.*
2. *The .... sector is responsible for converting raw materials into finished products.*
3. *Doctors, teachers, and transport workers belong to the .... sector.*
4. *Factories and industries are part of the .... sector of the economy.*
5. *The economic activities that do not produce goods but provide services are known as .... activities.*

C. True or False

1. *Farming and fishing are examples of tertiary sector activities.*
2. *The secondary sector depends on raw materials from the primary sector.*
3. *Banking and transport are considered primary sector activities.*
4. *The tertiary sector provides essential services that support economic growth.*
5. *Without the tertiary sector, industries and agriculture would face difficulties in selling and distribution of goods.*

D. Match Column A with Column B

	Column A		Column B
1.	Farming	(*a*)	Secondary
2.	Banking	(*b*)	Primary
3.	Textile manufacturing	(*c*)	Tertiary
4.	Teaching	(*d*)	Tertiary
5.	Mining	(*e*)	Primary

E. Very Short Answer Type Questions

Q. 1. *Mention the three groups into which economic activities are classified.*

Q. 2. *Production of oilseeds is a primary activity while production of oil from oilseeds is secondary. Why?*

Q. 3. *Classify the following activities into primary, secondary and tertiary:*

(*i*) Mobile service providers
(*ii*) Manufacturing of aeroplane and ships.
(*iii*) Forestry and logging
(*iv*) Air and rail services
(*v*) Florist selling bouquets
(*vi*) Farmer growing flowers
(*vii*) Schools and colleges
(*viii*) Retailers selling grocery
(*ix*) Woman making jute baskets
(*x*) Manufacturing of steel from iron ore.

F. Short Answer Type Questions

Q. 1. *Distinguish between primary, secondary and tertiary sector by giving example.*

Q. 2. *Name 5 activities which have come up in the last one decade.*

Q. 3. *Primary sector depends on secondary and tertiary sector. How?*

Q. 4. *How does formation of AMUL cooperative benefitted farmers?*

G. Long Answer Type Questions

Q. 1. *Show how primary, secondary and tertiary sectors are interdependent by giving examples.*

Q. 2. *Mention few activities of each sector undertaken at AMUL cooperative.*

H. Assertion and Reasoning Questions

There are two statements Assertion (A) and Reason (R) given. Mark your answer according to the code given below.

1. **Assertion (A):** Economic activities are classified into three sectors - primary, secondary and tertiary.

   Reason (R): Each sector plays a different role in the economy and is interdependent.

   (*a*) Both (A) and (R) are true but (R) is not the correct explanation of (A).
   (*b*) Both (A) and (R) are true and (R) is the correct explanation of (A).
   (*c*) (A) is true but (R) is false.
   (*d*) (A) is false but (R) is true.

2. **Assertion (A):** A country can develop without a strong tertiary sector.

   Reason (R): The tertiary sector includes essential services like education, healthcare and transport which improves living standards.

   (*a*) Both (A) and (R) are true but (R) is not the correct explanation of (A).
   (*b*) Both (A) and (R) are true and (R) is the correct explanation of (A).
   (*c*) (A) is true but (R) is false.
   (*d*) (A) is false but (R) is true.

NOTES

Golden®

SAMPLE PAPER–I

CLASS-VI

Time: 2:30 hours **Max. Marks: 60**

General Instructions:

(i) *This question paper is divided into five sections.*

(ii) *There are total 22 questions in this question paper. All questions are compulsory.*

(iii) *There is internal choice in some of the questions. Attempt only one of them.*

(iv) *Marks are indicated against each question.*

(v) *Section A, questions 1 to 9 are of 1 mark each.*

(vi) *Section B, questions 10 to 13 are of 3 marks each.*

(vii) *Section C, questions 14 to 19 are of 4 marks each.*

(viii) *Section D, questions 20 and 21 are of 5 marks each.*

(ix) *Section E, question number 22 is a map-based question which has two parts 22 (A) and 22 (B). It is of total 5 marks.*

SECTION A

Answer the question nos. 1–9 by choosing the correct option given below

1. *Which of the following is odd one out?* 1

(a) Physical Maps
(b) Thematic Maps
(c) Political Maps
(d) Circular Maps

2. *Highest mountain of the world is:* 1

(a) Kanchenjunga
(b) Mt. Everest
(c) Mt Aconcagua
(d) Mt Kilimanjaro

3. *The Great Bath has been discovered in ....* 1

(a) Lothal
(b) Harappa
(c) Mohenjo-daro
(d) Kalibangan.

4. *Which of these is not a cause of inequality?* 1

(a) Economic condition
(b) Belonging to a different religion
(c) Speaking one language and not another
(d) Constitution

5. *The term Jambudvipa refer to which tree_____* 1

(a) jamun (b) peepal
(c) mango (d) coconut

6. *The smaller extensions of Oceans is_____* 1

(a) gulf (b) island
(c) fauna (d) continents

7. *Match Column A with Column B.* 1

Column A	Column B
1. Estuary	(*a*) roof of the world
2. Plateau	(*b*) where river meets the sea
3. Gangetic Plain	(*c*) Tributary
4. Yamuna	(*d*) Rice

8. *Larger buildings used for storing products before they are sold used or rented out to shops are called:* 1

9. *Correct and rewrite the sentence.* 1

Amul products are not sold in other countries as it is a cooperative.

SECTION B

10. *Enumerate the importance of Zila Parishad.* 3

11. *Name the mountain that is not the part of any range. Give its one feature.* 3

12. *Distinguish between primary, secondary and tertiary sector by giving examples.* 1+2=3

13. *What are the sources of history? Why are they important?* 3

SECTION C

14. *Enumerate the works of Gram Panchayats? How has it helped grassroot democracy?* 4

15. *Can diversity be a cause of discrimination? Explain with example.* 4

16. *What is the difference between local time and standard time? Give an example in support of your answer.* 4

17. *Give a brief description about village Lakshmanpur.* 4

18. *Explain Mountains. Give example of two mountains.* 4

19. *Can we compare historians to detectives? Give reasons for your answer.* 4

SECTION D

20. *What are the challenges and opportunities of life associated with each landform?* 5

21. *How can various sources help us to understand history?* 5

SECTION E

22. A. *Three places A, B and C are marked on the map of the world.*

Identify these places with the help of following information and write the correct names. 1+1+1=3

A. It is the third-largest ocean, covering approximately 20% of the Earth's water surface and plays a vital role in the global climate and weather patterns, including the monsoon seasons in India and Southeast Asia.

B. This ocean is home to many island nations, including Hawaii, the Philippines, and New Zealand.

C. It's an ocean situated between the Americas, Europe, and Africa, connecting the Old World with the New World.

WORLD-PHYSICAL

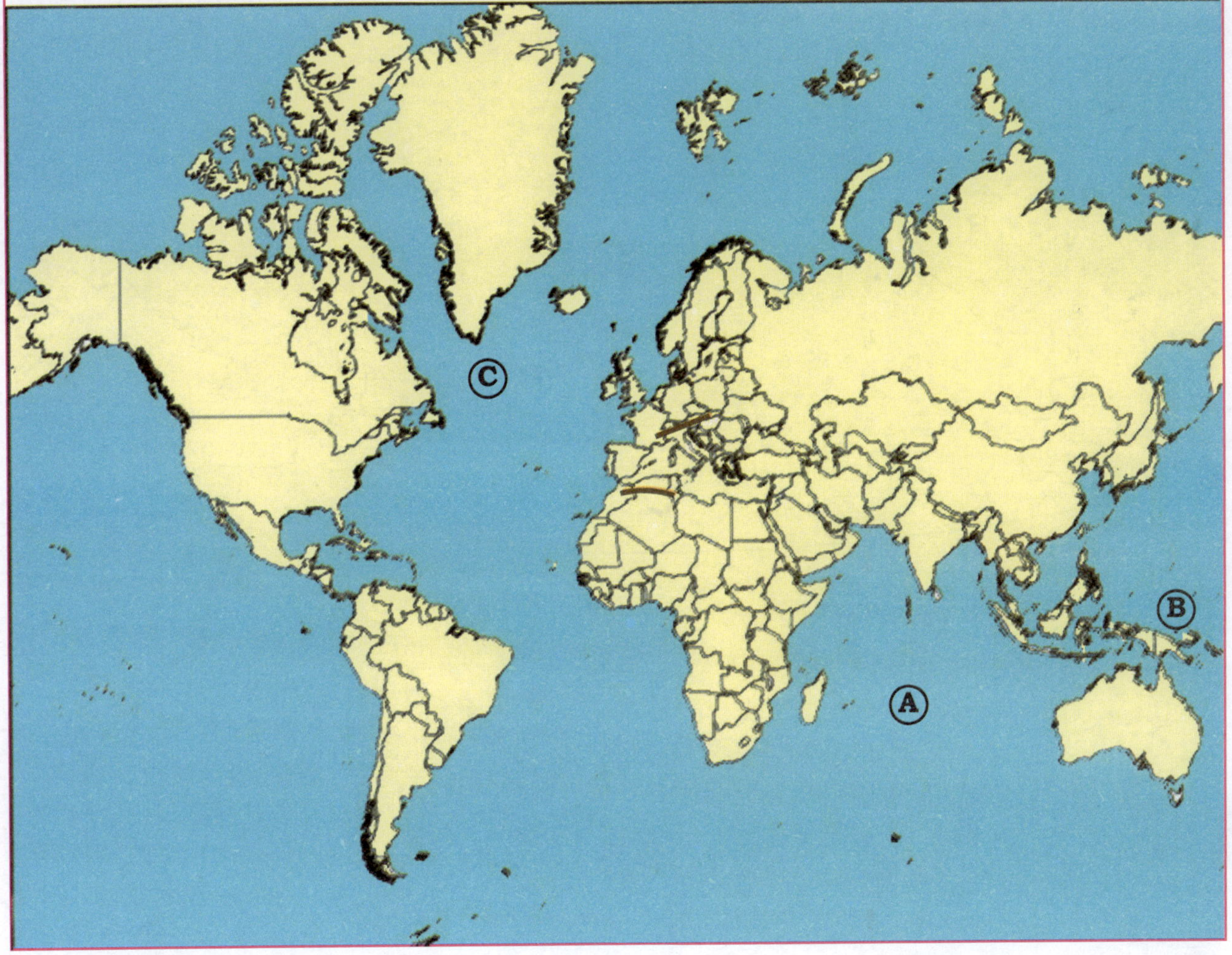

A. ____________________ **B.** ____________________ **C.** ____________________

22. B. *Locate and label the following on the map of India.* 1+1=2

1. Vindhya Range **2.** Ganga Plains

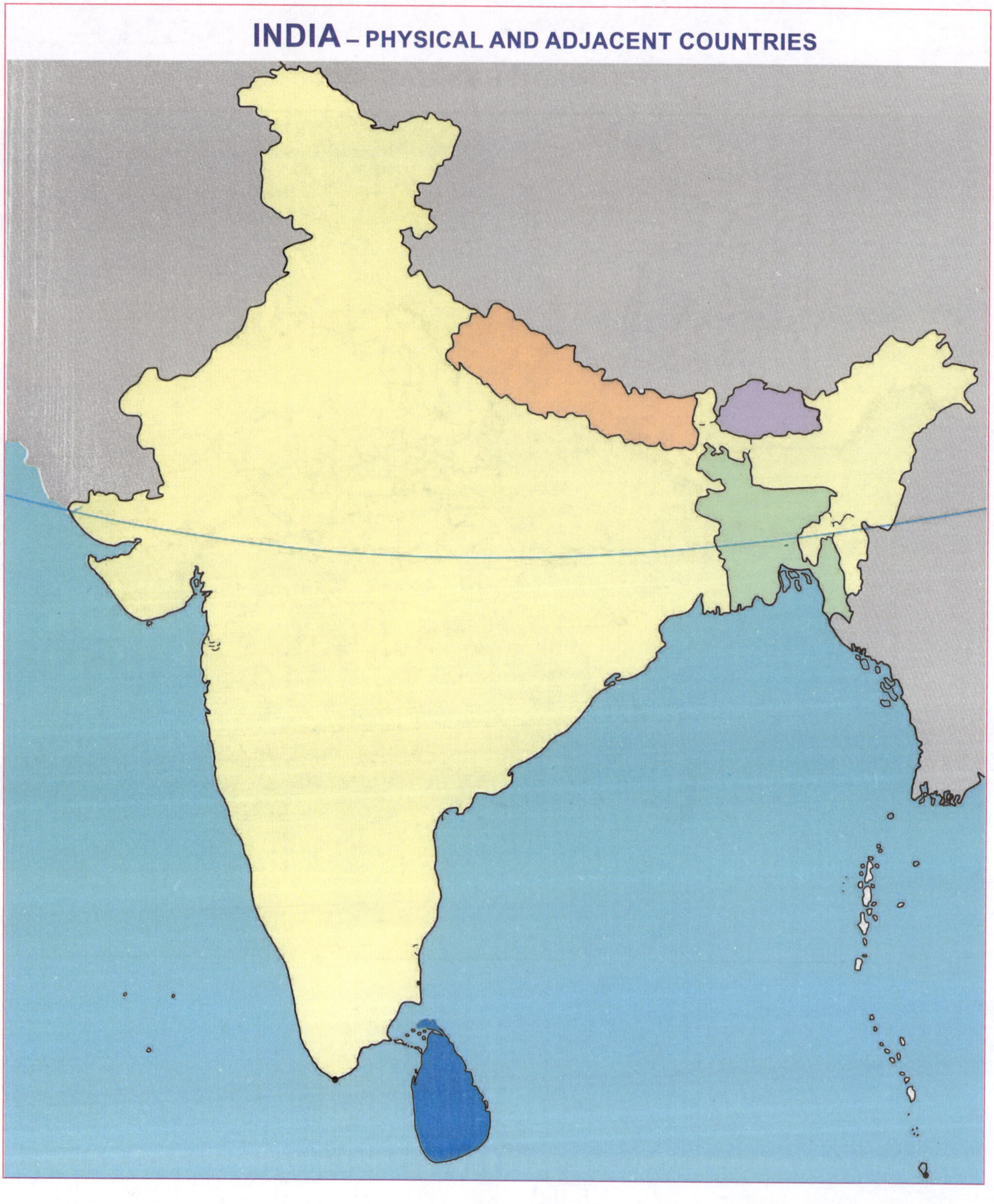

Golden®

SAMPLE PAPER–II

CLASS-VI

Time: 2:30 hours **Max. Marks: 60**

General Instructions:

(i) *This question paper is divided into five sections.*
(ii) *There are total 22 questions in this question paper. All questions are compulsory.*
(iii) *There is internal choice in some of the questions. Attempt only one of them.*
(iv) *Marks are indicated against each question.*
(v) *Section A, questions 1 to 9 are of 1 mark each.*
(vi) *Section B, questions 10 to 13 are of 3 marks each.*
(vii) *Section C, questions 14 to 19 are of 4 marks each.*
(viii) *Section D, questions 20 to 21 are of 5 marks each.*
(ix) *Section E, question number 22 is a map-based question which has two parts 22 (A) and 22 (B). It is of total 5 marks.*

SECTION A

Answer the question nos. 1–9 by choosing the correct option given below

1. *The exact replica of the Earth is:* 1

(a) map (b) sketch
(c) globe (d) plan.

2. *The shape of the Atlantic Ocean is like the alphabet:* 1

(a) A (b) C
(c) L (d) S.

3. *Extracting Pulp from the trees is a:* 1

(a) Primary Sector
(b) Secondary Sector
(c) Tertiary Sector
(d) Both Primary Sector and Secondary Sector.

4. *The city of Lothal was situated beside a river which was a tributary of:* 1

(a) Ganga (b) Sabarmati
(c) Narmada (d) Kaveri.

5. *The .... is an ancient text written by Kautilya.* 1

(a) Ramayana (b) Gita
(c) Young India
(d) Arthaśhāstra.

6. *Insurance, banking is the example of:* 1

(a) Primary Sector
(b) Secondary Sector
(c) Tertiary
(d) All of the above

7. Consider the statements given below: 1

Statement I: *The Panchayati Raj system works at three levels — from bottom up — the village, the block and the district. This is called a 'three-tier system' and works under the Central government.*

Statement II: *Together, these institutions' responsibilities cover almost all aspects of life in the district, from agriculture, housing, maintenance of roads, management of water resources.*

(*a*) (I) is correct and (II) is incorrect

(*b*) (I) is incorrect and (II) is correct

(*c*) Both (I) and (II) are incorrect

(*d*) Both (I) and (II) are correct

8. The French referred to India as 1

(*a*) Hind (*b*) Yintu

(*c*) Indoi (*d*) Inde

9. The following are known as store houses of minerals. 1

(*a*) Plateaus (*b*) Plains

(*c*) Deserts (*d*) Mountains.

SECTION B

10. *Explain the importance of the Panchayat Samiti.* 3

11. *Elaborate on how three sectors (Primary Sector, Secondary Sector and Tertiary Sector) are interdependent with each other?* 3

12. *Name the highest mountain in South India. Give its features.* 3

13. *Read the paragraph carefully and answer the following question—* 1+2=3

Mountains in some cases are very challenging as the areas are more susceptible to natural hazards and disasters, such as avalanches, landslides debris flow and floods from landslide dams. Mountains are very steep and rugged, which can impact daily life agriculture also. But then there are many opportunities with any mountain areas such as they are the store house of natural beauty and also the soil is fertile and very good for agriculture.

(*a*) *What are the challenges of mountain areas?*

(*b*) *What are its advantages?*

SECTION C

14. *Describe the composition of the Gram Panchayat.* 4

15. *Explain Gender Discrimination.* 4

16. *Compare and contrast parallels of latitude and meridians of longitude.* 4

17. *What differences do you notice between the governance system at the Central level and at the Panchayat level?* 4

18. *Explain the importance of Plateaus.* 4

19. *Explain the term BCE, CE, AD.* 4

SECTION D

20. *Explain different type of Heat Zones.* 5

21. *Elaborate the challenges faced by the early humans.* 5

SECTION E

22. A. *Three places A, B and C are marked on the map of the world. Identify these places with the help of following information and write the correct names.* 1+1+1=3

A. The Ocean, known as the Antarctic Ocean, surrounds Antarctica and extends north to the coast of South America, Africa, and Australia.

B. Located in the northernmost part of the world, surrounding the North Pole it's the smallest and shallowest of the world's five oceans.

C. The busiest ocean surrounded by America, Europe and Africa.

WORLD-PHYSICAL

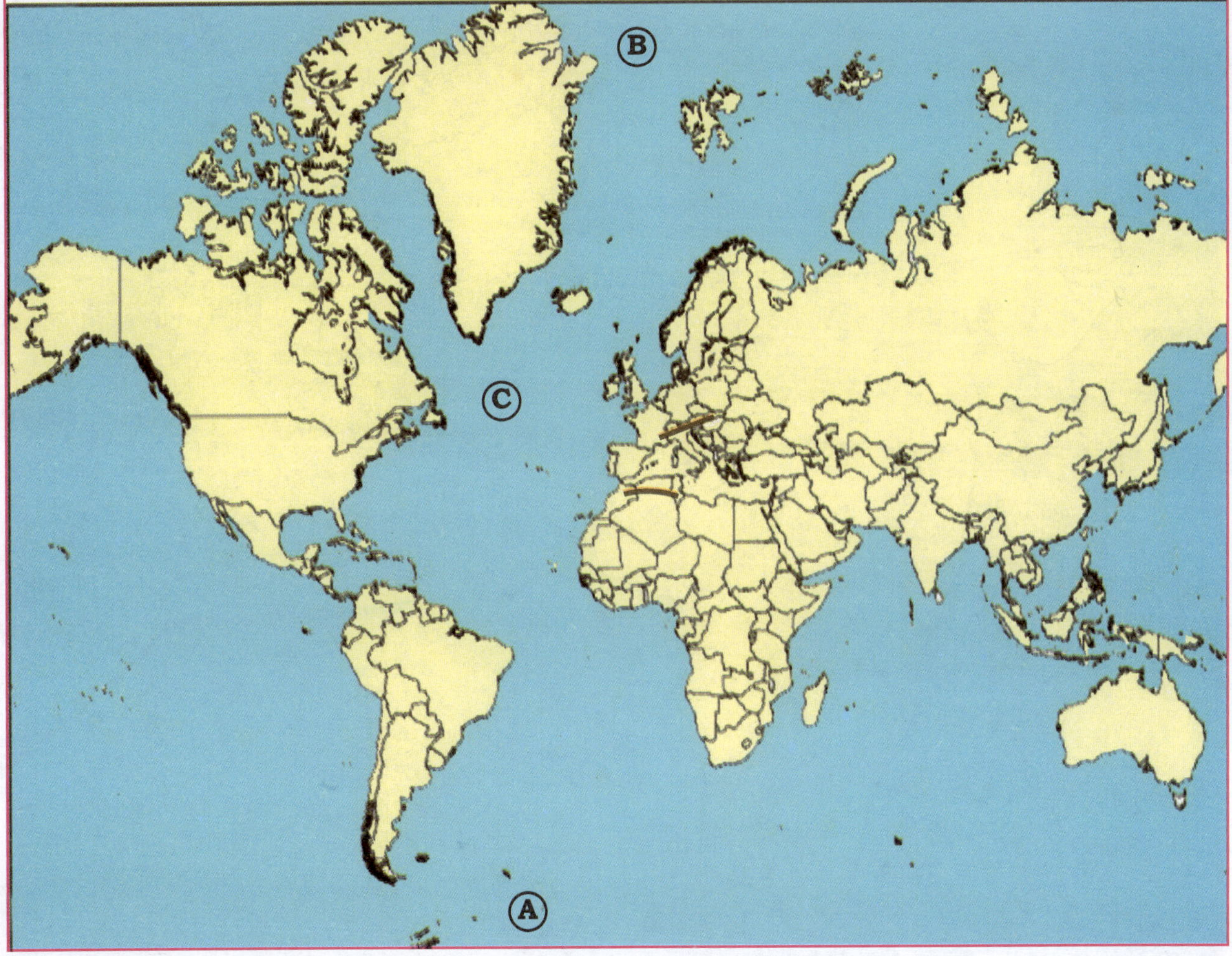

A. ____________ **B.** ____________ **C.** ____________

22 B. *Locate and label the following on the map of India* 1 + 1 = 2

(*a*) The Deccan Plateau (*b*) The Arabian Sea

INDIA – PHYSICAL AND ADJACENT COUNTRIES

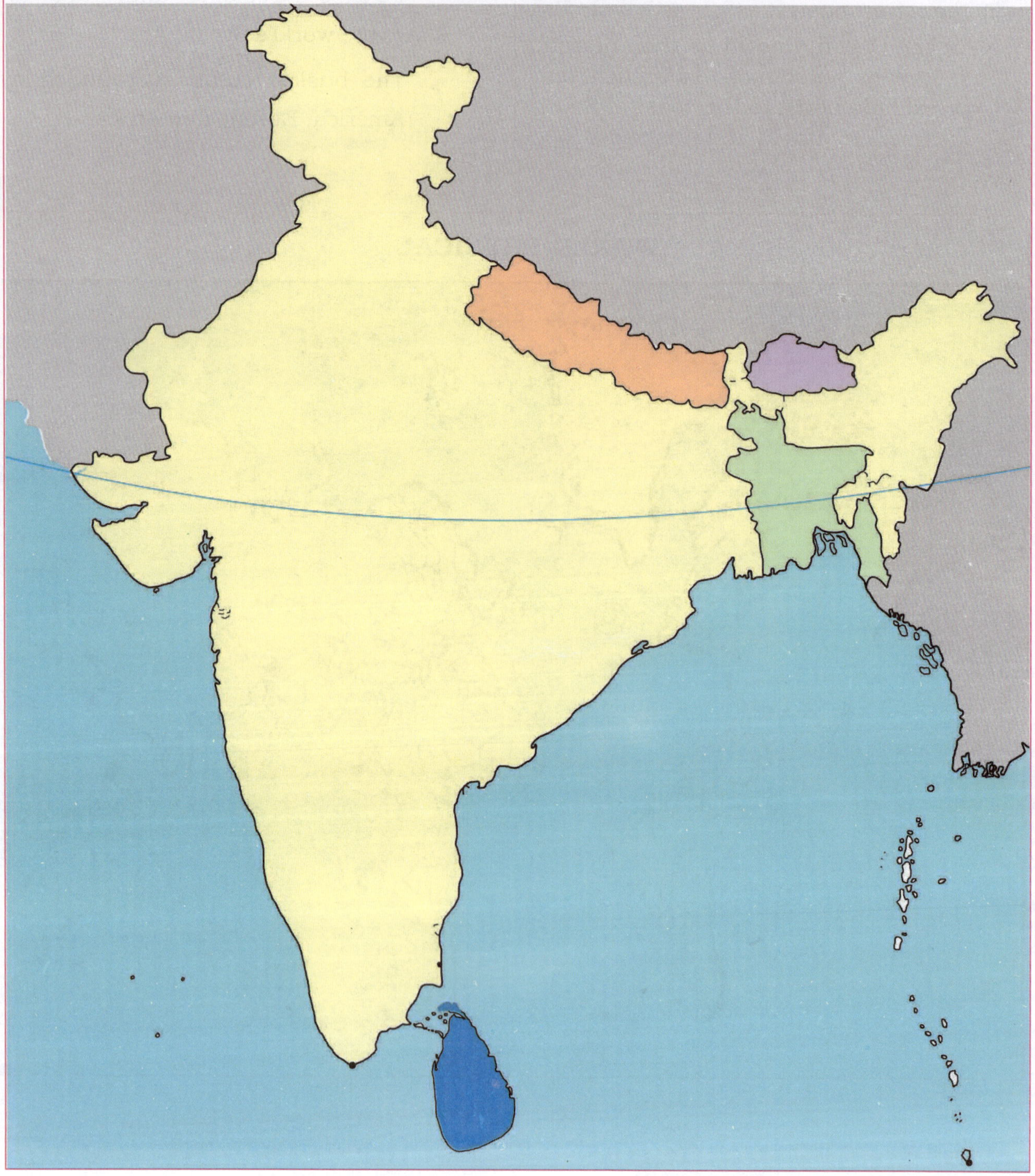

Golden®

SAMPLE PAPER–III

CLASS-VI

Time: 2:30 hours **Max. Marks: 60**

General Instructions:

(i) *This question paper is divided into five sections.*

(ii) *There are total 22 questions in this question paper. All questions are compulsory.*

(iii) *There is internal choice in some of the questions. Attempt only one of them.*

(iv) *Marks are indicated against each question.*

(v) *Section A, questions 1 to 9 are of 1 mark each.*

(vi) *Section B, questions 10 to 13 are of 3 marks each.*

(vii) *Section C, questions 14 to 19 are of 4 marks each.*

(viii) *Section D, questions 20 and 21 are of 5 marks each.*

(ix) *Section E, question number 22 is a map-based question which has two parts 22 (A) and 22 (B). It is of total 5 marks.*

SECTION A

Answer the question nos. 1–9 by choosing the correct option given below

1. ***The continent of Africa is bound by which of the following seas in the North.*** 1

(a) Bay of Bengal
(b) Caspian Sea
(c) Arabian Sea
(d) Mediterranean Sea

2. ***The highest peak in South India is:*** 1

(a) Nanda Devi
(b) Vindhyas
(c) Kanchenjunga
(d) Anamudi

3. ***Which metal did the Harappan use to make tools?*** 1

(a) Iron (b) Silver
(c) Gold (d) Bronze

4. ***Which of these groups of people did not usually live in cities, but the countryside?*** 1

(a) rulers
(b) craftsperson
(c) farmers and herders
(d) scribes.

5. ***The members of the gram-panchayat are generally elected for a term of:*** 1

(a) 1 year (b) No fixed term
(c) 5 years (d) 4 years.

6. *The Constitution was first written in:* 1

(*a*) English (*b*) Hindi
(*c*) Sanskrit (*d*) Tamil

7. *Assertion and Reason* 1

There are two statements marked as Assertion (A) and Reason (R). Mark your answer as per the codes provided below:

Assertion (A): *Like every village in India, the Lakshmanpur people have a system of local government called 'Panchayat'.*

Reason (R): *Panchayats bring governance closer to the people, making it possible for them to actively participate in decision-making processes.*

(*a*) Both (A) and (R) are true but (R) is not the correct explanation of (A)
(*b*) Both (A) and (R) are true and (R) is the correct explanation of (A)
(*c*) (A) is true but (R) is false
(*d*) (A) is false but (R) is true

8. *Why are the inhabitants of the Indus Valley Civilisation called Harappans?* 1

(*a*) They lived near the Sarasvati
(*b*) The city of Harappa was the first to be excavated
(*c*) They spoke the Harappan language
(*d*) They invented the first writing system

9. *Which of the following is a tertiary sector activity?* 1

(*a*) Manufacturing of laptop
(*b*) Fisherman catching fish
(*c*) Construction of house
(*d*) Repairing of computers

SECTION B

10. *Elaborate the functions of the Panchayat Secretary and the Patwari?* 3

11. *What is the significance of the Rig Veda?* 3

12. *How are economic activities different from non-economic activities?* 3

13. *Read the paragraph carefully and answer the following questions:* 1+2=3

Mountain is a place of pure nature with very low pollution. Terrace farming is practised on the slopes by cutting steps into the slope. Tourism is often an important source of income for the people living in the mountains. The crisp mountain air and scenic beauty attracts many tourists.

A. What form of farming is generally practised in mountain areas?

B. What is an important source of income for the people living in mountains?

SECTION C

14. *Explain the efforts of the Bal Panchayat in Maharashtra.* 4

15. *What are three levels of government? Examine their function.* 4

16. *Give examples of rivers sources or confluences from your region that are regarded sacred by any community?* 4

17. *Elaborate similarities that you notice between the governance system at the Central level and at the Panchayat level?* 4

18. *What are Plains? Give its importance.* 4

19. *How do historians calculate years between BCE and CE dates?* 4

SECTION D

20. *Enlist the features of Pacific Ocean.* 5

OR

Enlist the features of the Continent – Antarctica.

21. *How do you think understanding the past will help us understand the present world?* 5

SECTION E

22 A. *Three places A, B and C are marked on the map of the world. Identify these places with the help of following information and write their correct names on the line marked near them.* 1+1+1=3

A. It's the largest continental landmass on Earth and comprises two traditional continents: Europe and Asia.

B. The second-largest continent, covering approximately 30 million square kilometres and is home to the world's oldest human fossils, found in Ethiopia.

C. This continent, also known as Oceania or Australasia, includes: - Australia, New Zealand, Papua New Guinea, Pacific Island nations and - Tasmania and surrounding islands.

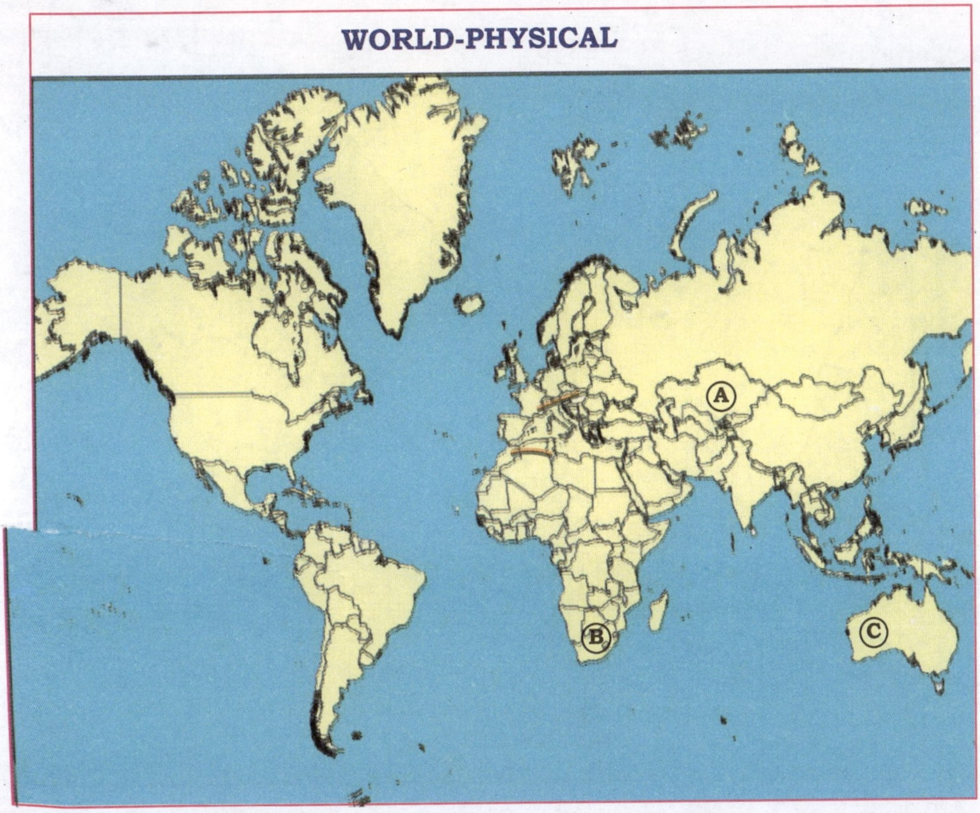

A. ____________________ **B.** ____________________ **C.** ____________________

22 B. *Locate and label the following with appropriate symbols on the map of India.* 1+1=2

1. Lothal
2. Kalibangan

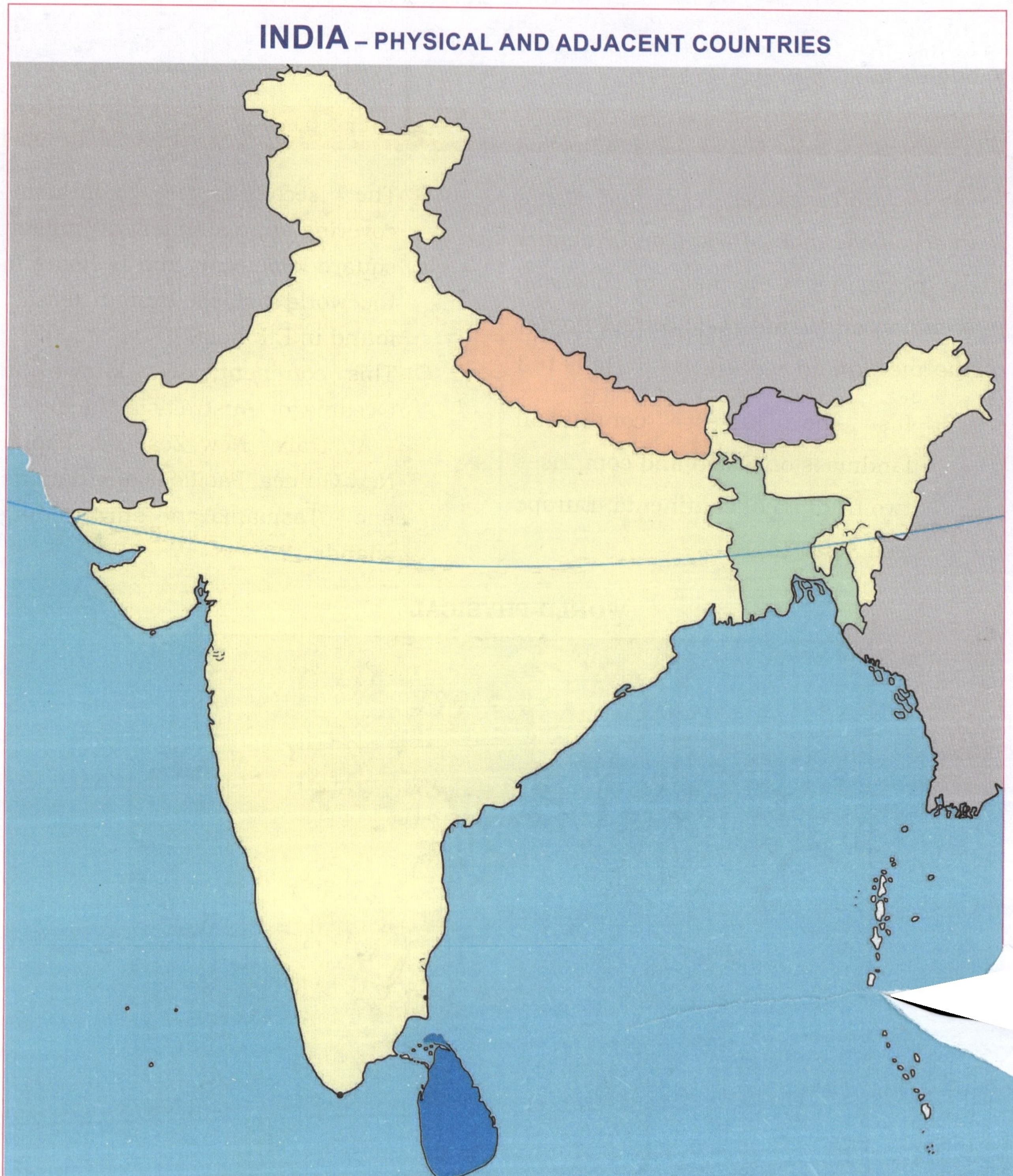